AA
Travellers' Guide To FRANCE

GAZETTEER
Compiled by the AA's Research Unit, Information Control in co-operation with AA Hotels Services, and generated by the AA's Establishment Data-base.

MAPS
Prepared by the Cartographic Department of
The Automobile Association
© The Automobile Association 1989

COVER ILLUSTRATION
KAG Design

HEAD OF ADVERTISEMENT SALES
Christopher Heard Tel 0256 20123 (ext 21544)

ADVERTISEMENT PRODUCTION
Karen Weeks Tel 0256 20123 (ext 21545)

FILMSETTING BY
William Clowes Ltd, Beccles, Suffolk

PRINTED AND BOUND IN GREAT BRITAIN BY
Richard Clay Ltd, Bungay, Suffolk

Every effort is made to ensure accuracy, but the publishers do not hold themselves responsible for any consequences that may arise from error or omissions. Whilst the contents are believed correct at the time of going to press, changes may have occurred since that time or will occur during the currency of this book.

© The Automobile Association 1989

All rights reserved. No part of this publication may be reproduced, stored in a retrieval system, or transmitted in any form or by any means – electronic, mechanical, photocopying, recording or otherwise – unless the written permission of the Publisher has been given beforehand.

Published by The Automobile Association, Basingstoke, Hampshire
RG21 2EA

ISBN 0 86145 7765
AA Reference: 10388

CONTENTS

5–26 ABC OF FRENCH MOTORING REGULATIONS AND GENERAL INFORMATION

From AA Service to Wheel chains, plus a note on Monaco and specimen letters for booking hotels

27 ROUTE PLANNING

An application form for details of the Overseas route service

29–33 ABOUT THE GAZETTEER

Contains general information about accommodation plus explanatory notes on the Accommodation and Garages within the gazetteer including an Example of a gazetteer entry

39–117 GAZETTEER

The gazetteer section contains Location maps followed by a gazetteer of hotels and garages

118–119 SYMBOLS AND ABBREVIATIONS

English, French, German, Italian and Spanish

120 ACCOMMODATION REPORT

If you take your car with Sally Line you'll sail from Ramsgate straight to our brand new terminal in Dunkerque.

A terminal that's strategically placed to set you straight onto the fast, toll-free roads of Europe direct to your holiday destination.

And because we have exclusive use of these ports there's no queueing to get on or off.

In fact, the only bottlenecks you'll find are those you can enjoy on board with our exeellent Smörgåsbord cuisine, in our welcoming bars. You'll also be able to choose from the widest range of duty-free goods across the Channel.

Add to this a children's play area and you'll find that we offer a lot more for a lot less when you compare our fares with other operators.

So if you want a smooth crossing followed by a drive that's 'plain sailing', call in at your nearest AA travel agency or send for your brochure today. Sally Line, FREEPOST, Ramsgate, Kent CT11 7BR.

Please send me the 1989 Sally Ferries & Holidays brochure.

Name

Address

Postcode

Please send to: Sally Line, FREEPOST, Ramsgate, Kent CT11 7BR.

AABI

TAKE SALLY FROM RAMSGATE TO DUNKERQUE AND IT'S PLAIN SAILING ACROSS EUROPE.

Sally LINE

WE'VE GOT IT RIGHT ACROSS THE CHANNEL

French ABC

MOTORING and GENERAL INFORMATION

Area *213,000 sq miles*
Population *54,300,000*
Local time *GMT + 1 (Summer GMT + 2)*
Monaco *See page 26*
Corsica A leaflet entitled *Motoring in Corsica* is available to AA members

International distinguishing sign

National flag
Vertical tricolour of blue, white and red

Motoring laws in France are just as wide and complicated as those in the UK, but they should cause little difficulty to the average British motorist. You should, however, take more care and extend greater courtesy than you would normally do at home, and bear in mind the essentials of good motoring – avoiding any behaviour likely to obstruct traffic, to endanger persons or cause damage to property. It is also important to remember that tourists are subject to the laws of the country in which they travel.

Make sure that you have clear all-round vision. See that your seat belts are securely mounted and not damaged and remember that in France their use is compulsory. If you are planning to tow a caravan, you will find further advice and information on campsites in the AA guide *Camping and Caravanning in Europe*.

As well as a current passport, a tourist temporarily importing a motor vehicle into France should always carry a valid full national driving licence, the registration document of the car, and evidence of insurance. The proper international distinguishing sign should be affixed to the rear of the vehicle. The appropriate papers must be carried at all times and secured against loss. The practice of spot checks on foreign cars is widespread, and to avoid inconvenience or a *police fine*, ensure that your papers are in order and that the international distinguishing sign is of the approved standard design.

Mechanical repairs and replacement parts can be expensive abroad. While not all breakdowns are avoidable, a vast number occur because the vehicle has not been prepared properly before the start of the journey. A holiday abroad involves many miles of hard driving over roads completely new to you, perhaps without the facilities you have come to take for granted in this country. Therefore you should give serious thought to the business of *preparing your vehicle for a holiday abroad*.

We recommend that your car undergoes a major service by a franchised dealer shortly before you holiday or tour abroad. In addition, it is advisable to carry out your own general check for any audible or visible defects.

It is not practical to provide a complete list of points to look for, but the *ABC* contains information under the following headings:

Automatic gearboxes
Automatic transmission fluid
Brakes
Cold weather touring
Direction indicators
Electrical
Engine and mechanical
Lights
Spares
Tyres
Warm climate touring

These, used in conjunction with the manufacturer's handbook, should ensure that no obvious faults are missed.

If AA members would like a thorough check of their car made by one of the AA's experienced engineers, any AA Centre can arrange this at a few days' notice. Our engineer will then submit a written report complete with a list of repairs required. There is a fee for this service. For more detailed information please ask for our leaflet *Tech 8*.

French ABC

AA SERVICE INCLUDING PORT AGENT

The Association has its own offices in Boulogne-sur-Mer and Calais and an appointed Port Agent in Cherbourg.

62201 Boulogne-sur-Mer The Automobile Association, Tour Damremont (18ème), Boulevard Chanzy BP No. 21 ☏21872121

62100 Calais The Automobile Association, Terminal Est ☏21964720

50100 Cherbourg (Port Agent) Agence Maritime Tellier, Gare Maritime ☏33204338; port office (when ferries operating), car ferry terminal ☏33204274.

See also *Town Plans of Boulogne-sur-Mer* page 51, *Calais* pages 54–55 and *Cherbourg* page 61.

ACCIDENTS

Fire ☏18 and police ☏17. For **ambulance** use the number given in the telephone box or, if no number is given, call the police (*Brigade de Gendarmerie*). Emergency telephone boxes are stationed every 20km on some roadways and are connected direct to the local police station. In the larger towns, emergency help can be obtained from the *police secours* (emergency assistance departments).

Motorists involved in a traffic accident must complete a *constat à l'amiable* before the vehicle is moved. If the vehicle has been seriously damaged, an expert's examination is advised prior to the return to the UK. The *constat à l'amiable* was introduced by the French insurance companies and represents the 'European Accident Statement Form'. It must be signed by the other party, but if a dispute arises and one of the parties involved should refuse to complete the *constat à l'amiable*, then the other party should immediately obtain a written report from a bailiff (*huissier*), which is known as a *constat d'huissier*. A bailiff can usually be found in any large town and charges a fee of *Fr*400 for preparing the report. Normally, the police are only called out to accidents where persons are injured, a driver is under the influence of alcohol, or the accident impedes traffic flow. When attending an accident, the police prepare a report know as a *procès verbal*.

After an accident, the French authorities, at their discretion, may request a surety payment to cover the court costs or fines. See also *Warning triangle/Hazard warning lights*, page 24.

AUTOMATIC GEARBOXES

When towing a caravan the fluid in an automatic gearbox becomes hotter and thinner, so there is more slip and more heat generated in the gearbox. Many manufacturers recommend the fitting of a gearbox oil cooler. Check with the manufacturer as to what is suitable for your car.

AUTOMATIC TRANSMISSION FLUID

Automatic transmission fluid is not always readily available, especially in some of the more remote areas, and tourists are advised to carry an emergency supply with them.

BBC WORLD SERVICE

If you wish to receive English language broadcasts whilst travelling abroad, BBC World Service transmissions can be heard in France. A full programme including current affairs, sport and music is available, with world news at approximately every hour. Most car radios operate on medium and long wave so BBC World Service programmes may normally be obtained by tuning to the following frequencies between the times mentioned:

KHz	Metres	Summer broadcasting times – GMT
1296	231	03.00–03.30, 06.00–06.30, 17.00–19.00, 22.00–23.15
648*	463	04.45–05.30, 06.00–10.30, 11.00–16.15, 19.00–03.45
198	1515	00.00–04.30

* 'BBC 648' is Europe's first trilingual radio station. It carries World Service programmes in English, but includes French and German

MOTORING and GENERAL INFORMATION

sequences, news for Europe and 'English by Radio' at certain times.

In some parts of France, it is possible to receive BBC national services (with the exception of Radio 3).

For more comprehensive information on BBC transmissions in France, write to BBC World Information Centre and Shop, Bush House, Strand, London WC2B 4PH.

BOATS

If you are taking any type of boat to France, check the requirements with the Royal Yachting Association (RYA). However, boat registration documentation is compulsory for all craft except very small craft under about 10ft. This documentation may be obtained from the Royal Yachting Association, RYA House, Romsey Road, Eastleigh, Hampshire SO5 4YA ☎ (0703) 629962. A Helmsman's (Overseas) Certificate of Competence is rarely needed, but is advisable for all inland waters except the canals. The certificate can be obtained from the above address, and is free to members of the RYA. Applications should be made well in advance. See also *Custom's Carnet de Passages en Douane* under *Customs regulations*, page 9, *Identification plate*, page 13 and *Insurance*, page 13.

BRAKES

Car brakes must always be in peak condition. Check both the level in the brake-fluid reservoir and the thickness of the brake lining/pad material. The brake fluid should be completely changed in accordance with the manufacturer's instructions, or at intervals of not more than 18 months or 18,000 miles. However, it is advisable to change the brake fluid, regardless of the foregoing, before departing on a Continental holiday, particularly if the journey includes travelling through a hilly or mountainous area.

BREAKDOWN

If your car breaks down, endeavour to move it to the side of the road or to a position where it will obstruct the traffic flow as little as possible. If the car is fitted with hazard warning lights, switch them on or, alternatively, place a warning triangle at the appropriate distance on the road behind the obstruction. If the vehicle breaks down on a motorway, telephone the police (*Brigade de Gendarmerie*) from an emergency telephone or service station. The police will contact a garage for you, but should it be necessary to move the vehicle from the motorway for repair, the choice of repair garage can be determined by the motorist. For breakdowns in Motorway Service/Motel or Filling Station areas, the call for assistance must originate from the area to the police. On all other roads, you are advised to seek local assistance as, at the present time, there is no nationwide road assistance service in France. See also *Warning triangle/Hazard warning lights*, page 24.

Motorists are advised to take out *AA 5-Star Service*, the overseas motoring emergency service, which includes breakdown and accident benefits, and personal travel insurance. It offers total security and peace of mind to all motorists travelling in Europe. Cover may be purchased by any motorist, although a small additional premium must be paid by non-members of the AA. Details and brochures may be obtained from AA Travel Agencies, AA Port Service Centres and AA Centres, or by telephoning 021-550 7648. *Note:* Members who have not purchased *AA 5-Star Service* prior to departure, and who subsequently require assistance, may request spare parts or vehicle recovery, but in this case the AA will require a deposit to cover estimated costs and a service fee prior to providing the service. All expenses must be reimbursed to the AA in addition to the service fee.

BRITISH EMBASSY/ CONSULATES

There are some fourteen British Consulates in France with varying degrees of status. The functions and office hours of Honorary Consuls are naturally more restricted than those of full-time officials. Generally, Consulates (and the consular section of the Embassy) stand ready to help British travellers in France, but there are limits to what they can do. A Consulate cannot pay your hotel, medical or any other bills, nor will they do the work of travel agents, information bureaux or police. Any loss or theft of property should be reported to the local police not the Consulate, and a statement obtained confirming the loss or theft. If you still need help, such as the issue of an emergency passport or guidance on how to transfer funds, contact the Consulate.

The British Embassy is located at 75008 Paris, 35 rue du Faubourg St Honoré ☎42669142; consular section 75008 Paris, 16 rue d'Anjou ☎42669142. There are British Consulates in Bordeaux, Lille, Lyons and Marseilles; there are

7

French ABC

British Consulates with Honorary Consuls in Boulogne-sur-Mer, Calais, Cherbourg, Dunkerque (Dunkirk), Le Havre, Nantes, Nice, Perpignan, St Malo-Dinard and Toulouse.

CLAIMS AGAINST THIRD PARTIES

The law and levels of damages in foreign countries are generally different to our own. It is important to remember this when considering making a claim against another motorist arising out of an accident abroad. Certain types of claims invariably present difficulties, the most common probably being that relating to the recovery of car-hire charges. Rarely are they recoverable in full under French law, and more often than not they are considerably reduced. Frequently, an 'immobilisation allowance' is allowed of a few francs per day, which will bear no relation at all to the actual cost of hiring a vehicle.

With regard to vehicle damage, it is usually necessary to have the claim substantiated by not only the estimate and receipted repairs account but also an engineer's report noting the damage caused, cost of labour, parts, etc. plus, of course, VAT. All other items of claim should be supported with documentary evidence. Otherwise, they may be rejected by the French Courts.

Claims for damages for personal injuries or death can be pursued against French third parties but the basis of settlement is different to that in the United Kingdom and it should be left to the experts.

The negotiation of claims against foreign insurers is extremely protracted, and translation of all documents slows down the process at each end. A delay of three months between sending a letter and receiving a reply from French insurers is not at all uncommon.

If you have taken out the AA's *5-Star Service* cover, at the AA's discretion, assistance will be given in pursuing uninsured loss claims against third parties arising out of a road accident in France. In this event, members should seek guidance and/or assistance from the AA as soon as possible.

COLD WEATHER TOURING

If you are planning a winter tour, make sure that you fit a high-temperature (winter) thermostat, and make sure that the strength of your antifreeze mixture is correct for the low temperatures likely to be encountered.

If you think you will need wheel chains, it is better to take them with you from home. They may be hired from the AA and further details are available from your nearest AA Centre.

Wheel chains fit over the driven wheels to enable them to grip on snow or icy surfaces. They are sometimes called *snow chains* or *anti-skid chains*. Full-length chains which fit right round a tyre are the most satisfactory, but they must be fitted correctly. Check that the chains do not foul your vehicle bodywork; if your vehicle has front-wheel-drive put the steering on full lock while checking. If your vehicle has radial tyres, it is essential that you contact the manufacturers of your vehicle and tyres for their recommendations in order to avoid damage to your tyres. Chains should only be used when necessary, as prolonged use on hard surfaces will damage the tyres.

Spiked or *studded tyres* are sometimes called *snow tyres*. They are tyres with rugged treads on to which spikes or studs have been fitted. For the best grip, they should be fitted to all wheels. The correct type of spiked or studded winter tyres will generally be more effective than chains. See also page 22.

CRASH, OR SAFETY, HELMETS

It is compulsory for drivers and passengers of all motorcycles (and motorised bicycles over 50cc) to wear crash, or safety, helmets.

CREDIT/CHARGE CARDS

Credit/charge cards may be used in France, but their use is subject to the 'conditions of use' set out by the issuing company who, on request, will provide full information. Establishments display the symbols of cards they accept, but it is not possible to produce any detailed lists. However, hotels which accept credit/charge cards are indicated in the Gazetteer (see page 30 for further information. See also *Petrol* page 19).

CURRENCY, INCLUDING BANKING HOURS

The unit of currency is the franc (*Fr*) divided into 100 *centimes*; at the time of going to press, £1 = *Fr*10.84.

MOTORING and GENERAL INFORMATION

Denominations of bank notes are *Fr*10, 20, 50, 100, 200, 500; standard coins are *Fr*1, 2, 10, 50 and 5, 10, 20, 50 *centimes*.

There is no restriction on the amount of foreign currency which may be taken into France. However, non-residents may only export the equivalent of *Fr*12,000 in local or foreign currencies when leaving the country, unless, of course, they imported more currency on entry and made the appropriate declaration on arrival. There are no restrictions on the export of travellers' cheques.

Banks In most large towns, banks are open from Monday to Friday 09.00–12.00hrs and 14.00–16.00hrs and closed on Saturday and Sunday; in the provinces, they are open from Tuesday to Saturday as above, and closed on Sunday and Monday. Banks close at midday on the day prior to a national holiday and all day on Monday if the holiday falls on a Tuesday.

The *Crédit Lyonnais* has offices at the Invalides air terminal in Paris for cashing travellers' cheques and the *Société Générale* has two offices at Orly airport, whilst at the Charles de Gaulle airport, exchange facilities are also available.

There is no limit to the amount of sterling notes you may take abroad. However, it is best to carry only enough currency for immediate expenses.

CUSTOMS REGULATIONS FOR FRANCE

Bona fide visitors to France can assume, as a general rule, that they may *temporarily* import personal articles duty-free, providing the following conditions are met:

a that the articles are for personal use, and are not to be sold or otherwise disposed of;
b that they may be considered as being in use, and in keeping with the personal status of the importer;
c that they are taken out when the importer leaves France, or
d that goods stay for no more than 6 months in any 12-month period, whichever is the earlier.

All articles which do not qualify under these conditions must be declared upon entry, otherwise you will be liable to penalties. Should you be taking a large number of personal effects with you, it would be a wise measure to prepare in advance an inventory to present to the Customs authorities on entry. Customs officers may withhold concessions at any time and ask you to deposit enough money to cover possible duty, especially on portable items of apparent high value. Any deposit paid (for which a receipt must be obtained) is likely to be high; it is recoverable (but only at the entry point at which it was paid) on leaving the country and exporting the item. Alternatively, the Customs may enter the item in your passport, and in these circumstances, it is important to remember to get the entry cancelled when the item is exported. For duty and tax-free allowances, see table page 10, but for **other goods** substitute pound sterling amounts in the table for *Fr*300 per person (*Fr*150 per person under 15 years of age) from a non-EEC country* and *Fr*2,400 per person (*Fr*620 per person under 15 years of age) from an EEC country.

A *temporarily imported motor vehicle, caravan, boat* or any other type of *trailer* is subject to strict control on entering France, attracting Customs duty and a variety of taxes; much depends on the circumstances and the period of the import and also upon the status of the importer. A person entering a country in which he has no residence, with a private vehicle for holiday or recreational purposes, and intending to export the vehicle within a short period, enjoys special privileges, and the normal formalities are reduced to an absolute minimum in the interests of tourism. However, a *Customs Carnet de Passages en Douane* is required for temporarily imported outboard engines exceeding 92cc (5cv as applied to marine engines), imported without the boats with which they are to be used, and for cycles with auxiliary motors up to 50cc which are new or show no signs of use. The *Carnet*, for which a charge is made, is a valuable document issued by the AA to its members, or as part of the *AA 5-Star Service* – further information may be obtained from most AA Centres and AA Port Service Centres. If you are issued with a *Carnet*, you must ensure that it is returned to the AA correctly discharged in order to avoid inconvenience and expense, possibly including payment of customs charges, at a later date. A temporarily imported vehicle, etc, should not:

a be left in France after the importer has left;
b be put at the disposal of a resident of France;
c be retained in France longer than the permitted period;
d be lent, sold, hired, given away, exchanged or otherwise disposed of.

People entering with a motor vehicle for a period of generally more than six months, or to take up residence, employment, any commercial activity, or with the intention of disposing of the vehicle should seek advice concerning their position well in advance of their departure. Most AA Centres will be pleased to help.

*Residents of the Channel Islands and the Isle of Man do not benefit from EEC allowances due to their fiscal regimes

CUSTOMS REGULATIONS FOR THE UNITED KINGDOM

If, when leaving Britain, you export any items of new appearance, such as watches, items of jewellery, cameras etc, particularly of foreign manufacture, which you bought in the UK, it is a good idea to carry the retailer's receipts with you, if they are available. In the absence of such receipts, you may be asked to make a written declaration of where the goods were obtained.

The exportation of certain goods *from the United Kingdom* is prohibited or restricted. These include: controlled drugs; most animals, birds and some plants; firearms and ammunition; strategic and technological equipment (including computers); photographic material over 60 years old, and antiques and collectors' items more than 50 years old.

When you *enter the United Kingdom*, you will pass through Customs. You must declare everything in excess of the duty and tax-free allowances (see table) which you have obtained outside the United Kingdom, or on the journey, and everything previously obtained free of duty or tax in the United Kingdom. You may not mix allowances between duty-free and non-duty-free sources within each heading, except for alcohol, which allows, for example, 1 litre of duty and tax-free spirits in addition to 5 litres of duty and tax-paid still wine. Currently, as a concession only, travellers may use their entitlement of alcoholic drinks not over 22% vol to import table wine, in addition to the set table wine allowance.

You must also declare any prohibited or restricted goods, and goods for commercial purposes. Don't be tempted to hide anything or to mislead the Customs! The penalties are severe, and articles which are not properly declared may be forfeit. If articles are hidden in a vehicle, that, too, becomes liable to forfeiture. Customs Officers are legally entitled to examine your luggage. Please co-operate with them if they ask to examine it. You are responsible for opening, unpacking and repacking your luggage.

The *importation* of certain goods *into the United Kingdom* is prohibited or restricted. These include: controlled drugs such as opium, morphine, heroin, cocaine, cannabis,

Goods obtained duty and tax-free in the EEC, or duty and tax-free on a ship or aircraft, or goods obtained outside the EEC	Duty and tax-free allowances	Goods obtained duty and tax-paid in the EEC
Tobacco products		
200	Cigarettes	300
	or	
100	Cigarillos	150
	or	
50	Cigars	75
	or	
250g	Tobacco	400g
Alcoholic drinks		
2 litres	Still table wine	5 litres
1 litre	Over 22% vol. (*eg* spirits and strong liqueurs)	1½ litres
	or	
2 litres	Not over 22% vol (*eg* low strength liqueurs or fortified wines or sparkling wines)	3 litres
	or	
2 litres	Still table wine	3 litres
Perfume		
50g		75g
Toilet water		
250cc		375cc
Other goods		
£32	but no more than: 50 litres of beer and 25 mechanical lighters	£250

Note
i Persons under 17 years of age are not entitled to duty and tax free allowances in respect of alcohol and tobacco.
ii Visitors to France entering from an EEC country may also import duty-free 1000g of coffee or 450g of coffee extract and 250g of tea or 80g of tea extract bought duty and tax paid; a reduced allowance applies if bought duty-free.

amphetamines, barbiturates and LSD (lysergide); counterfeit currency; firearms (including gas pistols, electric shock batons and similar weapons), ammunition, explosives (including fireworks) and flick knives; horror comics, indecent or obscene books, magazines, films, video tapes and other articles; animals* and birds, whether alive or dead (*eg* stuffed); certain articles derived from endangered species, including fur-skins, ivory, reptile leather and

MOTORING and GENERAL INFORMATION

goods made from them; meat and poultry and most of their products (whether or not cooked), including ham, bacon, sausage, pâté, eggs and milk; plants, parts thereof and plant produce, including trees and shrubs, potatoes and certain other vegetables, fruit, bulbs and seeds; wood with bark attached; certain fish and fish eggs (whether live or dead); bees; radio transmitters (*eg* citizens' band radios, walkie-talkies, etc) not approved for use in the UK.

Customs Notice No. 1 is available to all travellers at the point of entry, or on the boat, and contains useful information of which returning tourists should be aware. Details for drivers going through the *red* and *green channels* are enclosed in *Notice No. 1*. Copies of this can be obtained from HM Customs and Excise, CDE, Room 201, Dorset House, Stamford Street, London SE1 9PS.

*Note Cats, dogs and other mammals must not be landed unless a British import licence (rabies) has previously been issued.

DIMENSIONS AND WEIGHT RESTRICTIONS

Private **cars** and towed **trailers** or **caravans** are restricted to the following dimensions – height, no restriction, but 4 metres is a recommended maximum; width, 2.50 metres; length, 11 metres (excluding towing device). The maximum permitted overall length of vehicle/trailer or caravan combination is 18 metres.

If the weight of the trailer exceeds that of the towing vehicle, see also *Speed limits* page 22.

DIRECTION INDICATORS

All direction indicators should be working at 60–120 flashes per minute. Most standard car-flasher units will be overloaded by the extra lamps of a caravan or trailer, and a special heavy-duty unit or a relay device should be fitted.

DRINKING AND DRIVING

There is only one safe rule – **if you drink, don't drive.** The laws are strict and penalties severe.

DRIVING LICENCE

A valid UK or Republic of Ireland licence is acceptable in France. The minimum age at which a visitor may use a temporarily imported car or motorcycle (exceeding 80cc) is 18 years – for a motorcycle not exceeding 80cc it is 16 years. See also *Speed limits* page 22.

If your licence is due to expire before your anticipated return, it should be renewed in good time prior to your departure. The Driver and Vehicle Licensing Centre (in Northern Ireland the Licensing Authority) will accept an application two months before the expiry of your old licence.

In the Republic of Ireland, licensing authorities will accept an application one month before the expiry of your old licence.

ELECTRICAL INFORMATION

General The public electricity supply in France is predominantly AC (alternating current) of 220 volts (50 cycles) but can be as low as 110 volts. European circular two-pin plugs and screw-type bulbs are usually the rule. Useful electrical adaptors (not voltage transformers) which can be used in French shaver points and light bulb sockets are available in the UK, usually from the larger electrical appliance retailers.

Vehicle Check that all the connections are sound, and that the wiring is in good condition. Should any problems arise with the charging system, it is essential to obtain the services of a qualified auto-electrician.

EMERGENCY MESSAGES TO TOURISTS

In cases of emergency, the AA will assist in the passing on of messages to tourists. The AA can arrange for messages to be published in overseas editions of the *Daily Mail*, and in an extreme emergency (death or serious illness concerning next-of-kin) can arrange to have personal messages broadcast on Radio Monte Carlo. These messages are transmitted in French on 1400 metres long wave between 21.00 and 22.30hrs. Anyone wishing to use this service should contact their nearest AA Centre. Before you leave home, make sure your relatives understand the procedures to follow should an emergency occur.

11

French ABC

No guarantee can be given, either by the AA or by the *Daily Mail*, to trace the person concerned, and no responsibility can be accepted for the authenticity of messages.

ENGINE AND MECHANICAL

Consult your vehicle handbook for servicing intervals. Unless the engine oil has been changed recently, drain and refill with fresh oil and fit a new filter. Deal with any significant leaks by tightening up loose nuts and bolts and renewing faulty joints and seals.

Brands and grades of *engine oil* familiar to the British motorist are readily available in France. However, they will be much more expensive than in the UK and generally packed in 2-litre cans (3½pints). Motorists can usually assess the normal consumption of their car and carry what oil is likely to be required for the trip.

If you suspect that there is anything wrong with the engine, however insignificant it may seem, it should be dealt with straightaway. Even if everything seems in order, do not neglect such commonsense precautions as checking valve clearances, sparking plugs, and contact breaker points where fitted, and make sure that the distributor cap is sound. The fan belt should be checked for fraying and slackness. If any of these are showing signs of wear you should replace them.

Any obvious mechanical defects should be attended to at once. Look particularly for play in steering connections and wheel bearings and, where applicable, ensure that they are adequately greased. A car that has covered a high mileage will have absorbed a certain amount of dirt into the fuel system, and as breakdowns are often caused by dirt, it is essential that all filters (petrol and air) should be cleaned or renewed.

Owners should think twice about towing a caravan with a car that has already given appreciable service. Hard driving on motorways and in mountainous country puts an extra strain on ageing parts and items such as a burnt-out clutch can be very expensive to replace.

Check the cooling system for leaks and the correct proportion of anti-freeze and replace any perished hoses or suspect parts.

EUROCHEQUES

The Eurocheque scheme is a flexible money-transfer system operated by a network of European Banks, including France. All the major UK banks are part of the Uniform Eurocheque Scheme and you will be able to obtain from them a multi-currency chequebook enabling you to write cheques in *francs*. Approach your bankers well in advance of your departure for further information.

FERRY CROSSING

Motorists can cross the Channel to France by ship or hovercraft services. Short sea crossings operate from Dover to Boulogne (1hr 40mins) and Calais (1¼–1½hrs), and Folkestone to Boulogne (1hr 50mins). Longer Channel crossings operate from Ramsgate to Dunkerque (Dunkirk) (2½hrs), Newhaven to Dieppe (4hrs), Portsmouth to Le Havre (5¾–7½hrs) or Caen (5¼–7hrs) or *Cherbourg (4¾–6hrs) or St Malo (9–11hrs), *Poole to Cherbourg (4½hrs), Plymouth to Roscoff (6–6½hrs) and *Weymouth to Cherbourg (4–6hrs). Fast hovercraft services operate between Dover and Boulogne (40mins) or Calais (35mins).

In addition, car-sleeper trains operate from Boulogne, Calais and Dieppe to the south of the country.

* Summer *only* service

The AA provides a full information service on all sea, motorail and hovercraft services, and instant confirmation is available on many by ringing one of the numbers listed (Monday to Friday, 09.00–17.00hrs). Ring these numbers too if you want information and booking on French car-sleeper and ferry services.

The South East	☏01-930 2462 (for car ferry and motorail only)
The West & Wales	☏Bristol (0272) 264417
The Midlands	☏021-550 7648
The North	☏061-845 8551
Scotland and Northern Ireland	☏041-848 8674
Republic of Ireland	☏Dublin (0001) 833656

FIRE EXTINGUISHER

It is a wise precaution to equip your vehicle with a fire extinguisher when motoring abroad. An AA Fire Extinguisher may be purchased from your nearest AA Centre.

MOTORING and GENERAL INFORMATION

FIRST-AID KIT

It is a wise precaution to equip your vehicle with a first-aid kit when motoring abroad. An AA First-Aid Kit may be purchased from your nearest AA Centre.

h

HORN, USE OF

In built-up areas, the general rule is not to use horns unless safety demands it; in many large towns and resorts, as well as in areas indicated by the international sign (a horn inside a red circle, crossed through), the use of the horn is totally prohibited.

i

IDENTIFICATION PLATE

If a boat, caravan or trailer is taken abroad, it must have a unique chassis number for identification purposes. If your boat, caravan or trailer does not have a number, an *identification plate* may be purchased from the AA.

INSURANCE, INCLUDING CARAVAN INSURANCE

Third-party motor insurance is compulsory by law in France and you are strongly advised to ensure that you are adequately covered. Temporary policies may be obtained at the port of entry, but this is the most expensive way of effecting cover. It is best to seek early advice from your insurer regarding an extension of your full policy cover as it applies in the UK. Should you have any difficulty, *AA Insurance Services* will be pleased to help you. Third-party insurance is also recommended for all boats temporarily imported into France (see also *Boats* page 7).

An International motor insurance certificate or *Green Card*, although no longer necessary to enter France, is ready evidence that you are covered to the minimum extent demanded by local laws and the AA strongly recommends that you obtain one. It will be issued by your own insurer, upon payment of an additional premium, for extension of your UK policy cover to apply in France. The document will not be accepted until you have signed it. Green Cards are recognised by police and other authorities, and may save a great deal of inconvenience in the event of an accident. If you are towing a caravan or trailer, it will need separate insurance, and mention on your Green Card. Remember, the cover on a caravan or trailer associated with a Green Card is normally limited to third-party towing risks, so a separate policy (see *AA Caravan Plus* below) is advisable to cover accidental damage, fire or theft.

In accordance with a Common Market Directive, the production and inspection of Green Cards at the frontiers of Common Market countries are no longer legal requirements. However, the fact that Green Cards will not be inspected does not remove the necessity of having insurance cover as required by law in France.

Motorists can obtain expert advice through *AA Insurance Services* for all types of insurance. Several special schemes have been arranged with leading insurers to enable motorists to obtain wide insurance cover at economic premiums. One of these schemes, *AA Caravan Plus*, includes damage cover for caravans and their contents, including personal effects. While detached from the towing vehicle, protection against your legal liability to other persons arising out of the use of the caravan is also provided. Cover is extended to the Continent of Europe for up to 60 days in any period of insurance without extra charge. *AA Caravan Plus* also provides cover for camping equipment. Full details of *AA Caravan Plus* may be obtained from any AA Centre or direct from AA Insurance Services Ltd, PO Box 2AA, Newcastle upon Tyne NE99 2AA.

Finally, make sure that you are covered against damage in transit (*eg* on the ferry or motorail). Most comprehensive motor insurance policies provide adequate cover for transit between ports in the UK, but need to be extended to give this cover if travelling outside the UK. You are advised to check this aspect with your insurer before setting off on your journey.

INTERNATIONAL DISTINGUISHING SIGN

An international distinguishing sign of the approved pattern, oval with black letters on a white background, and size (GB at least 6.9in by 4.5in), must be displayed on a vertical surface at

13

French ABC

the rear of your vehicle (and caravan or trailer if you are towing one). These distinguishing signs signify the country of registration of the vehicle. Checks are made to ensure that a vehicle's nationality plate is in order. Fines are imposed for failing to display a nationality plate, or for not displaying the correct nationality plate.

l

LEVEL CROSSINGS

Practically all level crossings are indicated by international signs. Most guarded ones are of the lifting barrier type, sometimes with bells or flashing lights to give warning of an approaching train.

LIGHTS

For driving abroad, headlights should be altered so that the dipped beam does not dazzle oncoming drivers. The alteration can be made by fitting headlamp convertors (PVC mask sheets) or beam deflectors (clip-on lenses) which may be purchased from your nearest AA Centre. However, beam deflectors must not be used with halogen lamps. It is important to remember to remove the headlamp converters or beam deflectors as soon as you return to the UK.

In France, it is obligatory to use headlights, as driving on sidelights *only* is not permitted. In fog, mist or poor visibility during the day, either two fog lamps or two dipped headlights must be switched on, in addition to two sidelights. It is also compulsory for *motorcyclists* riding machines exceeding 125cc to use dipped headlights during the day. Failure to comply with this regulation will lead to an on-the-spot fine (see *Police deposits ('fines')* page 19). Headlight flashing is used only as a warning of approach, or a passing signal at night. In other circumstances, it is accepted as a sign of irritation and should be used with caution lest it is misunderstood.

It is recommended that visiting motorists equip their vehicle with a set of replacement bulbs; drivers unable to replace a faulty bulb when requested to do so by the police may be fined. An AA Emergency Auto Bulb Kit suitable for most makes of car, can be purchased from your nearest AA Centre. Alternatively, spare bulbs form a part of the AA Spares Kit (see *Spares* page 22). Visiting motorists are also advised to comply with the regulation which requires all locally registered vehicles to be equipped with headlights which show a yellow beam and, in the interests of safety and courtesy, visiting motorists are advised to comply. If you are able to use beam deflectors to alter your headlights for driving abroad, you can purchase deflectors with yellow lenses. However, with headlamp converters, it is necessary to coat the outer surface of the headlamp glass with a yellow plastic paint which is removable with a solvent. This headlamp paint may be purchased from your nearest AA Centre.

LIQUEFIED PETROLEUM GAS (LPG)

The availability of *LPG* in France makes a carefully planned tour with a converted vehicle feasible. Motorists regularly purchasing this fuel in the UK could possibly obtain a list of French garages selling *LPG* from their UK retailer.

When booking a ferry crossing, it is advisable to point out to the booking agent/ferry company that the vehicle runs on a dual-fuel system.

m

MEDICAL TREATMENT

Travellers who are in the habit of taking certain medicines should ensure they have a sufficient supply to last throughout their trip.

Those who suffer from certain diseases (diabetes or coronary artery diseases, for example) should get a letter from their doctor giving treatment details. Some doctors will understand a letter written in English, but it is better to have it translated into French. The AA cannot make such a translation.

Travellers who, for legitimate health reasons, carry drugs or appliances (*eg* hypodermic syringes) may have difficulty with Customs or other authorities. Others may have a dietary problem, which would be understood in hotels but for a language barrier: again it is better to have details translated into French. The letter(s) which such persons carry should, therefore, supply treatment details, a statement for Customs, and dietary requirements.

The UK has a reciprocal health agreement with France under which visitors can obtain urgently

MOTORING and GENERAL INFORMATION

needed medical treatment at reduced cost. However, the cover provided under this arrangement is not comprehensive, nor does it extend to **Monaco** where the **full** costs of medical care must be paid. Therefore, you are strongly advised to take out adequate insurance cover before leaving the UK such as that offered by *Personal Security* under the *AA 5-Star Service*.

Details of the reciprocal health agreement are in the DHSS leaflet *SA40*, '*The Traveller's Guide to Health – Before You Go*'. Free copies are available from local offices of the Department of Health and Social Security or from its Leaflets Unit at PO Box 21, Stanmore, Middlesex HA7 1AY ☎0800 555 777. The DHSS leaflet *SA40* incorporates an application form for a certificate of entitlement (*E111*) which is necessary to obtain treatment. Applicants should allow at least one month for the form to be processed, although in an emergency the *E111* can be obtained over the counter of the local DHSS office (residents of the Republic of Ireland must apply to their Regional Health Board for the *E111*). The DHSS leaflet *SA40* also gives advice about health precautions and international vaccination requirements.

Further information about health care precautions and how to deal with an emergency abroad is given in the DHSS leaflet *SA41*, '*The Traveller's Guide to Health – While You're Away*'. A free copy is also available from DHSS Leaflets, PO Box 21, Stanmore, Middlesex HA7 1AY ☎0800 555 777.

MINIBUS

A minibus constructed and equipped to carry 10 or more persons (including the driver*) and used outside the UK is subject to the regulations governing international bus and coach journeys. This will generally mean that the vehicle must be fitted with a tachograph, and documentation, in the form of a Driver's Certificate, Model Control Document and waybill obtained. For vehicles registered in Great Britain (England, Scotland and Wales), contact the authorities as follows:

   a   for Driver's Certificate, apply to the local Traffic Area Office of the Department of Transport;

   b   for Model Control Document and waybill, apply to the Bus and Coach Council, Sardinia House, 52 Lincoln's Inn Fields, London WC2A 3LZ ☎01-831 7546.

For vehicles registered in Northern Ireland, contact the Department of the Environment for Northern Ireland, Road Transport Department, Upper Galwally, Belfast BT8 4FY ☎(0232) 649044.

Residents of the Republic of Ireland should contact the Department of Labour, Mespil Road, Dublin 4 for details about tachographs, and the Government Publications Sales Office, Molesworth Street, Dublin 2 for information about documentation.

The above authorities should be contacted well in advance of your departure.

*Note: A minibus driver must be at least 21 years of age and hold a full driving licence valid for group 'A' or, if automatic transmission, group 'B'.

MIRRORS

When driving in France on the right, it is essential, as when driving on the left in the UK and Republic of Ireland, to have clear all-round vision. Ideally, external rear-view mirrors should be fitted to both sides of your vehicle, but certainly on the left to allow for driving on the right.

MOTORING CLUB

The *Alliance Internationale de Tourisme (AIT)* is the largest confederation of touring associations in the world, and it is through this body that the AA is affiliated to the *Association Française des Automobilistes (AFA)* whose office is at 9 rue Anatole-de-la-Forge, F-75017 Paris ☎42278200.

MOTORWAYS

There are about 4,110 miles of motorway (*Autoroute*) open, and more are under construction or in preparation. To join a motorway, follow signs with the international motorway symbol, or signs with the words '*par Autoroute*' added. Signs with the added words '*Péage*' or '*par Péage*' lead to toll roads. With the exception of a few sections into or around large cities, all *autoroutes* have a toll charged according to the distance travelled, *eg* toll charges for a single journey from Calais to Nice are about £33 for a car and about £49 for a car with caravan. On the majority of toll motorways, a travel ticket is issued on entry and the toll is paid on leaving the motorway. The travel ticket gives all relevant information about the toll charges, including the toll category of your vehicle. At the exit point, the ticket is handed in and the amount due shows up on an illuminated sign at the toll booth. On some motorways, the toll collection is automatic; have the correct amount ready to throw into the

15

French ABC

collecting basket. If change is required, use the marked separate lane.

Motorway restaurants The *L'Arche* restaurant chain was the first network of restaurants established on French motorways. The 21 restaurants are open all year at least 07.00–22.30hrs, and offer the prospect of a relaxing stop-over. Change facilities, a telephone, a baby's corner and playgrounds for children are always to be found. For more details see inside front cover.

Motorway telephones For assistance on a motorway, use one of the telephone boxes sited at 2.4km (1½ mile) intervals; they are connected to police stations. A leaflet entitled *Motorways in France* is available to AA members.

ORANGE BADGE SCHEME FOR DISABLED DRIVERS

There is no formal system of concessions in operation, and responsibility for parking in built-up areas rests with the local authorities. Any parking places reserved for the disabled are indicated by the international symbol. However, the police are instructed to show consideration where parking by the disabled is concerned. In some towns and cities including Paris, orange badge holders may be allowed to park at meter bays and pay only the initial charge.

As in the UK, the arrangements only apply to badge holders themselves and the concessions are not for the benefit of able-bodied friends or relatives. A non-entitled person who seeks to take advantage of the concessions by wrongfully displaying an orange badge will be liable to whatever penalties apply for unlawful parking.

OVERLOADING

This can create safety risks, and committing such an offence can involve *on-the-spot* fines (see *Police deposits ('fines')* page 19). It would also be a great inconvenience if your car was stopped because of overloading – you would not be allowed to proceed until the load had been reduced.

The maximum loaded weight, and its distribution between front and rear axles, is decided by the vehicle manufacturer, and if your owner's handbook does not give these facts, you should seek the advice of the manufacturer direct. There is a public weighbridge in all districts, and when the car is fully loaded (not forgetting the passengers, of course), use this to check that the vehicle is within the limits.

When loading a vehicle, care should be taken that no lights, reflectors or number plates are masked, and that the driver's view is in no way impaired. All luggage loaded on a roof-rack must be tightly secured, and should not upset the stability of the vehicle. Any projections beyond the front, rear, or sides of a vehicle, that might not be noticed by other drivers, must be clearly marked.

OVERTAKING

When overtaking on roads with two lanes or more in each direction, always signal your intention in good time, and after the manoeuvre, signal and return to the inside lane. Do *not* remain in any other lane. Failure to comply with this regulation will incur an *on-the-spot* fine (see *Police deposits ('fines')* page 19).

Always overtake on the left, and use your horn as a warning to the driver of the vehicle being overtaken (except in areas where the use of the horn is prohibited). Do not overtake whilst being overtaken or when a vehicle behind is preparing to overtake. Do not overtake at level crossings, at intersections, the crest of a hill or at pedestrian crossings. When being overtaken, keep well to the right and reduce speed if necessary – never increase speed.

PARKING

Regulations are similar to those in the UK. As a general rule, all prohibitions are indicated by road signs or by yellow markings on the kerb. It is prohibited to leave a vehicle parked in the same place for more than 24 consecutive hours in Paris and surrounding departments.

On some roads in built-up areas, parking is allowed from the 1st to the 15th day of each month on the side of the road where the numbers of the buildings are odd, and from the 16th to the last

CALAIS—So close you could touch it. Once the only landfall for Britons bound for the Continent and far and away the best route today.

Modern jumbo car ferries plus giant hovercraft provide a choice of over 100 crossings daily during the summer and never less than 50 off peak.

Take the shortest crossing between Dover and Calais. From 75 minutes by car ferry and from 30 minutes by hovercraft.

VIA Calais
—the shortest route to France

French ABC

day of the month on the side with even numbers. This is called *alternate unilateral parking*.

There are short-term parking areas known as *blue zones* in most principal towns; in these areas, discs must be used (placed against the windscreen) every day, except Sundays and Public holidays, between 09.00 and 12.30hrs and 14.30 and 19.00hrs. They permit parking for up to one hour. Discs are sold at police stations, but at tourist offices and some clubs and commercial firms they are available free of charge. There are *grey zones* where parking meters are in use; in these zones, a fee must be paid between 09.00 and 19.00hrs. Motorists using a ticket issued by an automatic machine must display the ticket on the inside of the windscreen or nearside front window of their car.

In **Paris**, cars towing caravans are prohibited from the *blue zone* between 14.00 and 20.30hrs. Cars towing trailers with an overall surface of 10sq metres or more may neither circulate nor park in the central *green zone* between 14.00 and 20.30hrs, except on Sundays and Public holidays. Vehicle combinations with an overall surface exceeding 16sq metres may neither circulate nor park in the *green zone* between 08.00 and 20.30hrs. Those wishing to cross Paris during these hours with vehicle/trailer combinations can use the Boulevard Périphérique, although the route is heavily congested, except during Public holiday periods. In some parts of the *green zone*, parking is completely forbidden. It is prohibited to park caravans, even for a limited period, not only in the *green zone* but in almost all areas of Paris.

Vehicles which are parked contrary to regulations are liable to be removed by the police at the owner's risk, and the driver will be liable for any costs incurred, including a heavy fine.

PASSENGERS

Children under 10 are not permitted to travel in a vehicle as front-seat passengers when rear seating is available.

For passenger-carrying vehicles constructed and equipped to carry more than 10 passengers, including the driver, there are special regulations. See *Minibus* page 15.

PASSPORTS

Each person must hold, or be named on, an *up-to-date* passport. Passports should be carried at all times and, as an extra precaution, a separate note kept of the number, date and place of issue. There are various types of British passports, including the standard or regular passport and the limited British Visitor's Passport.

Standard UK passports are issued to British Nationals, *ie* British Citizens, British Dependent Territories Citizens, British Overseas Citizens, British Nationals (Overseas), British Subjects, and British Protected Persons. Normally issued for a period of 10 years, a standard UK passport is valid for travel to all countries in the world. A family passport may cover the holder and children under 16. Children under 16 may be issued with a separate passport valid for 5 years and renewable for a further 5 years on application. Full information and application forms in respect of the standard UK passport may be obtained from a main Post Office or from one of the Passport Offices in Belfast, Douglas (Isle of Man), Glasgow, Liverpool, London, Newport (Gwent), Peterborough, St Helier (Jersey) and St Peter Port (Guernsey). Application for a standard passport should be made to the Passport Office appropriate for the area concerned, allowing at least one month, or between February and August (when most people apply for passports) – three months for passport formalities to be completed, and should be accompanied by the requisite documents and fees.

British Visitor's Passports are issued to British Citizens, British Dependent Territories Citizens or British Overseas Citizens over the age of 8, resident in the UK, Isle of Man or Channel Islands. Valid for one year only, they are acceptable for travel in France. A British Visitor's Passport issued to cover the holder, spouse and children under 16 may only be used by the first person named on the passport to travel alone. Children under 8 cannot have their own Visitor's Passport. Full information and application forms may be obtained from main Post Offices in Great Britain (England, Scotland and Wales) or Passport Offices in the Channel Islands, Isle of Man and Northern Ireland. However, Visitor's Passports or application forms for Visitor's Passports are NOT obtainable from Passport Offices in Great Britain. All applications for a Visitor's Passport must be submitted *in person* to a main Post Office, or Passport Office as appropriate. Provided the documents are in order and the fee is paid, the passport is issued immediately.

Irish Citizens resident in the Dublin Metropolitan area or in Northern Ireland should apply to the Passport Office, Dublin; if resident elsewhere in the Irish Republic, they should apply through the nearest Garda station. Irish citizens resident in Britain should apply to the Irish Embassy in London.

MOTORING and GENERAL INFORMATION

PEDESTRIAN CROSSINGS

In France, pedestrian crossings are known as *Passages Piétons* and identified by wide, white bands across the road. Pedestrians have right of way and motorists must slow down, and stop if necessary, to give way to pedestrians *who are crossing*.

PETROL

In the UK, the motorist uses a fuel recommended by the vehicle manufacturer, and this is related to a star method (2-star, 90 octane; 3-star, 93 octane; and 4-star, 97 octane). In France, petrol (*essence*) is graded as *Normale* or *Super* and visiting motorists should be careful to use a grade in the recommended range, as many modern engines designed to run on 4-star petrol are critical on carburation and ignition settings. Additionally, as *unleaded petrol* is now being sold, it is important to purchase the correct petrol. If a car designed to run on leaded petrol is filled with unleaded petrol, it will do no immediate harm, but ensure that the next fill is the correct type and grade. Any queries regarding the suitability of a vehicle for an unleaded fuel should be directed to the vehicle manufacturer or the manufacturer's agent. A leaflet containing further information on the subject of *Leaded and Unleaded Petrol in Europe* is available through AA Centres and AA Port Service Centres.

At the time of going to press, there are no supply problems and petrol is readily available throughout France. If a full tank is required, ask for *Faites le plein, s'il vous plaît*. The minimum amount of petrol which may be purchased is usually five litres (just over one gallon). It is advisable to keep the petrol tank topped up, particularly in remote areas or if wishing to make an early start when garages may be closed, but when doing this use a lockable filler cap as a security measure. Although petrol prices are not quoted, the current position can be checked with the AA before departure.

Credit cards The most widely accepted credit cards at petrol stations in France are Access, Eurocard/Mastercard and Visa; these can be used for purchases of petrol at main garages.

Duty-free petrol The petrol in the vehicle tank may be imported free of customs duty and tax.

Petrol (leaded) Essence Normale (90octane) and Essence Super (98 octane) grades.

Petrol (unleaded) is sold in France as Essence Super (95 octane). Pumps dispensing unleaded petrol are clearly marked with a sticker *super sans plomb* (super grade unleaded).

PHOTOGRAPHY

Photography is generally allowed without restriction, with the exception of photographs taken within the vicinity of military or government establishments. Signs are usually prominent where the use of cameras is prohibited, and are often a picture of a camera crossed by a diagonal line.

POLICE DEPOSITS ('FINES')

The French Police Authorities have the power to impose and collect *on-the-spot* deposits (often mistakenly called fines), for certain traffic offences such as speeding, failing to give priority or obey a traffic sign, and driving without lights at night or in fog. Such deposits must be paid in French francs, and the amount is often very high, even for minor offences (*eg* 600 francs). A deposit will be ordered when offenders cannot provide evidence of their employment or permanent residence in France. If it is not paid, the authorities have the power to impound the vehicle, and subsequently to sell it if the deposit remains unpaid. It is usually easier to pay the deposit, but do make sure that you obtain a receipt for it. Court proceedings are always taken on a subsequent date. Written notification of the court hearing will be sent prior to the date set, and you can appear in the court and give your explanation if you wish. If there is an acquittal, the deposit monies are returned to the motorist. If there is a conviction, the judge fixes the fine which is normally the amount of the deposit, so no more money need be paid. AA members who feel they require assistance in any matter involving local police can apply to the Legal Department of the national motoring organisation.

POLLUTION

Tourists should be aware that pollution of the sea-water at European coastal resorts, particularly on the shores of the Mediterranean, represents a severe health hazard. Not many popular resorts wish to admit to this, but others now realise the dangers and erect signs, albeit small ones, forbidding bathing. These signs would read as follows:

No bathing *Défense de se baigner*
Bathing prohibited *Il est défendu de se baigner*

19

French ABC

POSTAL INFORMATION

Mail Postcards *Fr*2; letters up to 20gm *Fr*2.20.

Post offices There are 17,500 post offices in France. They are open 09.00–12.00hrs and 14.00–17.00hrs Monday to Friday, and 09.00–12.00hrs Saturday. Opening hours of small offices in rural areas may vary. In Paris, the office at 52 rue du Louvre is open 24 hours a day.

POSTCHEQUES

Girobank current account holders who have a cheque guarantee card can use the *Girobank Postcheque* service when travelling in France.

Postcheques may be cashed at all post offices up to a maximum of *Fr*1200 per cheque. Counter positions are identified by the words *Paiement des mandats* or *Chèques postaux*. See *Postal information* for post office opening hours.

Further information may be obtained from: International Division, Girobank plc, Bootle, Merseyside GIR 0AA. ☎051-933 3330.

POSTE RESTANTE

If you are uncertain of having a precise address, you can be contacted through the local *poste restante*. Before leaving the UK, notify your friends of your approximate whereabouts at given times. If you expect mail, call with your passport at the main post office of the town where you are staying. To ensure that the arrival of correspondence will coincide with your stay, your correspondent should check with the Post Office regarding delivery times before posting. It is most important that the recipient's name be written in full: *eg* Mr Lazarus Perkins, Poste Restante, Nice, France. Do not use *Esq*.

PRIORITY INCLUDING ROUNDABOUTS

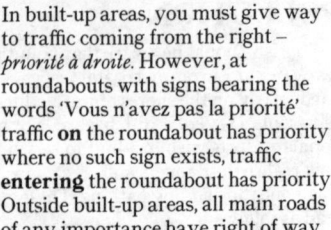

1. In built-up areas, you must give way to traffic coming from the right – *priorité à droite*. However, at roundabouts with signs bearing the words 'Vous n'avez pas la priorité' traffic **on** the roundabout has priority; where no such sign exists, traffic **entering** the roundabout has priority. Outside built-up areas, all main roads of any importance have right of way. This is indicated by a red bordered triangle showing a black cross on a white background with the words '*Passage Protégé*' underneath (1); or a red-bordered triangle showing a pointed black upright with horizontal bar on a white background (2); or a yellow square within a white square with points vertical (3).

PUBLIC HOLIDAYS

Public holidays, on which banks, offices and shops are closed, generally fall into two categories: those which are fixed on the calendar by some national festival or religious date and those which are movable. The latter (usually religious), are based on a movable Easter Sunday, and the actual dates for 1989 are given below. Further information about annual events and festivals may be obtained from the French Government Tourist Office, see page 23.

January 1 †(New Year's Day)
March 26 (Easter Sunday)
March 27 (Easter Monday)
May 1 (Labour Day)
May 4 (Ascension Day)
May 8 (VE Day)
May 14 (Whit Sunday)
May 15 (Whit Monday)
July 14 (National Holiday)
August 15 (Assumption)
November 1 (All Saints' Day)
November 11* (Armistice Day)
December 25 (Christmas Day)
* Saturday † Sunday

RADIO TELEPHONES/ CITIZENS' BAND RADIOS AND TRANSMITTERS IN TOURIST CARS ABROAD

There are restrictions and controls on the temporary importation and subsequent use of radio transmitters and radio telephones. Therefore, if your vehicle contains such equipment, whether fitted or portable, you should contact the AA for guidance.

MOTORING and GENERAL INFORMATION

REGISTRATION DOCUMENT

You must carry the original vehicle registration document with you. If, for any reason, your registration document has to be sent to the licensing authorities, you should bear in mind that, as processing can take some while, the document may not be available in time for your departure. Under these circumstances, a *Certificate of Registration (V379)* will normally be issued to cover the vehicle for international circulation purposes. It can be obtained free of charge from your nearest Vehicle Registration Office upon production of proof of identity (eg driving licence) and proof of ownership (eg bill of sale).

If you plan to use a borrowed, hired or leased vehicle, you should be aware that:
- **a** for a borrowed vehicle, the registration document must be accompanied by a letter of authority to use the vehicle from the registered keeper;
- **b** for a UK-registered hired or leased vehicle, the registration document will normally be retained by the hire company. Under these circumstances, a *Hired/Leased Vehicle Certificate (VE 103A)* should be used in its place; this may be purchased from the AA.

RELIGIOUS SERVICES

Refer to your religious organisation in the British Isles. A directory of British Protestant churches in Europe, North Africa and the Middle East, entitled *English Speaking Churches*, can be purchased from Intercon (Intercontinental Church Society), 175 Tower Bridge Road, London SE1 2AQ ☎01-407 4588.

The Intercontinental Church Society welcomes visitors from any denomination to English language services in the following centres:
06400 Cannes The Rev Canon Keith Anderson, Chaplain's Apartment, 'Residence Kent', rue Général Ferrie ☎93945461
60500 Chantilly The Rev John Fulton, 15F av Marie-Amelie ☎44585322
59140 Dunkerque The Rev Tony Rimmer, 130 rue de l'Ecole Maternelle ☎28633947
33310 Lormont The Rev Brian Eaves, 32 rue de Lormont Village (serving Bordeaux) ☎56063717
78600 Maisons-Laffitte 15 av Carnot (Paris area) ☎39623497
75008 Paris The Ven Brian Lea, 5 rue d'Aguesseau ☎47427088
69110 Sainte Foy-Les-Lyon The Rev Gerald Hovenden, Le Coteau, 38 Chemin de Taffignon (serving Lyon and Grenoble) ☎78596706
78000 Versailles The Rev Martin Oram, 31 rue du Pont Colbert ☎39514707

ROADS (INCLUDING HOLIDAY TRAFFIC)

France has a very comprehensive network of roads, the surfaces of which are normally good; exceptions are usually signposted *Chaussée déformée*. The camber is often severe and the edges rough.

During July and August and especially at weekends, traffic on main roads is likely to be very heavy. Special signs are erected to indicate alternative routes with the least traffic congestion. Wherever they appear, it is usually advantageous to follow them, although you cannot be absolutely sure of gaining time. The alternative routes are quiet, but they are not as wide as the main roads. They are **not** suitable for caravans.

A free road map showing the marked alternative routes, plus information centres and 24-hr petrol stations is available from service stations displaying the *Bison Futé* poster (a Red Indian chief in full war bonnet). These maps are also available from *Syndicats d'Initiative* and information offices.

Road number changes Following the 1974–78 decentralisation, when many secondary National highways were transferred to the Departments ('N' to 'D' roads; when N315 became D915, and N16 became D916, *etc*), further modifications to the road system are taking place. These latest changes involve about 4,000–5,000km on N-roads throughout France, and some irregularities may occur during the changeover period when the same road may have signs showing two different numbers.

Traffic lanes (Paris) There are special lanes for buses and taxis only in some streets; these are marked by a continuous yellow line painted one vehicle width from the kerb. Usually, buses and taxis in the special lane travel in the opposite direction to other traffic.

ROAD SIGNS

Most road signs are internationally agreed, and the majority will be familiar to the British motorist, but see *Priority including roundabouts* page 20.

Watch for road markings – do not cross a solid white or yellow line marked on the road centre.

21

French ABC

RULE OF THE ROAD

In France, drive on the right and overtake on the left.

SEAT BELTS

If your car is fitted with seat belts, it is compulsory to wear them. Failure to do so could result in an *on-the-spot* fine, see *Police deposits ('fines')* page 19.

SHOPPING HOURS

Most shops, including department stores, are open Monday to Saturday 09.00–18.30/19.00hrs; *food shops* open earlier at 07.00hrs, and some (*bakers* in particular), open on Sunday mornings. *Hypermarkets* generally remain open until 21.00/22.00hrs. However, outside the larger cities, you will find that many shops close all day, or a half-day, on Mondays. In *small towns* lunch-time closing can extend from 12.00 to 14.00hrs.

SPARES

The problem of what spares to carry is a difficult one; it depends on the vehicle and how long you are likely to be away. However, you should consider hiring an *AA Spares Kit* for your car; full information about this service is available from any AA Centre or AA Port Service Centre. AA Emergency Windscreens are also available for hire or purchase. In addition to the items contained in the spares kit, the following would also prove useful:

* a pair of windscreen wiper blades;
* a torch;
* a length of electrical cable;
* a fire extinguisher;
* an inner tube of the correct type;
* a tow rope;
* a roll of insulating or adhesive tape.

Remember that when ordering spare parts for dispatch abroad, you must be able to identify them as clearly as possible, and by the manufacturer's part numbers if known. When ordering spares, always quote the engine and chassis numbers of your car. See also *Lights*, page 14.

SPEED LIMITS

It is important to observe speed limits at all times. Offenders may be fined and driving licences confiscated on the spot, causing great inconvenience and possible expense. The limits may be varied by road signs, and where such signs are displayed, the lower limit should be accepted. At certain times, limits may also be temporarily varied, and information should be available at the frontier. It can be an offence to travel at so slow a speed as to obstruct traffic flow without good reason.

The beginning of a built-up area is indicated by a sign bearing the placename in blue letters on a light background; the end by the placename sign with a thin red line diagonally across it. Unless otherwise signposted, speed limits are:

Built-up areas 60kph (37mph)
Outside built-up areas on normal roads 90kph (56mph); on *dual-carriageways* separated by a central reservation 110kph (68mph).
On Motorways 130kph (80mph). **Note** The *minimum* speed in the fast lane on a level stretch of motorway during good daytime visibility is 80kph (49mph), and drivers travelling below this speed are liable to be fined. The *maximum* speed on *urban stretches of motorway* is 110kph (68mph).

In wet weather, speed limits outside built-up areas are reduced to 80kph (49mph), 100kph (62mph) and 110kph (68mph) on motorways.

These limits also apply to private cars towing a trailer or caravan, if the latter's weight does not exceed that of the car. However, if the weight of the trailer exceeds that of the car by less than 30% the speed limit is 65kph (39mph); if more than 30% the speed limit is 45kph (28mph). Additionally, these combinations must:

i Display a disc at the rear of the caravan/trailer showing the maximum speed.

ii Not be driven in the fast lane of a 3-lane motorway.

Both French residents and visitors to France, who have held a driving licence for less than one year, must not exceed 90kph (56mph) or any lower signposted limit when driving in France.

SPIKED OR STUDDED TYRES

Spiked or *studded tyres* must be used from 15 November to 15 March by vehicles with a total authorised laden weight not exceeding 3,500kg, provided that a speed of 90kph (56mph) is not exceeded. The speed-limitation disc bearing

MOTORING and GENERAL INFORMATION

the figure '90' is only obligatory for French-registered vehicles. See also *Cold weather touring*, page 8.

TELEPHONE

Insert coin **after** lifting receiver, dialling tone is a continuous tone. Generally, to make a local call use *Fr*1 coin, or *jeton* (special telephone coin bought from point where call is made), but 2 × 50 *centimes* required in some callboxes. Coins accepted are 50 *centimes* and *Fr*1, 5 or 10. Many telephone booths now take phonecards; you can buy the *télécarte* from post offices and where advertised on telephone booths.

Within France, to call one provincial number from another, or one Paris area number (Paris, Seine St Denis, Hauts de Seine and Val de Marne) from another, simply dial the 8-digit number. To call a Paris area number from the provinces, precede the 8-digit number with (161), and to call a provincial number from the Paris area precede the 8-digit number with (16).

To make a call *to the UK*, other than from a private phone, use an international callbox. Dial the code given below, the telephone dialling code (omitting the intial '0') followed by the number. For example, to call AA Basingstoke (0256) 20123, dial 19 44 256 20123. The highest value coin accepted is *Fr*10 and this should allow a reasonable period of uninterrupted conversation.

International callbox identification Metallic grey payphones. Cardphones.

Telephone rates The charge for a call to the UK is *Fr*0.5 for 11 seconds, with a surcharge if the call is made from an hotel. A reduced rate is available for calls made between 21.00–08.00hrs.
What to dial for the UK 19*44.
What to dial for the Irish Republic 19*353.
*Wait for second dialling tone.

TOURIST INFORMATION

The French Government Tourist Office maintains a full information service at 178 Piccadilly, London W1V 0AL (Mon–Fri) and will be pleased to answer any enquiries on touring in France. The telephone number is 01-491 7622 (for general enquiries) and 01-499 6911 (for the 24-hr recorded information service). See also *Paris* entry in gazetteer below.

Once in France, you should contact the local tourist office, *Syndicat d'Initiative*, which will be found in all larger towns and resorts. They are pleased to give advice on local events, amenities and excursions, and can also give specific information regarding bus timetables and local religious services (all denominations), not available in the UK.

A further source of information within the country is the *Accueil de France* (Welcome Office), who will also book hotel reservations within their area for the same night, or up to 7 days in advance **for personal callers only**. There are fewer of these offices, which are mainly located at important stations and airports. The hours of opening vary considerably, depending upon the district and the time of year. Generally, the offices are open 09.00–12.00hrs and 14.00–18.00hrs Monday to Saturday, but in popular resort areas *Syndicats d'Initiative* are sometimes open later and on Sunday mornings.

TRAFFIC LIGHTS

The three-colour system, as in the United Kingdom, is in operation, with the addition of miniatures set at eye-level and with the posts placed in irregular positions, sometimes over the roadway and possibly without a set on the opposite side of the junction. It must be stressed that the lights themselves are extremely dim, and easily missed – especially those overhead.

A *flashing amber light* is a warning that the intersection or junction is particularly dangerous.

A *flashing red light* indicates no entry, or may be used to mark obstacles.

TRAVELLERS CHEQUES

We recommend you take *Visa Travellers Cheques*. You can used them like cash, or change them for currency in just about any country in the world. If you should lose them, a reverse charge telephone call will put you in touch with Visa's world-wide instant refund service – there are over 60,000 locations in 166 countries, so help is never far away. Visa Travellers Cheques are available on demand from any AA Travel Agency for a cash payment.

TYRES

Inspect your tyres carefully; if you think they are likely to be more than three-quarters worn before you get back, it is better to replace them prior to your departure. If you notice uneven wear, scuffed treads or damaged walls, expert advice should be sought on whether the tyres are

23

French ABC

suitable for further use. The regulations in the UK governing tyres call for a minimum tread depth of 1mm over 75% of the width of the tyre all around the circumference, with the original tread pattern clearly visible on the remainder. French regulations are stricter: a minumum tread depth of 1mm over the whole width of the tyre around the circumference.

When checking tyre pressures, remember that if the car is heavily loaded the recommended pressures may have to be raised; this may also be required for high-speed driving. Check the recommendations in your handbook, but remember pressures can only be checked accurately when the tyres are cold. Do not forget the spare tyre.

VALUABLES

Tourists should pay particular attention to the security of their money and items of value whilst touring. Whenever possible, excess cash and travellers cheques should be left with the hotel management **against a receipt**.

It cannot be stressed too strongly that all valuables should be **removed** from a parked car, even if it is parked in a supervised car park or lock-up garage.

VEHICLE EXCISE LICENCE

It is advisable for all vehicles temporarily exported from the UK for a period of 12 months or less to continue to be currently taxed in the UK. If your vehicle excise licence (tax disc) is due to expire while you are abroad, you may apply by post before you leave to The Post Office for a tax disc up to 42 days in advance of the expiry date of your present disc. You should explain why you want the tax disc in advance, and ask for it to be posted to you before you leave, or to an address you will be staying at abroad. However, your application form must always be completed with your UK address. To find out which Post Office in your area offers this service, you should contact your local *Post Office Customer Service Unit* on the telephone number listed in your local telephone directory.

VISAS

A visa is not normally required by United Kingdom and Republic of Ireland passport holders visiting France for periods of three months or less. However, if you hold a passport of any other nationality, a UK passport not issued in this country, or are in any doubt at all about your position, you should check with the nearest French consulate.

VISITORS' REGISTRATION

All visitors must register with the local police. This is a formality, usually satisfied by the completion of a card or certificate when booking into an hotel, camp site or place offering accommodation. If staying with friends or relatives, it is usually the responsibility of the host to seek advice from the police within 24 hours of the arrival of guests.

For short holiday visits, the formalities are very simple, but if you intend staying for longer than three months you should make the appropriate enquiries before departure from the UK.

WARM-CLIMATE TOURING

In hot weather, and at high altitudes, excessive heat in the engine compartment can cause carburation problems. It is advisable, if you are taking a caravan, to consult the manufacturers of your towing vehicle about the limitations of the cooling system, and the operating temperature of the gearbox fluid if automatic transmission is fitted. See also *Automatic gearboxes* page 6.

WARNING TRIANGLE/ HAZARD WARNING LIGHTS

All vehicles temporarily imported into France, with the exception of two-wheelers, must be equipped with either a warning triangle or hazard warning lights†. However, as hazard

MOTORING and GENERAL INFORMATION

warning lights may become damaged or inoperative, it is recommended that a warning triangle always be carried. For vehicles over 3,500kg, warning must be given by at least a warning triangle. Hazard warning lights will only warn on the straight, having no effect at bends or rises in the road and for this reason, too, a warning triangle should always be carried.

The triangle should be placed on the road behind a stopped vehicle to warn traffic approaching from the rear that there is an obstruction ahead. A warning triangle should be used when a vehicle has stopped for any reason – not only breakdowns. The triangle should be placed 30m (33yds) behind the obstruction, but not in such a position as to present a danger to oncoming traffic, and be clearly visible from 100m (110yds) by day or night.

An AA Warning Triangle which complies with the latest International and European standards can be hired from the AA or bought in AA Travel Agencies, AA Centres or Port Service Centres.

†If your vehicle is equipped with hazard warning lights, it is also compulsory to use them if you are forced to drive temporarily at a greatly reduced speed. However, when slow moving traffic is established in an uninterrupted lane or lanes, this only applies to the last vehicle in the lane(s).

WEATHER INFORMATION (INCLUDING WINTER CONDITIONS)

Members of the public may telephone or call in at one of the Met. Office Weather Centres listed below, except where indicated otherwise. The Centres can provide information about local, national and Continental weather forecasts, but not road conditions.

Belfast *(telephone calls only)* ☎(08494) 22339
Bristol The Gaunts House, Denmark Street ☎(0272) 279298
Cardiff Southgate House, Wood Street ☎(0222) 397020
Glasgow 33 Bothwell Street ☎041-248 3451
Leeds Oak House, Park Lane ☎(0532) 451990
London 284–286 High Holborn ☎01-836 4311
Manchester Exchange Street, Stockport ☎061-477 1060
Newcastle upon Tyne 7th Floor, Newgate House, Newgate Street ☎091-232 6453
Norwich Rouen House, Rouen Road ☎(0603) 660779
Nottingham Main Road, Watnall ☎(0602) 384092
Plymouth *(telephone calls only)* ☎(0752) 402534
Southampton 160 High Street-below-bar ☎(0703) 228844

Met. Office Weather Centres are also being established in Aberdeen and Birmingham, but full details are not yet available.

If you require information about climate when planning your holidays, you should contact the French Government Tourist Office (see page 00) for information.

Winter conditions Although there are five mountain regions – the Vosges, Jura, Massif Central, Alps and Pyrenees – motoring in winter is not severely restricted. The main channels for south-bound traffic wanting to avoid the Alps and Massif Central are the A7 and N7 route along the Rhône Valley, the N20 from Limoges to Toulouse, and the highways farther west. Whenever possible, roads are swept and kept clear. However, during periods of thaw, some barred roads may be used by certain classes of traffic at the driver's risk; passenger vehicles without trailers being used privately may proceed provided they do not exceed 80kph (49mph).

Reports on the accessibility of mountain passes in France are received by the AA from the *European Road Information Centre* in Geneva. Additionally, during the winter months, and also under certain weather conditions, information is passed to the AA from France regarding the state of approach roads to the Continental Channel ports. To obtain information, ring the *AA Overseas Routes Unit* at Basingstoke during office hours, ☎(0256) 493748/493907, or the *AA London Operations Centre* (24-hr service) ☎01-954 7373, or enquire at the *AA Port Service Centre* before embarking.

Further information is contained in the leaflet entitled *Continental Weather and Motoring in Winter* which is available from the AA. See also *Cold weather touring* page 8.

WHEELCHAINS

These can be purchased from vehicle accessory shops in large towns. Wheel chains can be hired from some garages; however, they have only small supplies. See also *Cold weather touring*, page 8.

25

French and Monégasque ABC

MONACO

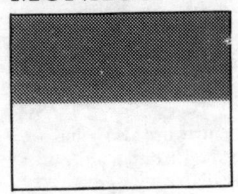

International distinguishing sign: **MC**

Area 8 sq miles
Population 28,000
National flag
Red over white in two stripes of equal breadth

The Principality of Monaco is an independent, soveriegn state, very much under the influence of France; its laws are similar to those of the major country. The official Monaco information centre in the UK is the Monaco Government Tourist and Convention Office, 50 Upper Brook Street, London W17 1PG ☎01-629 4712. Monaco is one large city/state, with Monaco Town and Monte Carlo the two towns.

Motoring regulations are the same as in France, but it should be stated that whilst caravans are permitted to pass through the Principality, they are not allowed to stop or park.

Specimen letters for booking hotels

Please use **block letters** and enclose an **International Reply Coupon**, obtainable from the Post Office. Be sure to include your own name and address clearly written.

English

Dear Sir
Please send me by return your terms with tax and service included, and confirm availability of accommodation with: Full Board/Half Board/Bed and Breakfast*
I would arrive on..
and leave on ....
I would need ....rooms with single bed with/without* bath/shower*
.... rooms with double bed with/without* bath/shower*
............................rooms with twin beds with/without* bath/shower*
.... cots in parents' room
We are ....adults
Our party also includes .... children; ....
boys aged ....years and .... girls aged .... years.
I look forward to receiving your reply and thank you in advance.

*delete where inapplicable.

French

Monsieur
Pourriez vous m'indiquer par retour si vous pouvez réserver et à quel tarif, taxe et service compris, pour un séjour en: Pension/Demi-pension/Chambre et petit déjeuner*
J'arriverais le..
et je repartirais le ....
Il me faudrait ....chambres à un lit d'une personne avec/sans*
....bain/douche*
.... chambres à grand lit avec/sans* bain/douche*
................................chambres à deux lits avec/sans* bain/douche*
.... lits d'enfants dans la chambre des parents.
Nous sommes............. adultes accompagnés de................. enfants; ....
garçons de..........ans et .... filles de .... ans.
J'attends vos renseignments et vous remercie par avance

*delete where inapplicable.

MOTORING and GENERAL INFORMATION

Route planning

EUROPEAN ROUTES SERVICE
Individually Prepared Routes to Your Own Requirements

The AA's Overseas Routes Unit has a comprehensive and unique database of road and route information built into the very latest computerised equipment.

The database includes all relevant information needed for an enjoyable, trouble-free route, including distance in miles and kilometres for estimating journey times.

A prepared route gives route numbers, road signs to follow, motorway services, landmarks, road and town descriptions, frontier opening times, etc.

Overseas Routes can supply you with any route you may require: scenic routes — direct routes — by-way routes — fast routes — coach routes — caravan routes — motorway routes — non-motorway routes — touring routes — special interest routes — and more.

You may believe you know the best route — we can confirm if you are correct or tell you if we believe you are wrong — and probably save you time and money.

Can we help you further?

If we can, please contact any AA Centre for a European Route application form. Alternatively, telephone Overseas Routes at Basingstoke (0256) 493748/493907, or complete the application form below, and we will send you full details of the European Routes Service and the prices charged.

Send the form below to:
Overseas Routes, The Automobile Association, Fanum House, Basingstoke, RG21 2EA.

Application form for details of the European Routes Service

(Complete in BLOCK CAPITALS)

Mr/Mrs/Ms/Miss/Title:　　　　Initials:　　　　Surname:

Address:

　　　　　　　　　　　　　　　　　　　Postcode:

Membership number (or 5-Star number, if any):　　Date of request:

(If you are not a Member of the AA an additional fee is payable unless you have paid the 5-Star non-members' service fee.)

Countries/places to be visited:

Date of departure:

27

AA
HIRE SERVICE

The Motoring Emergency Pack contains the following:

Booster Cable ● Fire Extinguisher
First-aid Kit ● Reflective Belt ● Tool Roll
Tow Rope ● Warning Triangle ● Spare Bulbs

Contact AA Hire Service, Snargate Street, Dover, Kent CT17 9XA
Telephone: Dover (0304) 203655.

Don't leave the country without one

AA
European Maps and Atlases

European Route Planning Maps

Series includes:
Scandinavia – Austria, Italy and Switzerland – Benelux and Germany – France – Spain and Portugal

Big Road Atlas Europe

A large format, full colour atlas covering 26 countries. Throughroute plans of 16 major cities.

DON'T CROSS THE CHANNEL WITHOUT ONE..

About the GAZETTEER

ACCOMMODATION

There is a large selection of hotels of all categories. The French Ministry of Tourism classifies hotels in five categories from one-star to four-star and four-star de luxe (see *Classification*). Local Tourist Information Offices (see page 23) can provide details of hotels and restaurants in the area.

Accueil de France Tourist Offices showing this sign will make hotel bookings for a very small fee **only for personal callers** and only for up to a week ahead. Bookings are made in the same town or at one of some 35 major towns and cities, including Calais, Le Havre and Rouen (open to 18.30hrs weekdays, sometimes later in season). The head office in Paris is the Office de Tourisme, 127 avenue des Champs-Elysées, Paris 8, open every day 09.00–20.00hrs; Sundays and Bank Holidays 09.00–18.00hrs.

Loisirs-Accueil In addition, many départements under the name of *Loisirs-Accueil* have a booking service for hotels and *gîtes*, usually charging no fee and with an English-speaking staff member.

Gîtes de France This is furnished accommodation in rural France, often at farms, for those who prefer to cater for themselves. There are some 23,000 gîtes in 4,000 villages, created with the financial support of the French Government and governed by a charter laid down by the Fédération Nationale de Gîtes de France. For information on membership, write to Gîtes de France, Department TF, 178 Piccadilly, London W1V 9DB, enclosing details of preferred regions, choice of dates and a stamped addressed envelope.

Logis de France These are privately owned, mostly family-run hotels equivalent to the one-star or two-star and some three-star categories. They are generally located off the beaten track, and offer a high standard for their type and good value for money. There are nearly 4,500 logis, some of which are listed in the gazetteer, and they are marked by the symbol L. There are none in Paris. A copy of the Logis Hotel Guide may be obtained in early March from the French Government Tourist Office, 178 Piccadilly, London W1V 0AL (against payment of 50p in stamps to cover postage and packing).

Relais Routiers These are restaurants situated on main roads providing a good meal at a reasonable price; some offer simple accommodation. The *Relais Routiers Guide* issued from February each year can be purchased through bookshops.

AA SIGNS

The AA issues signs on request to hotels listed in this Guide. You are advised, however, not to rely solely on the signs exhibited, but to check that the establishment still appears in this edition.

CHARGES

No prices are shown against individual hotels, but a price-banding chart appears at the beginning of the gazetteer. This shows the average *minimum* and *maximum* prices for *single* and *double* rooms within each classification, plus the average cost of breakfast and lunch/dinner. All average prices are expressed in **UK£ sterling** based on the rate of exchange at the time of going to press. For comparison, the current rate may be obtained from banks or from the national press. In the main, the average prices quoted should give a fairly accurate guide to hotel costs, but you are likely to find that accommodation is generally more expensive in Paris and some of the larger, more popular towns.

DPn indicates *demi-pension* (half-board) terms only available. This means that, in addition to the charge for rooms, guests are expected to pay for one main meal whether it is taken or not.

Pn indicates *full pension* (full board) terms only available.

Rates for rooms are usually officially controlled and must be displayed in each room, but this does not apply to the cost of meals.

Hotels are not required by law to exchange travellers cheques for guests, and many small hotels are unable to do so. You must expect to pay a higher rate of commission for this service at a hotel than you would at a bank.

About the GAZETTEER

CLASSIFICATION

Although the system of classification used in this Guide is similar to the AA system in this country, the variations in the traditions and customs of hotel-keeping in France often make identical grading difficult.

Hotels and motels are classified by stars. The definitions are intended to indicate the type of hotel rather than the degree of merit. Meals, service, and hours of service should be in keeping with the classification, and all establishments with restaurants must serve meals to non-residents and are expected to give good value for money.

★ Hotels simply furnished, but clean and well kept; **all** bedrooms with hot and cold running water; adequate bath and lavatory facilities.

★★ Hotels offering a higher standard of accommodation; adequate bath and lavatory facilities on all main floors, and some private bathrooms and/or showers.

★★★ Well-appointed hotels, with a large number of bedrooms with private bathrooms/showers.

★★★★ Exceptionally well-appointed hotels offering a very high standard of comfort and service with all bedrooms providing private bathrooms/showers.

★★★★★ Luxury hotels offering the highest international standards.

COMPLAINTS

You are advised to bring any criticism to the notice of the hotel management immediately. This will enable the matter to be dealt with promptly to the benefit of all concerned. If a personal approach fails, members should inform the AA. You are asked to state whether or not your name may be disclosed in any enquiries we may make.

CREDIT/CHARGE CARDS

The numbered boxes below indicate the credit/charge cards which the hotels accept

1 Access/Eurocard/Mastercard
2 American Express
3 Visa/Carte Bleue
4 Carte Blanche
5 Diners

It is advisable to check when booking to ensure that the cards are still accepted.

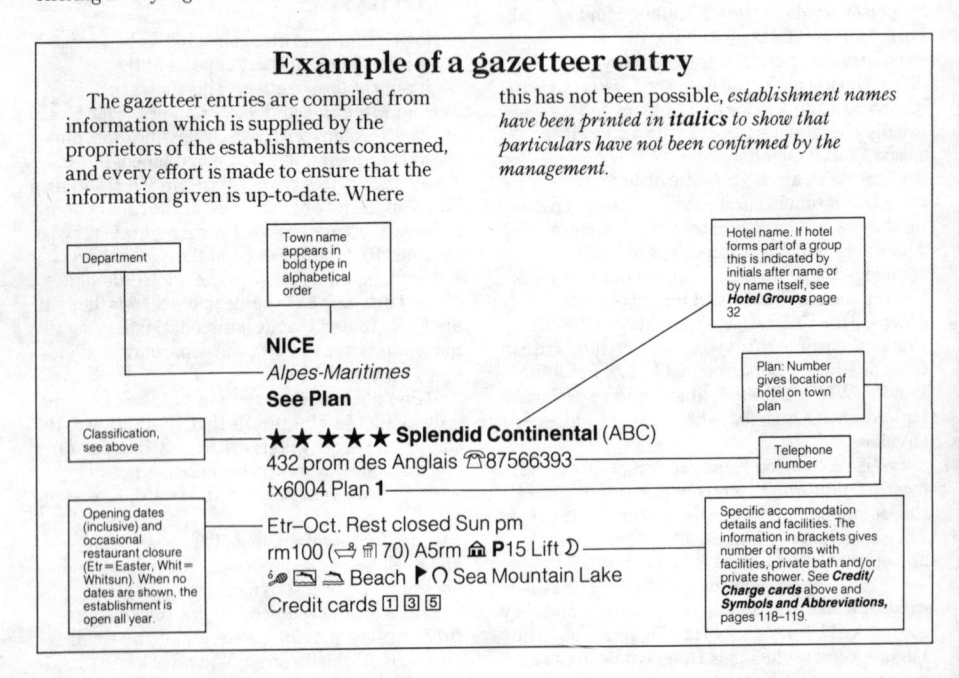

Example of a gazetteer entry

The gazetteer entries are compiled from information which is supplied by the proprietors of the establishments concerned, and every effort is made to ensure that the information given is up-to-date. Where this has not been possible, *establishment names have been printed in* **italics** *to show that particulars have not been confirmed by the management.*

Department

Town name appears in bold type in alphabetical order

Hotel name. If hotel forms part of a group this is indicated by initials after name or by name itself, see **Hotel Groups** page 32

NICE
Alpes-Maritimes
See Plan

Plan: Number gives location of hotel on town plan

Classification, see above

★★★★★ **Splendid Continental** (ABC)
432 prom des Anglais ☎87566393
tx6004 Plan **1**

Telephone number

Opening dates (inclusive) and occasional restaurant closure (Etr=Easter, Whit=Whitsun). When no dates are shown, the establishment is open all year.

Etr–Oct. Rest closed Sun pm
rm100 (⇆ ⋔ 70) A5rm 🛁 **P** 15 Lift ⅅ
🛎 🖼 ≋ Beach ▶ ○ Sea Mountain Lake
Credit cards 1 3 5

Specific accommodation details and facilities. The information in brackets gives number of rooms with facilities, private bath and/or private shower. See **Credit/Charge cards** above and **Symbols and Abbreviations**, pages 118–119.

30

CRUISE TO THE CONTINENT THIS SUMMER.

Now your continental holidays can really begin in style with P&O European Ferries.

With a heritage of great British seamanship and the most modern fleet on the Channel, we now have our new Superferries crossing from Dover to Calais in just 75 minutes.

You'll find the smooth, comfortable crossing so relaxing, you'll think your holiday has begun before you've even landed.

Find out more in our free colour brochure from your AA Travel Agent or P&O European Ferries, Brochure Dept, PO Box 12, Dover, Kent CT16 1LD, or ring (0304) 203388.

Why sail across the Channel when you can cruise across?

P&O European Ferries

DOVER-CALAIS, DOVER-BOULOGNE, DOVER-ZEEBRUGGE, DOVER-OSTEND, FELIXSTOWE-ZEEBRUGGE, PORTSMOUTH-LE HAVRE, PORTSMOUTH-CHERBOURG, CAIRNRYAN-LARNE.

About the GAZETTEER

HOTEL GROUPS

Below is a list of hotel groups and consortia.
Key to abbreviations and company/consortia reservation telephone numbers:

COMPANY	TELEPHONE
ALTEA	01-621 1962
Best Western (BW)	01-541 0033
Climat de France	01-434 4431
FAH/MINOTEL	(0253) 594185
Golden Tulip (GT)	01-847 3951
Hilton International	01-580 8197
Holiday Inns	01-722 7755
L'Horset	01-951 3990
IBIS	01-724 1000
Inter Continental (Intercont)	01-491 7181
Ladbroke Hotels	01-734 6000
MAP Hotels (MAP)	01-541 0033
Mercure	01-724 1000
Novotels	01-724 1000
Pullman	01-621 1962
Sofitel	01-724 1000
Steigenberger (SRS)	01-486 5754
Trusthouse Forte (THF)	01-567 3444

HOTELS

The list of hotels has been compiled from information given by members, by the motoring organisations, tourist offices, and from many other sources.

Your comments concerning the whole range of hotel information – whether included in this Guide or not, and whether in praise or in criticism – will always be most welcome; and all information will be treated in the strictest confidence.

LOCATION MAPS

The location maps (pages 34–38) use the following symbols to indicate adjoining countries:

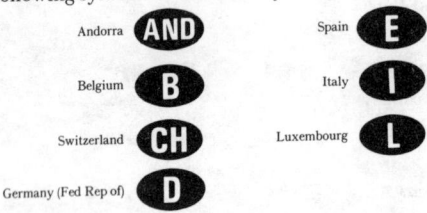

- Andorra **AND**
- Belgium **B**
- Switzerland **CH**
- Germany (Fed Rep of) **D**
- Spain **E**
- Italy **I**
- Luxembourg **L**

The maps are intended to assist the reader who wishes to stay in a certain area, by showing only those towns for which there is an entry in the gazetteer. Thus, someone wishing to stay in the Paris area will be able to select suitable towns by looking at the map. It must be emphasised that these maps are not intended to be used to find your way around the country, and we recommend readers should obtain the *AA Big Road Atlas of Europe*.

RESERVATIONS

The practice is the same in France as it is in this country – rooms are booked subject to their still being available when confirmation is received. It is therefore most important that confirmation should be sent to the hotel as soon as possible. Regrettably, many hotels will **not** accept bookings for **one** or **two** nights only. Sometimes, a deposit is required, which can be arranged through your bank. Many hotels do not hold reservations after 19.00hrs, and you should advise hotels if you anticipate a late arrival, or if you are unable to take up your booking for any reason. Unwanted rooms can then often be relet, and you will be saved the expense of paying for them, as a written, confirmed booking represents a legal contract.

Hotel telephone numbers are given in the gazetteer. In some entries, the name of the group operating the hotel is indicated, and a key to the abbreviations used may be found above, with the telephone numbers for reservations.

When writing direct to hotels abroad, it is advisable to enclose an *International Reply Coupon*; these are available from any post office. A specimen letter appears on page 26.

Double rooms may not be reduced in price when let to one person; however, a double room is generally cheaper than two rooms. Accommodation in an annexe may be of a different standard from rooms in the main hotel building; it is advisable to check the exact nature of the accommodation at the time of reservation.

TOWN PLANS

Listed below are major towns and cities for which there are town plans, followed by page numbers. A list of hotels showing the plan number can be found adjacent to the relevant plan. In addition, the appropriate plan number will appear following the telephone number in the hotel entry. These numbers correspond to the number on the plan, thereby giving the location of the hotel.

Boulogne	page 51	Le Havre	page 73
Calais	page 54	Nice	page 87
Cherbourg	page 61	Paris	pages 92–93
Dieppe	page 65		

About the GAZETTEER

GARAGES

The garages listed in the gazetteer are those which are most likely to be of help to members on tour, because of their situation and the services they have stated they can provide.

Their charges must be displayed on the premises so that they are clearly visible and legible. When you have had a repair carried out you should receive an invoice stating the labour charge, *ie* the hourly rate (displayed) multiplied by the time spent or the time shown on the time schedule for each operation and not just a lump sum. The price of supplies and spares should be shown separately. Parts which have been replaced must be returned to you, unless it is a routine replacement or the repair is carried out free during the guarantee period.

It cannot be emphasised too strongly that disputes with garages on the Continent must be settled on the spot. It has been the AA's experience that subsequent negotiations can seldom be brought to a satisfactory conclusion. Although the AA cannot accept responsibility for difficulties over repairs to members' cars, any unsatisfactory cases will be noted for amendment in any future editions of the Guide.

In selecting garages, preference has been given to those which provide a breakdown service (see below) and those accepting *AIT Credit Vouchers*. The number of garages holding each agency reflects, as far as possible, the relative popularity of the various makes of cars. Although firms normally specialise in the makes for which they are accredited agents, they do not necessarily hold stocks of spare parts. Certain garages will repair only the make of car for which they are officially agents as indicated in the text. The symbol 'P' indicates that the establishments undertake the garaging of cars.

A complete list of service agencies for your make of car is generally available through your own dealer. It has been found on occasions that some garages make extremely high charges for repairing tourists' cars; always ask for an estimate before authorising a repair.

BREAKDOWN SERVICE

The breakdown service of garages listed in the gazetteer is not free, and any assistance obtained must be paid for. The AA's free breakdown service for members operates in the United Kingdom and Republic of Ireland only. Therefore, motorists travelling abroad are advised to purchase *AA 5-Star Service*; see *Breakdown*, page 7 for further information.

HOURS OF OPENING

Generally hours of business are 08.00–18.00hrs except on Sundays and Public holidays when repairs, breakdown service, and petrol may be difficult to obtain. In August many garages close down completely for the annual holidays.

SERVICE AGENCIES

The service agencies held by garages are indicated by the following abbreviations:

Alf	Alfa Romeo
Ast	Aston Martin
Aud	Audi
BMW	BMW
RR	Bentley
Cit	Citroen
Dai	Daihatsu
DJ	Daimler/Jaguar
Fia	Fiat
For	Ford
Hon	Honda
Lan	Lancia
LR	Land Rover
Lot	Lotus
Maz	Mazda
Mer	Mercedes-Benz
Mit	Mitsubishi
Nis	Nissan
Ope	Opel
Peu	Peugeot
Por	Porsche
Ren	Renault
RR	Rolls-Royce
Rov	Rover Group
Saa	Saab
Sko	Skoda
Tal	Talbot
Toy	Toyota
Vau	Vauxhall
VW	Volkswagen
Vol	Volvo

33

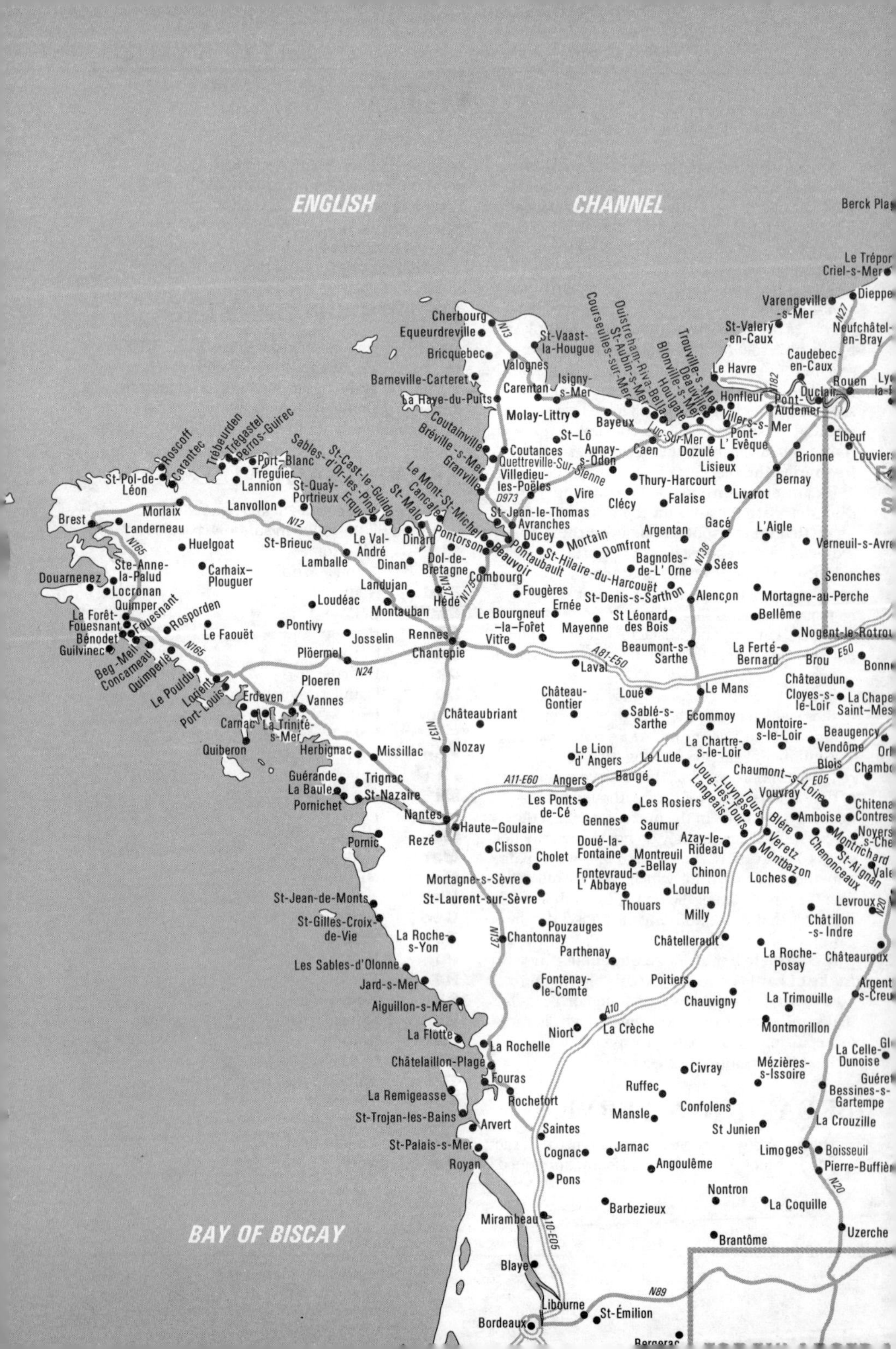
ENGLISH
CHANNEL
BAY OF BISCAY
Berck Plag
Le Trépor
Criel-s-Mer
Dieppe
Varengeville-s-Mer
St-Valery-en-Caux
Neufchâtel-en-Bray
N27
Caudebec-en-Caux
Rouen
Duclair
Le Havre
Honfleur
Pont-Audemer
Cherbourg
Equeurdreville
N13
St-Vaast-la-Hougue
Bricquebec
Valognes
Barneville-Carteret
Carentan
Isigny-s-Mer
La Haye-du-Puits
Molay-Littry
Bayeux
Courseulles-sur-Mer
St-Aubin-s-Mer
Ouistreham-Riva-Bella
Blonville-s-Mer
Houlgate
Deauville
Trouville-s-Mer
Villers-s-Mer
Luc-Sur-Mer
Caen
Dozulé
Pont-L' Evêque
Lisieux
Elbeuf
Brionne
Louviers
Bernay
Livarot
St-Lô
Aunay-s-Odon
Coutainville
Coutances
Quettreville-Sur-Sienne
Bréville-s-Mer
Granville
Villedieu-les-Poêles
D973
Thury-Harcourt
Falaise
Vire
Clécy
St-Jean-le-Thomas
Avranches
Ducey
Mortain
Argentan
Gacé
L'Aigle
Verneuil-s-Avre
Domfront
Bagnoles-de-L' Orne
Sées
N138
St-Hilaire-du-Harcouët
Pontaubault
Senonches
Mortagne-au-Perche
Alencon
St-Denis-s-Sarthon
Bellême
Nogent-le-Rotrou
Roscoff
Carantec
Trébeurden
Trégastel
Perros-Guirec
Port-Blanc
Treguier
Lannion
St-Pol-de-Léon
Sables-d'Or-les-Pins
St-Cast-le-Guildo
Erquy
St-Quay-Portrieux
Lanvollon
Morlaix
N12
St-Malo
Cancale
Le Mont-St-Michel
Pontorson
Beauvoir
Brest
Landerneau
N165
Huelgoat
St-Brieuc
Le Val-André
Dinard
Dinan
Lamballe
Dol-de-Bretagne
Combourg
N137
N175
Fougères
Ste-Anne-la-Palud
Douarnenez
Locronan
Carhaix-Plouguer
Landujan
Hédé
Ernée
Quimper
Loudéac
Montauban
Le Bourgneuf-la-Forêt
Mayenne
St Léonard des Bois
La Forêt-Fouesnant
Fouesnant
Rosporden
Pontivy
Bénodet
Le Faouët
Josselin
Rennes
Vitré
Guilvinec
Beg-Meil
Concarneau
Quimperlé
N165
Ploërmel
Chantepie
Beaumont-s-Sarthe
La Ferté-Bernard
Brou
E50
Bonn
N24
A81-E50
Laval
Le Pouldu
Lorient
Port-Louis
Ploeren
Vannes
Erdeven
Châteaudun
Château-Gontier
Loué
Le Mans
Cloyes-s-le-Loir
La Chape
Saint-Mes
Carnac
La Trinité-s-Mer
Châteaubriant
Sablé-s-Sarthe
Ecommoy
Quiberon
Herbignac
Missillac
Nozay
Montoire-s-le-Loir
Beaugency
Vendôme
Or
Le Lion d' Angers
Le Lude
La Chartre-s-le-Loir
Chamb
Blois
Guérande
Trignac
A11-E60
Angers
Baugé
Chaumont-s-Loire
E05
La Baule
St-Nazaire
Pornichet
Les Ponts-de-Cé
Joué-les-Tours
Luynes
Langeais
Tours
Vouvray
Chitena
Contres
Les Rosiers
Amboise
Nantes
Haute-Goulaine
Gennes
Saumur
Bléré
Montrichard
Noyers-s-Che
Pornic
Rezé
Clisson
Doué-la-Fontaine
Azay-le-Rideau
Veretz
Chenonceaux
Montbazon
St-Aignan
Vale
Cholet
Montreuil-Bellay
Mortagne-s-Sèvre
Fontevraud-L' Abbaye
Chinon
Loches
St-Laurent-sur-Sèvre
Loudun
St-Jean-de-Monts
Thouars
Levroux
N20
Milly
St-Gilles-Croix-de-Vie
Pouzauges
Châtillon-s-Indre
La Roche-s-Yon
N137
Chantonnay
Châtellerault
Parthenay
La Roche-Posay
Châteauroux
Les Sables-d'Olonne
Jard-s-Mer
Fontenay-le-Comte
Poitiers
Argent-s-Creu
Chauvigny
La Trimouille
Aiguillon-s-Mer
A10
Montmorillon
Niort
La Crèche
La Flotte
La Rochelle
La Celle-Dunoise
Gl
Châtelaillon-Plage
Civray
Mézières-s-Issoire
Fouras
Guéret
Ruffec
Bessines-s-Gartempe
La Remigeasse
Rochefort
Confolens
St-Trojan-les-Bains
Mansle
La Crouzille
Arvert
Saintes
St Junien
Jarnac
St-Palais-s-Mer
Cognac
Limoges
Boisseuil
Royan
Angoulême
Pierre-Buffièr
Pons
N20
Nontron
Barbezieux
La Coquille
Mirambeau
A10-E05
Uzerche
Brantôme
Blaye
N89
Libourne
St-Émilion
Bordeaux
Bergerac

Dunkerque
Calais
Bergues
Ardres
Wimereux
Tournehem
St-Omer
Le West
Boulogne-s-Mer
Aire-s-la-Lys
Tourcoing
Lille
Roubaix
Le Touquet
Beaurainville
Béthune
Noeux-les-Mines
Bully-les-Mines
Hesdin
St-Pol-s-Ternoise
Lens
Douai
Valenciennes
Frévent
Arras
Nampont Saint Martin
Abbeville
Henin-Beaumont
Cambrai
Bapaume
Le Nouvion-en-Thiérache
Louvroil
Albert
Hermies
Rancourt
Fourmies
Amiens
Fumay
Péronne
St-Quentin
Rocroi
Poix-de-Picardie
Vervins
Charleville-Mézières
Auvillers-les-Forges
Roye
La Fère
Noyon
Laon
Inor
Longwy
Longuyon
Rethel
Soissons
Reims
Thionville
Fère-en-Tardenois
Beaumont-s-Vesle
Étain
ENLARGED AREA
LAST MAP PAGE
THIS SECTION
Château-Thierry
Épernay
Sept-Saulx
Verdun
Forbach
Sarreguemines
St-Avold
Metz
Bonniel-s-Marne
Montmort
Châlons-s-Marne
Montmirail
Pont-a-Mousson
La Petite-Pierre
Haguenau
Sézanne
Commercy
Saverne
Vitry-le-François
Stainville
Toul
Nancy
Sarrebourg
Marlenheim
Romilly-s-Seine
St-Dizier
Méréville
Lunéville
Obersteigen
Arcis-s-Aube
Lingolsheim
Strasbourg
Obernai
Andlau
Pont-s-Yonne
Joinville
Nemours
Sens
Troyes
Dolancourt
Charmes
Neufchâteau
Villeneuve-s-Yonne
Souppes-s-Loing
Dordives
Pithiviers
Joigny
Migennes
Bar-s-Aube
Colombey-les-Deux-Eglises
Dompaire
Epinal
Les Trois-Epis
Fleury-les-Aubrais
Courtenay
St-Florentin
Bar-s-Seine
Chaumont
Contrexéville
Gérardmer
Colmar
Châteauneuf-s-Loire
Montargis
Polisot
Montigny-le-Roi
Remiremont
Neuf-Brisach
Olivet
La Ferté-St Aubin
Aillant-s-Tholon
Montigny-la-Resle
Foulain
Plombières-les-Bains
Rouffach
Sully-s-Loire
Auxerre
Tonnerre
Châtillon-s-Seine
St-Maurice-s-Moselle
Chablis
Langres
Luxeuil-les-Bains
Lutterbach
Le Rabot
Gien
Champs-sur-Yonne
Aisey-s-Seine
Mulhouse
Briare
L'Isle-s-Serein
Montbard
Combeaufontaine
Nouan-le-Fuzelier
Bonny-s-Loire
Semur-en-Auxois
Belfort
Sochaux
Altkirch
Vesoul
St-Louis
Salbris
St-Satur
Cosne-s-Loire
Avallon
Les Laumes
L'Isle-s-le-Doubs
Montbéliard
Lantin-Lanthenay
Pouilly-en-Auxois
Val-Suzon
Gray
Sancerre
Pouilly-s-Loire
Marsannay-la-Côte
Mehun-s-Yevre
Quarré-les-Tombes
Dijon
Pesmes
Recologne
Baume-les-Dames
Saulieu
Fixin
Goumois
Besançon
Chenôve
Auxonne
Arnay-le-Duc
Valdahon
Bourges
Nuits-St-Georges
Château-Chinon
Beaune
Dole
Issoudun
Nevers
Châtillon-en-Bazois
Mouthier-Haute-Pierre
Autun
Nolay
Chagny
St-Gervais-en-Vallière
Arbois
Le Veurdre
Chalon-s-Saône
Sellières
Pontarlier
Le Creusot
Poligny
Malbuisson
Jougne
Bourbon-Lancy
Buxy
St-Martin-en-Bresse
Champagnole
CH
Trévol
Sennecey-le-Grand
Beaurepaire-en-Bresse
Lons-le-Saunier
Moulins
Tournus
Paray-le-Monial
Clairvaux-les-Lacs
Morez
Montluçon
Digoin
Cluny
St-Amour
Charolles
Evian-les-Bains
Igé
Viriat
Oyonnax
St-Pourcain-s-Sioule
Mâcon
Gex
Thonon-les-Bains
Chambon-sur-Voueize
Bourg-en-Bresse
St-Genis-Pouilly
Morzine
Chaintres
Nantua
St-Germain-de-Joux
Gaillard
Les Gets
St-Éloy-les-Mines
Thoissey
Annemasse
Vichy
Roanne
Aubusson
Anse
St-Julien-en-Genevois
Sallanches
Renaison
Villefranche-s-Saône
Pont-d'Ain
Seyssel
Passy
Les Houches
Châtelguyon
St-Martin-Bellevue
Clermont-Ferrand
Thiers
Tarare
Pérouges
Ambérieu-en-Bugey
Bonneville
Chamonix-Mont-Blanc
Vaulx-en-Velin
Annecy
Veyrier-du-Lac
St-Gervais-les-Bains
Civrieux-d'Azergues
Sevrier
Talloires
Royat
Faverges
Megève
Lyon
Bourgoin-Jallieu
Le Mont-Dore
Lac Chambon
St-Etienne Airport
Chasse-s-Rhône
Yenne
Aix-les-Bains
Albertville
Bourg-St-Maurice
Chambéry
Ambert
Givors
Besse-en-Chandresse
Issoire
Villars
La Tour du Pin
Les Abrets
Moûtiers
St-Jean-de-Maurienne
St-Michael-de-Maurienne
Vienne
Pontcharra
La Chaise Dieu
St-Etienne
Roussillon
Charavines
Val d' Isère
Massiac
Firminy
Rive-de-Gier
Condrieu
Les Roches-de-Condrieu
St-Pierre-de-Chartreuse
Lanslevillard
Salers
Brioude
St-Rambert-dAlbon
Lanslebourg-Mont-Cenis
Grenoble
Tain L'Hermitage
Romans-s-Isère
Eybens
Valloire
Modane
Vic-s-Cère
St-Flour
Le Puy
Pont-de-L'Isere
Varces
Vizille
L'Alpe-
B
D
L
F
N1
A26
A2
E19
A1
E15
N43
A203
N44
A4
A4-E50
N4
N67
N19
A31
E21
A32
E25
A4-E25
N83
N57
N66
A35
A36
A26
A38
N5
A6
A40
N7
N9
N144
A72
E70
N89
A10
E05
A22
A42
D67
A48

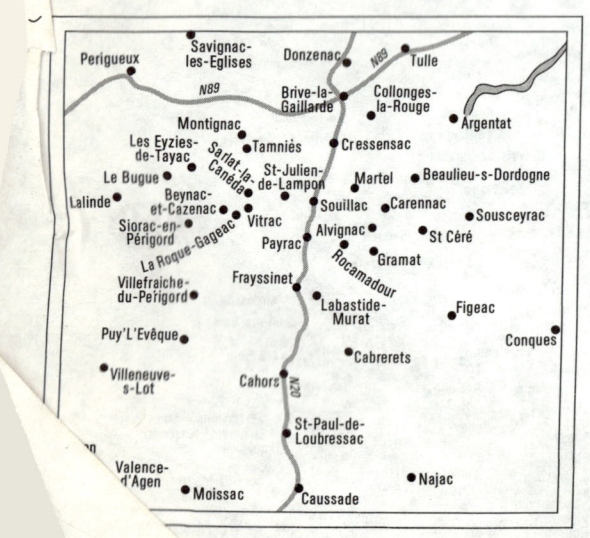

BAY OF BISCAY

Pons • Barbezieux • Nontron • La Coquille
Mirambeau • Brantôme • Uzerche
Blaye
Libourne • St-Émilion
Bordeaux • Bergerac
FOR ENLARGED AR
SEE INSET
Arcachon
Pyla-s-Mer
Parentis-en-Born
Belin-Beliet
Mimizan
Casteljaloux
Calignac
Barbotan-les-Thermes
Mont-de-Marsan
Condom • Castelsarrasin • Montauban • Cor
Soustons • Magescq • Villeneuve-de-Marsan • Vaïssac
Hossegor • Eugénie-les-Bains • Fleurance • Grisolles • Albi
Capbreton • Peyrehorade • Aire-s-l'Adour • Castéra-Verduzan • Lavaur
Bayonne • Auch • Toulouse • Castre
Biarritz • Anglet • Orthez • Colomiers
Bidart • Hendaye-Plage • Cambo-les-Bains • Pau • Muret
Guéthary • St-Jean-de-Luz • Navarrenx • Tarbes • Castelnaudary
Ascain • Ainhoa • Mauléon- • Oloron- • Lourdes • Bagnères- • St-Gaudens • Pamiers • Carcasso
St-Pée-s-Nivelle • Licharre • Ste-Marie • de-Bigorre • Argelès- • Arreau • St-Girons • Foix • Mirepoix
St-Étienne-de-Baïgorry • Etsaut • Gazost • St-Lary- • Luchon • Massat • Tarascon- • Quillan
St-Jean-Pied-de-Port • Soulan • s-Ariège
Ax-les-Thermes • Font-
Romeu

E

Périgueux • Savignac-les-Eglises • Donzenac • Tulle
Brive-la-Gaillarde • Collonges-la-Rouge
Montignac • Argentat
Les Eyzies-de-Tayac • Tamniès • Cressensac
Sarlat-la-Canéda • St-Julien-de-Lampon • Beaulieu-s-Dordogne
Le Bugue • Martel
Lalinde • Beynac-et-Cazenac • Souillac • Carennac
Siorac-en-Périgord • Vitrac • Alvignac • St Céré • Sousceyrac
La Roque-Gageac • Payrac • Gramat
Villefraîche-du-Périgord • Frayssinet • Rocamadour
Labastide-Murat • Figeac
Puy L'Evêque • Cabrerets • Conques
Villeneuve-s-Lot • Cahors
St-Paul-de-Loubressac
Valence-d'Agen • Moissac • Caussade • Najac

Digne
Château-Arnoux • St-André-les-Alpes
Châte
Castellane
Gréoux-les-Bains • Fayence
Bagnol-en-Fo
Draguignan
Trans-en-Provence • Le
St-Maximin-la-Ste-Baume • Le Luc • Ste-Maxime
Nans-les-Pins • Grimaud • Beauvallon
Bormes-les-Mimosas • Cro
Toulon • Hyères • Cavas
Sanary-s-Mer • Carqueiranne • Le Rayo
Cavaliere
Aiguabelle
Lavandou

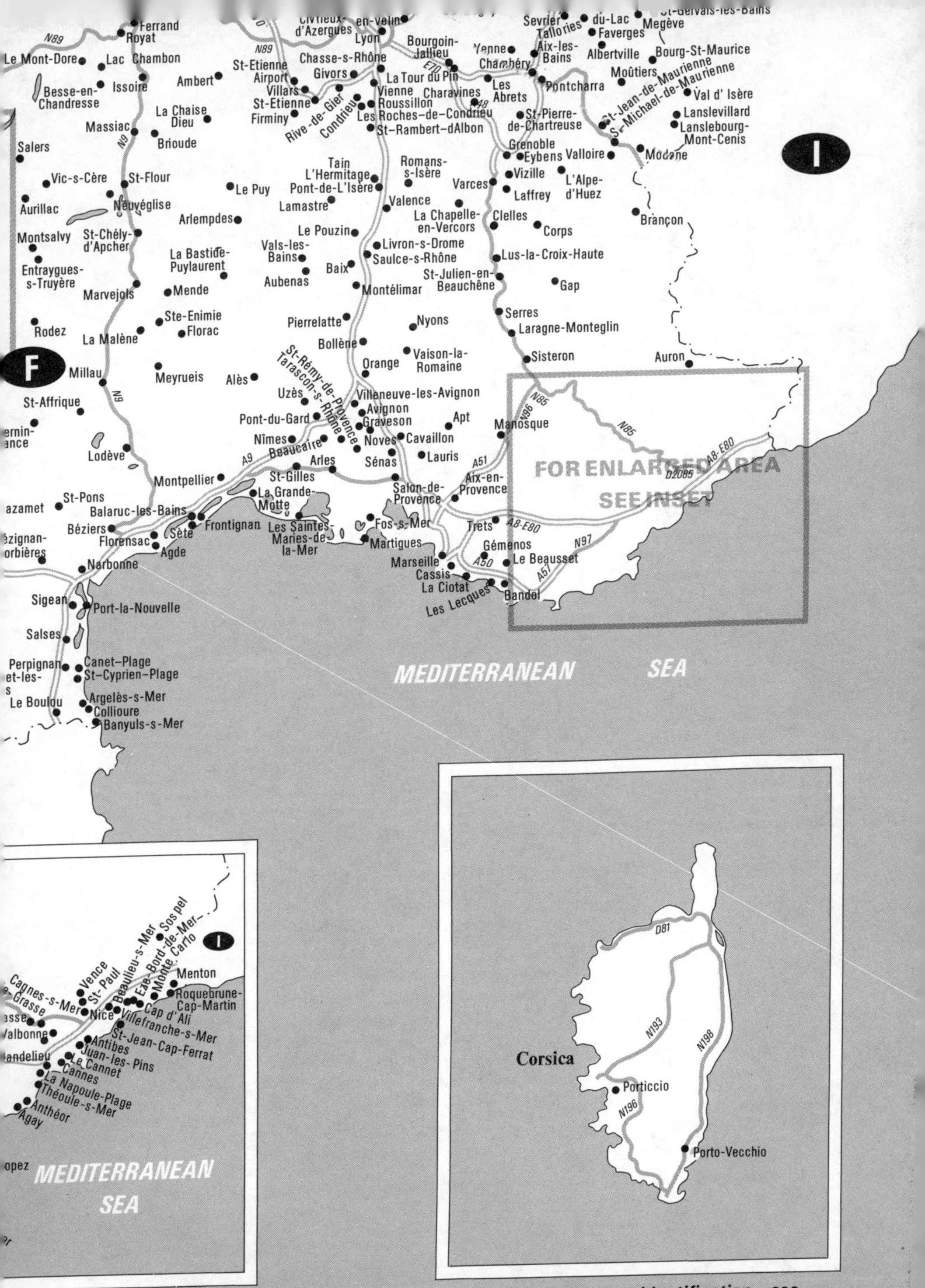

For key to country identification - see "About the gazetteer"

Beauvais
Ressons-s-Matz
Compiègne
N1
A1-E15
Nogent-s-Oise
Les Andelys
Creil
Villers Cotterêts
Senlis
Chantilly
Gaillon
A13-E05
Fontaine-Chaalis
Ermenonville
Survilliers-St-Witz
Charles-de-Gaulle
Airport
Pontoise
Montsoult
Pacy-s-Eure
Rolleboise
Ecouen
Gonesse
Évreux
Mantes-
la-Jolie
Les Mureaux
Meulan
Conflans-Ste-Honorine
Le Bourget
Airport
A4-E50
Argenteuil
Sannois
Montmorency
Sevran
Maisons-Laffitte
St-Denis
A13
E05
A104
Meaux
Orgeval
Montesson
Epinay-sur-Seine
Epone
Gennevilliers
Aulnay-sous-Bois
Ivry-la-Bataille
St-Germain-en Laye
Nanterre
Courbevoie
Levallois-Perret
Chelles
La Ferté-
sous-Jouarre
Bobingy
Noisiel
PARIS
Vaires-s-
Marne
Quincy-Voisins
Fontenay-
sous-Bois
Champs-
s-Marne
Plaisir
Suresnes
Houdan
Versailles
Nonancourt
Verrières-le-
Buisson
La Queue-
en-Brie
Buc
St-Quentin-en-
Yvelines
St-Aubin
Palaiseau
Rungis
Orsay
Dreux
Longjumeau
Orly Airport
Les Ulis
Viry-Châtillon
Rambouillet
Épinay-sur-Orge
Evry
St Michel
-sur-Orge
Corbeil-
Essonnes
A10
A6-E15
N19
Provins
Brétigny-sur-Orge
Melun
A11-E50
Ponthierry
Dourdan
A10-E05
Chartres
Barbizon
Fontainebleau

France

AVERAGE PRICES

	Single Room	Double Room	Breakfast	Lunch/Dinner
★★★★★	£80.25–£149	£113–£184.75	from £7.50	£23–£31
★★★★	£44.50–£66.75	£55.75–£81	£4.50–£5	£16–£23
★★★	£25.75–£34	£27–£40.25	£3–£3.50	£10.50–£16
★★	£16–£20.75	£23.50–£24.75	£2–£2.50	£7.25–£11.75
★	£9.50–£14.75	£12–£19	£1.50–£2	£6–£11.75

These prices are an average for each classification calculated at the exchange rate of *French francs* 10.84 = £1. Accommodation is likely to be more expensive in Paris and some of the more popular tourist areas. You are advised to confirm the current rate of exchange before your departure as there is likely to be some fluctuation since this table was compiled.

For additional information on French hotels, see page 29.
The department name follows the town name.
For information on making internal local telephone calls see page 23.
Abbreviations:

av	avenue
bd	boulevard
Cpt	Capitaine
Cdt	Commandant
espl	esplanade
fbg	faubourg
Gl	Général
Ml	Marshal, Maréchal
Mon	Monseigneur
pl	place
Prés	Président
Prof	Professeur
prom	promenade
r	rue
rte	route
sq	square

ABBEVILLE
Somme

★★ **Ibis** 234 rte d'Amiens ☎ 22248080 tx 145045
⇨🛏45 Lift
Credit Cards ①③

★ **Conde DPn** 14 pl de la Libération ☎ 22240633
⇨🛏7 P10
Credit Cards ②③

★ **Jean Bart** 5-7 r Ste-Catherine ☎ 22242171
Mar-Jan Closed :Rest closed Sun rm16(⇨🛏10) P10
Credit Cards ①②③

🍽 **Abbeville Automobile** 29 chaussée d'Hocquet ☎ 22240854 **P** For

🍽 **SADRA** 53 av R-Schumann ☎ 22243481 **P** Aud VW

ABRETS, LES
Isère

★ **Belle Etoile** L€ 4 r V-Hugo ☎ 76320497 rm15(⇨🛏8) 🍴 P Mountain

★ **Hostellerie Abrésienne** 34 r Gambetta (N75) ☎ 76320428
Closed :Rest closed Tue
rm22(⇨🛏5) 🍴 P25
Credit Cards ①③

AGAY
Var

🍽 **Agay** av du Gratadis ☎ 94820616 All makes

At **DRAMONT, LE**(2km SW)

★★★ **Sol et Mar** ☎ 94952560
Apr-15 Oct
⇨🛏47 P40 Lift ⌒ Beach Sea Mountain

AGDE
Hérault

🍽 **Four** 12 av Gl-de-Gaulle ☎ 67941141 Peu Tal

🍽 **Gare** 1 av V-Hugo ☎ 67942268 **P** All makes

At **CAP D'AGDE**(7km SE)

★★★★ **Matagor** r Trésor Royal ☎ 67260005 tx 480978
⇨🛏90 P60 Lift ⌒ Sea
Credit Cards ①②③⑤

★★ **Ibis** r du Tambour (n.rest) ☎ 67264666 tx 490034
⇨🛏30 🍴 P Lift (
Credit Cards ①③

At **TAMARISSIÈRE, LA**(4km SW D32E)

★★ **Tamarissière** 21 quai Théophile Cornu ☎ 67942087 tx 490225
15 Mar-Nov
⇨🛏34 A5rm ⌒ Sea
Credit Cards ①②③⑤

AGEN
Lot-et-Garonne

★★ **Château Jacobins** L€ 1 pl Jacobins ☎ 53470331 tx 560800
⇨🛏15 P20 (

★★ **Ibis** Ilot 5, bd Carnot ☎ 53473123 tx 541331
⇨🛏39 🍴 P
Credit Cards ①③

★★ **Périgord** L€ 42 pl XIV Juillet ☎ 53661001
⇨🛏21 Lift
Credit Cards ①③

🍽 **F Tastets** 182 bd de la Liberté ☎ 53471063 DJ

AIGLE, L'
Orne

★★★ **Dauphin** (MAP/BW) pl de la Halle ☎ 33244312 tx 170979
rm30(⇨🛏28) P8 (
Credit Cards ①②③⑤

AIGUEBELLE
Var

★★★★ **Roches Fleuries** (4 km on N599 to Le Lavandu) ☎ 94710507 tx 430023
Apr-early Oct
⇨🛏45 🍴 P ⌒ Beach Sea
Credit Cards ①②

★★ **Plage** ☎ 94058074
Etr-Sep
rm53(⇨🛏20) A31rm Sea

AIGUILLON-SUR-MER
Vendée

★★ **Port** 2 r Belle Vue ☎ 51564008
Mar-Oct
⇨🛏33 🍴 ⌒
Credit Card ③

AINHOA
Pyrénées-Atlantiques

★★★ **Argi-Eder** (MAP/BW) **DPn** rte de la Chapelle ☎ 59299104 tx 570067
Apr-15 Nov
⇨🛏36 A4rm P80 🍴 ⌒ Mountain
Credit Cards ①②③⑤

AIRE-SUR-L'ADOUR
Landes

🍽 **Tolerie** 65 av de Bordeaux ☎ 58716214 **P** Cit

AIRE-SUR-LA-LYS
Pas-de-Calais →

39

France

★ **Europ Hotel** 14 Grande Pl (n.rest)
☎ 21390432
rm14(⇨🛏13) 🍽 P8
Credit Cards ①②③

AISEY-SUR-SEINE
Côte-d'Or

★★ **Roy** 🆗 DPn ☎ 80932163
Closed Dec-1 Jan:Rest closed Tue
rm10(⇨🛏8) P10

AIX-EN-PROVENCE
Bouches-du-Rhône

★★★★ **Pullman le Pigonnet** 5 av Pigonnet (off N8 towards Marseille) ☎ 42590290 tx 410629
⇨🛏49 A14rm 🍽 P Lift ⊒
Credit Cards ①②③④⑤

★★★ **Manoir** 8 r d'Entrecasteaux (n.rest) ☎ 42262720
15 Feb-15 Jan
⇨🛏43 🍽 P Lift (
Credit Cards ①②③④⑤

★★★ **Novotel Beaumanoir** Résidence Beaumanoir (A8) ☎ 42274750 tx 400344
⇨🛏102 P Lift ⊒
Credit Cards ①②③⑤

★★★ **Novotel Sud** Périphérique Sud, Arc de Meyran ☎ 42279049 tx 420517
⇨🛏80 P100 Lift ♀ ⊒
Credit Cards ①②③⑤

★★★ **Paul Cézanne** 40 av V-Hugo (n.rest) ☎ 42263473
18 Jan-20 Dec
⇨🛏44 🍽 P Lift (
Credit Card ②

★★★ **Résidence Rotonde** 15 av des Belges (n.rest) ☎ 42262988 tx 410777
15 Jan – 15 Nov
⇨🛏42 🍽 P40 Lift (
Credit Cards ①②③⑤

★★ **Campanile** ZAC du Jas de Bouffan ☎ 42594073 tx 441273
⇨🛏47 P80 Lift
Credit Card ③

★★ **Ibis** chemin des Infirmeries ☎ 42279820 tx 420519
⇨🛏83 Lift
Credit Cards ①③

★★ **Renaissance** 4 bd de la République (n.rest) ☎ 42262422
⇨🛏36 P
Credit Card ③

At **EGUILLES**(11km NW)

★★ **Belvedere** quartier des Landons ☎ 42925292 tx 403521
⇨🛏38 A32rm P40 ⊒
Credit Cards ①②③⑤

At **MILLES, LES**(5km S off D9)

★ **Climat** r Ampère ☎ 42203077 tx 612141
⇨🛏38 P

AIX-LES-BAINS
Savoie

★★★ **Iles Britanniques** pl de l'Establisment Thermal ☎ 79610377
May-Sep
⇨🛏90 A10rm 🍽 P Lift (Mountain Lake

★★★ **International Rivollier** 18 av C-de-Gaulle ☎ 79352100 tx 320903
⇨🛏60 🍽 P10 Lift (Mountain
Credit Cards ①②③④⑤

★★★ **Manoir** 🆗 (Inter) 33 r Georges 1er ☎ 79614400 tx 980793
24 Jan-24 Dec
⇨🛏72 🍽 P10 Lift
Credit Cards ①③⑤

★★★ **Pastorale** 221 av Grand Port ☎ 79352536 tx 309709
Apr-Jan Closed :Rest closed Mon
⇨🛏30 P25 Lift Mountain
Credit Cards ①②③⑤

★★ **Campanile** av du Golf de Marlioz ☎ 79613066 tx 980090
⇨🛏43 P43
Credit Card ③

★★ **Cecil** 20 av Victoria (n.rest) ☎ 79350412
rm18(⇨🛏11) Lift Mountain

★★ **Paix** 🆗 11 r Lamartine ☎ 79350210 tx 980940
Mar-Nov
rm70(⇨🛏60) 🍽 P30 Lift (Mountain Lake
Credit Cards ③⑤

★★ **Parc** 28 r de Chambéry ☎ 79612911
mid Apr – Oct
rm50(⇨🛏18) 🍽 Lift (Mountain

★★ **Pavillon Rivollier** pl de la Gare ☎ 79351904
Etr-15 Oct
rm42(⇨🛏34) 🍽 P12 Lift (Mountain
Credit Cards ②③⑤

ALBERT
Somme

★ **Basilique** 🆗 DPn 3-5 r Gambetta ☎ 22750471
Closed :Rest closed Sun
rm10(⇨🛏8)
Credit Cards ①③

★ **Paix** 🆗 43 r V-Hugo ☎ 22750164
Closed 1-16 Feb
rm15(⇨🛏6) A3rm 🍽 P6
Credit Cards ①②③

ALBERTVILLE
Savoie

★★★ **Million** 8 pl de la Liberté ☎ 79322515 tx 306022
Closed :Rest closed Mon & Sun evening
rm28(⇨🛏27) 🍽 P12 Lift
Credit Cards ①②③⑤

★★ **Costaroche** 1 chemin P-du-Roy ☎ 79320202
⇨🛏20 P20 Mountain
Credit Cards ①③

ALBI
Tarn

★★★★ **Grand St-Antoine** (MAP/BW) 17 r St-Antoine ☎ 63540404 tx 520850
⇨🛏56 🍽 P25 Lift (♀ ⊒
Credit Cards ①②③⑤

★★★ **Chiffre** 50 r Séré de Rivières ☎ 63540460 tx 520411
⇨🛏40 🍽 P40 Lift (
Credit Cards ①②③⑤

★★ **Orléans** (FAH) pl Stalingrad ☎ 63541656 tx 521605
Closed 21 Dec-4 Jan: Rest closed Sun
⇨🛏62 Lift (
Credit Cards ①②③⑤

★ **Vieil Alby** DPn 25 r T-Lautrec ☎ 63541469
15 Jan-25 Jun & 8 Jul-25 Dec Closed :Rest closed Sun evening & Mon lunch
rm9(🛏5)
Credit Cards ①②③⑤

At **FONVIALANE**(3km N on N606)

★★★★ **Réserve** (Relais et Châteaux) DPn rte de Cordes ☎ 63607979 tx 520850
⇨🛏24 P30 (♀ ⊒
Credit Cards ①②③⑤

ALENÇON
Orne **See also ST-LÉONARD-DES-BOIS**

★★★ **Grand Cerf** 21 r St-Blaise ☎ 33260051 tx 772212
⇨🛏33 P20 Lift (
Credit Cards ①②③④

★★ **Campanile** rte de Paris ☎ 33295385 tx 171908
⇨🛏35 P35
Credit Card ③

★★ **France** 3 r St-Blaise (n.rest) ☎ 33262636
rm31(⇨🛏24) (
Credit Cards ①③

★★ **Gare** 🆗 50 av Wilson ☎ 33290393
Closed 27 Dec-4 Jan
rm22(⇨🛏20) 🍽 P22
Credit Cards ①②③⑤

★ **Industrie** 🆗 20-22 pl du Gl-de-Gaulle ☎ 33271930
rm9(🛏6) P15
Credit Cards ①③

★ **Paris** DPn 26 r D-Papin (opposite station) ☎ 33290164
Closed :Rest closed Fri-Sun
rm17(🛏8)🍽
Credit Cards ①③

ALÈS
Gard

★★★ **Mercure** 18 r E-Quinet ☎ 66522707 tx 480830
Closed :Rest closed Sun
⇨🛏75 P45 Lift
Credit Cards ①③⑤

🍽 **C Roux** av de Croupillac ☎ 66862626 P Peu

🍽 **Prairie** 4 av J-Guesde ☎ 66520261 AR LR

ALPE-D'HUEZ, L'
Isère

★★★ **Chamois d'Or** DPn r de Fontbelle ☎ 76803132
17 Dec-24 Apr
⇨🛏45 P25 Lift Mountain
Credit Card ③

★★★ **Ours Blanc** (MAP) av des Jeux ☎ 76803111 tx 320807

40

20 Dec-20 Apr
⇨🛏37 🍽 P40 Mountain
Credit Cards 1 2 3 5

ALTKIRCH
Haut-Rhin

★★ **Terrasse** L£ 44-46 r du 3e Zouave
☎ 89409802
rm22(⇨20) 🍽 P
Credit Cards 1 3 5

★ **Sundgovienne** L£ rte de Belfort (3.5km W on D4) ☎ 89409718
Feb-23 Dec
⇨🛏31 🍽 P50 Lift
Credit Cards 1 2 3 5

At **WALHEIM**(3.5km NE D432)
🏪 **Schmitt** 63b Grand' rue ☎ 89409162 P
All makes

ALVIGNAC
Lot

★★★ **Palladium** av de Padirac
☎ 65336023
May-15 Oct
⇨🛏25 A19rm P30 Lift ⇌ Mountain
Credit Cards 1 2 3 4 5

AMBÉRIEU-EN-BUGEY
Ain

★★★ **Savoie** (Inter) (2km N on D36)
☎ 74380690
Feb-23 Dec
⇨🛏45 P Lift

AMBERT
Puy-de-Dôme

★★ **Livradois** DPn 1 pl du Livradois
☎ 73821001
Closed :Rest closed Mon (out of season)
rm14(⇨🛏7) 🍽 P14 Mountain
Credit Cards 1 2 3 4 5

★ **Gare** 17 av de la Gare ☎ 73820027
15 Nov-15 Oct
rm22(⇨🛏14) 🍽 P12
Credit Cards 1 2 3 5

AMBOISE
Indre-et-Loire

★★★ **Novotel** 17 r des Sablonnières
☎ 47574207 tx 751203
⇨🛏121 P Lift 🏊 ⇌
Credit Cards 1 2 3 5

★★ **Château de Pray** DPn (2km NE on N751) ☎ 47572367
10 Feb-Dec
rm16(⇨🛏14) 🍽 P40
Credit Cards 1 2 3 5

★★ **Ibis** La Boitardière ☎ 47231023
⇨🛏70
Credit Cards 1 3

★★ **Lion d'Or** L£ DPn 17 quai C-Guinot
☎ 47570023
Apr-15 Nov
rm23(⇨🛏22) 🍽
Credit Cards 1 3

★★ **Parc** L£ 8 r L-da-Vinci ☎ 47570693
Mar-Oct
rm19(⇨🛏18) A1rm P30
Credit Cards 1 3

★ **Brèche Pn** 26 r J-Ferry ☎ 47570079
Closed :Rest closed Mon & 14 Nov-Etr
rm14(⇨🛏8) 🍽
Credit Cards 1 2 3 5

France

AMIENS
Somme

★★★ **Grand Hotel de l'Univers** 2 r de Noyon (n.rest) ☎ 22915251 tx 145070
⇨🛏41 P Lift
Credit Cards 1 2 3 4 5

★★ **Carlton-Belfort** 42 r de Noyon
☎ 22922644 tx 140754
⇨🛏36 Lift (
Credit Cards 1 2 3 4 5

★★ **Ibis** 'Le Centrum', r Ml-de-Lattre-de-Tassigny ☎ 22925733 tx 140765
⇨🛏94 Lift
Credit Cards 1 3

★★ **Nord-Sud** 11 r Gresset ☎ 22915903
rm26(⇨20)

★★ **Paix** 8 r de la République (n.rest)
☎ 22913921
Closed 16 Dec-14 Jan
rm26(⇨🛏11) P17

★★ **Prieure** 17 r Porion ☎ 22922767
⇨🛏11
Credit Cards 1 2 3 5

★ **Normandie** 1 bis r Lamartine (n.rest)
☎ 22917499
rm26(⇨🛏23) 🍽 P9
Credit Card 3

🏪 **Anciens Ets Leroux Frères** 48 r Gauthier de Rumilly ☎ 22953720 For

At **BOVES**(7km SE D934)
★★★ **Novotel Amiens Est** (CD934)
☎ 22462222 tx 140731
⇨🛏93 ⇌
Credit Cards 1 2 3 5

AMILLY See **MONTARGIS**

AMMERSCHWIHR See **COLMAR**

ANDELYS, LES
Eure

★★ **Chaîne d'Or** L£ 27 r Grande, pl St-Sauveur ☎ 32540031
Closed Jan
⇨🛏12 A1rm
Credit Card 3

★ **Normandie Pn** 1 r Grande ☎ 32541052
Closed Dec: Rest closed Wed & Thu
rm11(⇨🛏6) P12
Credit Card 1

ANDLAU
Bas-Rhin

★★ **Kastelberg** r du Gl-Koenig
☎ 88089783
Closed Xmas:Rest closed Nov-Mar
⇨🛏28 P30 Mountain
Credit Cards 1 3

ANDRÉZIEUX-BOUTHÉON See **ST-ÉTIENNE AIRPORT**

ANGERS
Maine-et-Loire

★★★ **Anjou** (MAP/BW) 1 bd Ml-Foch
☎ 41882482 tx 720521

Closed :Rest closed Sun
⇨🛏51 🍽 Lift (
Credit Cards 1 2 3 5

★★★ **Mercure** pl M-France ☎ 41603481
tx 722139
⇨🛏86 🍽 P53 Lift
Credit Cards 1 2 3 5

★★ **Boule d'Or** 27 bd Carnot ☎ 41437656
tx 720930
rm33(⇨🛏27) A5rm 🍽 P20
Credit Cards 1 3

★★ **Climat** r du Château-d'Orgemont
☎ 41663045
⇨🛏42 P50
Credit Cards 1 2 3

★★ **Croix de Guerre** 23 r Château-Gontier
☎ 41886659 tx 720930
rm29(⇨🛏28) 🍽 P35
Credit Cards 1 2 3 4

★★ **Fimotel** 23 r P-Bert ☎ 41881010
tx 722735
⇨🛏50 🍽 P50 Lift
Credit Cards 1 2 3 5

★★ **France** (FAH) 8 pl de la Gare
☎ 41884942 tx 720895
⇨🛏57 Lift (
Credit Cards 1 2 3 5

★★ **Ibis** r de la Poissonnerie ☎ 41861515
tx 720916
⇨🛏95 🍽 P Lift
Credit Cards 1 3

★★ **Progrès** (Inter) 26 r D-Papin (n.rest)
☎ 41881014 tx 720902
Apr-19 Dec
⇨🛏41 Lift
Credit Cards 1 2 3 5

★★ **Univers** 2 r de la Gare (n.rest)
☎ 41884358 tx 720930
⇨🛏45 P Lift (
Credit Cards 1 2 3 5

🏪 **Clogenson** 30 r Coste et Bellonte
☎ 41668266 P Peu Tal

🏪 **Rallye Service** 4 bis r St-Maurille
☎ 41880339 AR

ANGLET
Pyrénées-Atlantiques

★★★ **Chiberta et du Golf** (Inter) DPn 104
bd des Plages ☎ 59638830 tx 550637
⇨🛏80 P80 Lift ⇌ 🏖 Sea Lake
Credit Cards 1 2 3 5

★★ **Climat** bd du B.A.B ☎ 59529900
tx 572140
⇨🛏44 🍽 P50
Credit Cards 1 3

★★ **Ibis** 64 av d'Espagne (N10)
☎ 59034545 tx 560121
⇨🛏59 P Lift
Credit Cards 1 3

★ **Fauvettes** 69 r Moulin Barbot, à la Chambre d'Amour ☎ 59037558
Apr-Sep: Rest for guests only
rm11(⇨🛏3) 🍽 Sea

🏪 **J Iribarren** av de Cambo, Quartier Sutar
☎ 59423056 P

ANGOULÊME
Charente →

★★★ **Grand France** (Inter) 1 pl des Halles
☎ 45954795 tx 791020
rm60(⇨♪47) 🍴 P20 Lift (
Credit Cards 1 2 3 5

★★ **Epi d'Or** (Inter) 66 bd R-Chabasse
(n.rest) ☎ 45956764
⇨♪32 P25 Lift (
Credit Cards 1 2 3 5

★ **Flore** 414 rte de Bordeaux ☎ 45919346
tx 791573
rm40(♪14) A2rm 🍴 P20 (
Credit Cards 1 2 3 4 5

🛏 **Mathieux Automobiles** rte de Paris, Le
Gond Pontouvre ☎ 45680255 **P** For

At **CHAMPNIERS** (7km NE)
★★★ **Novotel Angoulême Nord** (N10)
☎ 45685322 tx 790153
⇨♪100 P100 Lift ⌿
Credit Cards 1 2 3 5

★★ **PM16** rte de Poitiers ☎ 45680322
tx 790345
Closed :Rest closed Mon midday
⇨♪41 P100 (
Credit Cards 1 2 3 5

ANNECY
Haute-Savoie See also TALLOIRES;
VEYRIER-DU-LAC

★★★ **Mercure Annecy Sud** rte d'Aix,
Seynod (N201) ☎ 50520966 tx 385303
⇨♪69 P100 ⌿ Mountain
Credit Cards 1 3 4 5

★★★ **Splendid** 4 quai E-Chappuis (n.rest)
☎ 50452000 tx 385233
⇨♪50 Lift Lake
Credit Cards 1 3

★★ **Campanile** Impasse de Crêts
☎ 50677466 tx 385565
⇨♪40 P40
Credit Card 3

★★ **Faisan Doré** L DPn 34 av d'Albigny
☎ 50230246
⇨♪40 🍴 Lift
Credit Cards 1 3

★★ **Ibis** quartier de la Manufacture, r de la
Gare ☎ 50454321 tx 385585
⇨♪83 Lift
Credit Cards 1 3

🛏 **Parmelan** av du Petit Port, Annecy-le-
Vieux ☎ 50231285 Ope

ANNEMASSE
Haute-Savoie See also GAILLARD

★★★ **Parc** (MAP/BW) 19 r de Genève
(n.rest) ☎ 50384460 tx 309034
⇨♪30 🍴 P Lift (Mountain
Credit Cards 1 2 3 5

★★ **Campanile** Parc d'Etremblères
☎ 50378485 tx 309511
⇨♪42 P42
Credit Card 3

★★ **National** (Inter) 10 pl J-Deffault (n.rest)
☎ 50920644
rm45(⇨42) 🍴 P24 Lift (Mountain
Credit Cards 2 5

ANSE
Rhône

🛏 **M Salel** 59 r Nationale ☎ 74670368

France

ANTHÉOR
Var

★★ **Réserve d'Anthéor Pn** (N98)
☎ 94448005
15 Feb-15 Oct
⇨♪13 P30 Lift Beach Sea
Credit Cards 1 2 3 5

ANTIBES
Alpes-Maritimes

★★★★ **Tananarive** rte de Nice (N7)
☎ 93333000
⇨♪50 🍴 P30 Lift ♪ ⌿ Sea Mountain

★★★ **First** 21 av des Chênes ☎ 93618737
tx 462466
Mar-Dec
⇨♪16 P (Sea Mountain
Credit Cards 1 2 3 4 5

★★★ **Mercator** 120 chemin des Groules,
Quartier de la Brague (4km N via N7)
(n.rest) ☎ 93335075
15 Dec-15 Nov
⇨♪18 A2rm P20 ♪
Credit Cards 1 2 3 5

★★ **Fimotel** 2599 rte de Grasse (4.5km W)
☎ 93744636 tx 461181
⇨♪75 P110 Lift ♪ ⌿ Sea Mountain
Credit Cards 1 2 3 5

🛏 **Boschini** 1650 av J-Grec ☎ 93335086
Peu Tal

🛏 **Dugommier** 16 bd Dugommier
☎ 93745999 **P** Ope Vau

🛏 **Molineri** chemin de St-Maymes
☎ 93616203 **P**

At **CAP D'ANTIBES**
★★★ **Gardiole** chemin de la Garoupe, Cap
d'Antibes ☎ 93613503
Closed 6 Nov-Feb
⇨♪21 A4rm P30
Credit Cards 1 2 3 5

★★ **Beau Site** 141 bd Kennedy (n.rest)
☎ 93615343
Apr-Oct
rm26(⇨♪24) A6rm P30 Sea Mountain

ANTONY
Hauts-de-Seine

★★ **Fimotel** r M-Berthelot ☎ 46682022
tx 206037
⇨♪42 P 30
Credit Cards 1 2 3 5

APPOIGNY See AUXERRE

APT
Vaucluse

★★★ **Ventoux** L DPn 67 av V-Hugo
☎ 90740758
⇨♪13 P6 Lift

🛏 **Germain** 56 av V-Hugo ☎ 90741017
For

ARBOIS
Jura

★★ **Messageries** L 2 r Courcelles (n.rest)
☎ 84661545
Mar-Nov
rm26(⇨♪14) 🍴 P10
Credit Cards 1 3

★ **Paris** L DPn 9 r de l'Hôtel-de-Ville
☎ 84660567
15 Mar-15 Nov
⇨♪18 A6rm 🍴 P4
Credit Cards 1 2 3 5

ARCACHON
Gironde See also PYLA-SUR-MER

★★★ **Arc** 89 bd Plage (n.rest)
☎ 56830685 tx 571044
⇨♪30 P40 Lift (⌿ Sea
Credit Cards 1 2 3 5

★★★ **Tamarins** 253 bd Côte d'Argent
(n.rest) ☎ 56545096
⇨♪28 A5rm Lift
Credit Cards 1 3

ARDRES
Pas-de-Calais

★★★ **Grand Clément Pn** pl du Gl-Leclerc
(n.rest) ☎ 21822525
Closed 16 Jan-14 Feb:Rest closed Mon
⇨♪17 🍴 P12
Credit Cards 1 2 3 5

★★ **Relais** L bd C-Senlecq ☎ 21354200
tx 130886
rm13(⇨♪12) A3rm P12
Credit Cards 1 2 3

★ **Chaumière** 67 av de Rouville (n.rest)
☎ 21354124
⇨♪12 P5

ARGELÈS-GAZOST
Hautes-Pyrénées

★ **Bernède** L (FAH) 51 r Ml-Foch
☎ 62970664 tx 531040
Feb-Oct
rm43(⇨♪40) P25 Lift Mountain
Credit Cards 1 2 3 5

★ **Mon Cottage** 3 r Yser ☎ 62970792
Apr-Sep
rm24(⇨18) A8rm P25 Lift Mountain

ARGELÈS-SUR-MER
Pyrénées-Orientales

★★★ **Plage des Pins** allée des Pins
☎ 68810905
28 May-Sep
⇨♪49 🍴 P49 Lift (♪ ⌿ Sea Mountain
Credit Cards 1 3

★ **Grand Commerce** L Pn 14 rte de
Collioure (N22) ☎ 68810033
Closed Jan
rm63 A23rm 🍴 P63 Lift ⌿
Credit Cards 1 2 3 5

ARGENTAN
Orne

★★ **Renaissance** L av de la 2e D-B
☎ 33361420
Closed Sun
rm15(⇨♪12) P30
Credit Cards 1 2 3 5

ARGENTAT
Corrèze

★★ **Gilbert** L av J-Vachal (n.rest)
☎ 55280162

42

5 Mar-Dec Closed :Rest closed Fri evening
& Sun lunch
rm30(⇌♠20) P Lift Mountain
Credit Cards [1][3][5]

☙ **Manaux** 1 rte de Tulle ☏ 55280332 **P** Peu

ARGENTEUIL
Val-d'Oise

★★ **Climat** bd Lenine, angle r du Perreux
☏ 39619805 tx 609372
⇌♠45 P51
Credit Cards [1][2][3][4]

★★ **Fimotel** 148 rte de Pontoise (N192)
☏ 34105200
⇌♠40 ☎ P80 Lift
Credit Cards [1][2][3][5]

ARGENTON-SUR-CREUSE
Indre

★★ **Manoir de Boisvillers** 11 r Moulin de Bord (n.rest) ☏ 54241388
Closed 21 Dec-14 Jan
rm14(⇌♠10) ☎ P13 ℂ
Credit Cards [1][2][3][5]

★ **France** ℡ **Pn** 8 r J-J-Rousseau
☏ 54240331
rm22(⇌♠13) A7rm ☎ P8
Credit Cards [1][2][3][5]

ARLEMPDES
Haute-Loire

★★ **Manoir** ℡ ☏ 71571714
Mar-Nov
rm17(♠11) Mountain

ARLES
Bouches-du-Rhône

★★★★ **Jules César** (Relais et Châteaux)
bd des Lices ☏ 90934320 tx 400239
Closed early Nov-21 Dec
⇌55 ☎ P10 ℂ ⇱
Credit Cards [1][2][3][4][5]

★★★ **Arlatan** 26 r Sauvage (n.rest)
☏ 90935666 tx 441203
rm49(⇌♠48) ☎ P25 Lift ℂ
Credit Cards [2][3][5]

★★★ **Cantarelles** Ville Vieille ☏ 90964410 tx 401582
19 May-15 Nov
⇌♠35 P30 ⇱
Credit Cards [1][2][3][5]

★★★ **Forum** 10 pl Forum (n.rest)
☏ 90934895
Mar-30 Oct
⇌♠45 P25 Lift ℂ ⇱

★★★ **Primotel** av de la 1ère Division F-Libre, Face de la Palais du Congrès
☏ 90939880 tx 401001
⇌♠148 P150 Lift ℘ ⇱
Credit Cards [1][2][3][5]

★★★ **Select** 35 bd G-Clemenceau
☏ 90960831
⇌♠24 ☎ Lift
Credit Cards [1][2][3][5]

★★ **Campanile** ZAD de Fourchon, r C-Chaplin ☏ 90499999 tx 403624
⇌♠40 P40
Credit Card [3]

★★ **Cloître** 18 r du Cloître (n.rest)
☏ 90962950

15 Mar-15 Nov
⇌♠33 A10rm
Credit Cards [2][3]

★★ **Ibis** quartier de Fourchon ☏ 90931674 tx 440201
⇌♠67 P Lift
Credit Cards [1][3]

★★ **Mireille** (Inter) 2 pl St-Pierre
☏ 90937074 tx 440308
Mar-15 Nov
⇌♠34 A4rm ☎ P60 ℂ ⇱
Credit Cards [1][2][3][5]

★★ **Montmajour et Le Rodin** (Inter) 84 rte de Tarasçon ☏ 90496910 tx 420776
⇌♠26 A20rm ☎ P Lift ⇱
Credit Cards [1][2][3][5]

★ **Mirador** (Inter) DPn 3 r Voltaire
☏ 90962805
10 Feb-5 Jan
⇌♠15 ☎

☙ **Margueritte** 89 av de Stalingrad
☏ 90960309 **P** For

At **RAPHÈLE-LES-ARLES**(8km SE N453)

★★★ **Auberge la Fenière** Voie Touristique 453 (8km SE on N453) ☏ 90984744 tx 441237
Closed :Rest closed Nov-20 Dec
⇌♠25 ☎ P30
Credit Cards [1][2][3][5]

ARMBOUTS-CAPPEL See **DUNKERQUE (DUNKIRK)**

ARNAGE See **MANS, LE**

ARNAY-LE-DUC
Côte-d'Or

★ **Terminus** ℡ **Pn** r Arquebuse
☏ 80900033
Closed 7 Jan-5 Feb:Rest closed Wed
rm12(⇌♠7) P12
Credit Cards [1][3]

ARRAS
Pas-de-Calais

★★★ **Univers** (Inter) 3 pl Croix Rouge
☏ 21713401
rm36(⇌♠29) A1rm P30 ℂ
Credit Cards [1][2][3]

★★ **Astoria** 12 pl Ml-Foch ☏ 21710814 tx 160768
rm31(⇌♠17) ℂ
Credit Cards [1][2][3][5]

★★ **Commerce** 24 r Gambetta (n.rest)
☏ 21711007
rm40(⇌♠18) ☎ P25 Lift ℂ

★★ **Moderne** (Inter) 1 bd Faidherbe (n.rest)
☏ 21233957 tx 133701
Closed 25 Dec-2 Jan
rm53(⇌50) Lift
Credit Cards [1][2][3][4][5]

★ **Chanzy** ℡ 8 r Chanzy ☏ 21710202
⇌♠24 ☎
Credit Cards [1][2][3][4][5]

☙ **Lievinoise Auto** 16 av P-Michonneau
☏ 21554242 **P** For

At **ST-NICHOLAS**(N off N17)

★★ **Campanile** Zone d'Emploi des Alouettes ☏ 21555630 tx 133616
⇌♠39 P50
Credit Cards [1][3]

ARREAU
Hautes-Pyrénées

★★ **Angleterre** ℡ **DPn** rte de Luchon
☏ 62986330
Jun-10 Oct & 26 Dec-15 Apr
⇌♠25 P30 Mountain
Credit Cards [1][3][5]

At **CADÉAC**(2km S)

★★ **Val d'Aure** rte de St-Lary ☏ 62986063
May-Sep 21 & Dec-15 Apr
⇌♠23 A4rm ☎ P30 ℘ Mountain
Credit Cards [1][3]

ARTIGUES See **BORDEAUX**

ARVERT
Charente-Maritime

★★ **Villa Fantaisie** ℡ **DPn** (n.rest)
☏ 46364009
Closed Feb:Rest closed Sun & Mon
rm23(⇌♠17) A10rm ☎ P6
Credit Cards [1][2][3]

ASCAIN
Pyrénées Atlantiques

★★ **Rhune Pn** pl d'Ascain ☏ 59540004 tx 570792
Closed 16 Jan-14 Mar
rm50(⇌♠48) A23rm P30 ⇱ Mountain
Credit Card [1]

ASSEVILLERS See **PÉRONNE**

ATHIS-MONS See **PARIS AIRPORTS** under **ORLY AIRPORT**

AUBENAS
Ardèche

★★ **Pinède** ℡ rte du Camping des Pins
☏ 75352588
⇌♠32 A10rm ☎ P80 ℘
Credit Cards [1][3]

AUBRES See **NYONS**

AUBUSSON
Creuse

★★ **France** ℡ (FAH) **Pn** 6 r Désportés
☏ 55651022
⇌♠21 ☎
Credit Cards [1][2][3][4][5]

★ **Lion d'Or Pn** pl d'Espagne ☏ 55661388
Closed :Rest closed Sun & Mon
rm11(⇌♠5) P

At **FOURNEAUX**(3km SW)

★★ **Tuilerie** (Inter) **Pn** ☏ 55662809
May-Oct
⇌♠24
Credit Cards [1][2][3][5]

☙ **G Durieux** 36 av de la Liberté
☏ 79050774 Fia Toy

AUCH
Gers

★★★ **France** ℡ (FAH) pl de la Libération
☏ 62050044 tx 520474
Closed :Rest closed Sun evening & Mon
⇌♠29 ☎ P Lift ⇱
Credit Cards [1][2][3]

★★ **Poste** (Inter) 5 r C-Desmoulins
☎ 62050236
⇨♪27🍴 P
Credit Cards 1 2 5

AULNAT AÉROPORT See **CLERMONT-FERRAND**

AULNAY-SOUS-BOIS
Seine
★★★ **Novotel Paris Aulnay-sous-Bois**
RN370 ☎ 48662297 tx 230121
⇨♪138 P280 Lift ⌇
Credit Cards 1 2 3 5

AUMALE
Seine-Maritime
★ **Dauphin Pn** 27 r St-Lazare ☎ 35934192
Closed 24 Dec-17 Jan:Rest closed Sun
rm11(⇨♪10) P6
Credit Cards 1 2 3
🍴 **Fertun** 3 av Foch ☎ 35934121 **P** Peu

AUNAY-SUR-ODON
Calvados
★ **Place** L 31776073
rm19(♪9) P50
Credit Cards 1 2
★ **St Michel** L **Pn** 6 & 8 r de Caen
☎ 31776316
rm7 P12
Credit Cards 1 3
🍴 **l'Odon** r de Caen ☎ 31776288 **P** Fia Lan

AURILLAC
Cantal
★★ **Grand Boreaux** L (MAP/BW) 2 av de la République (n.rest) ☎ 71480184 tx 990316
Closed 16 Dec-14 Jan
⇨♪37🍴 P Lift
Credit Cards 1 2 3 5

AURON
Alpes-Maritimes
★★★ **Pilon** L 93230015 tx 470300
20 Dec-15 Apr & Jul-Aug
⇨♪30 P30 Lift ⌇ Mountain
Credit Cards 1 2 3 5

AUTUN
Saône-et-Loire
★★ **Tête Noire** L **DPn** 1-3 r de l'Arquebuse ☎ 85522539
rm19🍴
Credit Card 3

AUVILLIERS-LES-FORGES
Ardennes
★★ **Lenoir** L Maubert ☎ 24543011
10 Mar-1 Feb Closed :Rest closed Fri
rm21(⇨♪18) A21rm P Lift
Credit Cards 1 2 3 4 5

AUXERRE
Yonne
★★★ **Clairions** L av de Worms
☎ 86468564 tx 800039
⇨♪62 P50 Lift ⌇
Credit Cards 1 2 3
★★★ **Maxime** L 2 quai de la Marine
☎ 86468564 tx 800039
⇨♪44 P Lift

France

★★ **Cygne** 14 r du 24-Août (n.rest)
☎ 86522651
⇨♪24🍴 P14
Credit Cards 1 2 3
★★ **Normandie** (Inter) 41 bd Vauban
(n.rest) ☎ 86525780
⇨♪47🍴 P50 Lift (
Credit Cards 1 2 3 4 5
★★ **Seignelay** L **Pn** 2 r du Pont
☎ 86520348
Closed 11 Jan-9 Feb
rm23(⇨♪14)🍴
Credit Cards 1 3

At **APPOIGNY**(9.5km NW N6)
★★ **Mercure** CD319 Lieu-dit-le Chaumois ☎ 86532500 tx 800095
⇨♪82 P120 ⌇
Credit Cards 1 2 3 5
★★ **Climat** chemin des Ruelles
☎ 86532711 tx 351888
⇨♪26 P30
Credit Cards 1 2 3

AUXONNE
Côte-d'Or
★ **Corbeau** L 1 r de Berbis ☎ 80311188
Closed 16 Dec-9 Jan:Rest closed Mon
⇨♪10 P10
Credit Cards 1 2 3 4 5

At **VILLERS-LES-POTS**(5km NW)
★★ **Auberge du Cheval Rouge** L
☎ 80314488
Closed :Rest closed Sat lunch & Sun evening
⇨♪10 P15
Credit Cards 1 2 3

AVALLON
Yonne
★★★★ **Poste** (Relais et Châteaux) 13 pl Vauban ☎ 86340612 tx 351806
Mar-Nov
rm23(⇨♪22)🍴 P23
Credit Cards 1 3 5
★★ **Moulin des Ruats DPn** Vallée du Cousin (4.5km W via D957 & D427) (n.rest) ☎ 86340774
15 Feb-15 Nov Closed :Rest closed Mon & Tue in season
⇨♪27 P25
Credit Cards 1 3 5
★★ **Relais Fleuri** L (5km E on N6)
☎ 86340285 tx 800084
⇨♪48 P48 ⌇ ⌇
Credit Cards 1 2 3 5

AVIGNON
Vaucluse See also **VILLENEUVE-LES-AVIGNON**
★★★ **Mercure Avignon Sud** rte Marseille-La Barbière ☎ 90889110 tx 431994
⇨♪105 P190 Lift ⌇
Credit Cards 1 2 3 5
★★★ **Novotel Avignon-Sud** rte de Marseille (N7) ☎ 90876236 tx 432878

⇨♪79🍴 P ⌇
Credit Cards 1 2 3 5
★★ **Angleterre** L 29 bd de Raspail (n.rest)
☎ 90863431
Closed 16 Dec-14 Jan
rm40(⇨♪36) P13 Lift
Credit Cards 1 3
★★ **Balladins** av du Grand Gigognan, Z.I. de Courtine ☎ 90868892
⇨♪38 P
Credit Cards 1 2 3
★★ **Ibis** angle av Montclar, bd St-Roch
☎ 90853838 tx 432502
⇨♪98 Lift
Credit Cards 1 3
★★ **Midi** (FAH/Inter) 25 r de la République (n.rest) ☎ 90821556 tx 431074
⇨♪57 Lift
Credit Cards 1 2 3 4 5
🍴 **Auto Service** 4 bd Limbert, 1 rte de Montfavet ☎ 90863958 AR
🍴 **EGSA** Centre des Affaires Cap Sud, rte de Marseille ☎ 90876322 Aud
🍴 **Scandolera** 1 bis rte de Morières
☎ 20821676 For

At **AVIGNON NORD AUTOROUTE JUNCTION A7**(8km E by D942)
★★★★ **Sofitel** L 90311643 tx 432869
⇨♪100 P150 Lift ⌇ ⌇
Credit Cards 1 2 3 5

At **MONTFAVET**(5.5km E)
★★ **Campanile** ZA du Clos de la Cristole
☎ 90899977 tx 432060
⇨♪42 P42
Credit Card 3
★ **Climat de l'Amandier** allée des Fenaisons ☎ 90881300
⇨♪30🍴 P40 Lift
★★ **Ibis** rte de Marseille (N 7), Zone de la Cristole ☎ 90871100 tx 432811
⇨♪69 Lift ⌇
Credit Cards 1 3

AVIGNON NORD AUTOROUTE JUNCTION A7 See **AVIGNON**

AVON See **FONTAINEBLEAU**

AVRANCHES
Manche
★★ **Croix d'Or DPn** 83 r de la Constitution
☎ 33580488
mid Mar-mid Nov
rm30(⇨♪25) A4rm🍴 P20
Credit Card 3
★★ **St-Michel DPn** 5 pl Gl-Patton
☎ 33580191
Etr-15 Nov Closed :Rest closed Sun evening & Mon
rm24(⇨♪16)🍴 P15
Credit Cards 1 3

AX-LES-THERMES
Ariège
★★★ **Royal Thermal**(MAP/BW) espl de Couloubret ☎ 61642251 tx 530955
rm68(⇨♪54) P30 Lift (Mountain
Credit Cards 1 2 3 5
★★ **Moderne** L 20 av du Dr-Gomma
☎ 61642024

44

Feb-Oct
⇌♁22🚗 Lift Mountain

★★ *Roy René* 🗝 **DPn** 11 av du Dr-Gomma
☏ 61642228
Jan-Oct
⇌♁29🚗 P18 Lift Mountain
Credit Cards ①②③

★ *Lauzeraie* prom du Couloubert (n.rest)
☏ 61642070
Jun-15 Nov
⇌♁33 P3 Lift Mountain
Credit Cards ①③

AZAY-LE-RIDEAU
Indre-et-Loire

★★ *Grand Monarque* 🗝 **DPn** pl de la République ☏ 47454008
rm28(⇌♁25) P12
Credit Cards ①②③

BAGNÈRES-DE-BIGORRE
Hautes-Pyrénées

★★ *Résidence* **Pn** Parc Thermal de Salut
☏ 62950397
Apr-15 Oct
⇌♁31 P70 ℘ ⇌ Mountain
Credit Cards ①③

★★ *Vignaux* 🗝 16 r de la République
☏ 62950341
rm15(⇌2)

BAGNEUX See **SAUMUR**

BAGNOLES-DE-L'ORNE
Orne

★★★ *Lutetia-Reine Astrid* (FAH) **DPn** P-Chalvet, pl du Gl-de-Gaulle ☏ 33379477
28 Mar-2 Nov
⇌♁34 A14rm
Credit Cards ①③⑤

★★ *Bois Joli* (FAH) av P du Rozier
☏ 33379277 tx 171782
Etr-Oct
rm20(⇌♁17) P15 Lift Lake
Credit Cards ①②③⑤

★★ *Ermitage* (Inter) 24 bd P-Chalvet (n.rest) ☏ 33379622
15 Apr-15 Oct
⇌♁39🚗 P12
Credit Card ③

BAGNOLET See **PARIS**

BAGNOLS-EN-FORÊT
Var

★★ *Auberge Bagnolaise* 🗝 rte Fayence
☏ 94406024
May-Sep
⇌♁8 P Mountain

BAIX
Ardèche

★★★ *Cardinale* (Relais et Châteaux) quai du Rhône ☏ 75858040 tx 346143
Mar-2 Jan
⇌♁15 A10rm P15 ⇌ Mountain
Credit Cards ②③⑤

BALARUC-LE-VIEUX
Hérault

★★ *Balladins* Zone Commerciale de Balaruc-le-Vieux ☏ 67801980 tx 649294
⇌♁38 P38

BANDOL
Var

France

★★★★ *Pullman Ile Rousse* **DPn** bd L-Lumière ☏ 94294686 tx 400372
⇌♁55🚗 Lift (⇌ Beach Sea
Credit Cards ①②③⑤

★★ *Baie* 62 r Marçon (n.rest) ☏ 94294082
⇌♁14 P5 (Sea
Credit Cards ①③

★★ *Golf* Plage de Renécros (n.rest)
☏ 94294583 tx 400383
Etr-Oct
rm24(⇌♁23) P25 (Beach Sea
Credit Cards ①③

★★ *Provençal* r des Écoles ☏ 94295211
tx 400308
⇌♁22🚗 (
Credit Cards ①②③⑤

★★ *Réserve* rte de Sanary ☏ 94294271
15 Jan-15 Nov
⇌♁16 P13 Sea
Credit Cards ①②③⑤

BANYULS-SUR-MER
Pyrénées-Orientales

★★★ *Catalan* rte Cerbère ☏ 68383244
Apr-Oct
⇌♁36🚗 P Lift ℘ ⇌ Sea Mountain
Credit Card ⑤

BAPAUME
Pas-de-Calais

★ *Paix* 11 av A-Guidet ☏ 21071103
Closed 21 Dec-4 Jan:Rest closed Sat
rm16(⇌9)🚗
Credit Cards ①②③

BARBEN, LA See **SALON-DE-PROVENCE**

BARBEREY See **TROYES AIRPORT**

BARBEZIEUX
Charente

★★ *Boule d'Or* 🗝 (Inter) **Pn** 11 bd Gambetta ☏ 45782272
⇌♁28 A2rm ⇌
Credit Cards ①②③④

🍽 *Alain Cougnon* rte de Chalais
☏ 45782976 **P** Peu Tal

At **BOIS VERT**(11km S on N10)
★★ *Venta* ☏ 45784095
⇌♁23🚗 P80 Lift ℘ ⇌
Credit Cards ①③

BARBIZON
Seine-et-Marne

★★★★★ *Bas-Breau* (Relais et Châteaux) **DPn** Grande Rue ☏ 60664005
tx 690953
Closed Jan-mid Feb
⇌♁19🚗 P (℘
Credit Cards ①②③

★★ *Charmettes* Grande Rue ☏ 60664021
Closed Feb
⇌♁39🚗 P26

BARBOTAN-LES-THERMES
Gers

★★ *Château-de-Bégue* (2km SW on N656)
☏ 62695008 tx 531918
2 May-Sep
rm14(⇌♁11)🚗 P50 Lift
Credit Card ③

BARENTIN See **ROUEN**

BARNEVILLE PLAGE See **BARNEVILLE-CARTERET**

BARNEVILLE-CARTERET
Manche

At **BARNEVILLE PLAGE**
★★ *Isles* 🗝 bd Maritime ☏ 33049076
Feb-25 Nov
rm35(⇌♁32) Sea
Credit Cards ①②③⑤

At **CARTERET**
★★ *Angleterre* 🗝 4 r de Paris
☏ 33538604
15 Mar-5 Nov
rm43(⇌23) P20 Sea
Credit Cards ①②③⑤

★★ *Marine* 🗝 2 r de Paris ☏ 33538331
15 Feb-15 Nov
⇌♁28 P15 Sea
Credit Cards ①③⑤

BAR-SUR-AUBE
Aube

★ *Commerce* 38 r Nationale ☏ 25270876
Closed Jan
rm15(⇌♁12)🚗 P15
Credit Cards ①②③⑤

BAR-SUR-SEINE
Aube

★★ *Barséquanais* 7 av Gl-Leclerc
☏ 25298275
15 Jan-15 Dec
rm28(⇌♁17) A10rm P30
Credit Cards ①②③

BASTIDE-PUYLAURENT, LA
Lozère

★★ *Pins* ☏ 66460007
Feb-Nov
⇌♁25 P20 Mountain
Credit Cards ①③

BAUGÉ
Maine-et-Loire

★ *Boule d'Or* 🗝 **DPn** 4 r du Cygne
☏ 41898212
15 Feb-15 Jan Closed :Rest closed Sun evening & Mon
rm12(⇌♁8)🚗
Credit Cards ①③

BAULE, LA
Loire-Atlantique

★★★ *Bellevue-Plage* 27 bd Océan
☏ 40602855 tx 710459F
Feb-Nov
⇌♁34 P27 Lift (Sea
Credit Cards ①②③

★★★ *Majestic* espl F-André (n.rest)
☏ 40602486
14 Apr-Sep
⇌♁67 P30 Lift (Sea
Credit Cards ②③⑤

★★ *Concorde* 1 av de la Concorde (n.rest)
☏ 40602309 →

France

Apr-Oct
⇨♆47 🕾 P8 Lift Sea
Credit Cards [1] [3]

★★ **Palmeraie** L♨ 7 allée Cormorans
☎ 40602441
26 Mar-Sep
⇨♆23
Credit Cards [1] [2] [3] [5]

★★ **Riviera** 16 av des Lilas (n.rest)
☎ 40602897
May-Sep
rm20(⇨♆16) P6
Credit Card [2]

★★ **Welcome** 7 av des Impairs (n.rest)
☎ 40603025
20 Mar-15 Oct
⇨♆18 Sea
Credit Cards [1] [3]

📨 **St-Atlantic** 33 av G-Clemencea ns
☎ 40602375 P AR

BAUME-LES-DAMES
Doubs

At **HYÈVRE-PAROISSE**(7km NE N83)

★★ **Ziss** N83 ☎ 81840788
Closed :Rest closed Sat lunch
⇨♆21 🕾 P7 Lift Mountain
Credit Cards [1] [2] [3]

BAVANS See **MONTBÉLIARD**

BAYEUX
Calvados

★★★ **Lion d'Or** L♨ 71 r St-Jean
☎ 31920690

22 Jan-19 Dec
rm29(⇨♆26) 🕾 P25 Lift ℂ
Credit Cards [1] [2] [3] [4] [5]

★★ **Bayeux** 9 r de Tardif (n.rest)
☎ 31927008 tx 171704
⇨♆31 🕾 P6
Credit Cards [1] [3]

★★ **Mogador** 20 r A-Chartier (n.rest)
☎ 33922458
⇨♆14
Credit Card [3]

BAYONNE
Pyrénées-Atlantiques

★★★ **Agora** av J-Rostand ☎ 59633090
tx 550621
⇨♆105 Lift
Credit Cards [1] [2] [3] [5]

★★ **Basses-Pyrénées** 12 r Tour de Sault
☎ 59590029 tx 541535
rm48(⇨♆25) A10rm 🕾 Lift ℂ Mountain
Credit Cards [1] [2] [3] [5]

★★ **Capagorry** (MAP/BW) 14 r Thiers
(n.rest) ☎ 59254822
rm48(⇨♆35) 🕾 P3 Lift ℂ
Credit Cards [1] [2] [3] [5]

📨 **Sajons** 36 allée des Marines
☎ 59254579 P

At **VILLEFRANQUE**(4km S)

★★★★ **Château de Larraldia**
☎ 59442000 tx 540831
Jun-3 Oct
⇨♆22 A4rm 🅿 🖃 🚙 Mountain
Credit Cards [1] [2] [3] [5]

BEAUCAIRE
Gard

★★★ **Vignes Blanches** rte de Nîmes
☎ 66591312 tx 480690
Apr-15 Oct
⇨♆62 P30 Lift 🚙
Credit Card [3]

BEAUGENCY
Loiret

★★ **Ecu de Bretagne** L♨ pl du Martroi
☎ 38446760 tx 306254
7 Mar-30 Jan
rm26(⇨♆17) A11rm 🕾 P30
Credit Cards [1] [2] [3] [5]

BEAULIEU-SUR-DORDOGNE
Corrèze

★★ **Central** L♨ DPn ☎ 55910134
15 Mar-15 Nov
rm30(⇨♆20) P20

★★ **Chasseing-Farges** L♨ pl du Champ de Mars ☎ 55911104
rm18(⇨♆11) A6rm 🕾
Credit Cards [1] [2]

BEAULIEU-SUR-MER
Alpes-Maritimes

HOTELLERIE DE LA DAGUE
77630 Barbizon/Fontainebleau
Tel.: 1 60 66 40 49

SITUATION 35 km from Paris. Access via motorway A6 (Paris-Lyon, Exit Fontainebleau) and RN 7 at the border of the Fontainebleau forest.

IMAGE A large hotel of recent construction respecting the image of Barbizon. Lots of heraldic shields and swords of copper, remind of the famous hunting-parties on horseback in this forest.

HOTEL ★★★ The chestnut-coloured (wood) panelling creates a warm atmosphere in those rooms overlooking the terrace. Private parking (lock-up) available to guests.

RESTAURANT A large stone fireplace decorated with brasses sits in the dining room. Candle-lit dinner, served on the shaded terraces in the Summer.

IN THE VILLAGE Three museums to visit, the Impressionist painters, the art galleries and the contemporary artists workshops. On the outskirts of the village, only 5 mins away are the Fontainebleau and Vaux-le-Vicomte châteaus the hall of Milly-la-Forêt, 18 hole golf courses, tennis courts and horse-riding for sport enthusiasts.

France

★★★★ **Réserve de Beaulieu Pn** 5 bd Gl-Leclerc ☏ 93010001 tx 470301
10 Jan-30 Nov
⇨🛏50🕭 P15 Lift (🔁 Sea
Credit Cards ② ③ ⑤

★★★★ **Métropole** (Relais et Châteaux) **Pn** bd Gl-Leclerc ☏ 93010008 tx 470304
20 Dec-20 Oct
⇨🛏50 P Lift (♪ 🔁 Beach Sea

★★★ **Victoria** 47 bd Marinoni
☏ 93010220 tx 470303
20 Dec-Sep
rm80(⇨🛏60) Lift (Sea Mountain

BEAUMONT-SUR-SARTHE
Sarthe

★ **Barque** 11 pl de la Libération
☏ 43970016
10 Jan-20 Dec
⇨🛏25 P12
Credit Cards ① ② ③

★ **Chemin de Fer** L꜀ La Gare ☏ 4397005
Nov-8 Feb & Mar-15 Oct
rm15(⇨2) A9rm 🕭 P
Credit Cards ① ③

🛵 **Thureau** rte Nationale 138
☏ 43970033 **P** Peu Tal

BEAUMONT-SUR-VESLE
Marne

★ **Maison du Champagne** L꜀ DPn
☏ 26039245
Nov-Jan & Mar-Sep Closed : Rest closed Sun evening & Mon
rm10(⇨🛏7) 🕭 P10
Credit Cards ① ② ③ ⑤

BEAUNE
Côte-d'Or

★★★ **Altea** Autoroute 6 ☏ 80214612 tx 350627
⇨🛏150
Credit Cards ① ② ③ ⑤

★★★ **Cep** 27 r Maufoux ☏ 80223548 tx 351256
14 Mar-Nov
⇨🛏46 A6rm 🕭 P Lift (
Credit Cards ① ② ③ ⑤

★★★ **Poste Pn** 5 bd Clemenceau
☏ 80220811 tx 350982
Apr-mid Nov
rm25(⇨🛏24) 🕭 P8 Lift (Mountain
Credit Cards ① ② ③ ⑤

★★ **Arcade** av du Gl-de-Gaulle, Rond-point de l'Europe ☏ 80227567 tx 351287
⇨🛏41 P20 Lift
Credit Cards ① ③

★★ **Balladins** ZA de la Chartreuse
☏ 05355575 tx 649394
rm38 P38
Credit Cards ① ② ③ ④ ⑤

★★ **Bourgogne** L꜀ av C-de-Gaulle
☏ 80222200 tx 350666
Feb-Dec
⇨🛏120 P120 Lift 🔁
Credit Cards ① ② ③ ⑤

★★ **Central** L꜀ **Pn** 2 r V-Millot ☏ 80247724
Seasonal
rm20(⇨🛏19)
Credit Cards ① ③

★★ **Climat** ZA de la Chartreuse
☏ 80227410 tx 351384
⇨🛏38 P30
Credit Cards ① ② ③

★★ **Samotel Pn** rte de Pommard (N74)
☏ 80223555 tx 350596
⇨🛏65 P65 🔁 Mountain
Credit Cards ① ② ③ ⑤

🛵 **Biais** 30 bd Foch ☏ 80247172 **P** Peu Tal

🛵 **Bolatre** 40 fbg Bretonnière
☏ 80222803 **P** Fia Lan

At **LADOIX-SERRIGNY**(5km NE)
★★ **Paulands** (n.rest) ☏ 80264105 tx 351293
rm21(⇨🛏20) P20 🔁
Credit Cards ① ③

At **MONTAGNY-LES-BEAUNE**(3km SE)
★★ **Campanile** rte de Verdun ☏ 80226550 tx 350156
⇨🛏42 P42
Credit Card ③

BEAURAINVILLE
Pas-de-Calais

★ **Val de Canche** L꜀ **Pn** ☏ 21903233
Jan 15-Dec 24 Closed : Rest closed Mon
rm10(⇨🛏4) 🕭 P10
Credit Cards ① ③

BEAUREPAIRE
Isère

★★ **Fiard** 25 r de la République
☏ 74846202
10 Feb-10 Jan
⇨🛏15 🕭 (
Credit Cards ① ② ③ ⑤

BEAUSSET, LE
Var

★★ **Auberge de la Gruppi** L꜀ **DPn** 46 rte Nationale 8 ☏ 94987018
Mar-Jan Closed : Rest closed Tue
rm12(🛏4)
Credit Cards ① ② ③ ④ ⑤

BEAUVAIS
Oise

★★★ **Chenal** 63 bd Gl-de-Gaulle (n.rest)
☏ 4450355 tx 145223
⇨🛏29 🕭 P5 Lift (
Credit Cards ① ② ③ ⑤

★★★ **Mercure** av Montaigne, ZAC St-Lazare ☏ 44020336 tx 150210
⇨🛏60 P120 🔁
Credit Cards ① ② ③ ⑤

★★ **Campanile** av Descartes ☏ 44052700 tx 150992
⇨🛏47 P47
Credit Card ③

★ **Commerce** L꜀ 11&13 r Chambiges (n.rest) ☏ 44481784
rm14(🛏6) 🕭 P4

★ **Palais** 9 r St-Nicolas (n.rest)
☏ 44451258

⇨🛏15 P4
Credit Cards ① ② ③ ④

BEAUVALLON
Var **See also STE-MAXIME**

★ **Marie Louise Pn** Guerrevieille
☏ 94960605
⇨🛏14 P8 Sea
Credit Cards ③ ⑤

BEAUVOIR
Manche

★★ **Gué de Beauvoir** Château de Beauvoir
☏ 33600923
Etr-Sep
rm21(⇨🛏10) P20
Credit Cards ① ③

BEG-MEIL
Finistère

★★ **Bretagne** ☏ 98949804
Apr-Sep Closed : Rest closed Tue
rm38(⇨🛏20) A18rm P100
Credit Cards ① ③

★★ **Thalamot** L꜀ Le Chemin Creux Fouesnant ☏ 98949738
23 Apr-2 Oct
rm35(⇨🛏29) A4rm
Credit Cards ① ② ③

BELFORT
Territoire-de-Belfort

★★★ **Altea Grand Lion** 2 r G Clemenceau
☏ 84211700 tx 360914
⇨🛏82 🕭 P150 Lift
Credit Cards ① ② ③ ⑤

★★ **Climat** r de l'As de Carreau
☏ 84220984 tx 361017
⇨🛏46 P30 Lift
Credit Cards ① ② ③

At **BESSONCOURT**(7km NE)
★★ **Campanile** Exchangeur Belfort Nord
☏ 84299442 tx 360724
⇨🛏46 P46
Credit Card ③

At **DANJOUTIN**(3km S)
★★★ **Mercure** r de Dr-Jacquot
☏ 84215501 tx 360801
⇨🛏80 P150 Lift 🔁
Credit Cards ① ② ③ ⑤

BELIN-BELIET
Gironde

★ **Alienor d'Aquitaine** L꜀ DPn ☏ 56880123
Mar-Nov
⇨🛏12 P20

🛵 **Garage Firmin Burgana** RN10
☏ 56880139 **P** Peu

BELLÊME
Orne

★ **Relais St Louis** 2 bd Bansart-des-Bois
☏ 33731221
20 Mar-Dec. Closed : Rest closed Wed
rm9(⇨🛏7) 🕭 P6

BELLERIVE-SUR-ALLIER See **VICHY**

BÉNODET
Finistère

★★ **Ancre de Marine** av l'Odet 6
☏ 98570529 →

France

15 Mar-5 Nov
rm25(⇨♄14) Sea
Credit Cards [1] [3]
★★ **Poste** (FAH) r de l'Église ☎ 98570109
tx 941818
Closed :Rest closed Mon
rm36(⇨♄32) A17rm 🛏 P10
Credit Cards [1] [2] [3] [4] [5]

BERCK-PLAGE
Pas-de-Calais

★★ **Homard Bleu DPn** 44-48 pl de l'Entonnoir ☎ 21090465
Closed :Rest closed Sun evening & Mon
⇨♄18
Credit Cards [1] [2] [3]

BERGERAC
Dordogne

★★ **Bordeaux L⁺** (Inter) 38 pl Gambetta ☎ 53571283 tx 550412
Feb-Nov
⇨♄42 🛏 P10 Lift (⊇
Credit Cards [1] [2] [3] [5]

★★ **Commerce L⁺** (FAH) 36 pl Gambetta ☎ 53273050 tx 541888
Mar-10 Feb Closed :Rest closed Sun evening
⇨♄30 Lift
Credit Cards [1] [2] [3] [5]

🍴 **Ets Jean Geraud** pl du Pont ☎ 53576272 Peu Tal

BERGUES
Nord **See also DUNKERQUE**

★★ **Motel 25** Autoroute Lille-Dunkerque ☎ 28687900 tx 132309
⇨♄42 🛏 P200 (℘ Lake
Credit Cards [1] [2] [3] [5]

★ **Tonnelier** 4 r de Mont-de-Piété ☎ 28687005
Closed :Rest closed Fri
rm11(♄7) 🛏 P7
Credit Cards [1] [3] [4]

BERNAY
Eure

★ **Angleterre et Cheval Blanc L⁺ DPn** 10 r Gl-de-Gaulle ☎ 32431259
rm23(⇨♄3) P50
Credit Cards [1] [2] [3] [5]

🍴 **Ets Lefèvre** rte de Broglie, RN138 ZI ☎ 32433428 **P** Peu Tal

BESANÇON
Doubs

★★★★ **Altea Parc Micaud** 3 av E-Droz ☎ 81801444 tx 360268
⇨♄95 P100 Lift
Credit Cards [1] [2] [3] [4] [5]

★★★ **Novotel** 22 bis r de Trey ☎ 81501466 tx 360009
⇨♄107 Lift ⊇
Credit Cards [1] [2] [3] [4] [5]

★★ **Balladins** r B-Russell ☎ 81515351
⇨♄28 P25
Credit Cards [1] [2] [3]

★★ **Ibis** 4 av Carnot ☎ 81803311 tx 361276
⇨♄66 Lift
Credit Cards [1] [3]

★ **Gambetta** 13 r Gambetta (n.rest) ☎ 81820233
rm26(⇨♄19)
Credit Cards [1] [2] [3] [5]

★ **Granvelle** 13 r de G-Lecourbe (n.rest) ☎ 81813392
rm26(⇨♄25) P15 (
Credit Cards [1] [2] [3] [5]

🍴 **Auto Dépannage** 9 r A-Fanart ☎ 81501332 **P** Cit

🍴 **Est Auto** 18 av Carnot ☎ 81808511 For

🍴 **M Morel** 48 r de Vesoul ☎ 81503673 **P** Peu Tal

At **CHÂTEAU-FARINE**(6km SW)

★★★ **Mercure** 159 r de Dôle (n.rest) ☎ 81520400 tx 360167
⇨♄59 P60 Lift ⊇
Credit Cards [1] [2] [5]

At **ÉCOLE-VALENTIN**(4.5km NW)

★★ **Campanile** ZAC de Valentin ☎ 81535222 tx 361172
⇨♄55 P55
Credit Card [3]

★★ **Climat** La Combe Oudotte ☎ 81880411 tx 361651
⇨♄43
Credit Cards [1] [2] [3]

BESSE-EN-CHANDESSE
Puy-de-Dôme

★★ **Beffroy** ☎ 73795008
Closed Nov
rm16(⇨♄14) ⊇ P

BESSINES-SUR-GARTEMPE
Haute-Vienne

★★★ **Toit de Chaume** (5km S on Limoges rd) (n.rest) ☎ 55760102
⇨♄20 🛏 P30 ⊇
Credit Cards [2] [3] [5]

★★ **Vallée L⁺ Pn** ☎ 55760166
Closed Feb: Rest closed Sun evening
rm20(⇨♄16) 🛏 P20
Credit Cards [1] [3]

BESSONCOURT **See BELFORT**

BÉTHUNE
Pas-de-Calais

★★ **Vieux Beffroi** 48 Grande pl ☎ 21681500 tx 134105
rm65(⇨♄59) A29rm 🛏 P120 Lift (℘
Credit Cards [1] [2] [5]

★ **Bernard et Gare L⁺** 3 pl de la Gare (n.rest) ☎ 21572002
rm33(⇨♄23) 🛏
Credit Cards [1] [2] [3] [5]

At **BEUVRY**(4km SE)

★★★ **France II** 11 r du Gl-Leclerc ☎ 21651100 tx 110691
⇨♄54 🛏 P160 Lift
Credit Cards [1] [2] [3] [5]

BEUVRY See **BÉTHUNE**

BEYNAC-ET-CAZENAC
Dordogne

★★ **Bonnet L⁺ DPn** ☎ 53295001
15 Apr-16 Oct
rm22(⇨♄20) 🛏 P40
Credit Cards [1] [3]

BEYNOST See **LYON**

BÉZIERS
Hérault

★★★ **Imperator** (Inter) 28 allée P-Riquet (n.rest) ☎ 67490225 tx 490608
⇨♄45 🛏 P Lift (
Credit Cards [1] [2] [3] [5]

★★ **Ibis** Echangeur Béziers-Est ☎ 67625514 tx 480938
⇨♄50 Lift
Credit Cards [1] [3]

BIARD See **POITIERS**

BIARRITZ
Pyrénées-Atlantiques

★★★★★ **Palais** 1 av de l'Impératrice ☎ 59240940 tx 57000
May-1 Nov
⇨♄140 P Lift (⊇ Sea
Credit Cards [1] [2] [3] [5]

★★★ **Miramar** av de l'Impératrice ☎ 59413000 tx 540831
⇨♄126 🛏 P35 Lift (⊇ Sea Mountain
Credit Cards [1] [2] [3] [4] [5]

★★★ **Regina & Golf** 52 av de l'Impératrice ☎ 59240960 tx 541330
⇨♄69 Lift (℘ Sea Mountain
Credit Cards [1] [2] [3] [4] [5]

★★★ **Windsor** (Inter) Grande Plage ☎ 59240852
15 Mar-15 Oct
⇨♄37 Lift (Sea
Credit Cards [1] [2] [3] [4]

★★ **Beau-Lieu** 3 espl du Port-Vieux (n.rest) ☎ 59242359
15 Feb-Dec
rm26(⇨♄18) Sea

★★ **Campanile** rte d'Espagne ☎ 59234041 tx 572120
⇨♄41 P41
Credit Card [3]

★ **Palacito** 1 r Gambetta (n.rest) ☎ 59240489
⇨♄26 Lift
Credit Cards [1] [2] [3]

🍴 **Darrort** 4 r Loeb ☎ 59410063 AR

BIDART
Pyrénées-Atlantiques

★★★ **Bidartea** (MAP/BW) rte d'Espagne N10 ☎ 59549468 tx 570820
Closed :Rest closed Mon in winter
⇨♄36 A6rm 🛏 Lift ⊇ Sea Mountain
Credit Cards [1] [2] [3] [5]

BLAGNAC See **TOULOUSE AIRPORT**

BLANGY-SUR-BRESLE
Seine-Maritime

★ **Poste Pn** 44 Grand' rue ☎ 35935020
15 Jan-15 Dec
rm12 P10
Credit Cards [1] [3]

48

★ *Ville* Pn 2 r Notre-Dame ☏ 35935157
Closed 6-26 Jul:Rest Sun
rm9(⇨☏8) A3rm
Credit Card ③

🍴 St-Denis 6 r St-Denis ☏ 35935042 P

BLAYE
Gironde

★★ *Citadelle* pl d'Armes ☏ 57421710
tx 540127
⇨☏21 A12rm P100 (⇨ Sea
Credit Cards ① ② ③ ⑤

BLERE
Indre-et-Loire

★ *Cher* Pn 9 r du Pont ☏ 47579919
⇨☏19 A8rm 🚗 P10
Credit Cards ① ③

BLÉRIOT-PLAGE
Pas-de-Calais

★ *Dunes* Pn N48 ☏ 21345430
rm13(⇨☏8) 🚗 P10
Credit Cards ② ③ ⑤

BLOIS
Loir-et-Cher

★★ *Campanile* r de la Vallée Maillard
☏ 54744466 tx 751628
⇨☏54 P54
Credit Card ③

★★ *Ibis* 15 r de la Vallée Maillard
☏ 54746060 tx 750959
⇨☏40 Lift
Credit Cards ① ③

★ *Bellay* L 12 r Minimes (n.rest)
☏ 54782362 tx 750135
rm12(⇨☏6) A2rm

★ *St-Jacques* pl de la Gare (n.rest)
☏ 54780415
rm33(⇨☏20)
Credit Cards ① ③

★ *Viennois* 5 quai A-Contant (n.rest)
☏ 54741280
15 Jan-15 Dec
rm26(⇨☏20) A15rm

🍴 *M Gueniot* 74 Levée des Tuileries
☏ 54789463 P

At **CHAUSSÉE ST-VICTOR, LA**(4km N)

★★★ *Novotel Blois l'Hermitage*
☏ 54783357 tx 750232
⇨☏116 P110 Lift ⇨ Lake
Credit Cards ① ② ③ ⑤

At **ST-GERVAIS-LA-FORÊT**(3km SE)

★★ *Balladins* r G-Melies ☏ 54426990
⇨☏36 P30
Credit Cards ① ② ③

At **VINEUIL**(4km SE)

★★ *Climat* 48 r des Quatre-Vents
☏ 54427022 tx 752302
⇨☏58 P20
Credit Cards ① ② ③

BLONVILLE-SUR-MER
Calvados

★ *Mer* L 93 av de la République (n.rest)
☏ 31879323
Feb-Nov
rm20(⇨☏14) P20 Sea
Credit Cards ① ③

France

BOBIGNY
Seine-St-Denis

★★ *Campanile* ZUP des Sablons, 304 av
P-V-Couturier ☏ 48313755 tx 233027
⇨☏120 P Lift
Credit Card ③

★★ *Ibis* 15 r H-Berlioz ☏ 48960730
tx 231452
⇨☏80 Lift
Credit Cards ① ③

BOCCA, LA See **CANNES**

BOIS-GUILLAUME See **ROUEN**

BOISSEUIL
Haute-Vienne

★ *Relais* ☏ 55711183
Closed 10-31 Dec
⇨☏13 A3rm P9

BOIS VERT See **BARBEZIEUX**

BOLLENBERG See **ROUFFACH**

BOLLÈNE
Vaucluse

★★ *Campanile* av T-Aubanel ☏ 90300042
tx 432017
⇨☏30 P30
Credit Card ③

BONNEUIL-SUR-MARNE
Val-de-Marne

★★ *Campanile* ZA des Petits Carreaux, 2
av des Bleuets ☏ 43777029 tx 211251
⇨☏50 P50
Credit Card ③

BONNEVAL
Eure-et-Loir

★★ *Bois Guibert* rte Nationale 10
☏ 37472233
rm17(⇨☏6) 🚗 P
Credit Cards ① ② ③

BONNEVILLE
Haute-Savoie

★★ *Sapeur* pl de l'Hôtel-de-Ville
☏ 50972068
Closed :Rest closed Mon
⇨☏18 P20 Lift Mountain

At **CONTAMINE-SUR-ARVE**(8km NW)

★ *Tourne-Bride* Pn ☏ 50036218
Closed :Rest closed Mon
rm7
Credit Card ①

BONNY-SUR-LOIRE
Loiret

★★ *Fimotel-Val De Loire* rte Nationale 7
☏ 38316462
⇨☏46 P70
Credit Cards ② ③ ⑤

🍴 *Parot* 139 Grande rue ☏ 38316332 P
Ren

BORDEAUX
Gironde

★★★★ *Aquitania Sofitel* Parc des
Expositions ☏ 56508380 tx 570557
⇨☏212 P1000 Lift (⇨ Lake
Credit Cards ① ② ③ ④ ⑤

★★★★ *Mercure Bordeaux le Lac* quartier
du Lac ☏ 56509030 tx 540077
⇨☏108 P Lift 🅿 ⇨ Lake
Credit Cards ② ⑤

★★★★ *Pullman Meriadeck* 5 r R-
Lateulade ☏ 56909237 tx 540565
⇨☏196 Lift
Credit Cards ① ② ③ ⑤

★★★ *Normandie* 7 cours 30-Juillot (n.rest)
☏ 56521680 tx 570481
⇨☏100 Lift (
Credit Cards ① ② ③ ⑤

★★★ *Novotel Bordeaux-le-Lac* quartier
du Lac ☏ 56509970 tx 570274
⇨☏173 P Lift ⇨ Lake
Credit Cards ① ② ③ ⑤

★★★ *Sofitel* Centre Hôtelier ☏ 56509014
tx 540097
⇨☏100 P Lift 🅿 ⇨
Credit Cards ① ② ③ ⑤

★ *Arcade* 60 r E-le-Roy ☏ 56909240
tx 550952
⇨☏140 Lift
Credit Card ③

★ *Bayonne* (Inter) 15 cours de
l'Intendance (n.rest) ☏ 56480088
Jan-15 Dec
rm37(⇨☏25) Lift
Credit Card ③

★★ *Campanile* quartier du Lac
☏ 56395454 tx 560425
⇨☏150 P150 Lake
Credit Card ③

★★ *Campaville* quartier du Lac (n.rest)
☏ 56399540 tx 572877
⇨☏41
Credit Card ③

★★ *Hotel Campaville* Angle cours
Clemenceau (n.rest) ☏ 56529898
tx 541079
⇨☏45
Credit Card ③

★★ *Ibis* 8 r A Becquerel, Parc Industriel,
Pessac ☏ 56072784 tx 572294
⇨☏87 P80 Lift
Credit Cards ① ③

★★ *Ibis Bordeaux-le-Lac* quartier du Lac
☏ 56509650 tx 550346
⇨☏119 Lift
Credit Cards ① ③

★★ *Sèze* 23 allées Tourny ☏ 56526554
tx 572808
rm25(⇨☏22) Lift (
Credit Cards ① ② ③ ④ ⑤

★ *Etche-Ona* (Inter) 11 r Mautrec (n.rest)
☏ 56443649 tx 570362
15 Jan-Dec
⇨☏33 Lift
Credit Cards ① ③

🍴 *P Mercier* 162-166 r de la Benauge
☏ 56862133 DJ Maz RR

🍴 *Ste Nouvelle* 107 r G-Bonnac
☏ 56968026 Peu Tal

🍴 *SAFI 33* 486 rte de Toulouse
☏ 56378008 P For

France

At **ARTIGUES**(7km NE)
★★ **Campanile** av J-F-Kennedy
☎ 56327332 tx 541745
⇨♪50 P50
Credit Card ③

At **BOUSCAT, LE**(4km NW)
★★ **Campanile** rte du Médoc ☎ 56283384
tx 571622
⇨♪50 P50
Credit Card ③

At **CESTAS**(15km SW)
★★ **Campanile** Aire de Service de
Bordeaux, Cestas A63 ☎ 56218068
tx 540408
⇨♪39 P39
Credit Card ③

At **GRADIGNAN**(6km SW)
★★ **Beausoleil** ☎ 56890048 tx 540322
Closed :Rest closed Sat
⇨♪32 🍴 P80 Lift
Credit Cards ①②③⑤

At **LORMONT**(5km NE)
★★ **Climat** Carrefour des 4 Pavillons (N10)
☎ 56329610 tx 612241
⇨♪38 P

At **MÉRIGNAC**(5km W on D106)
★★★ **Novotel Bordeaux Aéroport** av du
Prés-Kennedy ☎ 56341025 tx 540320
⇨♪100 P150 ⇌
Credit Cards ①②③⑤

★★ **Campanile** av du Prés-Kennedy
☎ 56344362 tx 550496
⇨♪47 P47
Credit Card ③

★★ **Fimotel** av du Prés-Kennedy
☎ 56343308 tx 541315
⇨♪60 P50 Lift ⇌
Credit Cards ②③⑤

★★ **Ibis Bordeaux Aéroport** av du Prés-
Kennedy ☎ 56341019 tx 541430
⇨♪64 Lift
Credit Cards ①③

BORMES-LES-MIMOSAS
Var

★★ **Safari** rte Stade (n.rest) ☎ 94710983
tx 404603
Apr-15 Oct
rm32(⇨30) 🍴 P50 🅿 ⇌ Sea
Credit Cards ①②③⑤

★ **Belle Vue** 🇱 pl Gambetta ☎ 94371515
Feb-Sep
rm14(♪13) Sea
Credit Card ①

BOSSONS, LES See **CHAMONIX-MONT-BLANC**

BOULOGNE-SUR-MER
Pas-de-Calais: See plan page 51 🅐🅐
Agent: see page 6. See also **PORTEL, LE**

★★ **Alexandra** 93 r Thiers ☎ 21305222
Plan **1**
Feb-Dec
⇨♪20 P ℂ
Credit Cards ①②③

★★ **Climat** pl Rouget-de-Lisle
☎ 21801450 tx 135570 Plan **2**

⇨♪47 P Lift ℂ
Credit Card ①

★★ **Faidherbe** 12 r Faidherbe (n.rest)
☎ 21316093 Plan **3**
⇨♪35 P10 Lift Sea

★★ **Ibis** (Inter) bd Diderot, quartier L-
Danremont ☎ 21301240 tx 160485 Plan **4**
⇨♪79 Lift
Credit Cards ①③

★★ **Lorraine** 7 pl de Lorraine (n.rest)
☎ 21313478 Plan **5**
rm21(⇨♪17)
Credit Cards ①③④⑤

★★ **Métropole** (Inter) 51 r Thiers (n.rest)
☎ 21315430 Plan **6**
5 Jan-20 Dec
rm27(⇨♪22)
Credit Cards ①②③④

★ **Hamiot** 1 r Faidherbe ☎ 21314420 Plan **7**
rm21 Lift
Credit Cards ①③

★ **Londres** 22 pl de France (n.rest)
☎ 21313563 Plan **8**
rm20(⇨♪16) P8 Lift
Credit Cards ①③

🛏 **Auto Channel** bd de la Liane
☎ 21920330 AR

🛏 **St-Christophe** 128 blvd de la Liane, ZI
☎ 211920911 Peu Tal

BOULOGNE-BILLANCOURT See **PARIS**

BOULOU, LE
Pyrénées-Orientales

🛏 **Noguer J** 1 r de Catalogne
☎ 68838057 Peu Tal

BOURBON-LANCY
Seine-et-Loire

★★ **Raymond** 🇱 DPn 8 r d'Autun
☎ 85891739
rm19(⇨♪12) 🍴 P19
Credit Cards ①③⑤

BOURDEILLES See **BRANTÔME**

BOURG-EN-BRESSE
Ain

★★★ **Logis de Brou** 132 bd de Brou
(n.rest) ☎ 74221155
⇨♪30 🍴 P10 Lift ℂ
Credit Cards ①②③⑤

★★★ **Prieuré** 49 bd de Brou (n.rest)
☎ 74224460
⇨♪14 🍴 P14 Lift ℂ
Credit Cards ①②③⑤

★★ **Chantecler** (MAP/BW) 10 av Bad
Kreuznach ☎ 74224488 tx 380468
⇨♪30 P30
Credit Cards ①②③④⑤

★★ **Ibis** ZAC de la Croix Blanche, bd Ch-
de-Gaulle ☎ 74225266 tx 900471
⇨♪62 Lift
Credit Cards ①③

🛏 **Mevnier** rte de Strasbourg, Viriat
☎ 74222080 P AR LR

BOURGES
Cher

★★ **Christina** 5 r Halle ☎ 48705650
rm76(⇨♪71) A4rm 🍴 Lift ℂ
Credit Cards ①②③④⑤

★★ **Monitel** 73 r Babes ☎ 48502362
tx 783397
Closed :Rest closed Sat lunch Sun evening
⇨♪48 P24 Lift
Credit Cards ①②③⑤

★★ **Poste** 22 r Moyenne (n.rest)
☎ 48700806
rm34(⇨♪22) A5rm 🍴 P12 Lift ℂ

★★ **St-Jean** 23 av M-Dormoy (n.rest)
☎ 48241348
Mar-Jan
rm26(⇨♪20) 🍴 P8 Lift
Credit Cards ①③

★★ **Tilleuls** (Inter) 7 pl de la Pyrotechnic
(n.rest) ☎ 48204904 tx 782026
⇨♪29 A9rm 🍴 P20
Credit Cards ①③⑤

🛏 **Carrosserie Berthot** 136 bis rte de
Nevers ☎ 48504210 P AR

🛏 **Service Auto Secours** 9 r Jacques
Brel, ZI du Plénéno ☎ 97370333 M/C P

At **ST-DOULCHARD**(2km S)
★★ **Campanile** le Detour du Pave
☎ 48702053 tx 780400
⇨♪42 P42
Credit Card ③

BOURGET AIRPORT, LE See **PARIS AIRPORTS**

BOURG-LÈS-VALENCE See **VALENCE**

BOURGNEUF-LA-FORÊT, LE
Mayenne

★ **Vieille Auberge** pl de l'Église
☎ 43371700
Feb-Dec Closed :Rest closed Sun evening
rm8(♪2) 🍴 P10
Credit Cards ①②③

BOURGOIN-JALLIEU
Isère

★★ **Campanile** ZAC de St-Hubert l'Isle,
d'Abeau Est ☎ 74270122 tx 308232
⇨♪50
Credit Card ③

★★ **Climat** 15 r E-Branly, ZAC de la
Maladière ☎ 74285229
⇨♪41 P50
Credit Cards ①③

🛏 **Giroud** rte de Lyon, Domarin
☎ 74283244 P AR

BOURG-ST-MAURICE
Savoie

★★ **Petit St-Bernard** 2 av du Stade
☎ 79070432
20 Dec-15 Apr & 28 Jun-15 Sep
rm24(⇨♪18) 🍴 P20 Mountain
Credit Cards ②③⑤

BOUSCAT, LE See **BORDEAUX**

BOVES See **AMIENS**

BOULOGNE

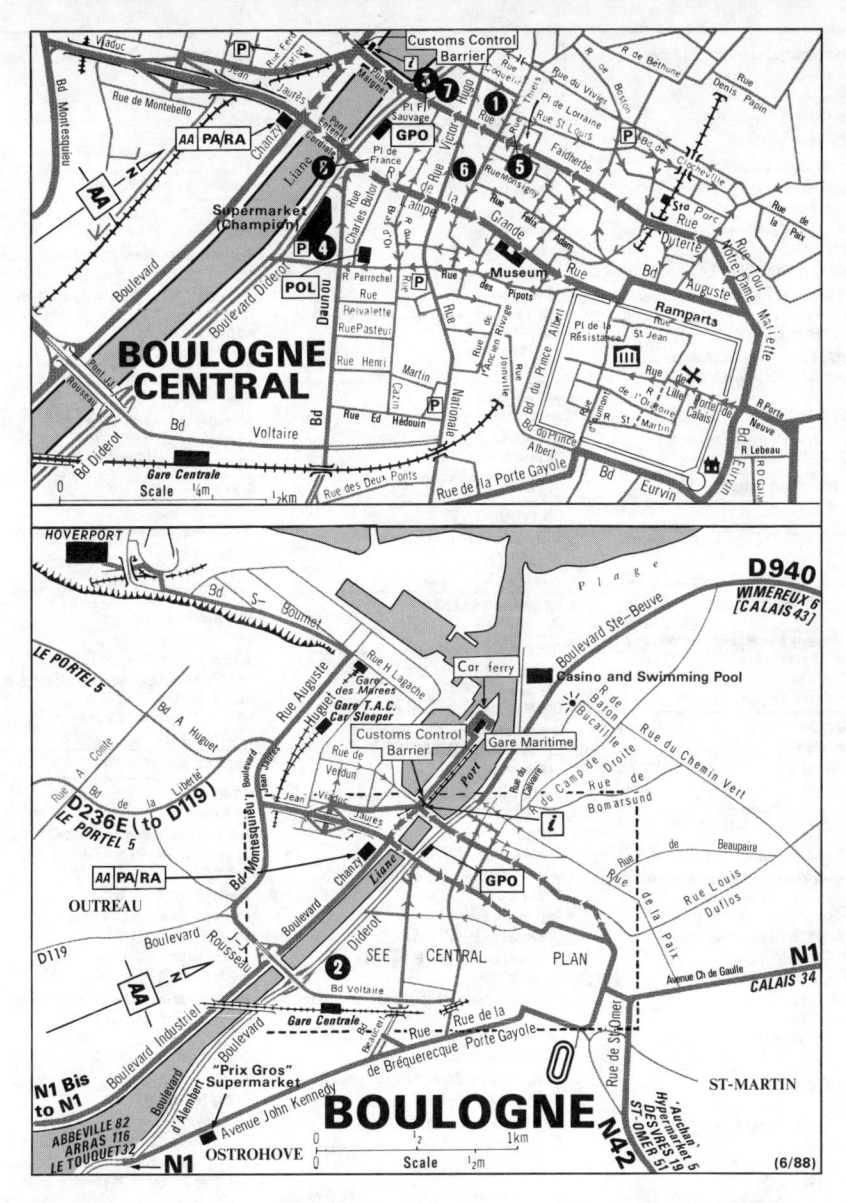

1	★★	Alexandra
2	★★	Climat
3	★★	Faidherbe
4	★★	Ibis
5	★★	Lorraine
6	★★	Métropole
7	★	Hamiot
8	★	Londres

BRANTÔME
Dordogne
★★★ *Chabrol* DPn 59 r Gambetta
☎ 53057015
Closed : Rest closed Sun & Mon in Winter
⇨♫20
Credit Cards ②③⑤

★★★ **Moulin de l'Abbaye** ☎ 53058022
tx 560570
May-Oct
⇨♫12 A3rm ☎P14
Credit Cards ①②③④

At **BOURDEILLES**(10km SW)
★★★ **Griffons** DPn (n.rest) ☎ 53037561
Apr-Sep Closed : Rest closed evenings
⇨♫10 ☎P10 ⌇ ⌇ Lake
Credit Cards ①②③⑤

BREST
Finistère
★★★ *Novotel de Brest* rte de Gouesnou,
ZAC de Kergaradec ☎ 98023283
tx 940470
⇨♫85 ⌇
Credit Cards ①②③⑤

51

France

★★★ **Sofitel Océania** 82 r de Siam ☎ 98806666 tx 940951
⇨🛏82 Lift
Credit Cards 1 2 3 5

At **GOUESNOU**(6km N)

★★ **Campanile** ZA d'Activités de Kergaradec, av du Baron ☎ 98416341 tx 941413
⇨🛏42 P42
Credit Card 3

At **PLOUGASTEL-DAOULAS**(9.5km SE)

★★ **Balladins** ☎ 98403200 tx 649394
⇨🛏38 P38
Credit Cards 1 2 3

★★ **Ibis Brest** rte de Quimper, quartier de Ty-Menez ☎ 98405028 tx 940731
⇨🛏45 Lift
Credit Cards 1 3

🍴 **Caroff** 2 r de Portzmoguer ☎ 98403732 Peu Tal

BRÉTIGNY-SUR-ORGE
Essone

★★ **Climat** ☎ 69019760
⇨🛏43 P ♿
Credit Cards 1 3

BRÉVILLE-SUR-MER
Manche

★★ **Mougine des Moulins à Vent** Les Moulins à Vent (n.rest) ☎ 33502241
⇨🛏7 P30 Sea
Credit Cards 1 3 5

BRIANÇON
Hautes-Alpes

★★ **Cristol** L Pn 6 rte d'Italie ☎ 92202011
15 Dec-15 Nov
⇨🛏16 🍴 P5 Mountain
Credit Cards 1 2 3 5

At **STE-CATHÉRINE**

★★★ **Mont Brison** 1 av Gl-de-Gaulle (n.rest) ☎ 92211455
15 Dec-2 Nov
rm44(⇨🛏29) P15 Lift Mountain
Credit Card 1

★★★ **Vauban Pn** 13 av Gl-de-Gaulle ☎ 92211211
20 Dec-10 Nov
rm44(⇨🛏38) 🍴 P25 Lift Mountain
Credit Cards 1 3

BRIARE
Loiret

★ **Cerf** 22 bd Buyser ☎ 38370080
Mar-15 Feb
rm20(⇨🛏8) A8rm 🍴 P20
Credit Cards 1 3

🍴 **SARL Relais Briarois Autos** 17 av de Lattre-de-Tassigny ☎ 38370161 P Aud

BRICQUEBEC
Manche

★ **Vieux Château** L DPn 4 cour du Château ☎ 33522449
⇨🛏22 A8rm 🍴 P25 ♿
Credit Cards 1 3

BRIDORÉ See **LOCHES**

BRIONNE
Eure

★ **Logis de Brionne** L Pn 1 pl St-Denis ☎ 32448173
Closed :Rest closed Sun evening & Mon
rm16(⇨🛏8) 🍴
Credit Cards 1 3

★ **Vieux Donjon Pn** 19 r de la Soie ☎ 32448062
Mar-15 Nov & 10 Dec-15 Feb Closed :Rest closed Mon
rm8(⇨🛏4) P20
Credit Cards 1 3

BRIOUDE
Haute-Loire

★★ **Brivas** L (Inter) rte de Puy ☎ 71501049 tx 392589
Closed 20 Nov-28 Dec
⇨🛏30 P100 Lift Mountain
Credit Cards 1 2 3 5

★★ **Moderne** L (FAH) 12 av V-Hugo ☎ 71500730
⇨🛏17 P17

BRIVE-LA-GAILLARDE
Corrèze

★★★★ **Mercure** rte Objat ☎ 55871503 tx 590096
⇨🛏57 P80 Lift ♿
Credit Cards 1 2 3 4 5

★★ **Campanile** av Gl-Pouyade ☎ 55868855 tx 590838
⇨🛏42 P42

★★ **Crémaillère** L 53 av de Paris ☎ 55743247
⇨🛏12
Credit Cards 1 2

★★ **Truffe Noir** 22 bd A-France ☎ 55743532
⇨🛏35 Lift ♿
Credit Cards 1 2 3 5

★ **Montauban** L 6 av E-Herriot ☎ 55240038
Feb-Dec Closed :Rest closed Mon midday & Fri evening
rm18(⇨🛏11) P18
Credit Cards 1 2 3

🍴 **G Cremoux** 20 av du Ml-Bugeaud ☎ 55236922 M/C P AR

🍴 **M Taurisson** 21-123 av de Toulouse ☎ 55244163 P BMW

At **VARETZ**(14km NW)

★★★ **Château de Castel Novel** L (Relais et Châteaux) Pn ☎ 55850001 tx 590065
7 May-15 Oct
⇨🛏37 A10rm P35 Lift (♿ ♿ 🏴 Mountain
Credit Cards 1 2 3

BRON See **LYON**

BROU
Eure-et-Loir

★ **Plat d'Etain** L pl des Halles ☎ 37470398
Closed Feb-4 Mar
rm20(⇨🛏10) A7rm 🍴 P10
Credit Cards 1 3

BUC
Yvelines

★★ **Climat** r L-Pasteur ☎ 39564811 tx 699220
⇨🛏43 P150 ♿
Credit Cards 1 2 3

BUCHÈRES See **TROYES**

BUGUE, LE
Dordogne

★★★ **Royal Vezère** (MAP/BW) pl H-de-Ville ☎ 53072001 tx 540710
May-Sep Closed :Rest closed midday Mon & Thu
⇨🛏53 🍴 Lift (♿
Credit Cards 1 2 3 5

BULLY-LES-MINES
Pas-de-Calais

★ **Moderne** 144 r de la Gare ☎ 21291422
⇨🛏36 🍴 P14
Credit Cards 1 2 3

BUXY
Saône-et-Loire

★ **Girardot** pl de la Gare ☎ 85920404
15 Mar-8 Feb
rm11(⇨🛏7) 🍴 P10 Lift
Credit Cards 1 3

CABRERETS
Lot

★ **Grottes DPn** ☎ 65312702
15 May-15 Oct Closed :Rest closed Sat midday (15 May-Jun)
rm18(⇨🛏9) A6rm P20 ♿
Credit Cards 1 3

CADÉAC See **ARREAU**

CAEN
Calvados

★★★★ **Relais des Gourmets** 15 r du Geôle ☎ 31860601 tx 171657
⇨🛏32 P Lift ♿
Credit Cards 1 2 3 4 5

★★★ **Malherbe** pl Ml-Foch (n.rest) ☎ 31844006 tx 170555
⇨🛏44 P100 Lift ♿
Credit Cards 1 2 3 4 5

★★★ **Moderne** (MAP/BW) 116 bd Gl-Leclerc ☎ 31860423 tx 171106
⇨🛏57 🍴 Lift ♿
Credit Cards 1 2 3 4 5

★★★ **Novotel** av de la Côte-de-Nacre ☎ 31930588 tx 170563
⇨🛏126 P200 Lift ♿
Credit Cards 1 2 3 5

★★ **Balladins** Zl de la Sphere (CD 60), rte de Lion-sur-Mer ☎ 314740000 tx 649394
⇨🛏38 P38
Credit Cards 1 2 3

★★ **Bristol** (Inter) 31 r du XI Novembre ☎ 31845976 tx 170234
rm25(⇨🛏24) P15 Lift
Credit Cards 1 2 3

★★ **Château** 5 av du 6-Juin (n.rest) ☎ 31861537
Closed 21 Dec-4 Jan
rm21(⇨🛏19) Lift
Credit Cards 1 3

52

★★ **Climat** av Montgomery, Quartier de la Folie, Couvrechef ☎ 31443636 tx 772141
⇨ඬ43 P43
Credit Cards [1] [2] [3]

★★ **Métropole** (Inter) 16 pl de la Gare ☎ 31822676 tx 170165
rm71(⇨ඬ64) P Lift

★ **Bernières** 50 r de Bernières ☎ 31860126
rm15(⇨ඬ12) (
Credit Cards [1] [3]

★ **St-Jean** 20 r des Martyrs (n.rest) ☎ 31862335
⇨ඬ15 P8

At **HÉROUVILLE-ST-CLAIR**

★★ **Campanile** Parc Tertiaire, bd du Bois ☎ 31952924 tx 170618
⇨ඬ43 P43
Credit Card [3]

★★ **Ibis** 4 quartier Savary ☎ 31935446 tx 170755
⇨ඬ89 Lift
Credit Cards [1] [3]

At **MONDEVILLE**(3.5km SE)

★★ **Fimotel** rte de Paris (N1) ☎ 31343700 tx 171514
⇨ඬ42 P Lift
Credit Cards [1] [2] [3] [5]

CAGNES-SUR-MER
Alpes-Maritimes

★★★ **Cagnard** (Relais et Châteaux) r Pontis Long ☎ 93207321 tx 462223
⇨ඬ20 A6rm P10 Lift Sea Mountain
Credit Cards [1] [2] [3] [5]

★★★ **Tierce** bd de la Plage/bd Kennedy ☎ 93200209
6 Dec-25 Oct
⇨ඬ23 🍴 P23 Lift (Sea Mountain

🛏 **Garage Amblard-Les Tritons** 115 rte de Nice ☎ 93310678 Peu

At **CROS-DE-CAGNES**(2km SE)

★★ **Horizon** 111 bd de la Plage (n.rest) ☎ 93310995
20 Dec-3 Nov
⇨ඬ44 P30 Lift Sea Mountain
Credit Cards [2] [3] [5]

At **VILLENEUVE-LOUBET-PLAGE**

★★ **Méditerranée** N98 (n.rest) ☎ 93200007
Closed Nov
⇨ඬ16 P16

CAHORS
Lot

★★★ **Wilson** 72 r Prés-Wilson (n.rest) ☎ 65354180 tx 533721
⇨ඬ36 P20 Lift
Credit Cards [1] [3] [4]

★★ **France** ⚐ (Inter) 252 av J-Jaurès (n.rest) ☎ 65351676 tx 520394
⇨ඬ80 🍴 P25 Lift
Credit Cards [1] [2] [3] [5]

★ **Terminus** ⚐ 5 av C-de-Freycinet ☎ 65352450
⇨ඬ31 🍴 P6 Lift (
Credit Cards [1] [3]

🛏 **Lacassagne** av A-de-Monsie ☎ 65354510 P

France

🛏 **Recuperautos** rte de Villefranche ☎ 65351516 **P**

At **LAROQUE-DES-ARC**(5km N)

★ **Beau Rivage** Laroque des Arcs ☎ 65221628
Etr-Oct
⇨ඬ16 P45 Lift
Credit Cards [1] [2] [3] [5]

CAISSARGUES-BOUILLARGUES
See **NÎMES**

CALAIS
Pas-de-Calais; **See plan page 54**
ℳ agent: **see page 6**

★★★ **Meurice** 5 r E-Roche ☎ 21345703
Plan 1
⇨ඬ40 A15rm 🍴 P25 Lift (
Credit Cards [2] [3] [5]

★★ **Bellevue** 25 pl d'Armes (n.rest) ☎ 21345375 tx 136702 Plan 2
rm56(⇨ඬ50) Lift (
Credit Cards [1] [2] [3] [5]

★★ **Campanile** r de Maubeuge, ZAC du Beau Marais ☎ 21343070 tx 135229 Plan 3
⇨ඬ42 P42
Credit Card [3]

★★ **CAP** quai du Danube ☎ 21961010
Plan 4
⇨ඬ48 P30
Credit Card [3]

★★ **Climat** Digue G-Berthe ☎ 21346464 tx 735300 Plan 5
⇨ඬ44 P45 Sea
Credit Cards [1] [2] [3]

★★ **George-V** (FAH/Inter) 36 r Royale ☎ 21976800 tx 135159 Plan 6
rm45(⇨ඬ40) P20 Lift
Credit Cards [1] [2] [3] [5]

★★ **Ibis** r Greuze, ZUP du Beau-Marais ☎ 21966969 tx 135004 Plan 7
⇨ඬ55 Lift
Credit Cards [1] [3]

★★ **Pacific** 40 r de Duc-de-Guise ☎ 21345024 Plan 8
⇨ඬ30 A10rm 🍴 P10 Lift
Credit Card [2]

★ **Beffroi** 10 r A-Gerschel (n.rest) ☎ 21344751 Plan 9
rm20(⇨ඬ13) P8 (
Credit Cards [1] [3] [5]

★ **Richelieu** 17 r Richelieu ☎ 21346160 tx 130886 Plan 10
rm15(⇨ඬ14) 🍴 P3 (
Credit Cards [1] [2] [3] [5]

★ **Sole Meunière** 53 r de la Mer (n.rest) ☎ 21343608 Plan 11
⇨ඬ14 P (Sea
Credit Cards [1] [3]

🛏 **Calais Nord** 361 av de St-Exupéry ☎ 21967242 Peu Tal

🛏 **L'Europe** 58 rte de St-Omer ☎ 21343575 For

🛏 **Station George V** 2-4 bd Clémenceau ☎ 21344004 **P** Peu Tal

CALIGNAC
Lot-et-Garonne

★ **Palmiers** ☎ 59247772
⇨ඬ25 P50 ≋

CAMBO-LES-BAINS
Pyrénées-Atlantiques

★ **Bellevue** r des Terrasses ☎ 59297322
15 Nov-1 Feb
⇨ඬ28 P Mountain
Credit Card [3]

CAMBRAI
Nord

★★★ **Beatus** 718 av de Paris (n.rest) ☎ 27814570 tx 820211
⇨ඬ26 🍴 P30 (
Credit Cards [1] [2] [3] [4] [5]

★★★ **Château de la Motte Fenelon** Sq du Château ☎ 27836138 tx 120285
rm33(⇨ඬ27) A26rm ♀ ≋
Credit Cards [2] [3] [5]

★★ **Campanile** rte de Bapaume ☎ 27816200 tx 820992
⇨ඬ42 P42
Credit Card [3]

★★ **Ibis** rte de Bapaume, Fontaine Notre-Dame ☎ 27835454 tx 135074
⇨ඬ51 Lift
Credit Cards [1] [3]

★★ **Mouton Blanc** 33 r A-Lorraine ☎ 27813016 tx 133365
rm31(⇨ඬ22) 🍴 P6 Lift
Credit Cards [1] [3]

★★ **Poste** 58-60 av de la Victoire (n.rest) ☎ 27813469
rm33(⇨ඬ32) 🍴 P10 Lift
Credit Cards [1] [3]

★ **France** 37 r Lille (n.rest) ☎ 27813880
Closed 26 Dec-1 Jan
rm24(⇨ඬ7)

CAMP-ST-LAURENT See **TOULON**

CANCALE
Ille-et-Vilaine

★★ **Continental** ⚐ **Pn** quai au Thomas ☎ 99896016
20 Mar-14 Nov
⇨ඬ20 Sea
Credit Cards [1] [3]

CANET-PLAGE
Pyrénées-Orientales

★★★ **Sables** r Vallée-du-Rhône ☎ 68802363 tx 505213
⇨ඬ41 A17rm P16 Lift ≋
Credit Cards [1] [2] [3] [5]

★★ **Mar-I-Cel** pl Centrale ☎ 68803216
Mar-Nov Closed :Rest closed Nov-Mar
⇨ඬ60 A11rm P30 Lift ≋ Sea Mountain
Credit Cards [1] [3] [5]

CANNES
Alpes-Maritimes

★★★★★ **Carlton** (Intercont) 58 bd Croisette ☎ 93689168 tx 470720
⇨ඬ355 🍴 P8 Lift (Beach
Credit Cards [1] [2] [3] [4] [5]

53

CALAIS

1	★★★	Meurice
2	★★	Bellevue
3	★★	Campanile
4	★★	CAP
5	★★	Climat
6	★★	George V
7	★★	Ibis
8	★★	Pacific
9	★	Beffroi
10	★	Richelieu
11	★	Sole Meunière

★★★★★ **Majestic** (SRS) 163 bd Croisette
☎ 93689100 tx 470475
mid Dec-mid Nov
⇌♠ 262 P80 Lift (♀ ☒ ⇌ ▶ Beach Sea
Credit Cards 1 2 5

★★★★★ **Martinez-Concorde** 73 bd Croisette (n.rest) ☎ 93689191 tx 470708
⇌♠ 420 A420rm P70 Lift (♀ ⇌ Beach
Credit Cards 1 2 3 4 5

★★★★ **Grand** 45 bd Croisette
☎ 93381545 tx 470727
⇌♠ 76 P36 Lift (Beach Sea Mountain
Credit Cards 1 2 3

★★★★ **Pullman Beach** 13 r du Canada
☎ 93382232 tx 470034
Jan-Oct
⇌♠ 95 ☎ Lift ⇌

★★★★ **Sofitel Méditerranée** 2 bd J-Hibert
☎ 93992275 tx 470728
Closed 20 Nov-21 Dec
⇌♠ 152 ☎ P24 Lift (⇌ Sea
Credit Cards 1 2 3 5

★★★ **Embassy** 6 r de Bone ☎ 93387902
tx 470081
⇌♠ 60 ☎ Lift
Credit Cards 1 2 3 5

★★★ **Savoy** 5 r F-Einesy ☎ 93381774
Closed 20 Dec-Oct
rm55(⇌48) Lift (
Credit Cards 2 5

★★ **Campanile** Aérodrome de Cannes-Mandelieu ☎ 93486941 tx 461570
⇌♠ 98 P60 ⇌
Credit Card 3

★★ **France** 85 r d'Antibes (n.rest)
☎ 93392334
⇌♠ 34 Lift Mountain
Credit Cards 1 2 3

★★ **Roches Fleuries** 92 r G-Clemenceau (n.rest) ☎ 93392878
28 Dec-13 Nov
rm24(⇌♠ 15) ☎ Lift Sea Mountain

At **BOCCA, LA**

★★ **Climat de France** 232 av F-Tonner
☎ 93902222 tx 970257
⇌♠ 45 P45 Lift ⇌
Credit Cards 1 2 3 5

▶◀ **Romeo** 4 bd J-Hibert, 22 av des Arlves
☎ 93475541 For

CANNET, LE
Alpes-Maritimes →

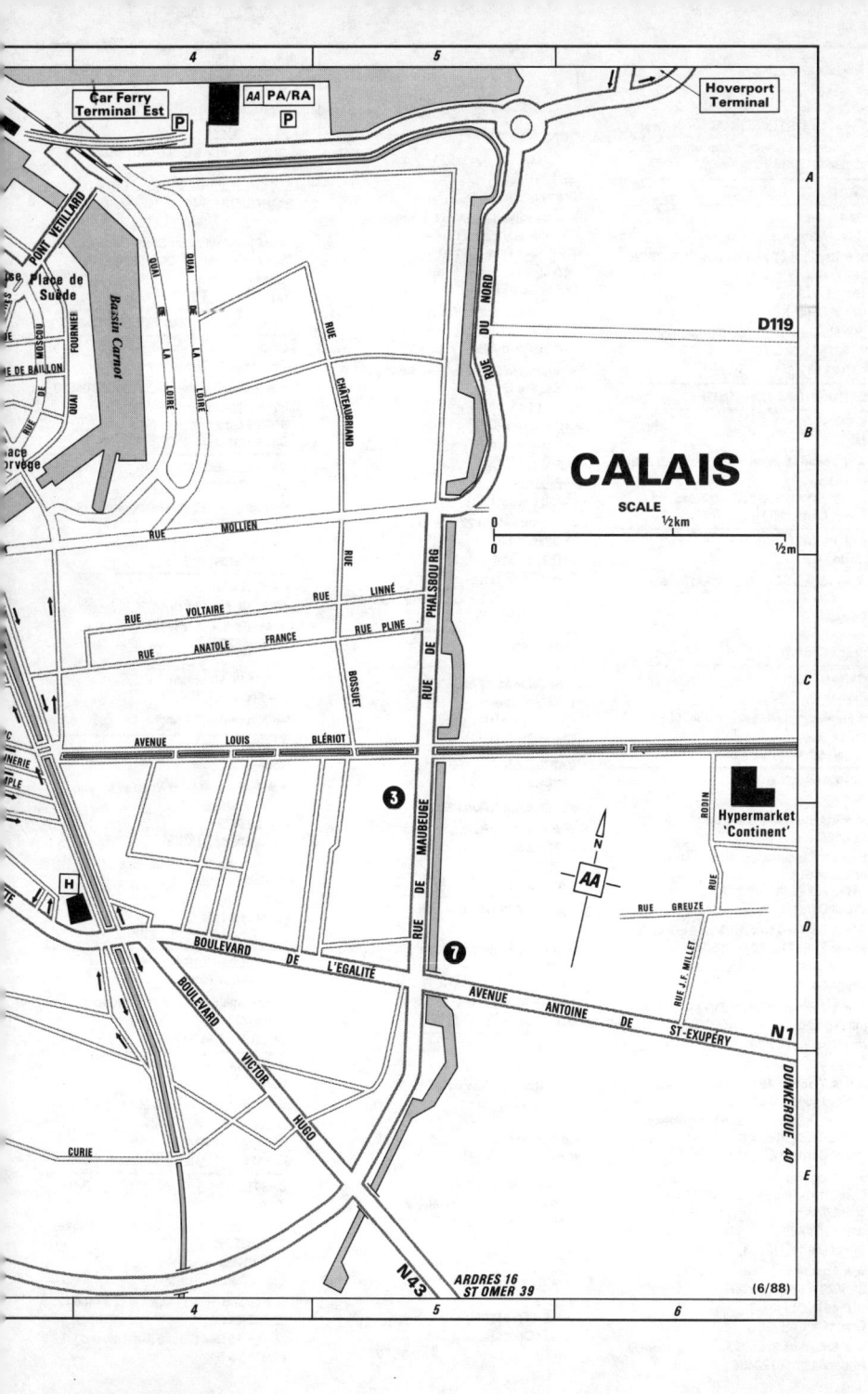

CALAIS

France

★★ **Ibis** 87 bd Carnot ☎ 93457976
tx 470095
⇨♠40 Lift
Credit Cards [1] [3]

🛢 **Europa** Bretelle Autoroute au Cannet
☎ 934351700 Alf Dai

CAP D'AGDE See AGDE

CAP D'AIL
Alpes-Maritimes

★★ **Cigogne** L r de la Gare ☎ 93782960
end Mar-Nov
⇨♠20 P10 Sea
Credit Card [3]

★★ **Miramar** 126 av du 3 Septembre
☎ 93780660
⇨♠27 P12 Sea

CAP D'ANTIBES See ANTIBES

CAPBRETON
Landes

★★ **Ocean** L av de la Plage ☎ 58721022
Mar-Oct
rm52(⇨♠43) A20rm P Lift (Sea
Credit Cards [1] [3] [5]

CAP FERRET
Gironde

★★ **Frégate** 34 av de l'Océan (n.rest)
☎ 56604162
Etr-Sep
⇨♠24 A4rm P8
Credit Cards [1] [2] [3] [5]

CARANTEC
Finistère

★ **Falaise** pl du Kelenn ☎ 98670053
Etr-20 Sep
rm24(⇨♠18) P35 Sea

CARCASSONNE
Aude

★★★★ **Domaine D'Auriac** rte St-Hilaire
☎ 68257222 tx 500385
Feb-Jan Closed :Rest closed Sun & Mon
(mid Oct-Etr)
⇨♠23 🍽 P Lift (🅿 ⇨ ▶
Credit Cards [1] [2] [3]

★★★ **Donjon** L (MAP/BW) 2 r Comte
Roger ☎ 68710880 tx 505012
⇨♠36 🍽 P70 Lift (Mountain
Credit Cards [1] [2] [3] [5]

★★★ **Terminus** (Inter) 2 av Ml-Joffre
(n.rest) ☎ 68252500 tx 500198
rm110(⇨92) 🍽 P30 Lift
Credit Cards [2] [3] [5]

★★★ **Vicomte** 18 r Camille St-Saëns
☎ 68714545 tx 500303
Closed :Rest closed Sun in high season
⇨♠59 P60 Lift (⇨ Beach
Credit Cards [1] [2] [3] [4] [5]

★★ **Aragon** (FAH/Inter) 15 Montée
Combéléran (n.rest) ☎ 68471631
tx 505076
⇨♠29 🍽 P29 ⇨
Credit Cards [1] [2] [3] [5]

★★ **Arcade** 5 sq Gambetta (n.rest)
☎ 68723737 tx 505227
⇨♠48 P20 Lift
Credit Card [3]

★★ **Balladins** ZI La Bouriette, 3 allée de
Roberval ☎ 68723534
⇨♠38 P40
Credit Cards [1] [2] [3]

★★ **Campanile** Centre Commercial
Salvaza, lieu-dit 'La Coustoune'
☎ 68724141 tx 505170
⇨♠42 P42
Credit Card [3]

★★ **Climat** 8 r des Côteaux de Pech-Mary
☎ 68711620
⇨♠26 P Mountain

★★ **Croque Sel** rte de Narbonne (N113)
☎ 68251415
⇨♠11 P11
Credit Cards [2] [3]

★★ **Ibis** rte de Barriac ☎ 68479835
tx 500554
⇨♠60 Lift
Credit Cards [1] [3]

★★ **Montesêgur** 27 allée d'Iéna
☎ 68253141
⇨♠21 P Lift (
Credit Cards [1] [2] [3] [5]

🛢 **Salvaza Automobiles** rte de Montréal
☎ 68251150 P For

CARENNAC
Lot

★ **Fenelon** L ☎ 65386767
10 Mar-25 Jan
rm19(⇨♠13) P19 Lake
Credit Cards [1] [3]

CARENTAN
Manche

At **VEYS, LES**(7km NE)

★★ **Aire de la Baie** Les Veys ☎ 33420099
tx 772085
⇨♠40 P50 🅿
Credit Cards [1] [2] [3] [5]

CARHAIX-PLOUGUER
Finistère

★★ **Gradlon** (Inter) 12 bd de la République
☎ 98931522
Closed 15 Dec-15 Jan
⇨♠45 🍽 P15 Lift 🅿
Credit Cards [2] [3] [5]

CARNAC
Morbihan

★★ **Armoric** 53 av de la Poste
☎ 97521347
Etr-15 Sep
⇨♠25 P56 🅿

At **CARNAC-PLAGE**

★★★ **Novotel Tal-Ar-Mor** av de
l'Atlantique ☎ 97521666 tx 950324
3 Jan-18 Nov
⇨♠106 P Lift ⇨

★★ **Celtique** 17 av Kermario ☎ 97521149
Feb-Oct
rm35(⇨♠31) P30 (
Credit Card [3]

★★ **Genêts** 45 av Kermario ☎ 97521101
1 Jun-25 Sep
rm31(⇨24) A4rm P10
Credit Cards [1] [3]

CARNAC-PLAGE See CARNAC

CARQUEFOU See NANTES

CARQUEIRANNE
Var

★★ **Plein Sud** av du Gl-de-Gaulle, rte des
Salettes (n.rest) ☎ 94585286
⇨♠17 P17 Sea
Credit Cards [1] [3]

CARTERET See BARNEVILLE-CARTERET

CASSIS
Bouches-du-Rhône

★★★ **Plage** pl Bestouan ☎ 420105870
20 Mar-25 Oct
⇨♠29 Lift (Sea
Credit Cards [1] [2] [3] [5]

CASTELJALOUX
Lot-et-Garonne

★ **Grand Cadets de Gascogne** L pl
Gambetta ☎ 53930059
rm15(⇨10) 🍽 P10 Lift
Credit Cards [1] [2] [3] [5]

CASTELLANE
Alpes-de-Haute-Provence

★ **Ma Petit Auberge** pl M-Sauvaire
☎ 92836206
Mar-Nov
⇨♠18 P5 Mountain
Credit Cards [1] [2] [3]

🛢 **Vincent** bd St-Michel ☎ 92836162 Peu

CASTELNAUDARY
Aude

★★ **Palmes** (MAP/BW) 10 av Ml-Foch
☎ 231710 tx 500372
⇨♠20 🍽 Lift
Credit Cards [1] [2] [3] [5]

★ **Fourcade** 14 r des Carmes
☎ 6821302108
10 Feb-5 Jan
rm14(⇨♠7) 🍽
Credit Cards [1] [2] [3] [4] [5]

CASTELSARRASIN
Tarn-et-Garonne

★ **Moderne** 54 r de l'Égalité (n.rest)
☎ 63323010
rm12(⇨♠7) 🍽 P12

CASTÉRA-VERDUZAN
Gers

★★ **Thermes** ☎ 62681307 tx 532915
18 Jan-Dec
rm48(⇨31) A8rm
Credit Cards [1] [2] [3] [5]

CASTRES
Tarn

★★ **Fimotel** ZI de la Chartreuse, (N622)
☎ 63598299
⇨♠40 P52 Mountain
Credit Cards [1] [2] [3] [5]

★★ **Grand** (Inter) 11 r de la Libération
☎ 63590030
15 Jan-15 Dec Closed :Rest closed Fri
evening & Sat

rm40(⇨🛏37) 🛌 Lift (Mountain Lake
Credit Cards [1][2][3][5]

CAUDEBEC-EN-CAUX
Seine-Maritime

★★★ **Marine** 18 quai Guilbaud
☎ 35962011 tx 770404
Closed : Rest closed Sun evening
⇨🛏27 🛌 P12 Lift
Credit Cards [1][2][3]

★★ **Normandie** L. quai Guilbaud
☎ 35962511
Closed Feb
⇨🛏16 P20
Credit Cards [1][2][3]

CAUSSADE
Tarn-et-Garonne

★★ **Dupont** 25 r Recollets ☎ 63650500
Closed Oct-Dec: Rest closed Sat midday
rm31(⇨🛏23) A8rm 🛌 P20 ₽
Credit Cards [1][3]

★★ **Larroque** L. av de la Gare
☎ 63931014
20 Jan-20 Dec Closed :Rest closed Sat
midday & Sun evening
rm27(⇨24) 🛌 P
Credit Cards [1][2][3][5]

CAVAILLON
Vaucluse

★★★ **Christel** Digue de Gd-Jardin (2km S)
☎ 90710779 tx 431547
⇨🛏109 P Lift

★★ **Toppin** L. (FAH) 70 cours Gambetta
☎ 90713042
⇨🛏32 🛌 P20
Credit Cards [1][2][3][5]

CAVALAIRE-SUR-MER
Var

★★ **Bonne Auberge** 400 av des Alliés, rte
Nationale ☎ 94640296
Etr-Oct
rm31(⇨24) P30

CAVALIÈRE
Var

★★★ **Surplage** ☎ 94058019
12 May-12 Oct
⇨🛏60 P36 Lift (🏖 Beach Sea
Credit Cards [1][3]

★★ **Cap Nègre** ☎ 94058046
May-28 Sep
⇨🛏32 🛌 P30 Lift Beach Sea Mountain

CELLE-DUNOISE, LA
Creuse

★ **Pascaud** L. ☎ 55891066
⇨🛏9 ₽ ∪

CERGY See PONTOISE

CESSON-SÉVIGNÉ See RENNES

CESTAS See BORDEAUX

CHABLIS
Yonne

★ **Étoile** 4 r des Moulins ☎ 86421050
Mar-Jan
rm15(⇨🛏8) 🛌 P9
Credit Cards [1][3]

CHAGNY
Saône-et-Loire

France

★★★ **Lameloise** 36 pl d'Armes
☎ 85870885 tx 801086
⇨🛏21 P20 Lift (
Credit Cards [1][3]

★★ **Capucines** 30 rte de Châlon
☎ 85870817
⇨🛏15 A4rm P50
Credit Cards [1][3]

★ **Paris** 6 r de Beaune ☎ 85870838
15 Feb-15 Nov
rm11(⇨🛏6) P12

At **CHASSEY-LE-CAMP**(6km W)

★★ **Auberge du Camp Romain**
☎ 85870991
Mar-Dec
⇨🛏26 🛌 P30 Mountain
Credit Cards [1][3]

CHAINTRÉ-LA-CHAPELLE-DE-GUINCHAY See MÂCON

CHAISE DIEU, LA
Haute-Loire

★★ **Tremblant** L. (D906) ☎ 71000185
15 Apr-15 Nov
rm28(⇨🛏18) 🛌 P20
Credit Cards [1][3]

CHALLES-LES-EAUX
Savoie

★★★ **Château** (MAP/BW) Montée du
Château ☎ 79728671 tx 309756
Feb-Nov
rm63(⇨50) ₽ ⇨ Mountain
Credit Cards [1][2][3][5]

★★ **Château de Trivier** ☎ 79850727
⇨🛏27 A13rm P150 Mountain
Credit Cards [1][2][3][5]

★★ **Climat** r J-Denarie ☎ 79703036
⇨🛏29 P Mountain
Credit Cards [1][3]

CHÂLONS-SUR-MARNE
Marne

★★ **Angleterre** 19 pl Mgr-Tissier
☎ 26682151 tx 842048
⇨🛏18 P12 (
Credit Cards [1][2][3][5]

★★ **Bristol** 77 av P-Sémard (n.rest)
☎ 26682463
⇨🛏24 🛌 P30 (
Credit Cards [1][3]

★★ **Ibis** rte de Sedan, Complex Agricole
☎ 26651665 tx 830595
⇨🛏40 Lift
Credit Cards [1][3]

★★ **Mont des Logès** r de Champagne
☎ 26673343
⇨🛏20 P150
Credit Cards [1][2][3][5]

★★ **Pasteur** 46 r Pasteur (n.rest)
☎ 26681000
⇨🛏29 P15
Credit Cards [1][3]

🛎 **Hall Automobiles** 34 av W-Churchill
☎ 26644937 For

🛎 **G Poiret** 16 ter r des Martyrs de la
Résistance ☎ 26680845 AR

At **COURTISOLS**(10.5km NE)

🛎 **Montel** 63 rte Nationale ☎ 26666004 P Ren

At **ÉPINE, L'**(8.5km E on N3)

★★ **Armes de Champagne** ☎ 26669679
tx 830998
Closed 6 Jan-9 Feb
⇨🛏40 A16rm 🛌 P (
Credit Cards [1][2][3]

CHALON-SUR-SAÔNE
Saône-et-Loire

★★★ **Mercure** Centre Commercial de la
Thalie, av de l'Europe ☎ 85465189
tx 800132
⇨🛏85 P50 Lift ⇨
Credit Cards [1][2][3][5]

★★★ **Royal** (MAP/BW) 8 r du Port Villiers
☎ 85481586 tx 801610
⇨🛏50 🛌 P18 Lift (
Credit Cards [1][2][3][5]

★★★ **St-Georges et Terminus** 32 av J-Jaurès ☎ 85482705 tx 800330
⇨🛏48 🛌 P Lift (
Credit Cards [2][3]

★★★ **St-Régis** (MAP/BW) 22 bd de la
République ☎ 85480728 tx 801624
⇨🛏40 🛌 Lift (
Credit Cards [1][2][3][5]

★★ **Ibis** Carrefour des Moirots (n.rest)
☎ 85466462 tx 800381
⇨🛏62 Lift
Credit Cards [1][3]

★★ **Rotonde** (n.rest) ☎ 85483593
rm32(🛏10) 🛌 P
Credit Cards [1][3]

★★ **St-Jean** 24 quai Gambetta (n.rest)
☎ 85484565
rm25(⇨🛏23) 🛌 Sea

★★ **St-Rémy** L. 89 r A-Martin, St-Rémy
(n.rest) ☎ 85483804 tx 800175
⇨🛏40 P30
Credit Cards [1][3][5]

🛎 **Moderne** r des P-d'Orient ☎ 85465212 Cit

🛎 **Soreva** 4 av Kennedy ☎ 85464945 For

At **CHAMPFORGEUIL**(4km NW)

★★ **Climat** ZAC des Blettrys (4km NW)
☎ 85644601 tx 692844
⇨🛏42

CHAMBÉRY
Savoie

★★★★ **Grand Hotel** 6 pl de la Gare
☎ 79695454 tx 320910
⇨🛏50 🛌 Lift (Mountain
Credit Cards [1][2][3][4][5]

★★★ **Art-Hotel** 12 r Sommeiller (n.rest)
☎ 79623726
⇨🛏40 🛌 Lift
Credit Cards [1][2][3][4][5]

★★★ **France** 22 fbg Reclus (n.rest)
☎ 79335118 tx 309689
⇨🛏48 🛌 P30 Lift Mountain
Credit Cards [1][2][3][5]

★★★ **Novotel** Le Cheminet ☏ 79692127
tx 320446
⇌♪103 P200 Lift ⇌ Mountain
Credit Cards ① ② ③ ⑤
★★ **Balladins** ZI Les Épinettes (n.rest)
☏ 05355575 tx 649394
rm38 P38
Credit Cards ① ② ③ ④ ⑤

At CHAMNORD
★★ **Ibis Chambéry** r E-Ducretet
☏ 79692836 tx 320457
⇌♪87 Lift
Credit Cards ① ③

CHAMBON, LAC
Puy-de-Dôme
★★ **Bellevue** L Lac Chambon
☏ 73886706
Apr-Sep
rm25(⇌♪23) A8rm Mountain Lake
★★ **Grillon** L Lac Chambon ☏ 73886066
Feb-Nov
rm20(⇌♪18) P20 Mountain Lake
Credit Cards ① ③

CHAMBON-SUR-VOUEIZE
Creuse
★★ *Etonneries* L 41 av G-Clemenceau
☏ 55821466
Mar-20 Dec
rm10(⇌♪6) P15 Mountain
Credit Cards ③ ⑤

CHAMBORD
Loir-et-Cher
★★ **Grand St-Michel** L **Pn** Face au
Château ☏ 54203131
20 Dec-12 Nov
rm40(⇌♪36) ☎ P25 (♪
Credit Cards ① ③

CHAMBOURCY See **ST-GERMAIN-EN-LAYE**

CHAMBRAY-LES-TOURS See **TOURS**

CHAMNORD See **CHAMBÉRY**

CHAMONIX-MONT-BLANC
Haute-Savoie
★★★★ **Croix Blanche** 7 r Vallot
☏ 50530011 tx 385614
Jul-Apr
rm34(⇌♪33) A20rm P12 Lift (
Credit Cards ① ② ③ ⑤
★★★ **Mont Blanc Pn** pl de l'Église
☏ 50530564 tx 385614
15 Dec-15 Oct
⇌♪50 ☎ P20 Lift (♪ ⇌ Mountain
Credit Cards ① ② ③ ④ ⑤
★★★ **Richemond** 228 r Dr-Paccard
☏ 50530885 tx 385417
20 Dec-16 Apr & 17 Jun-17 Sep
⇌♪53 P25 Lift (♪ ⇌ ▶ ☉ Mountain
Credit Cards ① ② ③ ④ ⑤

France

★★★ **Sapinière-Montana Pn** 102 r
Mummery ☏ 50530763 tx 30551
Dec-Apr & Jun-Sep
⇌♪30 ☎ P20 Lift (Mountain
Credit Cards ① ② ③ ⑤

At BOSSONS, LES(3.5km S)
★★ **Aiguille du Midi Pn** ☏ 50530065
Seasonal
rm50(⇌♪42) A16rm P80 Lift ♪ ⇌
Mountain
Credit Cards ① ③

CHAMPAGNAC
Cantal
★★ *Lavendès* L **DPn** Château le
Lavendès ☏ 71696279 tx 393160
Mar-Dec
⇌♪8 P20 ⇌ Mountain
Credit Cards ① ③

CHAMPAGNOLE
Jura
★★★ **Ripotot** 54 r Ml-Foch ☏ 84521545
15 Apr-15 Oct
rm60(⇌♪32) ☎ P30 Lift (♪
Credit Cards ① ② ③ ⑤

CHAMPFORGEUIL See **CHALON-SUR-SAÔNE**

CHAMPILLON See **ÉPERNAY**

CHAMPNIERS See **ANGOULÊME**

CHAMPS-SUR-MARNE
Seine-et-Marne
At ÉMERAINVILLE
★★ *Climat* Le Pave Neuf -(CD 51)
☏ 60063834 tx 612241
⇌♪38 P

CHAMPS-SUR-YONNE
Yonne
★★ **Ibis** Aire du Soleil Levant, A6 Venoy
(n.rest) ☏ 86403131 tx 351817
⇌♪72 P70
Credit Cards ① ③

CHANAS See **ROUSSILLON**

CHANTEPIE
Ille-et-Vilaine
★★ **Campanile** ZAC des deux Ruisseaux, r
de la Chalotais ☏ 99414444 tx 740436
⇌♪39 P39
Credit Card ③

CHANTILLY
Oise

★★ **Campanile** rte de Creil, (N16)
☏ 44573924 tx 140065
⇌♪50 P50
Credit Card ③
★ **Petit Vatel** ☏ 44570166
Closed end Dec
rm15(♪3)

At GOUVIEUX(3km SW)
★★★ **Château de Montvillar** Genne
☏ 44570514 tx 150212
⇌♪164 P300 Lift ♪ ⇌
Credit Cards ① ② ③
★★ **Balladins** rte de Creil ☏ 44581312
tx 649394
⇌♪38 P35
Credit Card ①

At LAMORLAYE(5km S)
★★★ **Hostellerie du Lys** 7ème Av
☏ 44212619 tx 150298
⇌♪35 A21rm P60 (
Credit Cards ① ② ③ ⑤

CHANTONNAY
Vendée
★★ *Moulin Neuf* L ☏ 51943027
⇌♪60 P ♪ ⇌ Lake
Credit Card ③
★ **Mouton** L 31 r Nationale ☏ 51943022
⇌♪11 ☎ P11
Credit Cards ① ② ③ ⑤

CHAPELLE-EN-VERCORS, LA
Drôme
★ **Bellier DPn** ☏ 75482003 tx 306022
18 Jun-25 Sep
rm12(⇌♪8) P12 Mountain
Credit Cards ① ② ③ ⑤

CHAPELLE-SAINT-MESMIN, LA
Loiret
★★ **Campanile** "Bel Air", r de l'Aquitaine
☏ 38722323 tx 783799
⇌♪52 P52
Credit Card ③
★★ *Fimotel* 7 r de l'Aquitaine ☏ 38437144
tx 781265
⇌♪42 P50 Lift
Credit Cards ① ② ③ ⑤

CHARAVINES
Isère
★★ **Hostellerie Lac Bleu** L ☏ 76066048
15 Mar-15 Oct
rm15(⇌♪10) P12 Mountain Lake
Credit Card ③

CHARBONNIÈRES-LES-BAINS See **LYON**

CHARLES-DE-GAULLE AIRPORT
See **PARIS AIRPORTS**

CHARLEVILLE-MÉZIÈRES
Ardennes

CHATEAU DE MONVILLARGENNE
HOTEL – RESTAURANT   60270 Chantilly-Gouvieux – Tel. 44.57.05.14 – Telex. 150 212 F

180 rooms with bathroom – TV with TUC 17 channels – radio alarm. 20 conference rooms for 5 to 300 persons.
Gastronomical restaurant – cocktail bar. The Golden Fork for Gastronomy 1987. Terrace – covered swimming
pool – sauna – tennis – 6 ha. park. Large car park.

★★★ **Cleves DPn** 43 r de l'Arquebuse
☎ 24331075 tx 841164
🛏♻49 P20 Lift
Credit Cards ①②③⑤

★★ **Campanile** ZAC du Moulin Blanc,
(N51) ☎ 24375455 tx 842821
🛏♻51 P51
Credit Cards ③⑤

At VILLERS-SEMEUSE(5km E)
★★★ **Mercure** r L-Michel ☎ 24375529
tx 840076
🛏♻68 P100 ⇌
Credit Cards ①②③⑤

CHARMES
Vosges
★ **Central** 🛗 4 r des Capucins ☎ 29380240
Jan-15 Feb & 28 Feb-31 Dec
🛏♻10 🍴 P
Credit Cards ①⑤

CHAROLLES
Saône-et-Loire
★★ **Moderne** 🛗 10 av de la Gare
☎ 85240702
Sep-28 Dec
rm18(🛏♻16) 🍴 P9
Credit Cards ②③⑤

CHARTRES
Eure-et-Loir
★★★ **Grand Monarque** (MAP/BW) 22 pl
des Epars ☎ 37210072 tx 760777
🛏♻46 A11rm 🍴 P30 Lift (
Credit Cards ①②③⑤
★★★ **Novotel** av M-Proust, Le Madeleine
☎ 37348030 tx 781298
🛏♻78 P120 Lift ⇌
Credit Cards ①②③⑤
★★ **Europ** 5 av M-Proust ☎ 37359111
tx 781284
🛏♻47 P150
Credit Card ②
★★ **Ibis Chartres Centre** pl de la Porte
Drouaise tx 789533
🛏♻79 P Lift
Credit Cards ①③
★★ **Poste** 🛗 3 r du Gl-König ☎ 37210427
tx 760533
rm60(🛏♻57) 🍴 Lift
Credit Cards ①②③⑤
★ **Ouest** 3 pl Sémard (n.rest) ☎ 37214327
rm29(🛏♻14) P10
Credit Cards ①③
🛌 **Mauger** 1 av de Sully, ZUP de la
Madeleine ☎ 37344411 **P** Peu Tal
🛌 **Paris-Brest** 80 r F-Lepine, Luisant
☎ 37281388 For

At LUCÉ(3km SW on N23)
★★ **Ibis** Impasse du Périgord (N 23)
☎ 37357600 tx 780348
🛏♻52 Lift
Credit Cards ①③
🛌 **Chartres Auto Sport** rte d'Illiers
☎ 37352479 AR LR

CHARTRE-SUR-LE-LOIR, LA
Sarthe
★★ **France** 🛗 **Pn** 20 pl de la République
☎ 43444016

France

15 Dec-15 Nov
🛏♻28 A12rm 🍴 P12 ♀
Credit Cards ①③

CHASSENEUIL-DU-POITOU
See **POITIERS**

CHASSE-SUR-RHÔNE
Isère
★★★ **Mercure Lyon Sud** CD4-Les Roues
☎ 78731394 tx 300625
🍴115 ⌂ Lift
Credit Cards ①②③⑤

CHASSEY-LE-CAMP See CHAGNY

CHÂTEAU-ARNOUX
Alpes-de-Haute-Provence
★★★ **Bonne Étape** (Relais et
Châteaux) **DPn** N85 ☎ 926640009
tx 430605
mid Feb-Jan
🛏♻18 🍴 P18 ⇌ Mountain Lake
Credit Cards ①②③⑤

CHÂTEAUBRIANT
Loire-Atlantique
★★★ **Hotellerie de la Ferrière** (FAH/Inter)
rte de Nantes ☎ 40280028 tx 701353
🛏♻25 A14rm P200 Lake
Credit Cards ①②③④⑤
★★ **Châteaubriand** 30 r du Il Novembre
(n.rest) ☎ 40281414 tx 721154
🛏♻37 P20 Lift
Credit Cards ①②③⑤
★ **Armor** 19 pl de la Motte (n.rest)
☎ 40811119
🛏♻20 Lift
Credit Cards ①②③⑤

CHÂTEAU-CHINON
Nièvre
★★ **Vieux Morvan** 🛗 6 pl Gudin
☎ 86850501
rm24(🛏♻16) Mountain
Credit Cards ①③

CHÂTEAU-D'OLONNE See SABLES-D'OLONNE, LES

CHÂTEAUDUN
Eure-et-Loir
★★ **Armorial** 59 r Gambetta (n.rest)
☎ 37451957
rm16(🛏♻13)
Credit Cards ①③
★★ **Beauce** (Inter) 50 r de Jallans (n.rest)
☎ 37451475
rm24(🛏♻18) 🍴 P10
Credit Cards ①③
★ **Rose** 🛗 **DPn** 12 r L-Licors ☎ 37452183
🛏♻7 🍴
Credit Cards ①③⑤
★ **Trois Pastoureaux** 31 r A-Gillet
☎ 37450162
rm10(🛏♻6) 🍴 P2
Credit Cards ①②③

CHÂTEAU-FARINE See BESANÇON

CHÂTEAUNEUF See NANS-LES-PINS

CHÂTEAUNEUF See **POUILLY-EN-AUXOIS**

CHÂTEAUNEUF-DE-GRASSE
Alpes-Maritimes
★★ **Campanile** Le Pré du Lac ☎ 93425555
tx 470092
🛏♻41 P41
Credit Card ③

CHÂTEAUNEUF-SUR-LOIRE
Loiret
★★ **Capitainerie DPn** 1 Grande rue
☎ 38584216
Mar-Jan
rm14(🛏♻12) P14
Credit Cards ①③④⑤
★ **Nouvel du Loiret** 🛗 **DPn** 4 pl A-Briand
☎ 38584228
Closed Jan
rm20(🛏♻11) 🍴 P20
Credit Cards ①②③⑤

CHÂTEAUROUX
Indre
★ **Central** 19 av de la Gare (n.rest)
☎ 54220100
5 Jan-22 Dec
rm11(♻8)
Credit Cards ①②③

CHÂTEAU-THIERRY
Aisne
★★ **Ile de France** (Inter) (2km N on rte de
Soissons) ☎ 23691012 tx 150666
Closed 21-28 Dec
rm56(🛏31) P100 Lift
Credit Cards ①②③⑤
★ **Girafe** pl A-Briand (n.rest) ☎ 23830206
rm30(🛏♻12) 🍴
Credit Cards ①③

At NOGENTEL(3.5km S D15)

CHÂTELAILLON-PLAGE
Charente-Maritime
★★ **Hermitage** 13 av G-Leclerc
☎ 46562097
🛏♻27 🍴 P20
Credit Cards ①②③
★★ **Hostellerie Select** 1 r G-Musset
☎ 46562431
Closed Nov
🛏♻21 P15
Credit Cards ①②③④⑤
★★ **Majestic** pl de St-Marsault
☎ 46562053
rm30(🛏♻29) 🍴
Credit Cards ①②③④⑤

CHÂTELGUYON
Puy-de-Dôme
★★★★ **Splendid** (MAP/Best Western) 5-7
r d'Angleterre ☎ 73860480 tx 990585
25 Apr-15 Oct
🛏♻93 P100 Lift ((⇌ Sea Lake
Credit Cards ①②③⑤
★★★ **International** r A-Punnet
☎ 73860672
Closed 27 Apr-5 Oct
rm68(🛏57) Lift ((
Credit Cards ①②③⑤

CHÂTELLERAULT
Vienne →

★★★ *Moderne* (MAP/BW) 74 bd Blossac
☎ 49213011 tx 791801
rm36(⇨9) 🚘 Lift (
Credit Cards 1 2 3 4 5

★★ *Croissant* 19 av Kennedy ☎ 49210177
rm19(⇨ 16) P
Credit Cards 1 3

★★ *Ibis* av Camille Plage, Quartier de la Forêt (n.rest) ☎ 49217577 tx 791488
⇨ 72 Lift
Credit Cards 1 3

★★ *Univers* 4 av G-Clemenceau
☎ 49212353
⇨ 30 🚘 Lift
Credit Cards 1 2 3

🛢 *Rousseau* 91 av L-Ripault ☎ 49210613
Peu Tal

🛢 *Tardy* 40-42 bd d'Estrées
☎ 49214344 **P** For

CHÂTILLON-EN-BAZOIS
Nièvre

★ *Poste* L DPn Grande rue ☎ 86841468
19 Jan-15 Dec
rm12(5) 🚘 P30
Credit Cards 3 4

CHÂTILLON-SUR-INDRE
Indre

★ *Auberge de la Tour* L DPn ☎ 54387217
1.2.88-15.12.88
rm11(⇨ 6) 🚘 P
Credit Cards 1 3

CHÂTILLON-SUR-SEINE
Côte-d'Or

★★ *Côte d'Or* Pn r C-Ronot ☎ 80911329
Closed 13 Dec-11 Jan
rm11(⇨ 8) 🚘 P6
Credit Cards 1 2 3 4 5

★★ *Sylvia* 9 av de la Gare (n.rest)
☎ 80910244
rm21(⇨ 15) A8rm 🚘 P25
Credit Cards 1 3

★ *Jura* Pn 19 r Dr-Robert (n.rest)
☎ 80912696
rm10(⇨ 6) P6
Credit Cards 1 3

CHATTANCOURT See VERDUN

CHAUMONT
Haute-Marne

★★★ *Terminus Reine* (MAP/BW) pl du Gl-de-Gaulle ☎ 25036666 tx 840920
rm68(⇨ 62) 🚘 P20 Lift (
Credit Cards 1 2 3 5

★★ *Grand Val* (Inter) rte de Langres (N19)
☎ 25039035
rm60(⇨ 35) 🚘 P15 Lift
Credit Cards 1 2 5

★ *France* 25 r Toupot de Beveaux
☎ 25030111
rm40(⇨ 30) 🚘 P
Credit Cards 1 2 3 5

🛢 *François* rte de Langres ☎ 25320888
M/C **P** For

CHAUMONT-SUR-LOIRE
Loir-et-Cher

★★★ *Château* DPn r du M-de-L-de-Tassigny ☎ 54209804

France

15 Mar-15 Nov
⇨ 15 P15 ⇨
Credit Cards 1 2 3 5

CHAUSSÉE ST-VICTOR, LA See BLOIS

CHAUVIGNY See NANCY

CHAUVIGNY
Vienne

★ *Lion d'Or* L 8 r du Marché ☎ 49463028
Closed 16 Dec-14 Jan
rm27(⇨ 21) A16rm P11
Credit Card 3

CHAVAGNE See CRÈCHE, LA

CHAVELOT See ÉPINAL

CHELLES
Seine-et-Marne

★★ *Climat Paris Est* r du Château-Gaillard
tx 691149
⇨ 30 P
Credit Cards 1 3

CHÊNEHUTTE-LES-TUFFEAUX
See SAUMUR

CHENONCEAUX
Indre-et-Loire

★★ *Bon Laboureur et Château* rte Nationale 75 ☎ 47239002
Mar-Nov
⇨ 26 🚘 P30
Credit Cards 1 2 3 5

★ *Roy* 9 r Dr-Bretonneau ☎ 47239017
7.2.88-12.11.88
rm42(⇨ 24) A12rm P13
Credit Cards 1 3

CHENÔVE
Côte-d'Or

★★ *Balladins* 18 r J-Moulin ☎ 80521511
tx 350282
⇨ 36 P14
Credit Cards 1 2 3 5

CHERBOURG
Manche
See Plan; M agent: see page 6

★★ *Beauséjour* 26 r Grande-Vallée (n.rest)
☎ 33531030 Plan **1**
rm27(⇨ 18) A18rm 🚘
Credit Cards 1 3

★★ *Chantereyne* Port de Plaisance (n.rest)
☎ 33930220 tx 111137 Plan **2**
⇨ 50 P40 Sea
Credit Cards 2 3 5

★★ *France* L 41 r MI-Foch ☎ 33531024
tx 170764 Plan **3**
8 Jan-20 Dec
rm50(⇨ 30) A9rm Lift
Credit Cards 1 3

★★ *Louvre* (Inter) 28 r de la Paix (n.rest)
☎ 33530228 tx 171132 Plan **5**
Closed 24-31 Dec
rm42(⇨ 32) 🚘 P12 Lift
Credit Cards 1 3

★ *Renaissance* 4 r de l'Église (n.rest)
☎ 33432390 Plan **6**
⇨ 12 P100
Credit Cards 1 3

🛢 *Accessoirauto* 124 r du Val-de-Saire
☎ 33442591 M/C **P**

🛢 *S A Lemasson* ZI av de l'Al-Lemonnier
☎ 33430522 For

At GLACERIE, LA(6km SE N13)

★★ *Campanile* r Montmartre ☎ 33434343
tx 171074
⇨ 43 P43

CHESNAY See PARIS

CHINON
Indre-et-Loire

★ *Boule d'Or* L 66 quai J-d'Arc
☎ 47930313
Feb-Nov
rm20(⇨ 13)
Credit Cards 1 2 3 5

★ *Gargantua* Pn 73 r Voltaire ☎ 47930474
15 Apr-Dec
rm13(⇨ 9) A3rm 🚘
Credit Cards 1 2 3 5

At MARCAY(7km S on D116)

★★★ *Château de Marcay* ☎ 47930347
tx 751475
15 Mar-Dec
⇨ 38 A11rm P50 Lift (♻ ⇨
Credit Cards 1 3 5

CHISSAY-EN-TOURAINE
See MONTRICHARD

CHITENAY
Loir-et-Cher

★ *Clé des Champs* rte de Fougères
☎ 54704203
Closed 12-21 Nov & 5 Jan-5 Feb
rm10(⇨ 3) P40
Credit Cards 1 3

CHOLET
Maine-et-Loire

★★★ *Fimotel* av Sables d'Olonne (2km S)
☎ 41624545
⇨ 42 🚘 P100 Lift
Credit Cards 2 3 5

★★ *Campanile* Parc de Carteron, sq de la Nouvelle France ☎ 41628679 tx 720318
⇨ 43 P43
Credit Card 3

CHONAS-L'AMBALLAN See VIENNE

CIBOURE See ST-JEAN-DE-LUZ

CIOTAT, LA
Bouches-du-Rhône

★★★ *Rose-Thé* 4 bd Beau Rivage
☎ 42830923
Apr-15 Oct
rm22(⇨ 14) P22 (Sea
Credit Cards 1 2 5

★★ *Rotonde* 44 bd de la République (n.rest) ☎ 42086750
rm32(11) P8 Lift
Credit Card 3

CIVRAY
Vienne

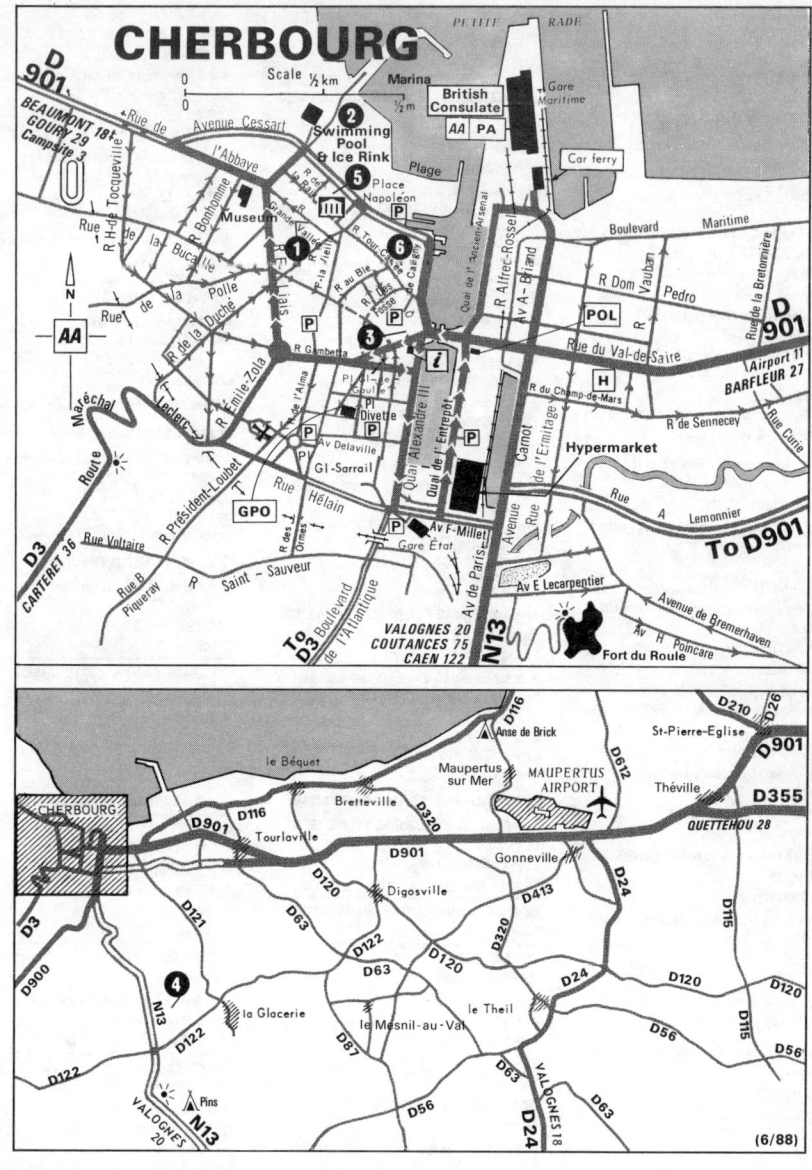

★★ **Davir** Comporte, St-Marcoux
☎ 49873195
⇌♪8☎P30 Lift Lake
Credit Cards [1] [3]

CIVRIEUX-D'AZERGUES
Rhône

★★ *Roseraie* L ☎ 78430178
⇌♪10☎
Credit Card [1]

CLAIRVAUX-LES-LACS
Jura

★ **Lac** Bonlieu ☎ 84255711
15 Dec-15 Nov
rm39(⇌6) P40
Credit Cards [1] [2] [3] [5]

CLAIX See **GRENOBLE**

CLÉCY
Calvados

★★ *Site Normand* L ☎ 31697105
tx 170234
Mar-Dec
⇌♪15 A6rm P
Credit Cards [1] [2] [3] [4] [5]

CHERBOURG

1	★★ Beauséjour
2	★★ Chantereyne
3	★★ France
4	★★ Campanile (At La Glacerie)
5	★★ Louvre
6	★ Renaissance

France

CLELLES
Isère
★★ **Ferrat** Pn ☎ 76344270
Mar-Nov
⇨♠17 A10rm ☎ P20 ⇨ Mountain
Credit Card [1]

CLÉON See **ELBEUF**

CLERMONT-FERRAND
Puy-de-Dôme
★★★★ **Altea Gergovia** Pn 82 bd Gergovia
☎ 73930575 tx 392658
⇨♠124 ☎ Lift Mountain
Credit Cards [1][2][3][5]

★★★ **Gallieni** 51 r Bonnabaud
☎ 73935969 tx 392779
⇨♠80 ☎ P85 Lift Mountain
Credit Cards [1][2][3][5]

★★★ **PLM Arverne** 16 pl Delille
☎ 73919206 tx 392741
⇨♠57 ☎ P Lift Mountain

★★★ **Relais Arcade** 19 r Colbert (n.rest)
☎ 73932566 tx 990125
⇨♠67 P10 Lift

★★ **Balladins** ZAC du Brezet-Est (n.rest)
☎ 05355575 tx 649394
rm38 P38
Credit Cards [1][2][3][4][5]

★★ **Campanile** r C-Guichard ☎ 73918891 tx 394166
⇨♠43 P43 Lift
Credit Card [3]

★★ **Ibis** bd A-Brugière, Quartière Montferrand ☎ 73230004 tx 392288
⇨♠52 Lift
Credit Cards [1][3]

★★ **Minimes** 10 r des Minimes (n.rest)
☎ 73933149
rm28(⇨♠15) P ⦅ Mountain
Credit Card [2]

★ **Foch** 22 r Ml-Foch (n.rest) ☎ 73934840
⇨♠19 P100
Credit Cards [1][2]

★ **Ravel** 8 r de Maringues (n.rest)
☎ 73915133
rm19(⇨♠11)
Credit Card [3]

◑ **Auvergne Auto** 3 r B-Palissy, ZI du Brezet ☎ 73917656 Ope

At **AULNAT AÉROPORT**(5km E)
★★ **Climat** ☎ 73927202
⇨♠42 P40
Credit Cards [1][2][3][5]

CLISSON
Loire-Atlantique
★ **Auberge de la Cascade** Gervaux
☎ 40540241
rm10(⇨♠5) P Lake
Credit Cards [1][3]

CLOYES-SUR-LE-LOIR
Eure-et-Loir
★★ **St-Jacques** 35 r Nationale ☎ 7985008
7 Feb-Nov Closed Rest Sun pm & Mon, Jul-Aug
⇨♠75 ☎ P12 Lift
⇨♠20 ☎ P20
Credit Card [3]

★ **St-Georges** 13 r du Temple ☎ 37985436
⇨♠11 ☎ P8
Credit Card [2]

◑ **Cassonnet** 37 r Nationale
☎ 37985190 **P** Peu Tal

CLUNY
Saône-et-Loire
★★ **Bourgogne** Pn pl de l'Abbaye
☎ 85590058
Mar-15 Sep
rm16(⇨♠15) ☎ P25
Credit Cards [1][2][3][5]

★★ **Moderne DP**n Pont de l'Étang
☎ 85590565
rm15(⇨♠13) ☎ P15 Lake
Credit Cards [1][2][3][5]

★ **Abbaye** Pn av de la Gare ☎ 85591114
3 Mar-28 Nov
rm16(⇨♠10) A4rm ☎ P15 Mountain
Credit Cards [1][3]

COGNAC
Charente
★★ **Auberge** 13 r Plumejeau ☎ 45320870
rm22(⇨♠20)
Credit Cards [1][2][3]

★★ **Moderne** 24 r Élysée-Mousnier, pl de la Sous Préfecture (n.rest) ☎ 45821953 tx 793105
6 Jan-20 Dec
rm40(⇨♠39) P15 Lift
Credit Cards [1][3][5]

At **ST-LAURENT-DE-COGNAC**(6km W)
★★ **Logis de Beaulieu** ☎ 45823050
tx 791020
⇨♠21 ☎ P ⦅ ⦆
Credit Cards [1][2][3][5]

COL-DE-CUREBOURSE See **VIC-SUR-CÈRE**

COLLIOURE
Pyrénées-Orientales
★★ **Madeloc** (Inter) r R-Rolland (n.rest)
☎ 68820756
Apr-15 Oct
⇨♠22 P18 Mountain
Credit Cards [1][2][3][5]

COLLONGES-LA-ROUGE
Corrèze
★ **Relais St-Jacques de Compostelle**
☎ 55254102
Feb-Nov
rm17(⇨♠7) A5rm
Credit Cards [1][2][3][5]

COLMAR
Haut-Rhin
★★★ **Altea Champs de Mars** 2 av de la Marne (n.rest) ☎ 89415454 tx 880928
⇨♠75 ☎ P12 Lift
Credit Cards [1][2][3][5]

★★★ **Novotel** 49 rte de Strasbourg
☎ 89414914 tx 880915

⇨♠66 ⇨ Mountain
Credit Cards [1][2][3][5]

★★★ **Terminus Bristol** (MAP/BW) 7 pl de la Gare ☎ 83235959 tx 880248
⇨♠70 P50 Lift ⦅
Credit Cards [1][2][3][5]

★★ **Campanile** ZI Nord, r des Frères-Lumière ☎ 89241818 tx 394166
⇨♠42 P42
Credit Card [3]

★★ **Climat** r du la 1 Armée Française
☎ 89411110
⇨♠43 P10 Lift
Credit Cards [1][2][3][5]

★★ **Turenne** 10 rte Bâle (n.rest)
☎ 89411226 tx 880959
⇨♠85 ☎ P Lift
Credit Cards [1][2][3][5]

◑ **Bolchert** 77 r Morat ☎ 89791125 For

At **AMMERSCHWIHR**(7km NW)
★ **Arbre Vert** Pn 7 r des Cigognes
☎ 89471223
25 Mar-10 Feb
rm13(⇨♠10)
Credit Cards [1][2][3][5]

At **KAYSERSBERG**(1km NW)
★★ **Remparts** r de la Flieh (n.rest)
☎ 89471212
⇨♠32 A6rm ☎ P20
Credit Cards [1][2][3]

COLOMBEY-LES-DEUX-ÉGLISES
Haute-Marne
★★★ **Dhuits** (MAP/BW) N19
☎ 25015010 tx 840920
⇨♠30 ☎ P40
Credit Cards [1][2][3][5]

COLOMBIER See **FRÉJUS**

COLOMIERS
Haute-Garonne
★★ **Fimotel** pl de la Gare, rte d'Auch
☎ 61789292 tx 531782
⇨♠42 P50 Lift
Credit Cards [1][2][3][5]

COMBEAUFONTAINE
Haute-Saône
★ **Balcon** rte de Paris ☎ 84921113
rm20(⇨♠17) ☎ P40
Credit Cards [1][2][3][4][5]

COMBOURG
Ille-et-Vilaine
★★ **Château & Voyageurs** (FAH) 1 pl Châteaubriand ☎ 99730038 tx 740901
20 Jan-15 Dec
rm33(⇨♠29) A9rm ☎ P15 Lake
Credit Cards [1][2][3][5]

COMPIÈGNE
Oise
★★ **Campanile** av de Huy (Rocade Sud)
☎ 44204235 tx 150088
⇨♠55 P55
Credit Card [3]

★★ **Harlay** 3 r Harlay (n.rest) ☎ 44230150 tx 145923
6 Jan-15 Dec
⇨♠20 P6 Lift
Credit Cards [1][2][3][5]

★★ **Ibis** 18 r E-Branly, Quartier de l' Université ☎ 44231627 tx 145991
⇨♔40 Lift
Credit Cards [1] [3]

🛏 **Thiry** Centre C-de-Venette
☎ 44832692 Aud VW

At **MARGNY**(2km W on D935)
🛏 **Depan' Nord** 189 r de Beauvais
☎ 44832883 P Dat
🛏 **Ille-de-France** 186 av O-Butin
☎ 44833232 P For

CONCARNEAU
Finistère

★★ **Grand** 1 av P-Guéguen (n.rest)
☎ 98970028
Etr-Oct
rm33(⇨♔22) P10 ℂ Sea

★★ **Sables Blancs** 🅻 **DPn** Plages des Sables ☎ 98970139
25 Mar-4 Nov
rm48(⇨♔42) Sea
Credit Cards [2] [3] [4] [5]

🛏 **B Tilly** 106 av de la Gare ☎ 98973500
For

CONCHE-DE-NAUZAN See ROYAN

CONDOM
Gers

★★ **Table des Cordeliers Pn** ☎ 62280368
rm21 ♿ P15 ⊃
Credit Card [3]

CONDRIEU
Rhône

★★★ **Beau Rivage** (Relais et Châteaux) 2 r Beau-Rivage ☎ 74595224 tx 308946
15 Feb-5 Jan
⇨♔26 🅿 Lake
Credit Cards [1] [2] [3] [5]

CONFLANS-STE-HONORINE
Yvelines

★★ **Campanile** Deviation RN184, r des Frères-Dammes ☎ 39192100 tx 699219
⇨♔50 P50
Credit Card [3]

CONFOLENS
Charente

★ **Belle Étoile** 🅻 **DPn** 151 bis rte d'Angoulême ☎ 45840235
Nov-Dec & Feb-Sep
rm14(⇨♔6) 🅿 P30

CONQUES
Aveyron

★ **Ste-Foy** ☎ 65698403
Etr-Oct
⇨♔21 P8
Credit Cards [1] [3]

CONTAMINE-SUR-ARVE
See **BONNEVILLE**

CONTRES
Loir-et-Cher

★★ **France** 🅻 **DPn** 33 r P-H-Mauger
☎ 54195014
Mar-Jan
rm40(⇨♔37) A3rm P20 ♘
Credit Cards [1] [3]

CONTREXEVILLE
Vosges

★★ **Campanile** rte du Lac-de-la-Folie
☎ 29080372 tx 960333
⇨♔31 P31 Lake
Credit Card [3]

★★ **Douze Apôtres** 25 r G-Thomson
☎ 29080412
Apr-15 Oct
⇨♔38 A12rm 🅿 P7 ℂ

COQUILLE, LA
Dordogne

★★ **Voyageurs** 🅻 r de la République (N21)
☎ 53528013
Apr-Oct
rm10(⇨♔7) 🅿 P8
Credit Cards [1] [2] [3] [5]

CORBEIL-ESSONNES
Essonne See also **EVRY**

★★ **Campanile** av P-Mantenant
☎ 60894145 tx 600934
⇨♔50 P50
Credit Card [3]

🛏 **Feray** 46 av du Mai 1945 ☎ 64979494
Ren

At **PLESSIS-CHENET, LE**(4km S)
★★ **Climat** 2 r Penhard ☎ 64938536
tx 692844
⇨♔50 P200
Credit Cards [1] [3] [4]

CORDES
Tarn

★★★ **Grand-Ecuyer** r Voltaire
☎ 63560103
Etr-Oct
⇨♔13

★★ **Hostellerie du Vieux Cordes** 🅻 r de la République ☎ 63560012 tx 530955
15 Feb-15 Jan
⇨♔21 🅿
Credit Cards [1] [2] [3] [5]

CORNEVILLE-SUR-RISLE See PONT-AUDEMER

CORPS
Isère

★★ **Poste** 🅻 pl de la Mairie ☎ 76300003
⇨♔20 A10rm 🅿 P30 Mountain
Credit Cards [1] [3] [4]

🛏 **R Rivière** pl Napoléon ☎ 76300113 M/C P Ren

CORSE (CORSICA)
PORTICCIO
Corse-du-Sud

★★★★ **Sofitel** Pointe de Porticcio
☎ 95250034 tx 460708
⇨♔100 P100 Lift ℂ ♘ ⊃ Beach Sea
Credit Cards [1] [2] [3] [5]

PORTO-VECCHIO
Corse-du-Sud

★★★ **Ziglione** (5km E on N158)
☎ 95700983
15 May-20 Sep
⇨♔32 P45 ℂ Beach Sea Mountain

COSNE-SUR-LOIRE
Nièvre

★★ **Grand Cerf Pn** 43 r St-Jacques
☎ 86280446
Closed 16 Dec-14 Jan
rm20(⇨♔13) 🅿
Credit Cards [1] [3]

COULANDON See MOULINS

COURBEVOIE
Hauts-de-Seine

★★★ **Novotel Paris – La Défense** 2 bd de Neuilly, Défense 1 ☎ 47781668 tx 630288
⇨♔280 Lift
Credit Cards [1] [2] [3] [5]

★★★ **Paris Penta** 18 r Baudin
☎ 47885051 tx 610470
⇨♔494 🅿 Lift ℂ
Credit Cards [1] [2] [3] [5]

COURSEULLES-SUR-MER
Calvados

★★ **Crémaillère** 🅻 bd de la Plage
☎ 31374673 tx 171952
⇨♔34 A25rm
Credit Cards [1] [2] [3] [5]

★★ **Paris** pl du 6-Juin ☎ 31374507
Apr-Sep
⇨♔30 P8 Sea
Credit Cards [1] [2] [3] [4] [5]

COURTABOEUF See ORSAY

COURTENAY
Loiret

🛏 **Chenardière** rte de Sens
☎ 38974194 P

COURTISOLS See CHÂLONS-SUR-MARNE

COUTAINVILLE
Manche

★ **Hardy** 🅻 **Pn** pl 28-Juillet ☎ 33470411
⇨♔17
Credit Cards [1] [2] [3] [5]

COUTANCES
Manche

★★★ **Cositel** (FAH) rte de Coutainville
☎ 33075164 tx 772003
⇨♔40 🅿 P100
Credit Cards [2] [3] [5]

★ **Moderne** (Inter) 25 bd Alsace-Lorraine
☎ 33451377
rm17(⇨♔11) 🅿 P25
Credit Cards [1] [3]

CRÈCHE, LA
Deux-Sèvres

★★ **Campanile** rte de Paris ☎ 49255622
tx 791216
⇨♔47 P47
Credit Card [3]

At **CHAVAGNE**(4km SW)
★★★ **Rocs** ☎ 49255038 tx 790632
⇨♔51 P ♘ ⊃
Credit Cards [1] [2] [3] [5]

CRÈCHES-SUR-SAÔNE See MÂCON

France

CREIL
Oise

★★ *Climat* r H-Bessemer ☏ 44244692 tx 692844
⇌♄42 P30
Credit Cards 1 3

◐ **Central** 9 r J-Jaurès ☏ 44554193 P AR

CRESSENSAC
Lot

★ *Chez Gilles* rte Nationale 20
☏ 65377006
rm25(⇌♄13) A19rm 🍴
Credit Cards 1 2 3 5

CRÉTEIL See**PARIS**

CREUSOT, LE
Saône-et-Loire

At **MONTCHANIN**(8km E off D28)

★★★ *Novotel* 30 r du Pont J-Rose
☏ 85785555 tx 800588
⇌♄87 P Lift ≈
Credit Cards 1 2 3 5

At **TORCY**(4km SE)

★★ *Balladins* 2 allée G-Defferre
☏ 60176309 tx 649394
⇌♄39 P40
Credit Cards 1 2 3

★★ *Fimotel* bd de Beaubourg ☏ 42615014 tx 215269
⇌♄42 P Lift
Credit Cards 1 2 3 5

CRIEL-SUR-MER
Seine-Maritime

★★ *Hostellerie de la Vielle Ferme* DPn 23 r de la Mer ☏ 35867218 tx 770303
Closed 3-31 Jan
rm35(⇌♄33) ℘
Credit Cards 1 2 3 5

CROIX-VALMER
Var

★★★ *Souleias* Plage de Gigaro
☏ 94796191 tx 970032
15 Apr-1 Nov
⇌♄47 P75 Lift (℘ ≈ Sea
Credit Cards 1 2 3 5

★★ *Mer* (2.5km SE on N559) ☏ 94796961
Apr-Sep
⇌♄31 P ≈ Beach Mountain

CROS-DE-CAGNES See **CAGNES-SUR-MER**

CROUZILLE, LA
Haute-Vienne

At **NANTIAT**

★★ *Relais St-Europe* ☏ 55399121
⇌♄19 P19 Mountain
Credit Cards 1 3

CUVILLY See **RESSONS-SUR-MATZ**

DAMMARIE-LES-LYS See **MELUN**

DANJOUTIN See **BELFORT**

DARDILLY See **LYON**

DEAUVILLE
Calvados

★★★★★ *Normandy* r J-Mermoz
☏ 31880921 tx 170617
⇌♄300 Lift (▶ Beach Sea
Credit Cards 1 2 3 5

★★★★★ *Royal* ☏ 31881641 tx 170549
Etr-Oct
⇌♄314 P80 Lift (℘ ≈ ▶ Beach Sea
Credit Cards 1 2 3 5

★★★ *Altea Port Deauville* bd Corniche (n.rest) ☏ 31886262 tx 170364
⇌♄72 P60 Lift Sea
Credit Cards 1 2 3 5

★★★ *Golf* ☏ 31881901 tx 170448
10 Apr-Oct
⇌♄175 P Lift ℘ ≈ ▶ Sea
Credit Cards 1 2 3 5

★★ *Ibis* 9 quai de la Marine ☏ 31983890 tx 171295
⇌♄94 🍴 P Lift
Credit Cards 1 3

At **TOUQUES**(2.5km S)

★★★ *Amirauté* (N834) ☏ 31889062 tx 171665
⇌♄20 P200 Lift ℘ ≈
Credit Cards 1 2 3 4 5

DIEPPE
Seine-Maritime See plan

★★★★ *Présidence* 1 bd de Verdun
☏ 35843131 tx 180865
rm89(⇌♄80) 🍴 P52 Lift (Sea
Credit Cards 1 2 3 5

★★★ *Aguado* 30 bd de Verdun (n.rest)
☏ 35842700 Plan **2**
⇌♄56 Lift Sea
Credit Cards 1 3

★★ *Select* 1 r Toustain, pl de la Barre (n.rest) ☏ 35841466 Plan **3**
rm25(⇌♄24) A3rm P6 Lift
Credit Cards 1 2 3

★★ *Windsor* 18 bd de Verdun
☏ 35841523 Plan **4**
25 Jan-20 Dec
rm47(⇌♄42) Lift Sea
Credit Cards 1 2 3 5

DIGNE
Alpes-de-Haute-Provence

★★ *Aiglon* 1 r de Provence
☏ 92310270
Feb-Apr
rm26(⇌♄5) P8 Mountain
Credit Cards 1 2 3 5

DIEPPE

1 ★★★★ Présidence
2 ★★★ Aguado
3 ★★ Select
4 ★★ Windsor

★★ *Mistre* 65 bd Gassendi ☏ 92310016
10 Jan-10 Dec Closed :Rest closed Sat
⇌♄19 🍴
Credit Cards 1 2 3

◐ **J P Pavot** 21 av du Mi-Juin
☏ 92313536 P Peu

◐ **Zerubia** ZI des Arches ☏ 92312551 AR

DIGOIN
Saône-et-Loire

★ *Gare* 79 av du Gl-De-Gaulle ☏ 85530304
Feb-Dec
⇌♄13 A4rm P20
Credit Cards 1 3 5

★ *Terminus* DPn 76 av du Gl-De-Gaulle
☏ 85532528
Feb-15 Jan
rm15(⇌♄12) 🍴 P14
Credit Cards 1 3

DIJON
Côte-d'Or

★★★★ *Altea Palais des Congrès* 22 bd de la Marne ☏ 80723113 tx 350293
⇌♄123 🍴 P100 Lift ≈
Credit Cards 1 2 3 5

★★★★ *Cloche* 14 pl Darcy ☏ 80301232 tx 350498
Closed :Rest closed Sun evening & Mon
⇌♄80 🍴 P60 Lift
Credit Cards 1 2 3 5

★★★ *Chapeau Rouge* (MAP/BW) 5 r Michelet ☏ 80302810 tx 350535
⇌♄33 P Lift
Credit Cards 1 2 3 4 5

★★★ *Urbis Dijon* 3 pl Grangier
☏ 80304400 tx 350606
⇌♄90 🍴 P Lift
Credit Cards 1 3

★★ *Hostellerie du Sauvage* 64 r Monge (n.rest) ☏ 80413121
rm21(⇌♄10) 🍴
Credit Card 3

★★ *Jura* (Inter) 14 av Ml-Foch (n.rest)
☏ 80416112 tx 350485
⇌♄80 🍴 P20 Lift (
Credit Cards 1 2 3 5

★ *Nord* 2 r Liberté ☏ 80305858 tx 351554
9 Jan-23 Dec
rm29(⇌♄25) 🍴 P
Credit Cards 1 2 3 5

◐ **Château d'Eau** 1 bd Fontaine des Suisses ☏ 80654034 P Peu Tal

◐ **J Faisca** 2 r du Champsaux Feves, Fontaine-lès-Dijon ☏ 80572523 P Ope

---

HOTEL DE L'ELEPHANT ★★
Mr and Mrs ROLAND JAMMET
Restaurant with fine gastronomy. ★★★
Rooms with every comfort — Terrace with view.
21, rue de la République
Tél. 29.09.43.36   Open: May-September   88260 DARNEY

Grills on a wood fire for your pleasure

95 GRILL courte·paille

**COURTE-PAILLE 95 relaxed halts
which make
your journey agreeable during
your trip in France**

OPEN DAILY
Without interruption
From 10 A.M.
to 10 P.M.

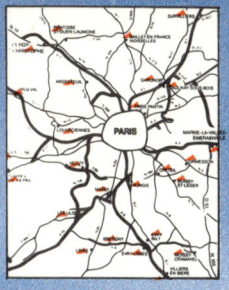

Paris Area

ADDITIONALLY, COURTE-PAILLE
proposes a special children's menu
at **33,50 FF***
for children under 12 years of Age.

COURTE-PAILLE is relaxation :
- a cosy, rustique, warm atmosphere
- a warm and sympathic welcome with a smile

COURTE-PAILLE gives you confidence :
- Grills prepared on a wood fire in front of you, at extremely reasonable prices (From 36,50 FF*)
- Uninterrupted service assured daily from 10 A.M. to 10 P.M.
- Large parking space
- Efficient Service to fit your itinerary.

In each COURTE-PAILLE, on your road, you should ask for a plan of addresses, or write to : SERARE -COURTE-PAILLE - CE 1412 F 91019 EVRY CEDEX FRANCE or Phone PARIS : (1) 60.77.92.20
* Prices on the 1st - 5 - 1988.

Studio Gérard Charroin 60 46 14 32

GRILL courte·paille

In all Courte-Paille Restaurants throughout France our charcoal grills are served 7 days a week from 10 a.m. to 10 p.m.

A salad is served with each meal at no extra charge

STARTERS

Plain andouillette ....
Country ham ....
Fresh white cheese with herbs ....
Two fried eggs ....

GRILLS

Grilled andouillette ....
Chicken leg ....
Loin lamb chop ....
Pork chop ....
Sirloin steak ....
Rib steak for two ....
Rumsteack ....
....

All grills are served with unlimited amount of chips

CHEESE • DESSERT

Yoghourt ....
Fresh white cheese with cream ....
Fresh white cheese with herbs ....
A selection of local cheeses ....
« Petite maison » ice-cream ....
Fresh fruit ....
Home-made apple tart ....
COURTE-PAILLE special ....

(vanilla ice-cream, black-currant sorbet and black-currant liqueur)

CHILDREN'S MENU
under 12's

COURTE-PAILLE salad ....
Hamburger or chicken leg ....
French fried potatoes ....
Apple tart or « Petite maison » ice cream ....

GRILL courte·paille

Water is available free of charge on request. We accept « luncheon Vouchers » and bank cards.

DIEPPE CENTRAL

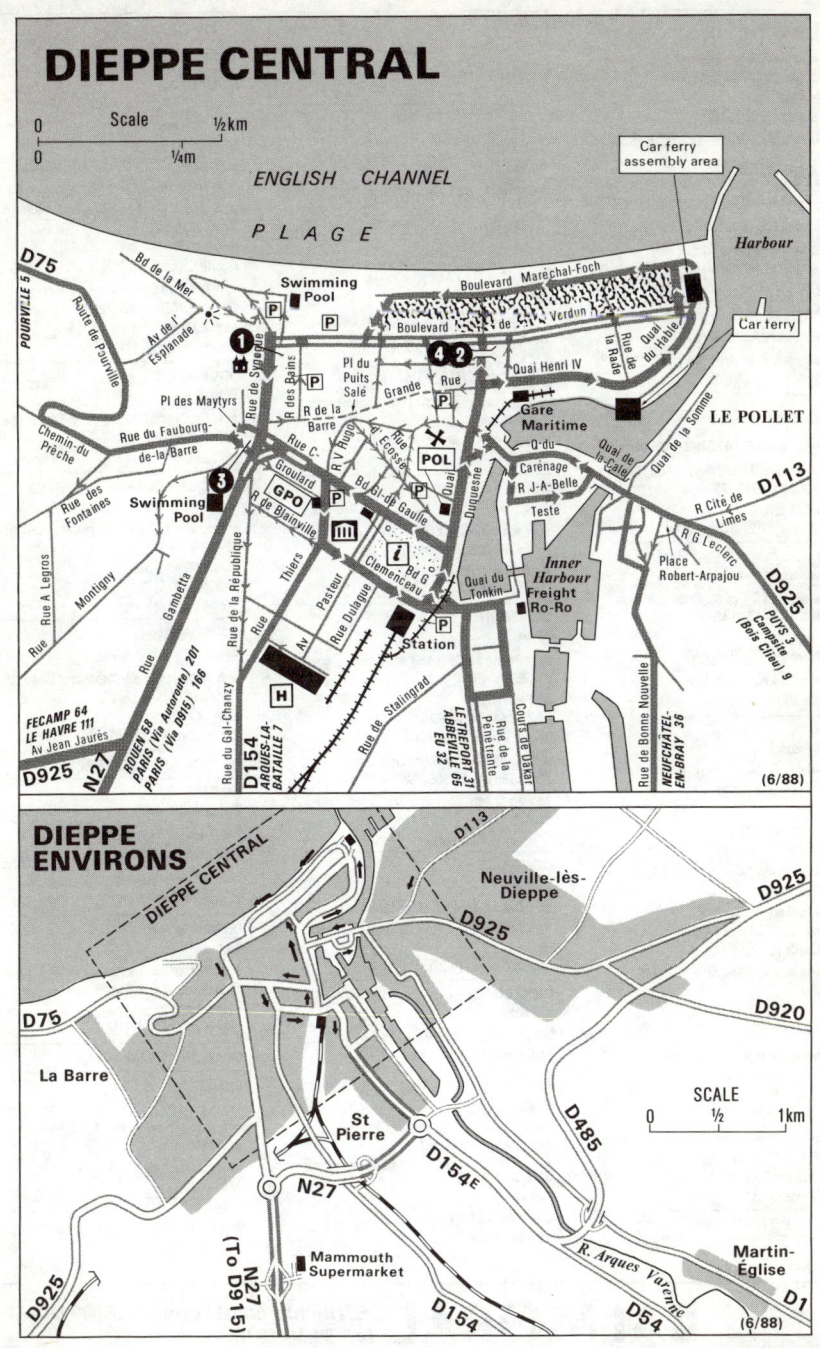

DIEPPE ENVIRONS

Lignier 3 r des G-Champs
☎ 80663905 **P** For

Monchpart 12 r Gagnereaux
☎ 80734111 For

Mont Blanc 2 av du Mont-Blanc
☎ 80664514 **P** Peu

SCA Bourgogne Auto Dijon Nord, r de Cracovie ☎ 80738116 Peu Tal

At **HAUTEVILLE-LÈS-DIJON**(7km NE D107)

★ *Musarde* **L** **DPn** ☎ 80562282
rm11(⇌♠8) P10
Credit Cards [1] [3] [5]

France

At PERRIGNY-LÈS-DIJON(9km S on N74)

★★★ **Novotel Dijon-Sud** rte de Beaune (N74) ☎ 80521422 tx 350728
⇨🛏124 P300 ⇨
Credit Cards [1][2][3][5]

★★ **Ibis** rte de Lyon-Beaune ☎ 80528645 tx 351510
⇨🛏48 Lift
Credit Cards [1][3]

At QUÉTIGNY(5km E CD 107b)

★★ **Climat** 14 av de Bourgogne ☎ 80460446 tx 692844
⇨🛏42 P
Credit Cards [1][3]

At ST-APOLLINAIRE(3km E)

★★ **Campanile** rte de Gray ☎ 80724328 tx 350566
⇨🛏50 P50
Credit Card [3]

At SENNECEY-LE-DIJON(3km SW)

★★★ **Flambée** (MAP/BW) rte de Genève ☎ 80473535 tx 350273
⇨🛏23 P45 Lift
Credit Cards [1][2][3][5]

DINAN
Côtes-du-Nord

★★ **Avaugour** L₺ 1 pl du Champs Clos ☎ 96390749 tx 950145
⇨🛏27 Lift
Credit Cards [1][2][3][4][5]

🚘 **Dinanaise Auto** rte de Ploubalay, Taden ☎ 96396495 **P** For

DINARD
Ille-et-Vilaine

★★★★ **Grand** 46 av George-V ☎ 99461028 tx 740522
23 Apr-6 Oct
⇨🛏100 🅿 P70 Lift Sea
Credit Cards [1][2][3]

★★ **Bains** 38 av George-V ☎ 99461311 tx 740802
15 Mar-15 Oct
rm39(⇨🛏35) P6 Lift ⟨ Sea
Credit Cards [2][3][5]

★★ **Climat** La Millière ☎ 99466955 tx 740300
⇨🛏42 A16rm P35 Sea
Credit Cards [1][3][4]

★★ **Emeraude Plage** 1 bd Albert Ier ☎ 99461579 tx 740802
Etr-Sep
rm59(⇨🛏53) A5rm 🅿 P20 Lift Sea

★★ **Printania** 5 av Georges-V ☎ 99461307
Etr-Sep
⇨🛏77 A30rm Sea
Credit Cards [2][3]

DIZY See ÉPERNAY

DOLANCOURT
Aube

★★ **Moulin du Landion DPn** ☎ 25261217
Jan-Nov
⇨🛏16 P35
Credit Cards [1][3][5]

DOL-DE-BRETAGNE
Ille-et-Vilaine

★★ **Bresche Arthur** L₺ (Inter) **DPn** bd Deminiac ☎ 99480144 tx 741369
⇨🛏24 🅿 P10
Credit Cards [1][2][3][4][5]

★★ **Bretagne** L₺ 17 pl Châteaubriand ☎ 99480203
rm29(⇨🛏14) 🅿 P6
Credit Cards [1][3]

DOLE
Jura

★★★ **Chandioux** (MAP/BW) pl Grévy ☎ 84790066 tx 360498
⇨🛏33 🅿 P23 ⟨
Credit Cards [1][2][3][4][5]

DOMFRONT
Orne

★★ **Poste** L₺ **DPn** 15 r Ml-Foch ☎ 33385100
25 Feb-15 Jan
rm29(⇨🛏14) 🅿 P20
Credit Cards [1][2][3][5]

★ **France** L₺ **Pn** r Mont St-Michel ☎ 33385144 tx 306022
14 Feb-6 Jan
rm22(⇨🛏9) P20 ⚲
Credit Cards [1][3]

DOMPAIRE
Vosges

★★ **Commerce** L₺ pl Ml-Leclerc ☎ 29365028
⇨🛏11
Credit Cards [1][2][3][4][5]

DONZENAC
Corrèze

🚘 **J N Chamournie** La Pause ☎ 55857876 **P** Peu Tal

At **ST-PARDOUX-L'ORTIGLER**(9km N off N20)

🚘 **M Dely** N20, St-Pardoux l'Ortigler ☎ 55845167 **P** Peu Tal

DORDIVES
Loiret

★★ **César** L₺ 8 r de la République ☎ 38927320

rm24(⇨🛏14) 🅿 P24
Credit Cards [1][2][5]

DOUAI
Nord

★★ **Climat** pl du Brossolette ☎ 27882997 tx 692844
⇨🛏42 P
Credit Cards [1][3]

★★ **Grand Cerf** 46 r St-Jacques ☎ 27887960
rm39(⇨🛏30) P ⟨
Credit Cards [1][2][3]

★★ **Urbis** pl St Ame, r de la Fonderie ☎ 27872727 tx 820220
⇨🛏42 P20 Lift
Credit Cards [1][2][3]

DOUARNENEZ
Finistère

★★ **Bretagne** 23 r Duguay-Trouin (n.rest) ☎ 98923044 tx 29100
⇨🛏27 Lift

DOUÉ-LA-FONTAINE
Maine-et-Loire

★ **Dagobert** L₺ **DPn** 14 pl Champ-de-Foire ☎ 41591444
Closed Dec & Jan
rm20(⇨🛏16) P
Credit Card [3]

DOURDAN
Essonne

★★★ **Blanche de Castille** pl des Halles ☎ 64596892 tx 690902
⇨🛏41 P40 Lift
Credit Cards [1][2][3]

DOUSSARD See FAVERGES

DOZULÉ
Calvados

🚘 **R Marci** fbg du Pont Mousse ☎ 31792041 **P** Peu

🚘 **St-Christophe** 102 Grande rue ☎ 31792036 **P** Ren

DRAGUIGNAN
Var

★★ **Col de l'Ange** (Inter) rte de Lorgues ☎ 94682301 tx 970423
⇨🛏30 P50 ⟨ ⇨ Mountain
Credit Cards [1][2][5]

DRAMONT, LE See AGAY

DREUX
Eure-et-Loir

★★ **Auberge Normande** L₺ 12 pl Metezeau ☎ 37500203
Closed :Rest closed Fri
⇨🛏16 P
Credit Cards [1][3]

★★ **Balladins** rte des Anglais ☎ 05355575 tx 649394

BALMORAL 26, rue Maréchal Leclerc – 35800 DINARD
Tel. 99.46.16.97

Open throughout the year. City centre. 100 m from the Casino, the beach and congress centre. Opposite the tennis court. **"Very quiet."** Hospitable environment, welcoming atmosphere, very comfortable. Colour TV + English channels, direct telephone line, "Minitel"-socket, electric porter. Member of the "Inter Hotel" and the "Destination Bretagne" chain.

Inter_hotel

rm38 P38
Credit Cards 1 2 3 4
★★ **Campanile** av W-Churchill
☎ 37426484 tx 783578
⇌♠42 P42
Credit Card 3
★★ **Climat** r de Nuisement ☎ 37467541
tx 692844
⇌♠26 P
Credit Cards 1 3
🛏 **Ouest** 51 av des Fenots ☎ 37461145
AR
🛏 **Perrin Freres** bd de l'Europe,
Vernouillet ☎ 37462331 **P** For

At **MONTREUIL**(8km NE)
★★ **Auberge Gué des Grues** ☎ 37435025
rm3(⇌2) P Lift

DUCEY
Manche
★★ **Ibis** St-Quentin-sur-Le-Homme
☎ 33604242 tx 171784
⇌♠42 P (
Credit Cards 1 3

DUCLAIR
Seine-Maritime
★★ **Poste** L̲ **Pn** 286 q de la Libération
☎ 35375004
Closed :Rest closed Sun evening & Mon
⇌♠24
Credit Cards 1 2 3

DUNKERQUE (DUNKIRK)
Nord
★★★★ **Altea Reuze** r J-Jaurès (n.rest)
☎ 28591111 tx 110587
⇌♠122 P3 Lift Sea
Credit Cards 1 2 3 5
★★★ **Borel** (Inter) 6 r l'Hermitte (n.rest)
☎ 28665180 tx 820050
⇌♠40 Lift
★★★ **Europ** (MAP/BW) 13 r de
Leughenaer ☎ 28662907 tx 120084
Closed :Rest closed Sun evening
⇌♠130 🍴 Lift
Credit Cards 1 2 3 4 5

At **ARMBOUTS-CAPPEL**(6km S)
★★★ **Mercure** Voie-Express, Bordure du
Lac ☎ 28607060 tx 820916
⇌♠64 🍴 P Lift 🏊 Lake
Credit Cards 1 2 3 5
★★ **Campanile** Bordure du Lac, Armbouts
Cappel ☎ 28646470 tx 132294
⇌♠42 P2

ECOUEN
Val-d'Oise
★★ **Campanile** La Redoute du Moulin
(N16) ☎ 39944600 tx 699594
⇌♠50 P50
Credit Card 3

ECULLY See **LYON**
EGUILLES See **AIX-EN-PROVENCE**

ELBEUF
Seine-Maritime
At **CLÉON**(5km N)
★★ **Campanile** r de l'Église ☎ 35813800
tx 172691

France

⇌♠42 P42
Credit Card 3
At **LONDE, LA**(5km NW D913)
🛏 **Maison Brulée** ☎ 35238055 **P** AR

ÉMERAINVILLE See **CHAMPS-SUR-MARNE**

ENGLOS See **LILLE**

ÉNTRAYGUES-SUR-TRUYÈRE
Aveyron
★★ **Truyère** L̲ ☎ 65445110
Apr-15 Nov Closed :Rest closed Mon
⇌♠26 🍴 P20 Lift Lake
Credit Cards 1 3

ÉPERNAY
Marne
★★★ **Berceaux** 13 r Berceaux (n.rest)
☎ 26553022 tx 842068
⇌♠32 🍴 P6 Lift (🔲
Credit Cards 1 2 5
★★★ **Champagne** 30 r Mercier
☎ 26553022 tx 842068
⇌♠32 🍴 P6 Lift (
Credit Cards 1 2 5
★★ **Climat** r de Lorraine ☎ 26541739
tx 842720
⇌♠34 P30 ⚘
Credit Cards 1 3
★★ **Pomme d'Or** 12 r E-Mercier (n.rest)
☎ 26531144 tx 841150
⇌♠26 Lift
Credit Card 1

At **CHAMPILLON**(6km N on N51)
★★★ **Royal Champagne** (Relais et
Châteaux) Bellevue ☎ 26511151 tx 830111
Closed 3wks Jan
⇌♠23 P (
Credit Cards 1 2 3 4 5

At **DIZY**(3km N)
★★ **Campanile** Les Terres Rouges
☎ 26553366 tx 842713
⇌♠42 P42
Credit Card 3

At **MOUSSY**(2.5km S)
★★ **Auberge Champenoise** L̲
☎ 26540318 tx 842743
rm35(⇌30) A8rm 🍴 P40 ⚘
Credit Card 1 3

At **VINAY**(6km S on n51)
★★★ **Briqueterie** rte de Sézanne
☎ 26541122 tx 842007
⇌♠42 P70
Credit Cards 1 2 3 4 5

ÉPINAL
Vosges
★★★ **Mercure** 13 pl Stein ☎ 29351868
tx 960277
⇌♠34 🍴 P10 Lift
Credit Cards 1 2 3 5

★★ **Campanile** r du M-Blanc, Bois-de-la-Voivre ☎ 29313838 tx 961107
⇌♠41 P41
Credit Card 3
★★ **Ibis** quai Ml-de-Contades ☎ 24642828
tx 850053
⇌♠60 🍴 P30 Lift
Credit Cards 1 3
🛏 **Grands Garages Spinaliens** 17 r du Ml-Lyautey ☎ 29824747 For
🛏 **Sessa** r A-Vitu ☎ 29341864 AR Vol

At **CHAVELOT**(8km N)
★★ **Climat** ☎ 29313940
⇌♠26

ÉPINAY-SUR-ORGE
Essonne
★★ **Campanile** r du Grand Vaux
☎ 64486020 tx 600148
⇌♠50 P50

ÉPINAY-SUR-SEINE
Seine-et-Denis
★★ **Ibis** av du 18 Juin 1940 ☎ 48298341
tx 614354
⇌♠64 Lift
Credit Cards 1 3

ÉPINE, L' See **CHÂLONS-SUR-MARNE**

EPONE
Yvelines
★★ **Routel** CD113 ☎ 30956870 tx 801059
⇌♠49 P ⚘

EQUEUDREVILLE
Manche
★★ **Climat** r de la Paix ☎ 33934294
⇌♠42 P40
Credit Cards 1 2 3 5

ERDEVEN
Morbihan
★★ **Auberge du Sous Bois** L̲ (FAH) rte de
Pont Lorois ☎ 97556610 tx 950581
Apr-10 Oct
⇌♠22 P50
Credit Cards 1 2 3 5

ERMENONVILLE
Oise
★★ **Auberge de la Croix d'Or** L̲ 2 r Prince
Radziwill ☎ 44540004
rm11(⇌9) P15
Credit Cards 1 3

ERNÉE
Mayenne
★★★ **Relais de Poste** L̲ 1 pl de l'Église
☎ 43052033 tx 730956
⇌♠35 🍴 P Lift
Credit Cards 1 3

ERQUY
Côtes-du-Nord
★ **Beauregard** L̲ bd de la Mer
☎ 96723003
rm17 A8rm P30 Sea
Credit Cards 1 2 5

ÉTAIN
Meuse
🛏 **Beauguitte** 87 r Poincaré
☎ 29871290 **P** Ren

67

France

ETSAUT
Pyrénées-Atlantiques
★ **Pyrénées** LE DPn ☎ 59348862
Jan-10 Nov
rm22(⇨↑14) A6rm 🍴 P4 Mountain
Credit Card [4]

EUGÉNIE-LES-BAINS
Landes
★★ **Climat** 4 chemin Communal
☎ 58511414
rm350(⇨↑70) P40
Credit Cards [1][3]

EVIAN-LES-BAINS
Haute-Savoie
★★★★★ **Royal** ☎ 50751400 tx 385759
15 Feb-15 Dec
⇨↑158 🍴 P102 Lift (♀ ⇌ Mountain Lake
Credit Cards [1][2][3][5]

★★★ **Bellevue** 6 r B-Moutardier
☎ 50750113
May-Sep
⇨↑50 P10 Lift (Lake
Credit Cards [1][3]

★★ **Mateirons** (Inter) ☎ 50750416
15 Mar-15 Oct
rm22(⇨↑18) P Mountain Lake
Credit Card [2]

ÉVREUX
Eure
★★ **Campanile** av W-Churchill
☎ 32337565 tx 771348
⇨↑42 P42
Credit Card [3]

★★ **Climat** Zone Tertiaire de la Madel
☎ 32311047 tx 770516
⇨↑42 P40
Credit Cards [1][3]

★★ **France** LE 29 r St-Thomas
☎ 32391337
⇨↑15 P8
Credit Cards [2][3]

★★ **Grenoble** 17 r St-Pierre (n.rest)
☎ 32330731
Closed Etr & Xmas
rm19(⇨↑16) ⇌
Credit Cards [1][3]

★★ **Ibis** av W-Churchill ☎ 32381636
tx 172748
⇨↑60 P60
Credit Cards [1][3]

★★ **Normandy** 37 r E-Féray ☎ 32331440
rm96(⇨↑26) 🍴 P20
Credit Cards [1][2][3][5]

★★ **Orme** LE (FAH) 13 r Lombards (n.rest)
☎ 32393412
rm43(⇨↑37) Lift
Credit Cards [1][2]

🏨 **Hôtel-de-Ville** 4 r G-Bernard
☎ 32395863 For

ÉVRY
Essonne See also CORBEIL-ESSONNES
★★ **Arcade** 16 cours Blaise-Pascal, Butte
Creuse ☎ 60782990 tx 601249
⇨↑100 🍴 Lift
Credit Cards [1][3]

★★ **Balladins** pl G-Crémieux, Quartier des
Epinettes ☎ 64972121 tx 649394
⇨↑28 P

★★ **Ibis** 1 av du Lac, Parc Yertiare du Bois
Briard ☎ 60777475 tx 691728
⇨↑135 Lift
Credit Cards [1][3]

★★ **Novotel Paris Évry** (A6) ☎ 60778270
tx 600685
⇨↑175 P100 Lift ⇌
Credit Cards [1][2][3][5]

EYBENS
Isère
★★ **Fimotel** 20 av J-Jaurès ☎ 76242312
tx 980371
⇨↑42 P35 Lift

ÉYZIES-DE-TAYAC, LES
Dordogne
★★★ **Cro-Magnon** (MAP/BW) DPn
☎ 53069706
28 Apr-10 Oct
⇨↑24 A8rm P30
Credit Cards [1][2][3][4][5]

★★ **Centenaire** LE (Relais et Châteaux) Pn
☎ 53069718 tx 541921
Apr-Nov Closed :Rest closed Tue midday
⇨↑26 A5rm 🍴 P30 Lift (⇌
Credit Cards [1][3]

★★ **Centre** LE Les Sireuils ☎ 53069713
Mar-Nov
⇨↑18
Credit Cards [1][3]

★★ **Glycines** Pn ☎ 53069707
mid Apr-3 Nov
⇨↑25 🍴 P3 ⇌ Sea Mountain
Credit Cards [1][2][3]

★ **France- Auberge de Musée** LE
☎ 53069723
26 Mar-10 Nov
rm29(⇨↑22) A13rm P29 Mountain Lake
Credit Cards [1][3]

🏨 **J C Dupuy** pl de la Port ☎ 53069732
Ren

ÉZE-BORD-DE-MER
Alpes-Maritimes
★★★★ **Cap Estel** Pn ☎ 93015044
tx 470305
Mar-Oct
⇨↑43 A6rm P50 Lift (🏖 ⇌ Beach Sea
Credit Cards [1][3]

★★ **Cap Roux** Basse Corniche (n.rest)
☎ 93015123
15 Mar-Sep
⇨↑30 P25 Lift Sea

FALAISE
Calvados
★★ **Normandie** 4 r Amiral Courbet
☎ 31901826
rm26(⇨↑16) 🍴
Credit Cards [1][3]

★★ **Poste** LE Pn 38 r G-Clemenceau
☎ 31901314

rm19(⇨↑13) 🍴 P8
Credit Cards [1][2][3]

FAOUËT, LE
Morbihan
★ **Croix d'Or** 9 pl Bellanger ☎ 97230733
15 Jan-15 Dec Closed :Rest closed Sat
rm16(⇨↑4) 🍴 P
Credit Cards [1][3]

FARLÈDE, LA *See* TOULON

FAVERGES
Haute-Savoie
★ **Parc** rte d'Albertville ☎ 50445025
⇨↑12 Mountain
Credit Card [1]

At **DOUSSARD**(7km NW)
★★ **Marceau** Marceau Dessus
☎ 50443011 tx 309346
Feb-Oct
⇨↑16 🍴 P30 ♀ Mountain Lake
Credit Cards [1][2][3][5]

FAVERGES-DE-LA-TOUR *See* TOUR-DU-PIN, LA

FAYENCE
Var
★★★ **Moulin de la Camandoule** DPn
chemin N D des Cypres ☎ 98760084
Mar-Jan
⇨↑11 P40 ⇌
Credit Cards [1][3][5]

🏨 **G Difant** Quartier Prés-Gaudin
☎ 94760740 P

At **TOURRETTES**(1km W)
★ **Grillon** N562 ☎ 94760296
⇨↑28 P30 (Mountain
Credit Cards [1][3]

FÈRE, LA
Aisne
★ **Tourelles** 51 r de la République (6km
from A26) (n.rest) ☎ 23563166
rm16(⇨↑8) 🍴 P12
Credit Cards [1][2][3]

FÈRE-EN-TARDENOIS
Aisne
★★★★ **Château** (Relais et Châteaux) DPn
☎ 23822113 tx 145526
Mar-Feb
⇨↑23 🍴 P ♀ ⛳
Credit Cards [1][2][3]

FERTÉ-BERNARD, LA
Sarthe
★★ **Climat** 43 bd Gl-de-Gaulle
☎ 43938470 tx 720435
⇨↑30 P30
Credit Cards [1][3]

FERTÉ-ST-AUBIN, LA
Loiret
★★ **Perron** (FAH) Pn 9 r du Gl-Leclerc
☎ 38765356 tx 782485
Closed 15-30 Jan
rm20(⇨↑17) P40
Credit Cards [1][2][3][5]

FERTÉ-SOUS-JOUARRE, LA
Seine-et-Marne
🏨 **Parc** 10 av de Montmiral
☎ 60229000 P Cit

68

France

FIGEAC
Lot
★★ ***Carmes*** L⸋ (FAH) enclos des Carmes
☎ 65342070 tx 520794
15 Jan-15 Dec
⇨📞32 P35 Lift ⸋
Credit Cards [1] [2] [3] [5]

FIRMINY
Loire
★★ ***Firm*** 37 r J-Jaurès ☎ 77560899
Closed Rest Sun pm
⇨📞20 (
Credit Cards [1] [2] [3] [4] [5]
★★ ***Table du Pavillon*** 4 av de la Gare
☎ 77560045
⇨📞22 🍴 P20 Lift
Credit Cards [1] [2] [3] [5]

FIXIN
Côte-D'or
★★ ***Chez Jeannette*** L⸋ Pn ☎ 80524589
25 Jan-23 Dec Closed : Rest closed Thu
rm11(📞9)
Credit Cards [1] [2] [3] [4] [5]

FLEURAC See **JARNAC**

FLEURANCE
Gers
★★ ***Fleurance*** rte d'Agen ☎ 62061485
20 Jan-10 Dec
⇨📞24 P60
Credit Cards [1] [2] [3] [5]

FLEURY-LES-AUBRAIS
Loiret
🛏 ***Société D.A.C.*** 50 r de la Halte, Saran
☎ 38734141 **P**

FLORAC
Lozère
★★ ***Parc*** 47 av J-Monestier ☎ 66450285
15 Mar-1 Dec
rm58(⇨📞41) A26rm 🍴 P45 Mountain
Credit Cards [2] [3] [4] [5]
★ ***Gorges du Tarn*** 48 r du Pêcher (n.rest)
☎ 66450063
May-Sep
rm31(⇨📞17) A12rm 🍴 P25 Mountain

FLORENSAC
Hérault
★★ ***Leonce*** L⸋ 2 pl de la République
☎ 67770305
Mar-20 Sep
rm14(⇨📞10) Lift
Credit Cards [1] [2] [3] [5]

FLOTTE, LA See **RÉ, ILE DE**

FOIX
Ariège
★★★ ***Barbacane*** 1 av de Lerida
☎ 61655044
Mar-Nov

⇨📞22 🍴 P18 Mountain
Credit Card [3]
★★★ ***Tourisme*** 2 cours I-Cros
☎ 616549121 tx 530955
⇨📞28 (
Credit Cards [1] [2] [3]

FONTAINEBLEAU
Seine-et-Marne
★★★ ***Aigle Noir*** (MAP/BW) 27 pl N-Bonaparte ☎ 64223265 tx 600080
⇨📞30 A4rm P Lift (
Credit Cards [1] [2] [3] [5]
★★ ***Ile de France*** L⸋ (Inter) 128 r de France
☎ 64228515 tx 690358
⇨📞25 P25 (
Credit Cards [1] [2] [3] [4] [5]
★★ ***Londres DPn*** 1 pl du Gl-de-Gaulle
☎ 64222021
Jan-20 Dec
rm22(⇨📞7) 🍴 P20
Credit Cards [1] [2]
★★ ***Toulouse*** 183 r Grande (n.rest)
☎ 64222273
20 Jan-20 Dec
rm18(⇨📞15) 🍴 (
Credit Cards [1] [3]
★ ***Forêt*** 79 av Prés-Roosevelt ☎ 64223926
rm26(⇨19) A9rm 🍴 P18 Lift (
Credit Cards [2] [3]
★ ***Neuville*** 196 r Grande ☎ 64222339
Closed Feb
⇨📞20 A4rm 🍴 P6
🛏 ***François 1er*** 9 r de la Chancellerie
☎ 64222034 For
🛏 ***St-Antoine*** 11 r de France
☎ 64223188 AR
At **AVON**(2km S)
★★ ***Fimotel*** 46 av F-Roosevelt
☎ 64223021 tx 693072
⇨📞42 P Lift
Credit Cards [1] [2] [3] [5]
At **URY**(6km SW on N51)
★★★ ***Novotel*** ☎ 64244825 tx 694153
⇨📞127 P150 ♿ ⸋
Credit Cards [1] [2] [3] [5]

FONTAINE-CHAALIS
Oise
★ ***Auberge de Fontaine DPn*** Grande Rue
☎ 44542022
3 Mar-30 Jan Closed Monday for dinner & Thursday

⇨📞8 P8
Credit Card [1]

FONTENAY-LE-COMTE
Vendée
★★ ***Rabelais*** L⸋ (Inter) rte Parthenay
☎ 51698620
⇨📞43 🍴 P50 ⸋
Credit Cards [1] [3] [5]
🛏 **M Breton** 61 rte de Nantes **P** For

FONTENAY-SOUS-BOIS
Val-de-Marne
★★ ***Climat*** r Rabelais ☎ 48762198
tx 629844
⇨📞42 P30
★★ ***Fimotel*** pl du Gl-de-Gaulle, av du Val-de-Fontenay ☎ 48766771 tx 232748
⇨📞100 Lift
Credit Cards [1] [2] [3] [5]

FONTEVRAUD-L'ABBAYE
Maine-et-Loire
★★ ***Croix Blanche*** L⸋ 7 pl Plantagenets
☎ 41517111
Closed 12-30 Nov
⇨📞22 P22

FONT-ROMEU
Pyrénées-Orientales
★★★ ***Bellevue*** av du Dr-Capelle
☎ 68300016
Closed Rest 15 Sep-15 Dec
rm65(⇨30) P (Mountain
★★★ ***Carlit*** ☎ 68300745 tx 375974
20 Dec-20 Apr & Jun-Oct
⇨📞58 Lift ⸋ Mountain
Credit Cards [1] [3]
★★ ***Pyrénées*** pl des Pyrénées
☎ 68300149
20 Dec-15 Apr & Jun-5 Nov
⇨📞40 Lift Mountain
Credit Cards [1] [2] [3]

FONVIALANE See **ALBI**

FORBACH
Moselle
★★ ***Fimotel*** r F-Barth ☎ 87870606
tx 861312
⇨📞42 P200 Lift ♿ ⸋ Mountain

FORÊT-FOUESNANT, LA
Finistère
★★ ***Baie*** L⸋ ☎ 98569735
rm20(⇨📞12) P Sea
Credit Cards [1] [2] [3]
★★★ ***Esperance*** pl Église ☎ 98569658
Apr-Sep
rm30(⇨📞24) A18rm P10 Sea
Credit Cards [1] [3]
★ ***Beauséjour*** 47 r de la Baie ☎ 98569718
25 Mar-15 Oct →

HOTEL DE LA **TERRASSE** *Logis de France*
Seaview
RESTAURANT — HOTEL ★★
Avenue de la Plage — 80790 MAHON-PLAGE. Tel.: 22.23.37.77
Close to the ornithological reserve of Marquenterre, a birds' paradise and the water games of Aqualand. Lift.

69

rm30(♪12) 🍴 P20 Sea
Credit Cards ① ③ ④

FOS-SUR-MER
Bouches-du-Rhône
★★★★ ***Camargue*** La Bastidonne, rte d'Istres ☎ 42050057 tx 410812
⇨♪130 ⊇
Credit Cards ① ② ③ ④ ⑤

FOUESNANT
Finistère
★★ **Pointe de Mousterlin** Pointe de Mousterlin ☎ 98560412
1 May-15 Oct
rm67(⇨♪55) A20rm P60 Lift ♫ Sea
Credit Cards ① ③

★ **Armorique** 🆒 ☎ 98560019
Mar-Oct
rm25(⇨♪14) A12rm P15
Credit Cards ① ③

🍴 **J L Bourhis** rte de Quimper ☎ 98560265 **P** Ren

🍴 **Merrien** rte de Quimper ☎ 98560017 **P** Peu Tal

FOUGÈRES
Ille-et-Vilaine
★★ **Mainotel** (N12) ☎ 99998155 tx 730856
⇨♪50 P ♫
Credit Cards ① ③

★★ **Voyageurs** 10 pl Gambetta ☎ 99990820 tx 730666
5 Jan-20 Dec Closed :Rest closed Sat
⇨♪37 A10rm 🍴 P6 Lift
Credit Cards ① ② ③ ④ ⑤

★ **Moderne** 🆒 15 r Tribunal ☎ 99990024
rm25(⇨♪21) 🍴 P18
Credit Cards ① ② ③ ④ ⑤

FOULAIN
Haute-Marne
★ **Chalet** 🆒 ☎ 25311111
Oct-15 Sep Closed :Rest closed Mon
rm12(⇨♪5) P7 ♫
Credit Cards ② ③ ⑤

FOURAS
Charente-Maritime
★★ **Grand Hotel des Bains DPn** 15 r Gl-Bruncher ☎ 46840344
12 May-25 Sep
rm36(⇨♪35) 🍴

FOURMETOT See **PONT-AUDEMER**

FOURMIES
Nord
★★ **Ibis** Étangs des Moines (n.rest) ☎ 27602154 tx 810172
⇨♪30
Credit Cards ① ③

FOURNEAUX See **AUBUSSON**

FRAYSSINET
Lot
★ **Bonne Auberge DPn** ☎ 65310002
Apr-Oct
⇨♪10 🍴 P15
Credit Cards ① ③

★ **Escale** 🆒 ☎ 65310001
15 Feb-Dec

France

⇨♪8 P20
Credit Cards ① ③
🍴 **Drianne** N 20 ☎ 65310017 **P** All makes

At **PONT-DE-RHODES**(1km N on N20)
★ **Relais** ☎ 65310016
Etr-15 Nov
⇨♪28 🍴 P50 ♫ ⊇

FRÉJUS
Var
★★★ ***St-Aygulf*** 214 rte Nationale 98 ☎ 65310016
15 Mar-15 Nov
⇨♪83 P Lift Sea Mountain
Credit Card ③

🍴 **Satac** N 7 ☎ 94514061 Ren

🍴 **Vagneur** 449 bd de la Mer ☎ 94513839 For

At **COLOMBIER**(3km W)
★★★ **Residences du Colombier** rte de Bagnols ☎ 94514592 tx 470328
Apr-Oct
⇨♪60 P120 (♫ ⊇ Mountain
Credit Cards ① ② ③ ④ ⑤

FRÉVENT
Pas-de-Calais
★ **Amiens** 🆒 7 r Doullens ☎ 21036543
rm10(⇨♪7) 🍴 P Lift ♫ 📺
Credit Cards ① ② ③

At **MONCHEL-SUR-CANCHE**(7.5km NW D340)
★★ **Vert Bocage** (n.rest) ☎ 21479675
⇨♪10 P60 Mountain Lake
Credit Card ①

FRONTIGNAN
Hérault
★★ **Balajan DPn** N112 ☎ 67481399
Closed Feb
rm21(⇨♪19) 🍴 P30 Mountain
Credit Cards ① ③

FUMAY
Ardennes
★★ ***Roches*** 393 av J-Jaurès ☎ 24411012
Apr-Nov
⇨♪31 P30 Mountain
Credit Cards ① ③ ⑤

GACÉ
Orne
★★★ ***Champs*** rte d'Alençon-Rouen ☎ 33355145
15 Feb-15 Nov
rm13(⇨♪11) P30 ♫ ⊇
Credit Cards ① ③ ④ ⑤

★★ **Morphée** 2 r de Lisieux (n.rest) ☎ 33355101
⇨♪10 P10
Credit Cards ① ② ③ ⑤

★ **Etoile d'Or** 60 Grande r ☎ 33355003
Mar-Jan Closed :Rest closed Sun evening & Mon

rm11(⇨♪4) 🍴 P8
Credit Cards ① ③

GAILLARD
Haute-Savoie See also **ANNEMASSE**
★★★ **Mercure** r des Jardins (exit Annemasse-B41) ☎ 50920525 tx 385835
⇨♪78 🍴 P100 Lift ⊇ Mountain
Credit Cards ① ② ③ ⑤

★★ **Climat** r R-Cassin, ZAC de la Châtelaine ☎ 50371922 tx 309931
⇨♪43 P50 Mountain
Credit Cards ① ② ③

GAILLON
Eure
🍴 **Poupardin** Côte-des-Sables ☎ 32530337 **P** All makes

GAP
Hautes-Alpes
★★ **Fons Régina** 🆒 Quartier de Fontreyme (N85) ☎ 92539899
rm20(⇨♪16) 🍴 P30 Mountain
Credit Cards ① ② ③ ⑤

★★ **Grille** 2 pl F-Euzière ☎ 92538484
5 Jan-5 Dec Closed :Rest closed Sun & Mon
⇨♪30 🍴 P4 Lift
Credit Cards ① ② ③ ⑤

★★ **Mokotel** Quartier Graffinel, rte de Marseille (n.rest) ☎ 92515782
⇨♪27 P27 Mountain
Credit Cards ① ② ③ ⑤

🍴 **Europ'auto** rte de Briançon ☎ 92520546 **P** For

🍴 **Verdun** 4 r P-Bert ☎ 92512618 **P** AR LR

At **PONT-SARRAZIN**(4km NE on N94)
🍴 **Berta** ☎ 92536730 **P** VW

GARDE, LA See **TOULON**

GARDE-ST-CAST, LA See **ST-CAST-LE-GUILDO**

GEISPOLSHEIM See **STRASBOURG**

GÉMENOS
Bouches-du-Rhône
★★★★ ***Relais de la Magdeleine*** rte d'Aix-en-Provence ☎ 42822005
Mar-Oct
⇨♪20 P40 ⊇ Mountain
Credit Cards ① ③

GENNES
Maine-et-Loire
★★ **Loire** 🆒 Pn ☎ 41518103
10 Feb-28 Dec Closed :Rest closed Mon evening & Tue
rm11(⇨♪7) 🍴 P12

★★ **Naulets d'Anjou** r Croix-de-Mission ☎ 41518188
Apr-2 Nov Closed :Rest closed Mon in high season
⇨♪20 🍴 P40 ♫
Credit Cards ① ③

GENNEVILLIERS
Hauts-de-Seine
★★ **Fimotel** Ilot des Chevrins ☎ 42615014 tx 215269

70

⇨♠60 P Lift
Credit Cards [1][2][3][5]

GENTILLY See **PARIS**

GÉRARDMER
Vosges
★★★★ **Grand Bragard** pl du Tilleul
☎ 29630631 tx 960964
⇨♠61 ♠ P60 Lift (⇨ Mountain
Credit Cards [1][2][3][5]
★★ **Parc** ℒ 12-14 av de la Ville-de-Vichy
☎ 29633243 tx 961408
Etr-Oct & Feb
⇨♠36 A14rm ♠ P30 Mountain Lake
Credit Cards [1][3]
★ **Echo de Ramberchamp** (n.rest)
☎ 29630227
20 Dec-15 Nov
rm16(⇨♠11) P30 Mountain Lake
At **SAUT-DES-CUVES**(3km NE N417)
★★★ **Saut-des-Cuves** ☎ 29633046
⇨♠27 ♠ Lift Mountain

GETS, LES
Haute-Savoie
★★★ **Marmotte** ℒ Pn ☎ 50797539
Seasonal
⇨♠45 Lift ℓ ⇨ Mountain
Credit Cards [1][2][3][5]

GEX
Ain
★ **Bellevue** av de la Gare ☎ 50415540
Feb-15 Dec
⇨♠22 ♠ P4 Mountain Lake

GIEN
Loiret
★★ **Rivage** ℒ DPn 1 quai de Nice
☎ 38672053
Closed :Rest closed 5 Feb-1 Mar
⇨♠22 P15
Credit Cards [1][2][3][5]

GIVORS
Rhône
★★ **Balladins** Centre Commercial de la
Vallée-du-Gier ☎ 72241556 tx 649394
⇨♠28 ♠ P28
Credit Cards [1][2][3]

GLACERIE, LA See **CHERBOURG**

GLÉNIC
Creuse
★★ **Moulin Noyé** Pn ☎ 55520911
tx 580064
Closed 15 Jan-15 Feb
rm32(⇨♠14) ♠ P8 Beach
Credit Cards [2][3][5]

GLUGES See **MARTEL**

GOLF LINKS See **TOUQUET-PARIS-PLAGE, LE**

GONESSE
Val-D'oise
★★ **Campanile** ZA Economiques de la
Grande, Couture ☎ 39857999 tx 609021
⇨♠50 P50
Credit Card [3]
★★ **Climat** La Croix-St-Benoît, r d'Aulnay
(off N370) ☎ 39874144

France

⇨♠66 P
Credit Card [1]
★★ **Ibis** Patte d'Oie-de-Gonesse (N 2)
(n.rest) ☎ 39872222 tx 609078
⇨♠41 Lift
Credit Cards [1][3]

GONFREVILLE-L'ORCHER See **HAVRE, LE**

GOUESNIÈRE, LA See **ST-MALO**

GOUESNOU See **BREST**

GOUMOIS
Doubs
★★ **Taillard** ℒ ☎ 81442075
Mar-Nov Closed :Rest closed Wed Mar & Oct
rm17(⇨♠16) P30 Mountain
Credit Cards [1][2][3][5]

GOUVIEUX See **CHANTILLY**

GRADIGNAN See **BORDEAUX**

GRAMAT
Lot
★★ **Centre** pl République ☎ 65387337
⇨♠14 ♠
Credit Cards [1][3]
★ **Lion d'Or** ℒ DPn pl République
☎ 65387318
15 Jan-15 Dec
⇨♠15 ♠ P12 Lift
Credit Cards [1][3]
At **RIGNAC**(4.5km NW)
★★★ **Château de Roumégouse** (Relais et Châteaux) ☎ 65336381 tx 532592
Apr-2 Nov Closed :Rest closed Tue
⇨♠14 P50
Credit Cards [1][3][5]

GRANDE-MOTTE, LA
Hérault
★★★★ **Altea Grande-Motte** r du Port
☎ 6756981 tx 480241
15 Mar-Nov
⇨♠135 P100 Lift ⇨ Sea
Credit Cards [1][2][3][4][5]

GRANVILLE
Manche
★★ **Bains** 19 r G-Clemenceau
☎ 33501731 tx 170600
⇨♠56 Lift (Sea
Credit Cards [1][2][3][5]
★★ **Poulain** av des Vendéens
☎ 33906499 P Ren

GRASSE
Alpes-Maritimes See also
CHÂTEAUNEUF-DE-GRASSE
★★ **Aromes** ℒ (N85) ☎ 93704201
Feb-Nov Closed :Rest closed Sat
⇨♠7 P32 Mountain
Credit Cards [1][3]
★★ **Ibis** r Martine Carol, rte de Cannes
(N85), Quartier St Claude ☎ 93707070
tx 462682

⇨♠65 P70 Lift ℓ ⇨ Mountain
Credit Cards [1][2][3]
Grasse Automobiles St-Christopher 6
bd E-Zola ☎ 93363650 Peu Tal
Montreal av des Marronniers
☎ 93700093 P Alf

GRAVESON
Bouches-du-Rhône
★★ **Mas des Amandiers** ℒ rte d'Avignon
(n.rest) ☎ 90958176
Mar-1 Nov
⇨♠21 ♠ P30 (ℓ ⇨ Mountain
Credit Cards [1][2][3][5]

GRAY
Haute-Saône
★★★ **Château de Rigny** DPn ☎ 84652501
tx 362926
⇨♠24 ♠ P80 ℓ ⇨
Credit Cards [1][2][3][5]
★★ **Bellevue** ℒ 1 av Carnot ☎ 84654776
Jan-Nov
rm15(⇨♠9) ♠ P8
Credit Cards [1][2][3][5]
★★ **Fer-a-Cheval** ℒ 4 av Carnot (n.rest)
☎ 84653255
4 Jan-24 Dec
rm46(⇨♠45) ♠ P35 Sea
Credit Cards [1][2][3][5]

GRENOBLE
Isère
★★★★ **Mercure** 1 av d'Innsbruck
☎ 76095427 tx 980470
⇨♠100 A60rm ♠ P140 Lift ⇨ Mountain
Credit Cards [1][2][3][5]
★★★★ **Park** 10 pl P-Mistral ☎ 76872911
tx 320767
2 Jan-Jul & 21 Aug-24 Dec Closed :Rest closed Sun midday
⇨♠59 ♠ Lift (Mountain
Credit Cards [1][2][3][5]
★★★ **Angleterre** 5 pl V-Hugo (n.rest)
☎ 76873721 tx 320297
⇨♠70 Lift Mountain
Credit Cards [1][2][3][5]
★★★ **Grand** (Inter) 5 r de la République
☎ 76444936 tx 980918
⇨♠72 Lift Mountain
Credit Cards [1][2][3][5]
★★★ **Terminus** 10 pl de la Gare (n.rest)
☎ 76872433 tx 320245
Closed Aug
⇨♠50 Lift
★★ **Alpazur** 59 av Alsace-Lorraine (n.rest)
☎ 76464280 tx 320868
⇨♠30 P
Credit Cards [1][2][3]
★★ **Dauphiné** 15 r du Dr-Schweitzer
☎ 76217612 tx 305551
⇨♠45 P50 ℓ Mountain
Credit Cards [1][3]
★★ **Fimotel** 20 av J-Jaurès, , Eybens
☎ 76242312 tx 980371
⇨♠42 P38 Lift Mountain
Credit Cards [1][2][3]
★★ **Gallia** 7 bd Ml-Joffre (n.rest)
☎ 76873921
Closed Clo Aug →

⇨🛏23 🍴 Lift
Credit Cards ①②③⑤

★★ **Ibis** Centre Commerciale.des Trois, Dauphins, r F-Poulat ☏ 76474849 tx 320890
⇨🛏71 Lift
Credit Cards ①③

★★ **Paris-Nice** 61 bd J-Vallier (n.rest) ☏ 76963618
rm29(⇨24) 🍴 P29 ₵
Credit Cards ①②③⑤

At **CLAIX**(10.5km S)

★★★ **Oiseaux** ☏ 76980774
Closed 15 Nov-15 Dec
⇨🛏20 🍴 P20 ⇨ Mountain
Credit Cards ①③

At **MEYLAN**(3km NE on N90)

★★ **Climat** chemin du Vieux-Chêne, Zirst de Meylan ☏ 76907690 tx 305551
⇨🛏38 P50 Mountain
Credit Cards ①③

At **PONT-DE-CLAIX**(8km S on N75)

★★ **Villancourt** cours St-André (n.rest) ☏ 76981854
⇨🛏33 🍴 P60 Lift ₵ Mountain
Credit Cards ①③

At **ST-ÉGRÈVE**(10km NW)

★★ **Campanile** av de l'Ille Brune ☏ 76755788 tx 980424
⇨🛏42 P42

At **VOREPPE**(12km NW)

★★★ **Novotel** Autoroute de Lyon ☏ 76508144 tx 320273
⇨🛏114 P150 Lift ⇨ Mountain
Credit Cards ①②③⑤

🍴 Echaillon 400 av de Juin 1940 ☏ 76502385 **P** Ren

GRÉOUX-LES-BAINS
Alpes-de-Haute-Provence

★★★ **Villa Borghèse** (MAP/BW) av des Thermes ☏ 92780091 tx 401513
Mar-Nov Closed :Rest closed 1Dec-1Mar
⇨🛏70 🍴 P30 Lift ₵ ♪ ✔ Mountain
Credit Cards ①②③⑤

GRIMAUD
Var

At **PORT-GRIMAUD**(5.5km E)

★★★ **Port** pl du Marché ☏ 94563618
⇨🛏20 P20 Lift Beach Sea
Credit Cards ①③⑤

GRISOLLES
Tarn-et-Garonne

★★ **Relais des Garrigues** ☏ 63303159
Closed 4 Jan-10 Feb
rm27(⇨20) 🍴 P40 ₵
Credit Card ②

GUÉRANDE
Loire-Atlantique

🍴 Cottais rte de la Turballe ☏ 40249039 **P** Peu Tal

GUÉRET
Creuse

★★ **Auclair** 19 av Senatorerie (n.rest) ☏ 55520826

France

15Feb-15Jan Closed :Rest closed Sun pm & Mon midday
rm33(⇨14) A5rm 🍴 P20
Credit Cards ①②③⑤

GUÉTHARY
Pyrénées-Atlantiques

★★ **Mariéna** av Mon-Mugabure (n.rest) ☏ 59265104
Jun-1 Oct
rm14(⇨5) P6 Sea

GUILLIERS
Morbihan

★★ **Relais du Porhoët** pl de l'Église ☏ 97744017
⇨🛏15 P15 ♪
Credit Cards ①②③⑤

GUILVINEC
Finistère

At **LECHIAGAT**(1km E)

★★ **Port** (FAH) ☏ 98581010 tx 941200
6 Jan-20 Dec
⇨🛏40 Sea
Credit Cards ①②③⑤

HAGUENAU
Bas-Rhin

★★ **Climat** rte de Bitche, chemin de Sandlach ☏ 33614219
rm7(⇨3) P
Credit Cards ①③⑤

HAMBYE
Manche

★ **Auberge de l'Abbaye** ☏ 33614219
rm7(⇨5) P8
Credit Cards ①③

HAUCONCOURT See **METZ**

HAUTE-GOULAINE
Loire-Atlantique

★★★ **Lande St-Martin** rte de Poitiers ☏ 40062006 tx 700520
rm40(⇨33) 🍴 P150 ₵ ✔
Credit Cards ①③

HAUTEVILLE-LÈS-DIJON See **DIJON**

HAVRE, LE
Seine-Maritime **See Plan**

★★★ **Bordeaux** (Inter) 147 r L-Brindeau (n.rest) ☏ 35226944 tx 190428 Plan **1**
⇨🛏31 Lift ₵ Lake
Credit Cards ①②③⑤

★★★ **Marly** (Inter) 121 r de Paris (n.rest) ☏ 35417248 tx 190369 Plan **2**
⇨🛏37 Lift ₵
Credit Cards ①②③⑤

★★★ **Mercure** chaussée d'Angoulême ☏ 35212345 tx 190749 Plan **3**
⇨🛏96 P Lift
Credit Cards ①②③④⑤

★★ **Foch** 4 r Caligny (n.rest) ☏ 35425960 tx 190359 Plan **6**
rm31(⇨21) P Lift

HAVRE, LE

1	★★★	Bordeaux
2	★★★	Marly
3	★★★	Mercure
4	★★	Campanile (At Gonfreville l'Orcher)
5	★★	Climat (At Montivilliers)
6	★★	Foch
7	★★	Ile de France
8	★★	Monaco
9	★★	Grand Parisien
10	★★	Petit Vatel
11	★★	Richelieu
12	★	Voltaire

★★ **Grand Parisien** (Inter) 1 cours de la République (n.rest) ☏ 35252383 tx 190369 Plan **9**
⇨🛏22 P22 Lift ₵ Sea
Credit Cards ①②③⑤

★★ **Ile de France** 104 r A-France (n.rest) ☏ 35424929 Plan **7**
rm16(⇨10)
Credit Cards ①③

★★ **Monaco** 16 r de Paris ☏ 35422101 Plan **8**
Mar-15 Feb
rm10(⇨7) P5 Sea

★★ **Petit Vatel** 86 r L-Brindeau (n.rest) ☏ (35)417207 Plan **10**
rm29(⇨27)
Credit Cards ①③

★★ **Richelieu** 132 r de Paris (n.rest) ☏ 35423871 Plan **11**
rm19(⇨12)
Credit Cards ①③

★ **Barrière d'Or** 365 bd de Graville ☏ 35304139
rm20(⇨19) 🍴
Credit Cards ①③

★ **Voltaire** 14 r Voltaire (n.rest) ☏ 35413091 Plan **12**
rm24(⇨16) P10
Credit Cards ①②③

At **GONFREVILLE-L'ORCHER**(10km E)

★★ **Campanile** Zone d'Activités du Camp Dolent ☏ 35514300 tx 771609 HAVRE, LE plan **4**
⇨🛏49 P49

At **MONTIVILLIERS**(7km NE)

★★ **Climat** ZAC de la Lézarde ☏ 35304139 tx 770346 HAVRE, LE plan **5**
⇨🛏38 P40
Credit Cards ①②③

At **STE-ADRESSE**(4km NW)

★★ **Phares** 29 r Gl-de-Gaulle (n.rest) ☏ 35463186
rm26(⇨18) 🍴 P12 ₵

HAYE-DU-PUITS, LA
Manche

★ **Gare** ᴸ DPn ☏ 33460422
Feb-Dec
rm12(🛏4)
Credit Cards ①③

HÉDE
Ille-et-Villaine

72

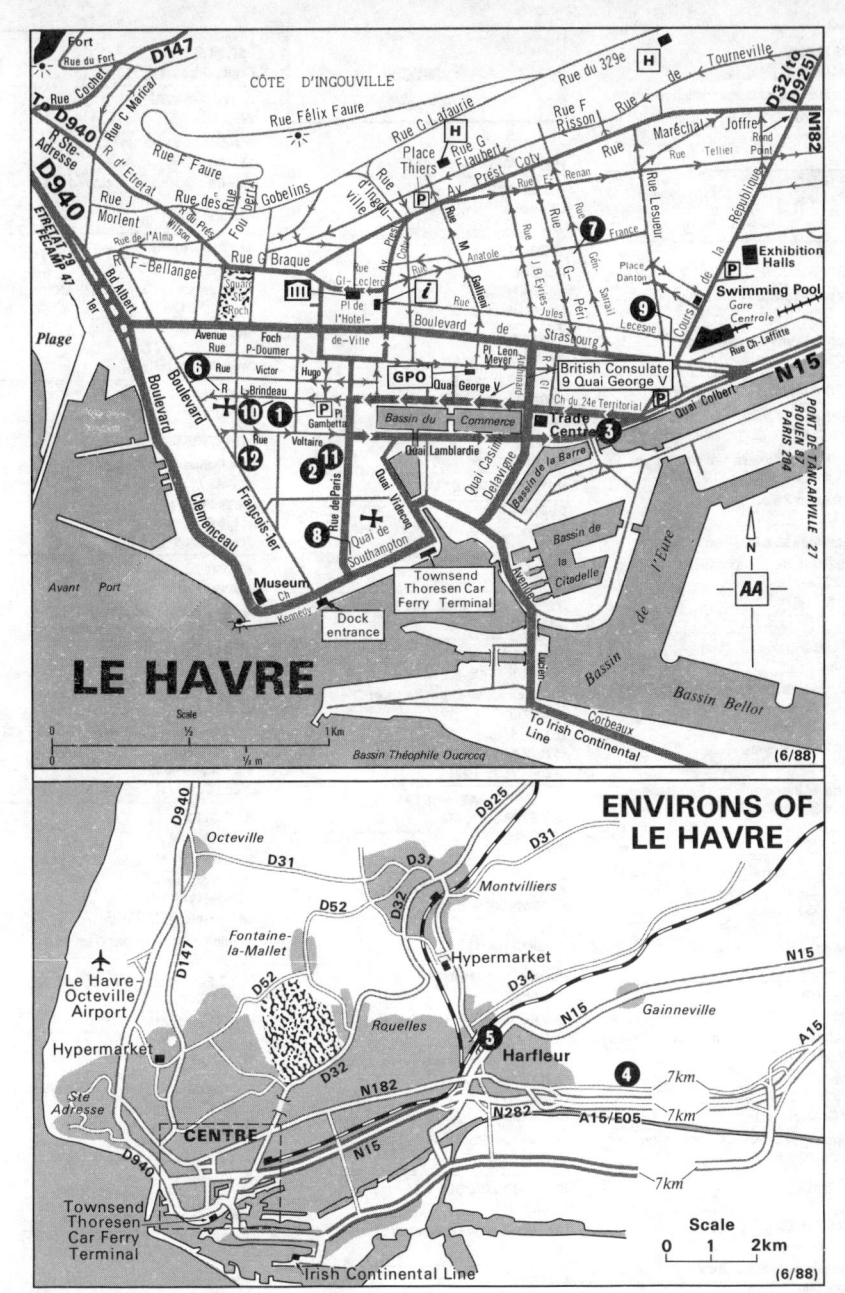

★★★ **Hostellerie du Vieux Moulin** L₣ Pn
rte Nationale 137 (n.rest) ☎ 99454570
Jan-20 Dec Closed :Rest closed Sun
evening & Mon
rm12(⇨11) ♠ P40
Credit Cards [1] [3] [5]

HENDAYE-PLAGE
Pyrénées-Atlantiques

★★★ **Liliac** 2 r des Clematites (n.rest)
☎ 59200245
25 Mar-Sep
⇨♠23 Lift
Credit Cards [1] [2] [3] [5]

★★★ **Paris** Rond-Point (n.rest)
☎ 59200506

Whit-Oct
⇨♠39 P15 Lift
Credit Cards [1] [3] [5]

HENIN-BEAUMONT
Pas-de-Calais
At **NOYELLES-GODAULT**(3km NE)

★★★ *Novotel Henin-Douai* Autoroute A1
☎ 21751601 tx 110352 →

France

⇨🛏79 P80 ⇔
Credit Cards ① ② ③ ⑤

★★ **Campanile** ZAC, rte de Beaumont
☎ 21762626 tx 134109
⇨🛏42 P42
Credit Card ③

HERBIGNAC
Loire-Atlantique

🚗 **Thudot** ☎ 40017107 **P** Cit

HERMIES
Pas-de-Calais

🚗 **Bachelet** 62 r d'Haurincourt
☎ 21074184 **P** Peu

🚗 **Central Mourcia** 13 Grand-Pl
☎ 21074010 **P** Ren

HÉROUVILLE-ST-CLAIR See **CAEN**

HESDIN
Pas-de-Calais

★★★ **Clery** Château d'Hesdin-l'Abbée
☎ 21831983 tx 135349
⇨🛏19 A8rm P40 ⟲
Credit Cards ① ② ③

★★ **Flandres** DPn 22 r d'Arras
☎ 21868021
8 Jan-20 Dec
rm14(⇨🛏12) 🍴 P8
Credit Cards ① ② ③

HONFLEUR
Calvados

★★★ **Ferme St-Siméon et Son Manoir**
(Relais et Châteaux) r A-Marais
☎ 31892361 tx 171031
⇨🛏38 P70 (ℛ Sea
Credit Cards ① ③

★★ **Cheval Blanc** quai des Passagers
☎ 31891349 tx 306022
Feb-Dec
⇨🛏35 Sea
Credit Cards ① ② ③

★★ **Dauphin** 10 pl P-Berthelot (n.rest)
☎ 31891553
Feb-Dec
⇨🛏30 A15rm
Credit Cards ① ③

HOSSEGOR
Landes

★★ **Beauséjour** av Genêts par av Tour-du-Lac ☎ 58435107
10 May-15 Oct
⇨🛏45 🍴 P12 Lift (⇔ Lake
Credit Card ③

★★ **Ermitage** allée des Pins Tranquilles
☎ 58435222
Jun-Sep
⇨🛏14 P ℛ

HOUCHES, LES
Haute-Savoie

★★ **Piste Bleue** rte les Chavants (n.rest)
☎ 50544066
rm25(⇨🛏19) Mountain

HOUDAN
Yvelines

★ **St-Christophe** 6 pl du Gl-de-Gaulle
☎ 30596161 tx 78550
⇨🛏9
Credit Card ③

HOUDEMONT See **NANCY**

HOULGATE
Calvados

★★ **Centre** 31 rue des Bains (n.rest)
☎ 31911815
Apr-Sept
rm22(⇨🛏19)
Credit Cards ① ③

HUELGOAT
Finistère

★★ **Triskel** 72 r des Cieux (n.rest)
☎ 98997185
Feb-15 Nov
⇨🛏10 P14
Credit Card ③

HUNINGUE See **ST-LOUIS**

HYÈRES
Var

🚗 **Fleschi** 7 rte de Toulon ☎ 94650283 **P** Fia

HYÈVRE-PAROISSE See **BAUME-LES-DAMES**

IGÉ
Saône-et-Loire

★★★ **Château d'Igé** (Relais et Châteaux)
☎ 85333399
15 Mar-5 Nov
⇨🛏12 A1rm 🍴 P16
Credit Cards ① ② ③ ⑤

ILLKIRCH-GRAFFENSTADEN
See **STRASBOURG**

INOR
Meuse

★ **Faisan Doré** r de l'Ecluse
☎ 29803545
⇨🛏13 P25
Credit Cards ① ③

ISIGNY-SUR-MER
Calvados

★★ **France** Pn 17 r Demagny
☎ 31220033
20 Jan-15 Dec Closed :Rest closed Fri in high season
rm19(⇨🛏14) P25 ⇔
Credit Cards ① ③

🚗 **Garage Etasse** 4 r de Littry
☎ 31220252 **P** Peu

ISLE-SUR-LE-DOUBS, L'
Doubs

🚗 **Marcoux** 64 r du Magny ☎ 81963154 **P** Ren

ISSOIRE
Puy-de-Dôme

★★ **Pariou** 18 av Kennedy ☎ 73892211
⇨🛏30 🍴 P18 Mountain
Credit Card ①

ISSOUDUN
Indre

★★ **France et Commerce** (FAH) 3 r P-Brossolette ☎ 54210065 tx 751422

⇨🛏24 🍴 P14
Credit Cards ① ② ③ ⑤

IVRY-LA-BATAILLE
Eure

★★ **Grand St-Martin** Pn 9 r Ezy
☎ 32364739
Feb-Dec Closed :Rest closed Mon
rm10(⇨🛏8)
Credit Cards ① ③

JARD-SUR-MER
Vendée

★★ **Parc de la Grange** (FAH) rte du Payré ☎ 51334488
May-Sept
⇨🛏60 A12rm (⇔
Credit Cards ① ② ③ ⑤

JARNAC
Charente

At **FLEURAC**(10km NE)

★★ **Domaine de Fleurac** (Inter)
☎ 45817822
Closed Nov
⇨🛏6 P40
Credit Cards ① ③ ⑤

JOIGNY
Yonne

★★★ **Côte St-Jacques** (Relais et Châteaux) Pn 14 fbg de Paris ☎ 86620970 tx 801458
5Feb88-2Jan89
⇨🛏30 A15rm 🍴 P12 Lift ⇔
Credit Cards ① ② ③ ⑤

★★ **Modern** (MAP/BW) 17 av R-Petit
☎ 86621628
⇨🛏21 🍴 P30 ℛ ⇔
Credit Cards ① ② ③ ④ ⑤

JOINVILLE
Haute-Marne

★ **Poste** (FAH) pl Grêve ☎ 95941263
10 Feb-10 Jan
rm11(⇨🛏7) 🍴 P10
Credit Cards ① ② ③ ⑤

★ **Soleil d'Or** 7 r des Capucins
☎ 25941566
Mar-7 Feb Closed :Rest closed Mon
⇨🛏11 🍴 P10
Credit Cards ① ② ③ ④ ⑤

JOSSELIN
Morbihan

★★ **Château** (Inter) 1 r Gl-de-Gaulle
☎ 97222011
rm36(⇨🛏28) 🍴 P30
Credit Cards ① ③

JOUÉ-LÉS-TOURS
Indre-et-Loire See also **TOURS**

★★ **Campanile** av du Lac, Les Bretonnières ☎ 47672489 tx 751683
⇨🛏49 P49
Credit Card ③

★★ **Château de Beaulieu** rte Villandry
☎ 47532026
⇨🛏19 A10rm P80
Credit Cards ① ③

★★ **Parc** (Inter) 17 bd Chinon (n.rest)
☎ 47251538
⇨🛏30 🍴 P30 Lift
Credit Cards ① ② ③

74

France

JOUGNE
Doubs

★ **Deux Saisons Pn** ☎ 81490004
Jun-Oct & 18 Dec-15 Apr
⇨♠21 🍽 P15 Lift Mountain
Credit Cards [1][3][5]

JUAN-LES-PINS
Alpes-Maritimes

★★★★ **Belles Rives** bd Littoral
☎ 93610279 tx 470984
end Mar-early Nov
⇨♠43 Lift (Beach Sea
Credit Cards [1][2][3]

★★★ **Juana** av G-Gallice, La Pinède
☎ 93610870 tx 470778
Apr-Oct
⇨♠50 P25 Lift (⇨ Beach Sea

★★★ **Apparthotel Astor** 61 chemin
Fournel Badine ☎ 93610738
⇨♠37 🍽 P15
Credit Cards [1][2][3][4][5]

★★★ **Helios** 3 av Daucheville ☎ 93615525
tx 970906
18 Apr-19 Oct
⇨♠70 🍽 P20 Lift (
Credit Cards [2][3][5]

★★ **Alexandra** r Pauline ☎ 93610136
1Apr-15Oct
rm20(⇨♠17) Beach
Credit Cards [1][3]

★★ **Cyrano** (Inter) av L-Gallet (n.rest)
☎ 93610483
Feb-15 Oct
⇨♠40 Lift (Beach Sea

★★ **Emeraude** 11 av Saramartel
☎ 93610967 tx 470673
Feb-end Nov
rm22(⇨♠20) 🍽 P6 Lift (Beach Mountain
Credit Cards [2][3][5]

★★ **Noailles** av Gallice ☎ 93611170
15 Jun-end Sept
rm22 🍽 Sea

★ **Midi** 93 bd Poincaré ☎ 93613516
4 Jan-20 Oct
rm23(⇨♠19) A8rm P12
Credit Card [3]

KAYSERSBERG See COLMAR

KREMLIN-BICÊTRE See PARIS

LA
Each name preceded by 'La' is listed under the name that follows it.

LABASTIDE-MURAT
Lot

★★ **Climat** ☎ 65211880
23 Jan-23 Dec
⇨♠20
Credit Cards [1][2][3][4][5]

LABÈGE See TOULOUSE

LADOIX-SERRIGNY See BEAUNE

LAFFREY
Isère

★★ **Grand Lac** Ŀ ☎ 76571290
May-Sep
⇨♠27 A19rm Mountain Lake

LALINDE
Dordogne

★★ **Château** Ŀ Pn r Verdun ☎ 53610182
10 Mar-15 Nov Closed :Rest closed Fri
⇨♠8 Lake
Credit Cards [1][3][5]

★★ **Résidence** 3 r Prof-Testut (n.rest)
☎ 53611081
May-Sep
⇨♠11

🍴 **Arbaudie** pl de l'Église ☎ 53610022 M/
C P Peu Tal

LAMASTRE
Ardèche

★★★ **Midi** pl Seignobos ☎ 75064150
Mar-15 Dec
rm18(⇨♠15) 🍽 P10
Credit Cards [1][2][3][5]

🍴 **Rugani** av de la Gare ☎ 75064220 P
Peu Tal

🍴 **Traversier** rte de Tournon
☎ 75064212 P Peu Tal

LAMBALLE
Côtes-du-Nord

★★ **Angleterre** Ŀ (FAH/Inter) 29 bd Jobert
☎ 96310016 tx 740994
⇨♠22 A13rm 🍽 P10 Lift
Credit Cards [2][3][5]

★★ **Auberge du Manoir des Portes** La Poterie ☎ 96311362
Mar-Jan Closed Rest Mon
⇨♠16 P20
Credit Cards [1][2][5]

★★ **Tour d'Argent** Ŀ 2 r du Dr-Lavergne
☎ 96310137
Closed :Rest closed Sat
rm31(⇨♠25) A16rm 🍽 P6
Credit Cards [1][2][3][5]

LAMORLAYE See CHANTILLY

LAMPAUL-GUIMILIAU
Finistère

★★ **Enclos** Ŀ ☎ 98687708 tx 29230
⇨♠36 P

LANÇON-PROVENCE See SALON-DE-PROVENCE

LANDERNEAU
Finistère

★★ **Clos du Pontic** Ŀ r du Pontic
☎ 98215091 tx 641155
Closed :Rest closed Sat midday & Sun
rm38(⇨♠21) P60 ⌒

★★ **Ibis** BP 151 Mescoat ☎ 98213132
tx 940878
⇨♠42 Lift
Credit Cards [1][3]

LANDUJAN See MONTAUBAN DE BRETAGNE

LANESTER See LORIENT

LANGEAIS
Indre-et-Loir

★★ **Hosten** Ŀ 2 r Gambetta ☎ 47967063
⇨♠12 🍽 P10
Credit Cards [1][2][3][5]

LANGRES
Haute-Marne

★★ **Europe** Ŀ DPn 23 r Diderot
☎ 25871088
Closed May-21 Oct:Rest closed Sun pm, Mon midday
rm28(⇨♠26) A9rm 🍽 P20
Credit Cards [1][2][3][5]

★★ **Lion d'Or** rte de Vesoul ☎ 25870330
Closed Jan
⇨♠14 🍽 P25 Lake
Credit Cards [1][2][3]

★ **Cheval Blanc** 4 r de l'Estres ☎ 25870700
4 Feb-4 Jan
rm23(⇨♠22) A8rm 🍽 P12
Credit Cards [1][2][3][5]

LANNION
Côtes-du-Nord

★★ **Climat** rte de Perros-Guirec
☎ 96487018
⇨♠47 P50
Credit Cards [1][2][3]

🍴 **Corre** rte de Perros-Guirec
☎ 96484541 For

LANSLEBOURG-MONT-CENIS
Savoie

★★★ **Alpazur** Ŀ ☎ 79059369 tx 980213
Jun-20 Sep & 20 Dec-20 Apr
⇨♠24 🍽 P10 Mountain
Credit Cards [1][2][3][5]

★ **Relais des Deux Cols** Ŀ 73 Val Cenis
☎ 79059283
Seasonal
rm30(⇨♠25) A10rm 🍽 P5 (⇨ Mountain
Credit Cards [1][2][3][5]

LANSLEVILLARD
Savoie

★★ **Étoile des Neiges** Lanslevillard
☎ 79059041 tx 309678 →

HOTEL SAINTE VALERIE ★★★ NN

Rue de l'Oratoire — 06160 Juan-les-Pins — Tel: 93.61.07.15

RESTAURANT — PERSONAL SERVICE — ABSOLUTE QUIETNESS AND REST IN THE OASIS CONSTITUTED BY ITS GARDENS.

Close to the casino, the harbour and the private beach of the hotel.

France

15 May-15 Sep & 15 Dec-15 Apr
⇨🛏24 🍴 P20 Mountain
Credit Cards 1 3

LANVOLLON
Côtes-du-Nord

At PLEHEDEL

★★★ *Château de Coatguelen* (Relais et Châteaux) ☎ 96223124 tx 741300
5 Apr-5 Jan Closed :Rest Tue & Wed am
⇨🛏16 P40 ♀ ⇨ ▶ ∪ Lake
Credit Cards 1 2 3 5

LAON
Aisne

★★ **Angleterre** (Inter) 10 Bd Lyon
☎ 23230462 tx 145580
rm30(⇨🛏15) 🍴 P10 Lift ℂ
Credit Cards 1 2 3 4 5

★★ **Bannière de France** Pn 1 r de F-Roosevelt ☎ 23232144
Closed 20 Dec-15 Jan & 1 May
rm19(⇨🛏13) 🍴 P
Credit Cards 1 2 3 5

★★ *Fimotel* ZAC Ile de France (N2)
☎ 23201811
⇨🛏40 P60 Lift
Credit Cards 1 2 3 5

★ *Chevaliers* 3 r Serurier ☎ 23234378
Closed 15-30Feb&10-20Aug:Rest closed for dinner
rm15(⇨🛏10)
Credit Cards 1 3

🚗 S.I.C.B 121 av de Belgique
☎ 23791408 P For

🚗 Tuppin 132 av M-France ☎ 23235036
Peu Tal

LARAGNE-MONTEGLIN
Hautes-Alpes

★ **Terrasses** 🛏 av Provence ☎ 92650854
May-Oct
rm17(⇨🛏8) 🍴 P12 Mountain
Credit Cards 1 2 3 4

LAROQUE-DES-ARC See CAHORS

LAUMES, LES
Côte-d'Or

★★ **Lesprit** 🛏 ☎ 80960046
⇨🛏24 🍴 P15
Credit Cards 1 3

LAURIS
Vaucluse

★★ *Chaumière* 🛏 pl du Portail
☎ 90082025
15 Feb-15 Jan Closed :Rest closed Tue & Wed lunch
⇨🛏12 P Mountain Lake
Credit Cards 1 2 3 5

LAVAL
Mayenne

★★ **Campanile** bd Duguesclin
☎ 43690400 tx 722633
⇨🛏42 P42
Credit Card 3

★★ **Climat** bd des Trappistines
☎ 78566434
rm42 P42 ♀
Credit Cards 1 3

★★ **Ibis** rte de Mayenne ☎ 43538182
tx 721094
⇨🛏51 Lift
Credit Cards 1 3

LAVANDOU, LE
Var

★★★ **Calanque** 62 av Gl-de-Gaulle (n.rest)
☎ 94710595
Etr-Oct
⇨🛏38 Lift Sea
Credit Cards 1 2 3 4 5

★ **Petite Bohème** DPn av F-Roosevelt
☎ 94711030
6 May-10 Oct
rm20(⇨🛏18) A4rm 🍴 Sea
Credit Cards 1 3

LAVAUR
Tarn

At ST-LIEUX-LES-LAVAUR(11km NW)

★★ **Château** ☎ 63416087
⇨🛏12 P25 ℂ

LAVERNAY See RECOLOGNE

LAXOU See NANCY

LE
Each name preceded by 'Le'is listed under the name that follows it.

LECHIAGAT See GUILVINEC

LECQUES, LES
Var

★★★ **Grand** Les Lecques Plage
☎ 94262301 tx 400165
May- Oct
rm58(⇨🛏53) P50 Lift ♀ Sea
Credit Cards 1 2 3 4 5

LECTOURE
Gers

★★ **Bastard** r Lagrange ☎ 62688244
1 Mar-31 Jan Closed :Rest closed Sun dinner & Mon
⇨🛏29 P25
Credit Cards 1 2 3 5

LENS
Pas-de-Calais

★★ **Campanile** Zone d'Activités, rte de la Bassée ☎ 21288282 tx 134089
⇨🛏51 P51
Credit Card 3

At LIÉVIN(4km W)

★★ **Climat** r S-Goulet ☎ 21282222
tx 134430
⇨🛏26 P30
Credit Cards 1 2 3

At VENDIN-LE-VIEL(6km NE)

★★ *Lensotel* Centre Commercial Lens 11
☎ 21786453 tx 120324
⇨🛏70 P70 Lift ⇨
Credit Cards 1 2 3 4 5

LES
Each name preceded by 'Les' is listed under the name that follows it.

LESCAR See PAU

LESQUIN See LILLE AIRPORT

LEVROUX
Indre

★★ **Cloche et St-Jacques** 🛏 DPn
r Nationale ☎ 54357043
Closed :Rest closed Mon evening & Tue
rm26(⇨🛏21) A14rm P5
Credit Cards 1 3

LIBOURNE
Gironde

★★ **Climat** Le Port du Noyer ☎ 57514141
tx 541707
⇨🛏42 P
Credit Cards 1 3

★★ **Loubat** 32 r Chanzy ☎ 57511758
tx 540436
rm25(⇨🛏23) 🍴 P6
Credit Cards 1 2 3

🚗 Solica Port du Noyer Arveyres
☎ 57513496 For

LIÉVIN See LENS

LILLE
Nord

★★★ **Bellevue** 5 r J-Roisin (n.rest)
☎ 20574564 tx 120790
⇨🛏80 P Lift
Credit Cards 1 2 3

★★★ **Carlton** (MAP/Inter) 3 r de Paris (n.rest) ☎ 20552411 tx 110400
rm65(⇨🛏60) P100 Lift ℂ
Credit Cards 1 2 3 5

★★★ *Royal* (Inter) 2 bd Carnot
☎ 20510511 tx 820575
rm102(⇨🛏98) P Lift
Credit Cards 1 2 3 5

★★ **Campanile** r C-Borda ☎ 20533055
tx 136203
⇨🛏49 P49
Credit Card 3

HOTEL – RESTAURANT DE LA MER ★ NN
22770 LANCIEUX – Tel.: 96.86.22.07 – Open 1.3 – 24.12
25 rooms, 7 with bathroom and WC, 7 with shower and WC, prices from 100 FF to 210 FF, full board from 160 FF to 220 FF, half-board from 130 FF to 170 FF. Restaurant from 60 FF to 130 FF and à la carte.
ENGLISH SPOKEN – Credit cards: Eurocard, C.B.

★★ **Ibis** Le Forum, av Charles, St Venant
☎ 20554444 tx 136950
⇌ ᴒ 151 🍴 P40 Lift
Credit Cards [1] [3]

★★ **Urbis** 21 r Lepelletier (n.rest)
☎ 20062195 tx 136846
⇌ ᴒ 60 P15 Lift
Credit Cards [1] [3]

At **ENGLOS**(7.5km W)

★★★ **Mercure** Autoroute Lille-Dunkerque
☎ 20923015 tx 820302
⇌ ᴒ 90 A20rm P200 ♗ ⌧
Credit Cards [1] [2] [3] [5]

★★★ **Novotel Lille Lomme** Autoroute A25
(n.rest) ☎ 20070999 tx 132120
⇌ ᴒ 124 P ⌧
Credit Cards [1] [2] [3] [5]

At **MARCQ-EN-BAROEUL**(4.5km N)

★★★★ **Holiday Inn** bd de la Marne
☎ 20721730 tx 132785
⇌ ᴒ 125 P50 Lift ⌧
Credit Cards [1] [2] [3] [4] [5]

🔧 **Flandres Automobiles** 607 av de la République ☎ 20550770 **P** For

LILLE AIRPORT

At **LESQUIN**(8km SE)

★★★★ **Holiday Inn** 110 r J-Jaurés
☎ 20979202 tx 132051
⇌ ᴒ 213 P400 Lift ⌧ Beach
Credit Cards [1] [2] [3] [5]

★★★ **Novotel Lille Aéroport** Autoroute A1
☎ 20979225 tx 820519
⇌ ᴒ 92 P100 ⌧
Credit Cards [1] [2] [3] [5]

LIMOGES
Haute-Vienne

★★★★ **Royal Limousin** 1 pl de la République ☎ 55346530 tx 580771
⇌ ᴒ 75 P Lift
Credit Cards [1] [2] [3] [5]

★★★ **Luk** 29 pl Jourdan ☎ 55334400 tx 580704
Closed :Rest closed Sat lunch & Sun
⇌ ᴒ 55 Lift ⦅
Credit Cards [1] [2] [3] [5]

★★ **Campanile** Le Moulin Pinard, r H-Giffard ☎ 55373562 tx 590909
⇌ ᴒ 42 P42
Credit Card [3]

★★ **Ibis Limoges** r F-Bastiat, ZAC Industrielle Nord 2 ☎ 55375014 tx 580009
⇌ ᴒ 76 Lift
Credit Cards [1] [3]

★★ **Jourdan** (Inter) 2 av du Gl-de-Gaulle ☎ 55774962 tx 580121
rm41(⇌ ᴒ 40) Lift ⦅
Credit Cards [1] [2] [3] [5]

★★ **Urbis** 6 bd V-Hugo (n.rest)
☎ 55790330 tx 580731
⇌ ᴒ 68 Lift
Credit Cards [1] [3]

★ **Relais Lamartine** 10 r des Cooperateurs (n.rest) ☎ 55775339
rm20(⇌ ᴒ 10) 🍴

LINGOLSHEIM
Basse-Rhin

France

★★ **Campanile** Parc des Tanneries, 305 rte de Schirmelic ☎ 88781010 tx 880454
⇌ ᴒ 50 P50
Credit Card [3]

LION D'ANGERS, LE
Maine-et-Loire

★ **Voyageurs DPn** 2 r Gl-Leclerc
☎ 41953008
15 Feb-1 Oct & 1 Nov-15 Jan
rm13(⇌ ᴒ 5) 🍴 P10
Credit Cards [1] [2] [3] [5]

LISIEUX
Calvados

★★★ **Gardens** rte de Paris (N13)
☎ 31611717 tx 170065
⇌ ᴒ 70 P70 ⌧
Credit Cards [1] [2] [3] [5]

★★★ **Grand Normandie** Ⓛ (Inter) 11 bis r au Char ☎ 31621605 tx 170269
May-1 Oct
⇌ ᴒ 70 🍴 Lift
Credit Cards [1] [2] [3] [4] [5]

★★★ **Place** (MAP/BW) 67 r H-Chéron (n.rest) ☎ 31311744 tx 171862
⇌ ᴒ 33 🍴 P30 Lift
Credit Cards [1] [2] [3] [5]

★★ **Lourdes** 4 r au Char (n.rest)
☎ 31311948
rm33(⇌ ᴒ 32) 🍴 Lift
Credit Cards [1] [2] [3]

★ **Coupe d'Or** 49 r Pont-Mortain
☎ 31311684 tx 772163
rm18(⇌ ᴒ 14) P
Credit Cards [1] [2] [3] [4] [5]

🔧 **Lorant** 61 bd Ste-Anne ☎ 31310071 **P** Peu Tal

🔧 **Pays d'Auge** 62 r du Gl-Leclerc ☎ 31311614 AR

LIVAROT
Calvados

★ **Vivier** Ⓛ pl de la Mairie ☎ 31635029
rm11(⇌ ᴒ 7) P20
Credit Cards [1] [3]

LIVRON-SUR-DRÔME
Drôme

🔧 **Gimenez** Elf Station (N7)
☎ 75616778 **P** All makes

LIVRY-GARGAN See **PARIS**

LOCHES
Indre-et-Loire

★ **France Pn** 6 r Picois ☎ 47590032 tx 750020
Feb-Dec
rm20(⇌ ᴒ 18) 🍴 P20
Credit Cards [1] [3] [5]

At **BRIDORÉ**(14km S)

★★★ **Barbe Bleue Pn** Oizay ☎ 47947269
Closed :Rest closed Tue
⇌ ᴒ 10 P30 ♗

LOCRONAN
Finistère

★★ **Prieure** Ⓛ DPn 11 r de Prieure
☎ 98917089
rm15(⇌ ᴒ 11) P25
Credit Cards [1] [3]

LODÈVE
Hérault

★★ **Croix Blanche** 6 av de Fumel
☎ 67441087
Apr-1 Dec
rm32(⇌ ᴒ 23) 🍴 P30
Credit Cards [1] [3]

LONDE, LA See **ELBEUF**

LONGJUMEAU
Essonne

At **SAULX-LES-CHARTREUX**

★★ **Climat** Le Pont Neuf ☎ 64480900 tx 600609
⇌ ᴒ 54 P100
Credit Cards [1] [2] [3]

LONGUYON
Meurthe-et-Moselle

★★ **Lorraine** Ⓛ (Inter) Face Gare
☎ 82265007 tx 861718
Feb-Dec Closed :Rest closed Tue
rm15(⇌ ᴒ 12)
Credit Cards [1] [2] [3] [5]

LONGWY
Meurthe-et-Moselle

★★ **Fimotel** (N52) ☎ 82231419 tx 861270
⇌ ᴒ 42 P60 Lift
Credit Cards [2] [5]

LONS-LE-SAUNIER
Jura

★★ **Genève** 19 pl XI Novembre
☎ 84241911
rm40(⇌ ᴒ 30) 🍴 P10 Lift
Credit Cards [1] [2] [5]

🔧 **Lecourbe** 58 bis r Lecourbe
☎ 84472013 M/C **P** For

🔧 **Thevenod** rte de Champagnole-Perrigny ☎ 84244158 Aud VW

LORIENT
Morbihan

★★★ **Mercure** 31 pl J-Ferry ☎ 97213573 tx 950810
⇌ ᴒ 58 Lift
Credit Cards [1] [2] [3] [5]

At **LANESTER**(5km NE)

★★★ **Novotel** Zone Commerciale de Bellevue ☎ 97760216 tx 950026
⇌ ᴒ 88 P80 ⌧
Credit Cards [1] [2] [3] [5]

★★ **Climat** ZA-Lann Sevelin ☎ 97764641
⇌ ᴒ 39 P50
Credit Cards [1] [3] [4]

★★ **Ibis** Zone Commerciale de Bellevue (n.rest) ☎ 97764022
⇌ ᴒ 40 Lift
Credit Cards [1] [3]

LORMONT See **BORDEAUX**

LOUDÉAC
Côtes-du-Nord →

★ **Voyageurs** 10 r Cadelac ☎ 96280047
15 Jan-20 Dec Closed :Rest closed Sat
rm29(⇨♠25) 🚗 P7 Lift
Credit Cards ①②③⑤

LOUDUN
Vienne

★★★ **Mercure** 40 av Leuze (n.rest)
☎ 49981922
⇨♠29 Lift
Credit Cards ①②③⑤

LOUÉ
Sarthe

★★★ **Ricordeau** (Relais et Châteaux) **DPn**
11 r Libération ☎ 43884003 tx 722013
Closed Dec-3 Jan
rm22(⇨♠19) A8rm 🚗 P15 ⌂ ⌂
Credit Cards ①②③⑤

LOURDES
Hautes-Pyrénées

★★★ **Grotte** (MAP/BW) 66 r de la Grotte
☎ 62945887 tx 531937
Etr-20 Oct
⇨♠83 🚗 P25 Lift (
Credit Cards ①②③⑤

★★ **Ibis** chaussée Marensin ☎ 62943838
tx 521409
⇨♠88 Lift
Credit Cards ①③

★★ **Provençale** (Inter) 4 r Baron Duprat
☎ 62943134 tx 520257
⇨♠46 Lift (Mountain
Credit Cards ①②③④⑤

LOUVIERS
Eure

At **ST-PIERRE-DU-VAUVRAY**(8km E)

★★★ **Hostellerie de St-Pierre DPn**
☎ 32599329
1 Mar-31 Dec Closed :Rest closed Tue
⇨♠14 P40 Lift ♪ Lake
Credit Cards ①③

At **VAL-DE-REUIL**(4km N A13)

★★★ **Altea** Lieu dit les Clouets
☎ 32590909 tx 180540
⇨♠58 P100 Lift ♪ ⌂
Credit Cards ①②③⑤

At **VIRONVAY**(4km SE)

★★ **Saisons** ☎ 32400256
Closed :Rest closed Sun evening
⇨♠20 🚗 P30 ♪
Credit Cards ①②③

LOUVROIL
Nord

★★★ **Mercure** rte d'Avesnes (N2)
☎ 27649373 tx 110696
Closed :Rest closed Sat & Sun
⇨♠59 ⌂
Credit Cards ①②③⑤

LUC, LE
Var

★ **Hostellerie du Parc** 1 r J-Jaurès
☎ 94607001
⇨♠12 P20
Credit Cards ①②③⑤

LUCÉ See **CHARTRES**

LUCHON
Haute-Garonne

France

★★★ **Poste & Golf** 29 allées d'Etigny
☎ 61790040 tx 520018
Closed 21 Oct-19 Dec
rm63(⇨♠59) 🚗 P Lift Mountain

★★ **Bains** (Inter) 75 allées d'Etigny
☎ 61790058 tx 521437
Feb-20 Oct
rm53(⇨♠48) P15 Lift Mountain
Credit Card ②

LUÇON
Vendée

★★ **Grand Hotel du Croissant**
☎ 51561115
Nov-Sep Closed :Rest closed Sun in low season
rm40(⇨♠33) 🚗 P10

LUC-SUR-MER
Calvados

★★ **Grand Casino** 3 r Guynemer
☎ 31973237
Apr-Sep
⇨♠30 P30 Lift ⌂ Sea
Credit Cards ①②③④⑤

LUDE, LE
Sarthe

★★ **Maine** **DPn** 24 rte Saumur
☎ 43946054
⇨♠24 🚗 P60
Credit Cards ①②⑤

LUDRES See **NANCY**

LUNÉVILLE
Meurthe-et-Moselle

★★ **Europe** 56 r d'Alsace (n.rest)
☎ 83741234
rm30(⇨♠22) P15
Credit Cards ①③

LUS-LA-CROIX-HAUTE
Drôme

★ **Chamousset** **DPn** ☎ 92585112
rm20(⇨♠15) 🚗 P15 Mountain
Credit Cards ②③

★ **Touring** 75 rte Nationale ☎ 92585001
Closed :Rest closed Sun
rm10(⇨5) Mountain

LUTTERBACH
Haut-Rhin

★★ **Campanile** 10 r Pfastatt ☎ 89536655
tx 881432
⇨♠53 P53
Credit Card ③

LUXEUIL-LES-BAINS
Haute-Saône

★★ **Beau Site** 18 r Thermes (n.rest)
☎ 84401467
Closed 24 Dec-2 Jan
⇨♠39 A11rm 🚗 P35
Credit Cards ①③

LUYNES
Indre-et-Loire

★★★★ **Domaine de Beauvois DPn**
☎ 47555011 tx 750204

---

10 Mar-10 Jan
⇨♠38 A2rm P20 Lift (♪ ⌂
Credit Cards ①③

LYON
Rhône See also **CHASSE-SUR-RHÔNE**

★★★★ **Grand Concorde** 11 r Grôlée
☎ 78425621 tx 330244
⇨♠140 🚗 P15 Lift (
Credit Cards ①②③⑤

★★★★ **Holiday Inn Crowne Plaza Lyon Atlas** r de Bonnel 29 ☎ 72619090
tx 330703
⇨♠156 P156 Lift (
Credit Cards ①②③⑤

★★★★ **Pullman Part-Dieu** 129 r Servient, Part Dieu Nord ☎ 78629412 tx 380088
⇨♠245 🚗 P Lift (
Credit Cards ①②③⑤

★★★★ **Royal** (MAP/BW) 20 pl Bellecour
☎ 78375731 tx 310785
⇨♠90 🚗 Lift
Credit Cards ①②③⑤

★★★★ **Sofitel** 20 quai Gailleton
☎ 78427250 tx 330225
⇨♠200 P100 Lift (
Credit Cards ①②③④⑤

★★★ **Beaux-Arts** (MAP/BW) 75 r Près-Herriot (n.rest) ☎ 78380950 tx 330442
⇨♠79 Lift
Credit Cards ①②③⑤

★★★ **Bordeaux et du Parc** (Inter) 1 r du Belier (n.rest) ☎ 78375873 tx 330355
⇨♠80 Lift
Credit Cards ①②③⑤

★★★ **Carlton** (MAP/BW) 4 r Jussieu (n.rest) ☎ 78425651 tx 310787
rm87(♠83) 🚗 P6 Lift
Credit Cards ①②③⑤

★★★ **Terminus Lyon Perrache** 12 cours de Verdun ☎ 78375811 tx 330500
⇨♠130 🚗 P100 Lift (Mountain
Credit Cards ①②③⑤

★★ **Campaville** 17 pl Carnot ☎ 78374847
tx 305660
⇨♠108 Lift
Credit Card ③

★★ **Globe & Cecil** (Inter) 21 r Gasparin (n.rest) ☎ 78425895 tx 305184
rm65(⇨♠53) Lift
Credit Cards ①②③⑤

★★ **Ibis Lyon La Part-Diéu Sud** pl Renaudel ☎ 78954211 tx 310847
⇨♠144 Lift
Credit Cards ①③

★★ **Moderne** 15 r Dubois (n.rest)
☎ 78422183 tx 330949
rm31(⇨♠26) P2 Lift
Credit Cards ①③

★★ **Urbis** 51 r de l'Université (n.rest)
☎ 78727842 tx 340455
⇨♠53 🚗 P10 Lift (
Credit Cards ①②③

🅿 **Gallieni** 47 av Berthelot ☎ 78720227 **P** For

At **BEYNOST**

★★★ **Ibis Lyon Est Beynost** Autoroute A42, Sortie N5 ☎ 78554088 tx 305215

⇌🛏25
Credit Cards [1] [3]
At **BRON**(10km SE)
★★★ **Novotel Lyon Aéroport** r L-Terray
☎ 78269748 tx 340781
⇌🛏191 P350 Lift ≋
Credit Cards [1] [2] [3] [5]
★★ **Campaville** quartier Rebufer, r
Maryse-Bastie ☎ 78262540 tx 305160
⇌🛏50 P60
★★ **Climat** Aéroport de Lyon ☎ 78265076
tx 375941
⇌🛏38 P40
Credit Cards [1] [2] [3]
★★ **Ibis Hostel** 36 av de Doyen J-Lepine
☎ 78543134 tx 380694
Closed :Rest closed 7 July
⇌🛏140 Lift
Credit Cards [1] [3]
At **CHARBONNIÈRES-LES-BAINS**(8km
NW on N7)
★★★ **Mercure** 78 bis rte de Paris (RN7)
☎ 78347279 tx 900972
⇌🛏60 🍴 P20 ≋
Credit Cards [1] [2] [3] [4] [5]
At **DARDILLY**(10km on N6)
★★★★ **Lyon-Nord** (MAP/BW) Porte de
Lyon ☎ 78357020 tx 900006
⇌🛏205 P300 Lift 🍴 Mountain
Credit Cards [1] [2] [3] [5]
★★★ **Mercure Lyon La Part-Dieu** 47 bd
Vivier-Merle ☎ 72341812 tx 306469
⇌🛏124 P Lift
★★★ **Mercure Lyon Nord** Porte de Lyon
(A6)
⇌🛏175 🍴 P200 ♪ ≋
Credit Cards [2] [3] [5]
★★★ **Novotel Lyon Nord** Porte de Lyon
(A6) ☎ 78351341 tx 330962
⇌🛏107 P110 Lift ≋
Credit Cards [1] [2] [3] [5]
★★ **Campanile** Porte de Lyon Nord
☎ 78354844 tx 310155
⇌🛏43 P43
Credit Card [3]
★★ **Climat** Porte de Lyon Nord
☎ 78359847
⇌🛏38 P
Credit Card [1]
★★ **Ibis Lyon Nord** Porte de Lyon (A6)
☎ 78543134 tx 305250
⇌🛏47 🍴
Credit Cards [1] [3]
At **ECULLY**(7.5km NW)
★★ **Campanile** av de Guy de Collongue
☎ 78331693 tx 310154
⇌🛏50 P50
Credit Card [3]
At **STE-FOY-LES-LYONS**(6km SW)
★★ **Campanile** Chemin de la Croix-Pivort
☎ 78593233 tx 305850
⇌🛏50 P50
Credit Card [3]
★★ **Provences** Ⓛ 10 pl St-Luc
☎ 78250155
⇌🛏14 P (

France

At **ST-GENIS-LAVAL**(10km SW)
★★ *Climat* chemin de Chazelle
☎ 78566434 tx 692844
⇌🛏42 P42 ♪
Credit Cards [1] [0]
At **SATOLAS AIRPORT**(18km SW)
★★ *Climat* Zone de Frêt ☎ 78409644
tx 612241
⇌🛏36 P
LYONS-LA-FORÊT
Eure
★★ **Licorne** Ⓛ pl Benserade ☎ 32496202
25 Jan-15 Dec
rm21(⇌🛏17) A2rm 🍴 P20
Credit Cards [1] [2] [3] [5]
MÂCON
Saône-et-Loire
★★★★ **Altea Mâcon** 26 r de Coubertin
☎ 85382606 tx 800830
⇌🛏63 P60 Lift ♪ ≋ Sea
Credit Cards [1] [2] [3] [5]
★★★ **Novotel Mâcon Nord** Autoroute A6
☎ 85360080 tx 800869F
⇌🛏115 P130 ≋
Credit Cards [1] [2] [3] [5]
★★ **Bellevue** (MAP/BW) 416-420 quai
Lamartine ☎ 853870507 tx 800837
rm25(⇌🛏23) 🍴 P23 Lift (
Credit Cards [1] [2] [3] [5]
★★ *Champs Elysées* (Inter) 6 r V-Hugo, 2
pl de la Barre ☎ 85383657 tx 351940
rm50(⇌🛏37) 🍴 Lift
Credit Cards [1] [2] [3] [5]
★★ **Europe et d'Angleterre** 92-109 quai J-
Jaurès (n.rest) ☎ 85382794
Feb-Oct
rm31(⇌17) 🍴 P18
Credit Cards [1] [2] [3] [5]
★★ *Genève* (Inter) 1 r Bigonnet
☎ 85381810 tx 351934
rm63(⇌🛏51) 🍴 Lift
Credit Cards [1] [2] [5]
★★ **Terminus** Ⓛ (FAH) 91 r V-Hugo
☎ 85391711 tx 351938
⇌🛏48 🍴 P15 Lift (
Credit Cards [1] [2] [3] [5]
🍴 **Bois** 39 r Lacretelle ☎ 85386431 P AR
🍴 **Chauvot** r J-Mermox, 'Les Bruyères'
☎ 85349898 P Ope Vol
🍴 **Corsin** 25 rte de Lyon ☎ 85387333 For
🍴 **Duval** 53 rte de Lyon ☎ 85348000 P
Fia Mer
🍴 **Mâcon Auto** 5 r du Concours
☎ 85389320 P Dat
At **CHAINTRÉ-LA-CHAPELLE-DE-
GUINCHAY**(14km SW)
★★ **Ibis Mâcon Sud** les Bouchardes
☎ 85365160 tx 351926
⇌🛏45 Lift
Credit Cards [1] [3]

At **CRÈCHES-SUR-SAÔNE**(0.5km NW)
★★ **Château de la Barge** ☎ 85371204
Closed :Rest closed Sat & Sun (out of
season)
rm23(⇌🛏21) P36 Lift
Credit Cards [1] [2] [3] [5]
🍴 **Perrin** (N 6) ☎ 85371261 P Ren
🍴 **Romand** (N 6) ☎ 85371137 P Peu
At **ST-ALBAIN**(10km N)
★★★ *Mercure* (A6) ☎ 85331900
tx 800881
⇌🛏100 🍴 Lift ≋
At **SANCÉ-LE-MÂCON**(4km N)
★★★ *Vielle Ferme* (N6) ☎ 85384693
⇌🛏32 ≋
Credit Cards [3] [5]
★★ **Balladins** ZAC des Platrières
☎ 05355575 tx 649394
rm38 P38
Credit Cards [1] [2] [3]
★★ *Climat* ZAC des Platières, r du 19 Mars
1962 ☎ 85392133 tx 692844
⇌🛏42 P
Credit Cards [1] [3]
MAGESCQ
Landes
★ **Relais de la Poste** Ⓛ ☎ 58477025
24 Dec-11 Nov Closed :Rest closed Mon
evening & Tue
⇌🛏12 🍴 P40 ♪ ≋
Credit Cards [1] [2] [3] [5]
MAISONS-LAFFITTE
Yvelines
★★★ *Climat* r de Paris ☎ 34460123
tx 692844
⇌🛏42 P
MALBUISSON
Doubs
★★★ *Lac* ☎ 81693480 tx 360713
rm54(⇌48) 🍴 P Lift Mountain Lake
MALÈNE, LA
Lozère
★★★ **Manoir de Montesquiou Pn**
☎ 66485112
Apr-Oct
⇌🛏12 P10 Mountain Lake
Credit Card [5]
MANDELIEU
Alpes-Maritimes
★ **Esterel** 1625 av de Fréjus (n.rest)
☎ 93499220
⇌🛏22 P25 Mountain
★ **Pavillon des Sports** rte de Fréjus (n.rest)
☎ 93495086
⇌🛏11 P20
MANOSQUE
Alpes-de-Haute-Provence
★★ **Campanile** Ⓛ rte de Voix, (N96)
☎ 92875900 tx 405915
⇌🛏30 P30
Credit Card [3]
🍴 **Renardat** 237 av F-Mistral
☎ 92878790 Peu
MANS, LE
Sarthe →

France

★★★★ **Concorde** 16 av Gl-Leclerc
☎ 43241230 tx 720487
rm68(⇨↑55) 🅿 P55 Lift
Credit Cards [1][2][3][4][5]

★★★ **Moderne** 14 r Bourg-Belé
☎ 43247920
⇨↑32 A18rm 🅿 P20 (
Credit Cards [1][2][3][5]

★★★ **Novotel le Mans Est** ZAC les Sablons, bd R-Schumann ☎ 43852680 tx 720706
⇨↑94 P200 Lift ⇨
Credit Cards [1][2][5]

★★ **Chantecler** 50 r Pelouse ☎ 43245853 tx 722941
Closed :Rest closed Sun (23 Dec-3 Jan)
rm37(⇨↑35) P22 Lift
Credit Cards [1][3]

★★ **Climat** Les Grues Rogues
☎ 43213121
⇨↑26 P40
Credit Cards [1][3]

★★ **Fimotel** 17 r de la Pointe, Rocade Sud
☎ 43722720 tx 722092
⇨↑42 P50 Lift ↑
Credit Cards [1][2][3][5]

★★ **Hotel Ibis** angle quai Ledru-Rollin, 4 r des Ah Ah ☎ 43231823 tx 722035
⇨↑83 🅿 P Lift
Credit Cards [1][3]

★★ **Ibis** r C-Marot ☎ 43861414 tx 720651
⇨↑49 Lift
Credit Cards [1][3]

At **ARNAGE**(9km S via N23)

★★ **Balladins** Zone d'Activité de la Rivière, D 147 ☎ 35355575 tx 649394
rm38 P38
Credit Cards [1][2][4][5]

★★ **Campanile** La Gêmerie, bd P-le-Faucheux ☎ 43218121 tx 722803
⇨↑42 P42
Credit Card [3]

MANSLE
Charente

🐟 **Central** Grand' rue ☎ 45222006 P Peu Tal

🐟 **Suire-Huguet** rte Nationale
☎ 45203031 M/C P Peu Tal

MANTES-LA-JOLIE
Yvelines

★★ **Climat** r M-Tabu ☎ 30330370
⇨↑41 P41 Lake

★★ **Ibis** allée des Martinets, ZAC des Brosses, Magnanville ☎ 30926565 tx 695358
⇨↑52 Lift
Credit Cards [1][3]

MARCAY See **CHINON**

MARCQ-EN-BAROEUL See **LILLE**

MARGNY See **COMPIÈGNE**

MARGUERITTES See **NÎMES**

MARIGNANE See **MARSEILLE AIRPORT**

MARLENHEIM
Bas-Rhin

France

★★ **Cerf** 30 r du Gl-de-Gaulle (n.rest)
☎ 88877373
Closed except early Jan
rm19 P
Credit Cards [2][3]

★★ **Hostellerie Reeb** L (N4) ☎ 88875270
⇨↑35 🅿 P100
Credit Cards [1][2][3][5]

MARSANNAY-LA-CÔTE
Côte-d'Or

★★ **Bimotel** Dijon Sud, (RN74), Couchey
☎ 80521266 tx 350121
⇨↑58 P158 ♪ ⇨
Credit Cards [1][2][3][5]

★★ **Campanile** Zone d'Activités Acti-Sud
☎ 80526201 tx 351400
⇨↑50 P50
Credit Card [3]

MARSEILLE
Bouches-du-Rhône

★★★★ **Altea** Centre Bourse, r Neuve St-Martin ☎ 91919129 tx 401886
⇨↑200 P150 Lift
Credit Cards [1][2][3][5]

★★★★ **Grand & Noailles** (MAP/BW) 66 Canebière ☎ 91549148 tx 430609
⇨↑70 P Lift
Credit Cards [1][2][3][4][5]

★★★★ **Sofitel Vieux-Port** 36 bd C-Livron
☎ 91529019 tx 401270
⇨↑222 🅿 P160 Lift ⇨ Sea
Credit Cards [1][2][3][5]

★★★ **St-Georges** 10 r du Cpt-Dessemond (n.rest) ☎ 91525692
⇨↑27 Lift (Sea
Credit Cards [1][2][3][5]

★★ **Fimotel** 25 bd Rabatau ☎ 91256666 tx 402672
⇨↑90 🅿 P70 Lift
Credit Cards [1][2][3][5]

★★ **Ibis** angle av E-Triolet et av J-Marliey
☎ 91723434 tx 420845
⇨↑88 🅿 P38 Lift ♪ ⇨ ∪
Credit Cards [1][3]

★★ **Ibis Marseille Prado** 6 r de Cassis
☎ 91257373 tx 400362
⇨↑118 🅿 P Lift
Credit Cards [1][3]

★★ **Urbis** 48 r Sainte ☎ 91547373 tx 420808
⇨↑148 🅿 P45 Lift (
Credit Card [1]

🐟 **Auto Diffusion** 36 bd National
☎ 91620805 P For

🐟 **Ciotti** 11 r J-B-Astir ☎ 91497534 P

🐟 **Touchard** 151 av Montolivet
☎ 91661239 M/C P

At **PENNE-ST-MENET, LA**(10km E of A52)

★★★ **Novotel Marseille Est** (A52)
☎ 91439060 tx 400667
⇨↑131 P150 Lift ♪ ⇨
Credit Cards [1][3][5]

MARSEILLE AIRPORT

At **MARIGNANE**(8km NW)

★★★★ **Sofitel** ☎ 42899102 tx 401980
⇨↑180 P135 Lift (♪ ⇨
Credit Cards [1][2][3][4][5]

★★ **Ibis** av du 8 Mai 1945 ☎ 42883535 tx 440052
⇨↑36
Credit Cards [1][3]

At **VITROLLES**(8km N)

★★★ **Novotel Marseille Aéroport** (A7)
☎ 42899044 tx 420670
⇨↑163 🅿 P250 Lift ⇨
Credit Cards [1][2][3][5]

★★ **Campanile** Le Griffon, rte d'Aix-en-Provence ☎ 42892511 tx 402722
⇨↑44
Credit Card [3]

★★ **Climat** ZI de Couperigne, (CD20)
☎ 42752300
⇨↑41 P45 Lift

MARTEL
Lot

At **GLUGES**(5km SE N681)

★★ **Falaises** DPn ☎ 65373359
Mar-Nov
rm15(⇨↑13) P Mountain
Credit Cards [1][3]

MARTIGUES
Bouches-du-Rhône

★★ **Campanile** ZAC de Canto-Perdrix, bd de Tholon
⇨↑42 P42
Credit Card [3]

★★ **Fimotel** Z I de Caronte, av Nobre
☎ 42818494 tx 441405
⇨↑40 P60 Lift
Credit Cards [1][2][3][5]

MARVEJOLS
Lozère

★ **Paix** L 2 av de Brazza ☎ 66321017
⇨↑19 🅿 P6
Credit Cards [1][3]

MASSAT
Ariège

★★ **Trois Seigneurs** av de St-Girons
☎ 61969589
Etr-Oct
⇨↑25 A10rm P80 Mountain

MASSIAC
Cantal

★★ **Poste** (FAH) av de C-Ferrand (N9)
☎ 71230201 tx 990989
20 Dec-10 Nov Closed :Rest closed Wed
rm36(⇨↑26) 🅿 P30 Lift ⇨
Credit Cards [1][2][3][5]

MAULÉON-LICHARRE
Pyrénées-Atlantiques

★★ **Bidegain** 13 r de la Navarre
☎ 59281605
15 Jan-15 Dec
rm30(⇨↑14) 🅿 P15 (Mountain
Credit Cards [1][2][3][5]

MAYENNE
Mayenne

★★ **Grand** L? (FAH) 2 r Ambroise-de-Loré
☎ 43009600 tx 722622
18 Jan-23 Dec
rm30(⇨♠23) 🅿 P40
Credit Cards ①②③

★ **Croix Couverte** L? rte de Paris
☎ 43043248
Closed :Rest closed Sun evening (Oct-May)
⇨♠13 🅿 P60
Credit Card ①

🞄 **P Legros** 15 r du Guesclin ☎ 43041627
For

MAZAMET
Tarn

★★★ **Grand Balcon** sq G-Tournier
☎ 63610115 tx 520411
⇨♠24 🅿 P
Credit Cards ①②③⑤

MEAUX
Seine-et-Marne

★★ **Climat** 32 av de la Victoire
☎ 64331547 tx 690020
⇨♠60 P80
Credit Cards ①②③

★★ **Sirène** 33 r Gl-Leclerc ☎ 64340780
rm19(⇨♠14) P20
Credit Cards ②③⑤

🞄 **Cornillon** 45 r Cornillon ☎ 64340558 P
All makes

MEGÈVE
Haute-Savoie

★★★★ **Mont Blanc** (Inter) pl de l'Église
☎ 50212002 tx 385854
15 Jun-Etr
⇨♠50 A17rm 🅿 P40 Lift (♪ 🖼 Mountain
Credit Cards ①②③⑤

★★★ **Parc** d'Arly (n.rest) ☎ 50210574
Xmas, Etr & end Jun-mid Sep
⇨♠48 P40 Lift (Mountain

MEHUN-SUR-YEVRE
Cher

★ **Croix Blanche Pn** 164 r J d'Arc
☎ 48573001
Closed :Rest closed Sun evening & Mon
rm19(⇨♠15) 🅿 P24
Credit Cards ①③

MELUN
Seine-et-Marne **See also PONTHIERRY**

★★★ **Grand Monarque Concorde** rte Fontainebleau ☎ 64390440 tx 690140
⇨♠50 🅿 P100 Lift (♪ ⇨
Credit Cards ①②③⑤

★★ **Climat** 338 r R-Hervillard, Vaux-le-Pénil ☎ 64527181 tx 693140
⇨♠43 P50
Credit Cards ①②③

★★ **Ibis** av de Meaux ☎ 60684245
tx 691779
⇨♠74 Lift
Credit Cards ①③

At **DAMMARIE-LES-LYS**(5km SW)

★★ **Campanile** 346 r C-de-Gaulle
☎ 64375151 tx 691621
⇨♠50 P50
Credit Card ③

France

At **VERT-ST-DENIS**(NW on N6)

★★ **Balladins** av du Bois Vert ☎ 64416666
⇨♠38
Credit Cards ①②③

MENDE
Lozère

★★ **Lion d'Or**(MAP/BW) 12 bd Britexte
☎ 66491666 tx 480302
Mar-Nov Closed :Rest closed Sun
⇨♠40 P70 Lift ⇨ Mountain

★★ **Paris** 2 bd du Soubeyran (n.rest)
☎ 66650003
25 Mar-15 Nov
rm45 🅿 P15 Lift Mountain

MENTON
Alpes-Maritimes

★★★ **Aiglon** 7 av de la Madone (n.rest)
☎ 93575555
20 Dec-4 Nov
rm32(⇨♠26) P20 Lift (⇨ Sea Mountain
Credit Cards ①②③⑤

★★★ **Europ** 35 av de Verdun (n.rest)
☎ 93355992 tx 470673
⇨♠33 🅿 P Lift
Credit Cards ①②③⑤

★★★ **Méditerranée** 5 r de la République
☎ 93282525 tx 461361
⇨♠90 🅿 P40 Lift
Credit Cards ①②③⑤

★★★ **Napoléon Pn** 29 Porte de France
☎ 93358950 tx 470312
Dec-Oct
⇨♠40 P Lift 🖼 ⇨ Sea Mountain
Credit Cards ①②③⑤

★★★ **Parc** 11 av de Verdun ☎ 93576666
tx 470673
20 Dec-Sep
⇨♠72 P30 Lift (
Credit Cards ①③

★★★ **Princess & Richmond** 617 prom du Soleil (n.rest) ☎ 93358020
19 Dec-4 Nov
⇨♠45 🅿 Lift (Sea
Credit Cards ①②③⑤

★★ **El Paradiso** (Inter) 71 Porte de France
☎ 93357402
Jan-Oct
⇨♠42 P Lift (

★★ **Floréal Pn** cours de Centenaire (n.rest)
☎ 93357581
10 Dec-10 Oct
rm58(⇨♠36) P14 Lift

★★ **Londres** 15 av Carnot ☎ 93357462
20 Dec-Oct Closed :Rest closed Wed
rm26(⇨♠20) 🅿 Lift
Credit Cards ①③

★★ **Prince de Galles** 4 av Gl-de-Gaulle
(n.rest) ☎ 93282121 tx 462540
⇨♠68 P10 Lift (Sea
Credit Cards ①②③⑤

★★ **Rives d'Azur** prom Ml-Joffre
☎ 93576760

20 Dec-Sep
⇨♠36 P6 Lift (Sea Mountain
Credit Card ①

🞄 **Idéal** 1 av Riviera ☎ 93357920 For

MÉRÉVILLE
Meurthe-et-Moselle

★★ **Maison Carrée** L? ☎ 83470923
tx 961052
⇨♠21 🅿 P25 ♪
Credit Cards ①②③

MÉRIGNAC See BORDEAUX

METZ
Moselle

★★★★ **Altea St-Thiébault** 29 pl St-Thiébault ☎ 87361769 tx 930417
⇨♠112 P40 Lift
Credit Cards ①②③④⑤

★★★ **Novotel Metz-Centre** Centre St-Jacques, pl des Paraîges ☎ 87745727
tx 930328
⇨♠90 🅿 P42 Lift ⇨
Credit Cards ①②③⑤

★★★ **Royal Concorde** 23 av Foch
☎ 87668111 tx 860425
rm73(⇨♠63) P7 Lift
Credit Cards ①②③④⑤

★★ **Campanile** Parc d'Activités de Queuleu, bd de la Défuse ☎ 87751311
tx 861597
⇨♠49 P49
Credit Card ③

★★ **Ibis** r Chambière, quartier du Pontiffroy ☎ 87310173 tx 930278
⇨♠79 Lift
Credit Cards ①③

★★ **Urbis** 3 bis r Vauban ☎ 87755343
tx 930281
⇨♠72 🅿 P Lift
Credit Cards ①③

★ **Lutèce** L? 11 r de Paris ☎ 87309725
15 Jan-21 Dec
rm20(⇨♠9) 🅿
Credit Cards ①②③

🞄 **Jacquot** 2 r P-Boileau ☎ 87325290
Peu Tal

At **HAUCONCOURT**(9.5km N A31)

★★★ **Novotel** (A31) ☎ 87804111
tx 860191
⇨♠132 P250 Lift ⇨
Credit Cards ①②③⑤

At **TALANGÉ**(5km N)

★★ **Climat** La Ponte, r des Allies
☎ 87721311 tx 861731
⇨♠38 P
Credit Cards ①②③

At **WOIPPY**(5km NW)

★★★ **Mercure** r du Port-Gambetta
☎ 87325279 tx 860891
⇨♠83 P120 Lift
Credit Cards ①②③⑤

MEULAN
Yvelines

★★★ **Mercure** Lieu dit Ile Belle
☎ 34746363 tx 695295
⇨♠69 Lift ♪ 🖼 ⇨
Credit Cards ①②③⑤

France

MEYLAN See **GRENOBLE**

MEYRUEIS
Lozère
★★★ **Château d'Ayres** (1.5km E via D57)
☎ 66456010
15 Apr-15 Oct
⇨♦24 P24 ℓ ℛ ∪ Mountain
Credit Cards ①②③⑤

★★ **Renaissance** (Inter) **Pn** ☎ 66456019
20 Mar-15 Nov
⇨♦20 Mountain
Credit Cards ①②③⑤

MÉZIÈRE-SUR-ISSOIRE
Haute-Vienne
✉ **A Boos** rte de Bellac ☎ 55683028 **P**
For

MIGENNES
Yonne
★★ **Gare et l'Escale** ☎ 86802099
rm12(⇨♦7) ☎ P8
Credit Cards ①②③⑤

★★ **Paris** ⊾ 57 av J-Jaurès ☎ 86802322
17 Jan-22 Jul & 22 Aug-Dec
⇨♦9 P6
Credit Cards ①③

MILLAU
Aveyron
★★★ **International** 1 pl de la Tine
☎ 65602066 tx 520629
Closed : Rest closed Sun evening & Mon (winter)
⇨♦110 ☎ P55 Lift ℓ Mountain
Credit Cards ①②③⑤

★★ **Moderne** 11 av J-Jaurès ☎ 65605923
tx 520629
Apr-Oct
☎ P55 Lift ℓ Mountain
Credit Cards ①②③⑤

★ **Causses** ⊾ 56 av J-Jaurès ☎ 65600319
Closed : Rest closed Sat & Sun evening (winter)
rm22(⇨♦14) ☎ P4

★ **Paris & Poste** 10 av A-Merle
☎ 65600052
3 Jan-15 Nov
rm22(⇨♦15) P14 Lift
Credit Cards ③⑤

✉ **G Alric** rte de Montpellier
☎ 65604144 **P** For

✉ **J Pineau** 161 av de Cates ☎ 65600855
M/C **P** All makes

✉ **H Pujol** 85 av J-Jaurès ☎ 65600921
Peu Tal

MILLES, LES See **AIX-EN-PROVENCE**

MILLY
Indre-et-Loire
★ **Château de Milly** rte de Richelieu et Châtellerault ☎ 47956456
Mar-Jan Closed : Rest closed Thu (out of season)
rm15(⇨♦13) ☎ P ∪
Credit Cards ①②③⑤

MIMIZAN
Landes
✉ **J Poisson** 48 av de Bordeaux
☎ 58090873 Ren

At **MIMIZAN-PLAGE**
★★ **Côte d'Argent Pn** 4 av M-Martin
☎ 58091522
20 May-Sep
⇨♦40 A33rm P70 Lift ℓ Sea
Credit Cards ①②③⑤

MIMIZAN-PLAGE See **MIMIZAN**
MIRAIL, LE See **TOULOUSE**

MIRAMBEAU
Charente-Maritime
★ **Union** r Principale ☎ 46496164
rm9(♦1) A2rm ☎ P10
Credit Cards ①③

✉ **Gauvin** 1 av C-Jourdain ☎ 46496185 **P**
For

MIREPOIX
Ariège
★ **Commerce** ⊾ **Pn** cours du Dr-Chabaud
☎ 61681029
Feb-Dec
rm31 A10rm ☎ P7
Credit Cards ①③⑤

MISSILLAC
Loire-Atlantique
★★★ **Golf de la Bretesche** (1km W via D2)
☎ 40883005
Mar-Jan
⇨♦27 ℛ ⇨ ⊧ Lake
Credit Cards ①③

MODANE
Savoie

At **FOURNEAUX**(3km SW)
★★ **Tuilerie** (Inter) **Pn** ☎ 55662809
May-Oct
⇨♦24
Credit Cards ①②③⑤

✉ **G Durieux** 36 av de la Liberté
☎ 79050774 Fia Toy

MOISSAC
Tarn-et-Garonne
★★★ **Moulin** (MAP) 1 pl du Moulin
☎ 63040355 tx 521615
⇨♦57 P50 Lift ℓ Sea
Credit Cards ①②③

★★ **Pont Napoléon DPn** 2 allée Montebello
☎ 63040155
5 Feb-5 Jun & 25 Jun-5 Jan
rm14(⇨♦11) ☎ Lake
Credit Cards ①③

MOLAY-LITTRY, LE
Calvados
★★★ **Château de Molay** (MAP/BW) rte d'Isigny ☎ 31229082 tx 171912
Mar-Nov
⇨♦40 A8rm P60 Lift ℓ ℛ ⇨ Beach
Credit Cards ①②③④⑤

MONCHEL-SUR-CANCHE See **FRÉVENT**
MONDEVILLE See **CAEN**
MONTAGNY-LES-BEAUNE See **BEAUNE**

MONTARGIS
Loiret
★ **Tour d'Auvergne** ⊾ 20 r J-Jaurès
☎ 38850116
Mar-Jan Closed : Rest closed Fri
rm14(⇨♦12) ☎ P10
Credit Cards ①②③④⑤

At **AMILLY**(5km S)
★★ **Climat** av d'Antibes ☎ 38982021
⇨♦26 P40
Credit Cards ①②③⑤

MONTAUBAN
Tarn-et-Garonne
★★ **Midi** ⊾ (Inter) 12 r Notre-Dame
☎ 63631723 tx 631705
rm62(⇨♦59) A14rm ☎ P60 Lift ℓ
Credit Cards ①②③④⑤

★★ **Orsay** (FAH) Face Gare ☎ 63660666
tx 520362
Closed : Rest closed Sun
⇨♦20 ☎ P Lift
Credit Cards ①②③⑤

✉ **Denayrolles** 878 av J-Moulin
☎ 63036202 M/C **P** AR Hon

At **MONTBETON**(3km W)
★★★ **Coulandrières Pn** rte Castelsarrasin
☎ 63674747 tx 520200
⇨♦21 P60 ℓ ⇨
Credit Cards ①②③⑤

MONTAUBAN-DE-BRETAGNE
Ille-et-Vilaine

At **LANDUJAN**(7km NE)
★★★ **Château de Lauville** ☎ 99072114
Mar-Jan
⇨♦6 P10 ⇨ ∪
Credit Cards ①③

MONTBARD
Côte-D'or
★★ **Gare** 10 r Ml-Foch, pl de la Gare
(n.rest) ☎ 80920212
rm20(⇨♦16) ☎ P12
Credit Cards ①③

★ **Ecu** ⊾ (FAH) 7 r A-Carré ☎ 80921166
tx 351102
rm25(⇨♦24) ☎ P8
Credit Cards ①②③⑤

MONTBAZON
Indre-et-Loire
★★★★★ **Château d'Artigny** (Relais et Châteaux) (2km SW via D17) ☎ 47262424
tx 750900
11 Jan-Nov
⇨♦53 A22rm P Lift ℛ ⇨ ⊧
Credit Card ③

★★★ **Tortinière** (1.5km N) ☎ 47260019
tx 752186
Mar-15 Nov Closed : Rest closed Tue/Wed midday (Mar/15 Oct-15 Nov)
⇨♦21 A10rm P50 ℛ ⇨ Lake
Credit Cards ①③

At **MONTS**(8km W)
★ **Sporting** ⊾ ☎ 47267015
8 Mar-15 Sep & Oct-15 Feb
rm13(⇨♦4) A2rm P25
Credit Cards ①⑤

France

MONTBÉLIARD
Doubs

★★ **Ibis** r J-Foillet, ZAC du Pied d'Egouttes
☎ 81902158 tx 361555
⇨♠42 Lift
Credit Cards [1] [3]

At **BAVANS**(2.5km SW)
🛏 **Esso** 85 Grande rue ☎ 81962659 **P** Peu

MONTBETON See **MONTAUBAN**

MONTCABRIER See **PUY-L'ÉVÊQUE**

MONTCHANIN See **CREUSOT, LE**

MONT-DE-MARSAN
Landes

★★★ **Richelieu** 3 r Wlerick ☎ 58061020 tx 550238
Closed :Rest closed winter & Sat
rm70(⇨♠50) 🍴 Lift 《
Credit Cards [1] [2] [3] [5]

🛏 **Continental** 839 av de Ml-Foch
☎ 58063232 AR

🛏 **Hiroire Automobiles** bd d'Alingsas
☎ 58753662 **P** For

MONT-DORE, LE
Puy-de-Dôme

★★★ **Carlina** Les Pradets ☎ 7365042
⇨♠50 🍴 P17 Lift 《 Mountain
Credit Cards [1] [2] [3] [4] [5]

At **PIED-DU-SANCY**(4km S on N683)
★★ **Puy-Ferrand** L̲ ☎ 73651899 tx 990332
20 Dec-Sep
⇨♠42 P70 Lift Mountain
Credit Cards [1] [2] [3] [5]

MONTE-CARLO BEACH See **MONTE CARLO**

MONTÉLIMAR
Drôme

★★★ **Relais de l'Empereur** pl Marx-Dormoy ☎ 75012900 tx 345537
22 Dec-11 Nov
rm40(⇨♠26) 🍴 P25 《
Credit Cards [1] [2] [3] [5]

★★ **Climat** 8 bd du Pêcher ☎ 75530770
⇨♠44 P Lift

★★ **Sphinx** 19 bd Desmarais (n.rest)
☎ 75018664
⇨♠25 🍴 P20
Credit Cards [1] [2] [3]

★ **Beausoleil** L̲ 14 bd Pêcher, pl d'Armes (n.rest) ☎ 75011980
rm16(⇨♠14) P14
Credit Cards [1] [3]

At **SAUZET**(9km NE on D6)
🛏 **M Chaix** ☎ 75467170 **P** Ren

MONTESSON
Yvelines

★★ **Campanile** 9 r du Chant des Oiseaux
☎ 30716334 tx 698906
⇨♠42 P42
Credit Card [3]

MONTFAVET See **AVIGNON**

MONTIGNAC
Dordogne

★★★ **Château de Puy Robert Pn**
☎ 53519213 tx 330616
11 May-15 Oct
⇨♠38 P30 Lift 《 🍴 Mountain
Credit Cards [1] [2] [3] [5]

★ **Soleil d'Or** 16 r IV Septembre
☎ 53518022
⇨♠38 P30 🍴
Credit Cards [1] [2]

MONTIGNY-LA-RESLE
Yonne

★★ **Soleil d'Or** L̲ **Pn** ☎ 86418121
1 Dec-30 Oct Closed :Rest closed Mon
⇨♠11 A4rm P15 ♪
Credit Cards [1] [2] [3] [5]

MONTIGNY-LE-ROI
Haute-Marne

★★ **Moderne** (Inter) av de Neufchâteau
☎ 25903018 tx 830349
rm13 🍴 P25 Mountain
Credit Cards [1] [3]

🛏 **Flagez** N 74 ☎ 25903034 M/C Peu Tal Fia

MONTIVILLIERS See **HAVRE, LE**

MONTLUCON
Allier

★★★ **Terminus** 47 av M-Dormoy (n.rest)
☎ 70052893
rm43 🍴 Lift
Credit Cards [1] [2] [5]

★★ **Château St-Jean** Parc St-Jean
☎ 70050465
rm8(⇨♠5) 🍴 P

🛏 **Bouronnais** 10 r P-Semard
☎ 70053437 **P** Peu Tal

MONTMERLE-SUR-SAÔNE
Ain

★★ **Rivage** L̲ 12 r du Pont ☎ 74693392
Closed :Rest closed Mon
⇨♠21 A8rm 🍴 P30
Credit Cards [1] [2] [3]

MONTMIRAIL
Marne

★ **Vert Galant** 2 pl Vert-Galant ☎ 26812017
rm12(♠3) **P**6
Credit Cards [1] [3]

MONTMORENCY
Val-d'Oise

★★ **Boscotel Montmorency** 42 rte de Domont ☎ 34170002 tx 699886
⇨♠42 P50 Lift
Credit Cards [1] [3] [4]

MONTMORILLON
Vienne

★★ **France Mercier Pn** 2 bd de Strasbourg
☎ 49910051
10 Feb-31 Dec Closed :Rest closed Sun Lunch & Mon
rm29(⇨♠19)
Credit Cards [1] [2] [3] [4]

MONTMORT
Marne

★★ **Place** L̲ 3 pl Berthelot ☎ 26591038
rm30(⇨♠24) A5rm P15
Credit Cards [1] [3]

MONTOIRE-SUR-LE-LOIR
Loire-et-Cher

★★ **Cheval Rouge** L̲ **Pn** pl M1-Foch
☎ 54850705
Mar-Jan Closed :Rest closed Tue eve & Wed
rm17(⇨♠12) 🍴 P10
Credit Cards [1] [2] [3]

MONTPELLIER
Hérault

★★★★ **Altea Antigone** 218 r de Bastion-Ventadour, quartier le Polygone
☎ 67646566 tx 480362
Closed :Rest closed Sat lunchtime & Sun
⇨♠116 🍴 P10 Lift
Credit Cards [1] [2] [3] [5]

★★★★ **Métropole** (MAP/BW) 3 r C-René
☎ 67581122 tx 480410
rm92(⇨♠90) 🍴 Lift 《
Credit Cards [1] [2] [3] [5]

★★★★ **Sofitel** Le Triangle (n.rest)
☎ 67540404 tx 480140
⇨♠98 Lift
Credit Cards [1] [2] [3] [5]

★★★ **Mercure Montpellier Est** 662 av de Pompignane ☎ 67655024 tx 480656
⇨♠122 P Lift 🍴

★★★ **Novotel** 125 bis av de Palavas
☎ 67640404 tx 490433
⇨♠97 P100 Lift 🍴
Credit Cards [1] [2] [3] [5]

★★ **Campanile** Lieudit "Terre du Mas de Sorrés", av du Mas-d'Argelliers
☎ 67587980 tx 485427
⇨♠50 P50
Credit Card [3]

★★ **Hotel Campanile** ZAC du Millénaire, r du Mas-de-Carbonnier ☎ 67648585 tx 485659
⇨♠84 P
Credit Card [3]

★★ **Climat** r de Caducée ☎ 67524333 tx 85693
⇨♠42 P80
Credit Cards [1] [3] [5]

★★ **Ibis** rte de Palavas ☎ 67588230 tx 480578
⇨♠165 Lift
Credit Cards [1] [3]

🛏 **Imbert** rte de Sète, St Jean de Vedars
☎ 67424622 **P** Ren

MONTREUIL See **DREUX**

MONTREUIL
Pas-de-Calais

★★★ **Château de Montreuil** (Relais et Châteaux) 4 chaussée des Capucins
☎ 21815304 tx 135205
Feb – Mid Dec Closed :Rest closed Thu Lunch
⇨♠14 A3rm 🍴 P8 《
Credit Cards [1] [3] [4]

★ **Central Pn** 7-9 r du Change ☎ 21861604
24 Jan-23 Dec →

rm11(⇨♙5) A3rm 🅿
Credit Cards 1 2 3

MONTREUIL-BELLAY
Maine-et-Loire

★ **Splendid** L£ **Pn** r Dr-Gaudrez
☎ 41523021
Closed :Rest closed 3-4 Jan
rm20(⇨19) A20rm P40 ⟶
Credit Cards 1 3

MONTRICHARD
Loir-et-Cher

★★ **Bellevue** L£ (Inter) quai du Cher
☎ 54320617 tx 751673
⇨♙29 P Lift ₽ 🖃 ⟶
Credit Cards 1 2 3 5

★★ **Tête-Noire Pn** rte de Tours
☎ 54320555
7 Feb-2 Jan Closed :Rest closed Fri 15 Oct-15 Mar
rm38(⇨♙31) A9rm P10
Credit Cards 1 3

At CHISSAY-EN-TOURAINE(6km W)

★★★ **Château Menaudière Pn** rte Amboise ☎ 54320244 tx 751246
Mid Mar-Beg Dec
⇨♙25 A8rm P30 ₽
Credit Cards 1 2 3 5

MONTROUGE See **PARIS**

MONTS See **MONTBAZON**

MONT-ST-AIGNAN See **ROUEN**

MONTSALVY
Cantal

★★ **Nord** L£ (Inter) pl du Barry
☎ 71492003
1 Apr-31 Dec
rm26(⇨♙22) P15
Credit Cards 1 2 3 4 5

MONTSOULT
Val d'Oise

★★★ **Novotel Château de Maffiers**
☎ 34739305 tx 695701
⇨♙80 P200 ₽ ⟶
Credit Cards 1 2 3 5

MONT-ST-MICHEL, LE
Manche

★★ **Digue** La Digue (2km S) ☎ 33601402 tx 170157
⇨♙35 P50 ⟶ Sea
Credit Cards 1 2 3 5

★★ **K** L£ La Digue (2km S on D976)
☎ 33601418 tx 170537
Etr-Nov
⇨♙60
Credit Card 2

★★ **Mère Poulard** L£ (Inter) ☎ 33601401 tx 170197
⇨♙27 A14rm Sea
Credit Cards 1 2 3 5

MORANGIS See **PARIS AIRPORTS** under **ORLY AIRPORT**

MOREZ
Jura

★★ **Central Modern** 106 r de La République ☎ 84330307
Closed 15 Jul-15 Aug

France

rm47(⇨♙18) A24rm 🅿 P Mountain
Credit Cards 1 3

MORLAIX
Finistère

★★★ **Grand Hotel d'Europe** (FAH) 1 r d'Aiguillon ☎ 98621199 tx 940696
15 Jan-20 Dec
rm68(⇨55) Lift
Credit Cards 2 3 4 5

★ **Fontaine** rte de Lannion (n.rest)
☎ 98620955
20 Mar-12 Feb
⇨♙35 P50
Credit Cards 1 3

MORTAGNE-AU-PERCHE
Orne

★ **Tribunal** L£ 4 pl du Palais ☎ 33250477 tx 170841
rm19(⇨♙13) A9rm 🅿 P30
Credit Cards 1 3

MORTAGNE-SUR-SÈVRE
Vendée

★★★ **France** L£ (FAH) 4 pl du Dr-Pichat
☎ 51650337 tx 711403
15 Aug-31 Jul
⇨♙25 P40 Lift ₽ 🖃
Credit Cards 1 2 3 5

MORTAIN
Manche

★ **Cascades Pn** 16 r du Bassin
☎ 33590003
3 Jan-20 Dec Closed :Rest closed Sun dinner & Mon
rm13(⇨♙7)
Credit Cards 1 2 3

MORZINE
Haute-Savoie

★★★ **Carlina Pn** av J-Plane ☎ 50790103 tx 365596
15 Dec-15 Apr & Jul-Aug
⇨♙22 🅿 P10 Mountain
Credit Cards 1 2 3 5

★★★ **Dahu** ☎ 50791112 tx 309514
15 Jun-15 Sep & 15 Dec-15 Apr
⇨♙26 🅿 P20 Lift ⟶ Mountain
Credit Card 3

MOULINS
Allier

★★★ **Paris** (Relais et Châteaux) 21 r de Paris ☎ 70440058 tx 394853
⇨♙27 🅿 P20 Lift ₵
Credit Cards 1 2 3 4 5

★★ **Ibis** Angle de la rte de Lyon(N7)/bd, Primaire ☎ 70467112 tx 090638
⇨♙43 Lift
Credit Cards 1 3

★★ **Moderne** (Inter) 9 pl J-Moulin
☎ 70440506 tx 392968
⇨♙44 🅿 P30 Lift ₵
Credit Cards 1 3

★★ **Parc** L£ 31 av Gl-Leclerc ☎ 70441225

⇨♙28 A5rm 🅿 P25 ₵
Credit Card 3

At COULANDON(7km W)

★★ **Chalet** ☎ 70445008
1 Feb-31 Oct Closed :Rest closed lunch time
⇨♙25 A16rm P30
Credit Cards 1 2 3 5

MOUSSY See **ÉPERNAY**

MOUTHIER-HAUTE-PIERRE
Doubs

★★ **Cascade** L£ DPn
1 Feb-1 Dec
⇨♙23 🅿 P19 Mountain
Credit Cards 1 3

MOÛTIERS
Savoie

★★ **Ibis** Colline de Champoulet
☎ 79242711 tx 980611
⇨♙62 Lift
Credit Cards 1 3

MULHOUSE
Haut-Rhin

★★★★ **Altea de la Tour** 4 pl Gl-de-Gaulle
☎ 89460123 tx 881807
⇨♙96 P Lift
Credit Cards 1 2 3 4 5

★★ **Balladins** Z Industrielle, Ile Napoléon Ouest ☎ 05355575 tx 649394
rm38 P38
Credit Cards 1 2 3 4 5

At RIXHEIM

🚗 **Ott et Wetzel** rte de Mulhouse 37, Rixheim ☎ 89440137 P AR DJ LR

At SAUSHEIM(6km NE D422)

★★★★ **Sofitel** R N 422A ☎ 89447575 tx 881311
⇨♙100 Lift ₽ ⟶
Credit Cards 1 2 3 5

★★★ **Mercure** Ile Napoléon ☎ 89618787 tx 881757
⇨♙97 P150 Lift ₽ ⟶
Credit Cards 1 2 3 5

★★★ **Novotel** r de l'Ile Napoléon
☎ 89618484 tx 881673
⇨♙77 P100 ₽ ⟶ ▶
Credit Cards 1 2 3 5

★★ **Ibis** rte de Sausheim Est, Ille Napoléon
☎ 89618383 tx 881970
⇨♙76 Lift
Credit Cards 1 3

At WITTENHEIM(6km NW)

★★ **Climat** r des Milleportuis ☎ 89535331 tx 881775
⇨♙43 P ⟶ Mountain
Credit Cards 1 2 3

MUREAUX, LES
Yvelines

★★ **Climat** ZAC du Grand Ouest CD 43, r des Pleiades ☎ 24747250 tx 399958
⇨♙42 P50
Credit Cards 1 3

MURET
Haute-Garonne

🚗 **Ste Cie Automobile** L'Escouplette (N117) ☎ 61510330 P For

84

MUS
Gard
★★ **Auberge de la Paillère** ☎ 66351333
Closed :Rest closed Sun dinner & Mon
⇌8 P8
Credit Cards 1 2 3 5

MUY, LE
Var
🍴 **St-Roch** ☎ 94451067 P CIT

NAJAC
Aveyron
★★ **Belle Rive** LE DPn ☎ 65297390
Apr-Oct
rm40(⇌38) A10rm 🛏 P30 ⇋ Mountain
Credit Cards 2 3 5
★★ **Oustal del Barry** LE DPn pl du Bourg
☎ 65297432
1 Apr-1 Nov
rm21(⇌17) 🛏 P15 Lift ♀ Mountain
Credit Cards 1 3

NAMPONT-ST-MARTIN
Somme
★★ **Peupleraie** (N1) ☎ 22299811
Closed 1-15 Jan
⇌40 🛏 P

NANCY
Meurthe-et-Moselle
★★★★ **Grand** (Relais et Châteaux) 2 pl Stanislas ☎ 83350301 tx 960367
⇌54 Lift ℂ
Credit Cards 1 2 3 5
★★★ **Agora** 6 r Piroux ☎ 83355805 tx 960034
⇌78 Lift
Credit Cards 1 2 3 5
★★★ **Altea Thiers** 11 r R-Poincaré, pl Thiers ☎ 83356101 tx 960034
⇌112 P40 Lift
Credit Cards 1 2 3 5
★★ **Albert 1er/Astoria** (Inter) 3 r Armée-Patton (n.rest) ☎ 83403124 tx 850895
rm123(⇌103) P Lift
Credit Cards 1 2 3 4 5
★★ **Central** 6 r R-Poincaré (n.rest)
☎ 83322124 tx 850895
rm68(⇌60) Lift
Credit Cards 1 3 4
★ **Américain** 3 pl A-Maginot (n.rest)
☎ 83322853 tx 961052
rm51 P Lift ℂ
Credit Cards 1 2 3 4 5
★ **Poincaré** 81 r R-Poincaré (n.rest)
☎ 83402599
rm25(⇌7)
Credit Cards 1 3
🍴 **H Gras** 11 r A Lebrun ☎ 83365175 For

At **CHAUVIGNY**(4km SW)
★★ **Balladins** Z I les Clairs Chênes, D974 ☎ 83576363
⇌28 P20
Credit Card 3

At **HOUDEMONT**(6km S)
★★★ **Novotel Nancy Sud** rte d'Épinal, N57 ☎ 83561025 tx 961184
⇌86 P150 ⇋
Credit Cards 1 2 3 5

France

At **LAXOU**(3km SW)
★★★ **Mercure** 2 r de la Saône
☎ 83964221 tx 850036
⇌99 P Lift ⇋
★★★ **Novotel Nancy Ouest** N4
☎ 83966746 tx 850988
⇌119 P160 Lift ⇋
Credit Cards 1 2 3 5
🍴 **Nancy Laxou Automobiles** 21 av de la Résistance ☎ 83984343 M/C For

At **LUDRES**(8km S)
★★ **Climat** ZI de Ludres ☎ 83542113 tx 961043
⇌38 P40
Credit Cards 1 2 3

At **VANDOEUVRE-LES-NANCY**(4km S)
★★★ **Campanile** ZAC de Brabois, 1 av de la Forêt-de-Haye ☎ 83514151 tx 960604
⇌42 P42
Credit Card 3

NANS-LES-PINS
Var

At **CHÂTEAUNEUF**(3.5km N)
★★★ **Châteauneuf** (Relais et Châteaux)
☎ 94789006 tx 400747
Apr-Nov
⇌32 P50 ⇋ ♟ Mountain
Credit Cards 1 2 3 5

NANTES
Loire-Atlantique
★★★★ **Pullman Beaulieu** 3 r du Dr-Zamenhof ☎ 40471058
⇌150 🛏 P70 Lift
Credit Cards 1 2 3 5
★★★★ **Sofitel** r A-Millerand ☎ 40476103
⇌100 P150 Lift ♀ ⇋ Sea
Credit Cards 1 2 3 5
★★★ **Central** (MAP) 4 r du Couëdic
☎ 40200935 tx 700666
⇌120 Lift ℂ
Credit Cards 1 2 3 5
★★★ **Mercure** RN165 Direction Vannes-La-Baule ☎ 40852317 tx 711823
⇌54 P ♀ ⇋
★★ **Astoria** 11 r Richebourg (n.rest)
☎ 40743990
⇌45 🛏 P25 Lift ℂ
Credit Card 1 3
★★ **Bourgogne** 9 allée du Cdt-Charcot (n.rest) ☎ 40740334 tx 701405
Closed 10 days Xmas
⇌43 Lift ℂ
Credit Cards 1 2 3 5
★★ **Graslin** (FAH) 1 r Piron (off pl Graslin) (n.rest) ☎ 40697291 tx 701619
⇌47 Lift
Credit Cards 1 2 3
★ **Ibis** 3 allée Baco ☎ 40202120 tx 701382
⇌104 🛏 P30 Lift Sea
Credit Card 1 3

🍴 **Dao** 14 r G-Clemenceau ☎ 40746666 P All makes

At **CARQUEFOU**(4km NE)
★★★ **Altea Carquefou** Le Petit Bel Air, rte de Paris (N23 exit A11) ☎ 40302924 tx 710962
⇌79 P Lift ℂ ⇋
★★★ **Novotel Nantes Carquefou** allée des Sapins ☎ 40526464 tx 711175
⇌98 P250 ⇋
Credit Cards 1 2 3 5
★★ **Balladins** CD 337, Petit Bel Air
☎ 05355575 tx 649394
rm38 P38
Credit Cards 1 2 3 4 5
★★ **Campanile** bd des Pastureaux
☎ 40300182 tx 701393
⇌77 P77
Credit Card 3
★★ **Climat** CD337, Petit Bel Air
☎ 40303336
⇌42 P40
Credit Cards 1 3

At **ST-HERBLAIN**(8km W)
★★ **Balladins** rte de St-Étienne-de-Montluc ☎ 40920410 tx 649394
⇌38 P38
Credit Cards 1 2 3
★★ **Campanile** rte de St-Étienne-de-Montluc ☎ 40921533 tx 711063
⇌50 P50
Credit Card 3

NANTIAT See **CROUZILLE, LA**

NANTUA
Ain
★★★ **France** DPn 44 r Dr-Mercier
☎ 74750055
20 Dec-Oct
⇌19 🛏 P Mountain
Credit Cards 1 2 3

NAPOULE-PLAGE, LA
Alpes-Maritimes
★★★★ **Ermitage du Riou** (MAP/BW) bd de Mer ☎ 93499556 tx 470072
⇌42 A5rm 🛏 P30 Lift ℂ ⇋ Sea Mountain
Credit Cards 1 2 3 5

NARBONNE
Aude
★★★ **Midi** LE av de Toulouse ☎ 68410462 tx 500401
3 Jan-Nov
rm47(⇌36) P30 Lift ℂ
Credit Cards 1 2 3 5
★★★ **Novotel Narbonne Sud** quartier Plaisance, rte d'Espagne ☎ 68415952 tx 500480
⇌96 P100 Lift ⇋
Credit Cards 1 2 3 5
★★ **Climat** ZI de Plaisance, chemin de Tuileries ☎ 68410490 tx 505085
⇌40 P60
Credit Cards 1 2 3
★★ **Ibis** Quartier Plaisance ☎ 68411441 tx 500480
⇌44 🛏 P Lift
Credit Cards 1 3

★★ *Languedoc* (MAP/BW) 22 bd Gambetta ☎ 68651474 tx 605167
rm45(⇨🛏32) Lift (
Credit Cards [1][2][3][5]

★★ *Résidence* 6 r Premier-Mai (n.rest)
☎ 86321941 tx 500441
Closed 3 Jan-2 Feb
⇨🛏26 🍴 (
Credit Cards [1][3]

★ *Lion D'Or* L 39 av P-Sémard
☎ 68320692
Closed :Rest Sun (in low season)
⇨🛏27 🍴 P6
Credit Cards [1][2][3][5]

🛏 G *Deirieu* 43 r P-L-Courier
☎ 68320838 M/C Cit

🛏 *Fraisse* 33 av de Toulouse
☎ 68422915 AR

🛏 *Jansana* r d'Aoste Razimbaud
☎ 68321869 P Peu Tal

🛏 *Lopez* 180 av de Bordeaux
☎ 68421631 P All makes

At **NARBONNE-PLAGE**(1.5km E)
★★ *Caravelle* L bd du Front-de-Mer
☎ 68498038
Etr-Oct
⇨🛏24 P25 Sea
Credit Cards [1][3]

At **ORNAISONS**(14km W)
★★★ *Relais Val d'Orbieu* ☎ 68271072
⇨🛏15 A6rm P25 ♪ ⚐ ⤴ Mountain
Credit Cards [1][2][3][4][5]

NARBONNE-PLAGE See **NARBONNE**

NAVARRENX
Pyrénées-Atlantiques
★★ *Commerce* (Inter) r Principale
☎ 59665016
Closed Jan:Rest closed Mon
⇨🛏29 A12rm 🍴 P30 Lift
Credit Cards [1][3]

NEMOURS
Seine-et-Marne
★★★ *Altea Darvault* L'Aire-de-Service (A6) (2Km SE on A6) (n.rest) ☎ 64281032 tx 690243
⇨🛏102 P
Credit Cards [1][2][3][5]

★★★ *Ecu de France Pn* 3 r de Paris
☎ 64281154
rm28(⇨🛏22) 🍴 P10
Credit Cards [1][3]

★★ *Ibis* r des Moires, ZI de Nemours
☎ 64288800 tx 600212
⇨🛏42 Lift
Credit Cards [1][3]

★ *Roches* av d'Ormesson, St-Pierre
☎ 64280143
⇨🛏12 A6rm 🍴 P8
Credit Cards [1][2][3][5]

★ *St-Pierre* av Carnot 12 (n.rest)
☎ 64280157
15 Mar-28 Feb
rm25(⇨🛏13) 🍴 P30
Credit Cards [1][3]

NEUF-BRISACH
Haut-Rhin

France

At **VOGELGRUN**(5km E on N415)
★★ *Européan* ☎ 89725157 tx 880215
Closed Feb Rest Sun dinner & Mon
⇨🛏23 🍴 P30
Credit Cards [1][2][3][5]

NEUFCHÂTEL-EN-BRAY
Seine-Maritime
★★ *Grand Cerf Pn* 9 Grande Rue
☎ 35930002
18 Jan-18 Dec Closed :Rest closed Sun dinner & Mon
⇨🛏12 P5
Credit Cards [1][3]

🛏 *Lechopier* 31 Grande Rue, St-Pierre
☎ 35930082 M/C P Ren

NEUILLY-SUR-SEINE See **PARIS**

NEUVÉGLISE
Cantal
🛏 *Sauret* ☎ 71238090 P

NEUVILLE-LES-BEAULIEU
Ardennes
★ *Bois* L RN43 ☎ 24543255
1 Feb-15 Dec Closed :Rest closed Mon lunch
⇨🛏10 P
Credit Cards [1][2][3][5]

NEVERS
Nièvre
★★★ *Diane* (MAP/BW) 38 r du Midi
☎ 86572810 tx 801021
4 Jan-20 Dec
⇨🛏30 🍴 Lift (
Credit Cards [1][2][3][4][5]

★★★ *Loire* quai Medine ☎ 86615092 tx 801112
Closed :Rest closed 10 Dec-15 Jan
⇨🛏60 P Lift
★★ *Climat* 25 bd V-Hugo ☎ 86214288 tx 800579
⇨🛏53 🍴 P50 Lift
Credit Cards [1][2][3]

★★ *Folie* L rte des Saulaies ☎ 86570531
rm39(⇨🛏29) P100 ⤴
Credit Cards [1][3]

★★ *Ibis* RN7 r du Plateau de la Bonne Dame ☎ 86375600 tx 800221
⇨🛏53 P60
Credit Cards [1][3]

★★ *Molière* L 25 r Molière (n.rest)
☎ 86572996
15 Jan-15 Dec
⇨🛏18 P12
Credit Cards [1][2]

★ *Morvan* L 28 r Mouësse ☎ 86611416
Closed 3 wks in Jan & Jul
rm11(🛏7) P12

★ *Ste-Marie* 25 r Petit-Mouësse
☎ 86611002
Closed :Rest closed Mon
rm17(⇨🛏8) A9rm 🍴 P35
Credit Card [1]

At **VARENNES-VAUZELLES**(5km N)
★★ *Etape Coqvert* ☎ 86380972 tx 801059
⇨🛏42 P30 ♪
Credit Cards [1][3][4]

NICE
Alpes-Maritimes See plan
★★★★★ *Négresco* (SRS) 37 prom des Anglais ☎ 93883951 tx 460040 Plan **1**
⇨🛏150 🍴 P30 Lift (Beach Sea
Credit Cards [1][2][3][4][5]

★★★★ *Atlantic* 12 bd V-Hugo
☎ 93884015 tx 460840 Plan **2**
⇨🛏123 P14 Lift
Credit Cards [1][2][3][5]

★★★★ *Holiday Inn* 179 bd R-Cassin
☎ 93839192 tx 970202 Plan **3**
⇨🛏151 🍴 P150 Lift ⤴ Sea
Credit Cards [1][2][3][4][5]

★★★★ *Pullman Nice* 28 av Notre-Dame (n.rest) ☎ 93803024 tx 470662 Plan **4**
⇨🛏201 P Lift (⤴ Mountain
Credit Cards [1][2][3][5]

★★★★ *Sofitel Splendid* 50 bd V-Hugo
☎ 93886954 tx 460938 Plan **5**
⇨🛏130 🍴 P28 Lift ⤴ Mountain
Credit Cards [1][2][3][4][5]

★★★★ *Westminster Concorde* 27 prom des Anglais ☎ 93882944 tx 460872 Plan **6**
⇨🛏110 Lift (Sea
Credit Cards [1][2][3][5]

★★★ *Bedford* (Inter) 45 r du Ml-Joffre
☎ 93822839 tx 970086 Plan **7**
⇨🛏50 Lift

★★★ *Brice* 44 r du Ml-Joffre ☎ 93881444 tx 470658 Plan **8**
⇨🛏60 Lift (
Credit Cards [1][3][5]

★★★ *Continental Massena* 58 r Gioffredo (n.rest) ☎ 93854925 tx 470192 Plan **9**
⇨🛏116 🍴 P14 Lift
Credit Cards [1][3][4][5]

★★★ *Gounod* 3 r Gounod (n.rest)
☎ 93882620 tx 461705 Plan **10**
⇨🛏50 🍴 P Lift (⤴
Credit Cards [1][2][3][4][5]

★★★ *Locarno* 4 av des Baumettes (n.rest)
☎ 93962800 tx 970015 Plan **11**
rm48(⇨🛏47) 🍴 P12 Lift
Credit Cards [1][2][3][5]

★★★ *Malmaison* (MAP/BW) 48 bd V-Hugo
☎ 93876256 tx 470410 Plan **12**
Closed :Rest closed Sun evening
⇨🛏46 Lift
Credit Cards [1][2][3][4][5]

★★★ *Massenet* 11 r Massenet (n.rest)
☎ 93871131 Plan **13**
⇨🛏46 🍴 P22 Lift (
Credit Cards [1][3]

★★★ *Mercure* 2 r Halevy (n.rest)
☎ 93823088 tx 970656 Plan **14**
⇨🛏124 P300 Lift Sea
Credit Cards [1][2][3][4][5]

★★★ *Napoléon* 6 r Grimaldi (n.rest)
☎ 93877007 tx 460949 Plan **15**
⇨🛏84 Lift (
Credit Cards [1][2][3][5]

★★★ *Windsor* 11 r Dalpozzo ☎ 93885935 tx 970072 Plan **17** →

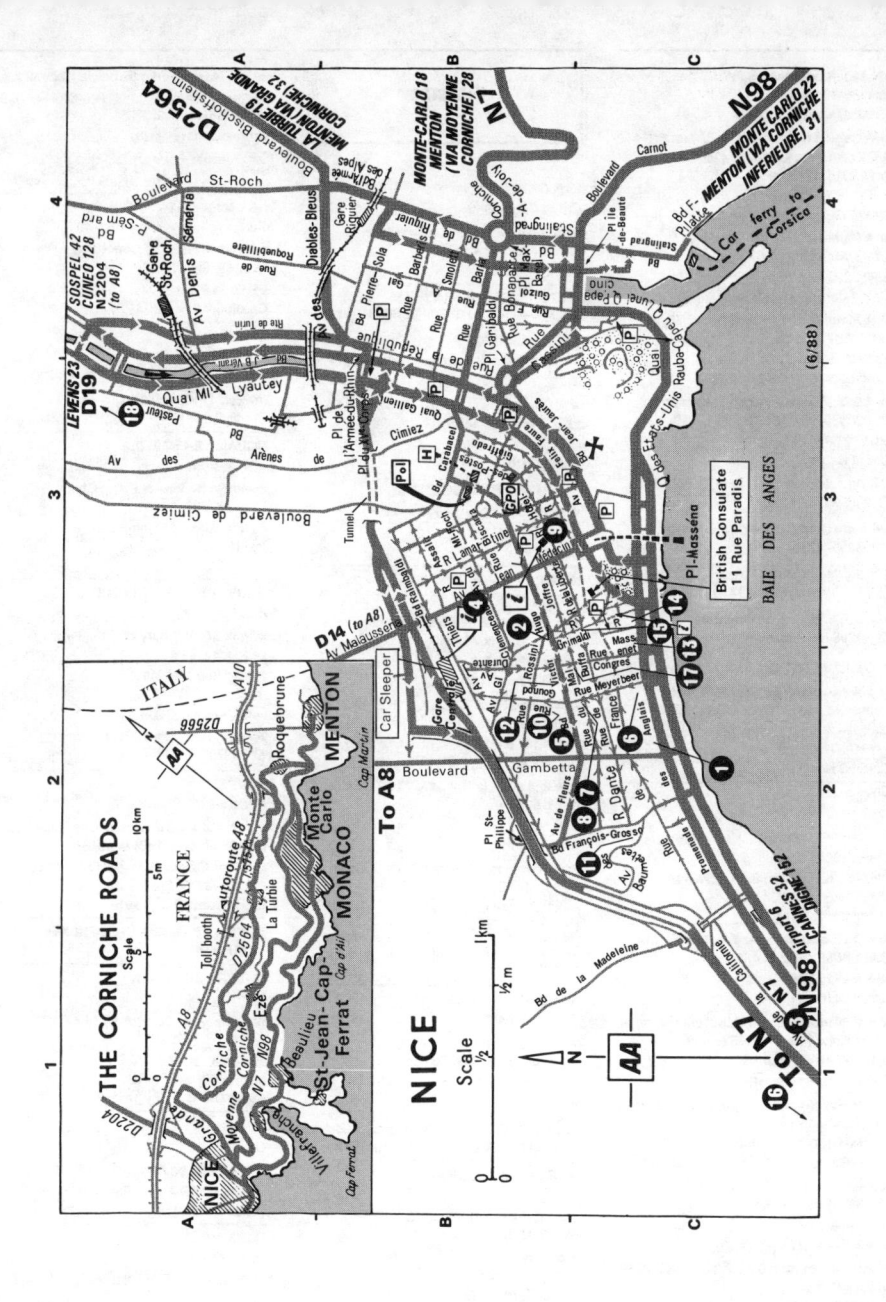

NICE

1	★★★★★ Négresco	7	★★★ Bedford	14	★★★ Mercure
2	★★★★ Atlantic	8	★★★ Brice	15	★★★ Napoléon
3	★★★★ Holiday Inn	9	★★★ Continental Massena	16	★★★ Novotel Nice Cap 3000 (At St-Laurent du Var)
4	★★★★ Pullman Nice	10	★★★ Gounod		
5	★★★★ Sofitel Splendid	11	★★★ Locarno	17	★★★ Windsor
6	★★★★ Westminster Concorde	12	★★★ Malmaison	18	★★ Fimotel
		13	★★★ Massenet		

France

Closed :Rest closed Sun
⇨♑65 P3 Lift (
Credit Cards 1 2 3 5

★★ **Campanile** quartier de l'Aéroport, 459-461 Prom des Anglais ☎ 47571111 tx 610016
⇨♑170 P Lift Sea
Credit Card 3

★★ **Climat** 232 rte de Grenoble
☎ 93718080 tx 470673
⇨♑72 🍴 P40 Lift
Credit Cards 1 2 3

★★ **Fimotel** bd Pasteur ☎ 93807676 tx 460507 Plan **18**
⇨♑82 🍴 P20 Lift ⇨
Credit Cards 1 2 3 5

★★ **Ibis** 350 bd Corniglion Molinier
☎ 93833030 tx 461285
⇨♑127 P70 Lift Sea
Credit Cards 1 2 3

🏨 **Albert-1er** 5 r Cronstadt, 06000 NICE
☎ 93883935 Vol Toy

🏨 **Cote d'Azur** 370 rte de Grenoble
☎ 93298787 **P**

🏨 **Delfinauto** 49 bd Gl Lousis-Delfino
☎ 93550452 M/C Peu Tal

🏨 **D.T.A.** 297 rte de Grenoble
☎ 93298489 **P** All makes

At **ST-LAURENT-DU-VAR**(7km SW off N7)

★★★ **Novotel Nice Cap 3000** av de Verdun ☎ 93316115 tx 470643 NICE plan **16**
⇨♑103 P100 Lift ⇨
Credit Cards 1 2 3 4 5

NÎMES
Gard

★★★★ **Imperator** quai de la Fontaine
☎ 66219030 tx 490235
Closed :Rest closed Sat lunchtime
⇨♑62 A3rm 🍴 P24 Lift (
Credit Cards 1 2 3 5

★★★ **Cheval Blanc et des Arènes** (MAP/BW) ☎ 66672003 tx 480856
⇨♑96 P120 ⇨
Credit Cards 1 2 5

★★★ **Mercure Nîmes Ouest** chemin de l'Hostellerie ☎ 66841455 tx 490746
⇨♑100 P100 Lift 🎱 ⇨
Credit Cards 1 2 3 4 5

★★★ **Novotel Nîmes Ouest** 124 chemin de l'Hostellerie ☎ 66846020 tx 480675
⇨♑96 P120 ⇨
Credit Cards 1 2 3 5

★★ **Balladins** ZAC Ville Active
☎ 05355575 tx 649394
rm38 P38
Credit Cards 1 2 3 4 5

★★ **Carrière** (Inter) 6 r Grizot ☎ 66672489 tx 490580
rm55(♑28) 🍴 Lift
Credit Cards 3 5

★★ **Climat** chemin de la Careirasse
☎ 66842152 tx 485201
⇨♑44 P ⇨
Credit Cards 1 2 3

★★ **Ibis** chemin de l'Hostellerie
☎ 66380065 tx 490180

⇨♑108 Lift
Credit Cards 1 3

★ **Louvre** 2 Sq de la Couronne
☎ 66672275 tx 480218
⇨♑33 P Lift (
Credit Cards 1 2 3 4 5

🏨 **Fricon** 175 rte d'Alès ☎ 66231911 M/C **P**

At **CAISSARGUES-BOUILLARGUES**(4km S)

★★ **Campanile** chemin de la Carréras
☎ 66842705 tx 480510
⇨♑50 P50
Credit Card 3

At **MARGUERITTES**(7km NE)

★★ **Marguerittes** rte d'Avignon
☎ 66260123
⇨♑48 P

NIORT
Deux-Sèvres

★★★ **Brèche** 8 av Bujault (n.rest)
☎ 49244178 tx 792343
rm50(⇨♑44) Lift
Credit Cards 1 2 3 5

★★ **Grand** 32 av Paris (n.rest) ☎ 49242221 tx 791502
⇨♑40 🍴 P Lift (
Credit Cards 1 2 3 4 5

★★ **Ibis** av de la Rochelle ☎ 49735454 tx 791635
⇨♑40 Lift
Credit Cards 1 3

★★ **Terminus** LE (FAH) 82 r de la Gare
☎ 49240038
rm43(⇨♑39) Lift (🎱
Credit Cards 1 5

🏨 **Geneve** 117 av de Nantes
☎ 49734519 **P** For

NOEUX-LES-MINES
Pas-de-Calais

★★ **Tourterelles** LE (FAH) 374 rte Nationale ☎ 21669075 tx 134338
Closed :Rest closed Sat lunch & Sun
rm18(⇨♑16) P30
Credit Cards 1 2 3 5

NOGENTEL See **CHÂTEAU-THIERRY**

NOGENT-LE-ROTROU
Eure-et-Loir

★★ **Dauphin** 39 r Villette-Gate
☎ 37521730
Mar-Nov
rm26(⇨11) 🍴 P12
Credit Cards 1 3

NOISIEL
Seine-et-Marne

★★ **Climat** 50 cours des Roches, NOISIEL
☎ 60061540
⇨♑58 P Lift
Credit Cards 1 2 3 5

NOLAY
Côte-D'or

★ **Ste-Marie** LE DPn 36 r de la République
☎ 80217319
rm12(♑4) A5rm 🍴 P12
Credit Cards 2 3 5

🏨 **Fourrier Freres** rte de Beaune
☎ 80217219 **P** Peu Tal

NONANCOURT
Eure

★ **Grand Cerf** LE 17 Grand' rue
☎ 32581527
⇨♑6 🍴 P
Credit Cards 1 2 3 5

NONTRON
Dordogne

★★ **Grand** 3 pl A-Agard ☎ 53561122
rm26(⇨♑18) 🍴 P30 Lift (
Credit Cards 1 3

NOUAN-LE-FUZELIER
Loir-et-Cher

★ **Moulin de Villiers** Pn rte Chaon
☎ 54887227
20 Mar-Aug & 15 Sep-3 Jan
rm11(⇨♑9) P20 Lake
Credit Cards 1 3

NOUVION-EN-THIÉRACHE, LE
Aisne

★ **Paix** 37 r V-Vicary ☎ 23970455
15 Feb-14 Jul & Aug-20 Dec Closed :Rest closed Sun evening
rm23(⇨♑12) P12
Credit Cards 1 3

🏨 **Sarl Hannecart** 36 r V-Vicary
☎ 23970105 **P** Peu

NOVES
Bouches-du-Rhône

★★★ **Auberge de Noves** DPn (2Km NW on D28) ☎ 90941921 tx 431312
Mar-Dec Closed :Rest closed Wed Lunch
⇨♑22 🍴 P50 Lift (🎱 ⇨ Mountain
Credit Cards 1 2 3 5

NOYELLES-GODAULT See **HENIN-BEAUMONT**

NOYERS-SUR-CHER
Loir-et-Cher

★ **Touraine et Sologne** LE DPn RN76 et RN675 ☎ 54751523
20 Feb-4 Jan
rm14(⇨♑12) P35
Credit Cards 1 2 3

NOYON
Oise

★ **St-Eloi** 81 bd Carnot ☎ 44440149
rm30(⇨♑26) A15rm P20
Credit Cards 1 3

NOZAY
Loire-Atlantique

★ **Gergaud** LE 12 rte Nantes ☎ 40794754
rm8(⇨♑6) P20

NUITS-ST-GEORGES
Côtes-d'Or

★★ **Ibis** 1 av Chamblolland ☎ 80611717 tx 350954
⇨♑52 Lift
Credit Cards 1 3

🏨 **Aubin** rte de Dijon ☎ 80670385 **P** Mer

France

Grands Crus rte de Dijon
☎ 80610223 P Peu

NYONS
Drôme

★★ **Colombet** pl de la Libération
☎ 75260366
5 Jan-5 Nov
rm30(⇨ℕ20) 🍴 P6 Lift (Mountain

At **AUBRES**(3km NE D94)

★★ **Auberge du Vieux Village** rte de Gap
☎ 75261289
Closed :Rest closed Sun Lunch
⇨ℕ24 P30 ⇨ Mountain
Credit Cards [1][2][3][5]

OBERNAI
Bas-Rhin

★★ **Duc d'Alsace** L 6 pl de la Gare (n.rest)
☎ 88955534 tx 880200
rm17(⇨ℕ15) 🍴 P4
Credit Cards [1][2][3][5]

OBERSTEIGEN
Bas-Rhin

★★ **Belle Vue DPn** 16 rte de Dabo
☎ 88873239
Closed Jan 11-19 Feb
⇨ℕ36 A4rm 🍴 P40 Lift ⇨ Mountain
Credit Cards [1][2][3][5]

OLÉRON, ILE D'
Charente-Maritime

REMIGEASSE, LA

★★★ **Grand Large** (Relais et Châteaux) pl de la Remigeasse ☎ 46753789 tx 790395
Apr-Oct
⇨ℕ31 P31 ₽ 🏊 Beach Sea
Credit Card [3]

ST-TROJAN-LES-BAINS

★★★ **Novotel** plage du Gatseau
☎ 4676246 tx 790910
⇨ℕ80 Lift ₽ 🏊 Sea
Credit Cards [1][2][3][5]

OLIVET
Loire

★★★★ **Altea Reine Blanche** r de la Reine Blanche ☎ 28664051 tx 760926
10Jan-23Dec Closed Rest:sat lunch
⇨ℕ65 P100 Lift ₽
Credit Cards [1][2][5]

★★ **Climat** ZAC de la rte de Bourges
☎ 38692055 tx 692844
⇨ℕ42 P

★★ **Rivage DPn** 635 r de la Reine Blanche
☎ 38660293 tx 760926
⇨ℕ20 P40 ₽
Credit Cards [1][2][3][5]

OLORON-STE-MARIE
Pyrénées-Atlantiques

★★ **Béarn** 4 pl de la Mairie ☎ 59390099
⇨ℕ29 🍴 P Lift
Credit Cards [1][2][3][5]

ORANGE
Vaucluse

★★★ **Altea** rte de Caderousse
☎ 96342410 tx 431550
⇨ℕ98 P ⇨

★★ **Boscotel** (Inter) rte de Caderousse
☎ 90344750 tx 431405
⇨ℕ57 P100
Credit Cards [1][2][3][5]

★★ **ibis** rte de Caderousse, Le Jonquier
☎ 90343535 tx 432752
⇨ℕ44 P50 🍴
Credit Cards [1][3]

★★ **Louvre & Terminus** 89 av F-Mistral
☎ 90341008 tx 431195
5 Jan-20 Dec Closed :Rest closed Sun Lunch
⇨ℕ34 ₽ P6 Lift (
Credit Cards [1][3]

Adiasse I r Capty (rte de Camaret)
☎ 90340387 All makes

Amepper 788 av MI-Foch
☎ 90341234 P Ope Vau

Cretalles quartier de Condoulet
☎ 201345305 P Mer

ORGEVAL
Yvelines

★★★ **Novotel** RN13/D113 ☎ 39759760
tx 697174
⇨ℕ119 P Lift ₽
Credit Cards [1][2][3][5]

★★ **Moulin d'Orgeval** ☎ 39758574
tx 689036
⇨ℕ14 P ₽ Lake
Credit Cards [1][2][3]

ORLÉANS
Loiret See also **CHAPELLE-SAINT-MESMIN, LA**

★★★★ **Sofitel** 44-46 quai Barentin
☎ 38621739 tx 780073
⇨ℕ110 P Lift (⇨

★★★ **Cedres** (Inter) 17 r du MI-Foch
☎ 38622292 tx 782314
rm36(⇨ℕ32) Lift (

★★ **Arcade** 4 r MI-Foch ☎ 28542311
tx 7806629
⇨ℕ125 🍴 P25
Credit Card [1]

★★ **Marguerite** L 14 pl Vieux-Marché (n.rest) ☎ 385374321
rm25(⇨ℕ17) P Lift
Credit Card [1]

★★ **Terminus** 40 r de la République (n.rest)
☎ 38532464 tx 782230
⇨ℕ50 P50 Lift
Credit Cards [1][2][3][5]

Lion Fort 51 r Porte St-Jean
☎ 38625829 P AR LR

At **SARAN**(2km NW on A10)

★★ **Campanile** 744 rte Nationale 20
☎ 38736666 tx 783692
⇨ℕ50 P50
Credit Card [3]

★★ **ibis** ☎ 38733993 tx 760902
⇨ℕ104 Lift
Credit Cards [1][3]

At **SOURCE, LA**(10km S)

★★★ **Novotel** 2 r H-De-Balzac
☎ 38630428 tx 760619
⇨ℕ119 P150 Lift ₽ ⇨
Credit Cards [1][2][3][5]

★★ **Campanile** 326 r Châteaubriand
☎ 38635820 tx 781228
⇨ℕ42 P42

ORLY AIRPORT See **PARIS AIRPORTS**

ORNAISONS See **NARBONNE**

ORSAY
Essonne

At **COURTABOEUF**(3km S on D35)

★★★ **Mercure Paris Orsay** av du Parana, Z A Courtaboeuf ☎ 69076396 tx 691247
⇨ℕ108 Lift ⇨
Credit Cards [1][2][3][5]

★★ **Climat** av du Cap Horn, ZA de Courtboeuf ☎ 69281420 tx 692844
⇨ℕ26
Credit Cards [1][3]

At **SACLAY**(6km N)

★★★ **Novotel** r C-Thomassin, Christ-de-Saclay ☎ 69418140 tx 601856
⇨ℕ134 P Lift ₽ ⇨
Credit Cards [1][2][3][5]

ORTHEZ
Pyrénées-Atlantiques

★★ **Climat** r du Soulor ☎ (6)594460123
tx 692844
⇨ℕ24

OUISTREHAM-RIVA-BELLA
Calvados

★★ **Univers** L pl du Gl-de-Gaulle
☎ 31971216 tx 170352
⇨ℕ18 A10rm P30 Sea
Credit Cards [1][2][3][5]

Relais des Pommiers rte de Caen
☎ 31961088 P

OYONNAX
Ain

★ **Nouvel** 31 r R-Nicod (n.rest) ☎ 74772811
rm37(⇨ℕ18) 🍴 P20 Lift
Credit Cards [1][3]

PACY-SUR-EURE
Eure

★★ **Etape** 1 r Isambard ☎ 32369277
rm9(⇨5) 🍴 P20
Credit Cards [1][3]

Lepée 92-102 r Isambard
☎ 32360673 P For

PALAISEAU
Essonne

★★★ **Novotel** 18-20 r E-Baudot, Zone d'Activité de Massy ☎ 69208491 tx 691595
⇨ℕ151 P200 Lift ⇨
Credit Cards [1][2][3][5]

PAMIERS
Ariège

★★ **Parc** L 12 r Piconniers ☎ 61670258
Closed :Rest closed Mon
rm13(⇨ℕ12) 🍴
Credit Cards [1][3]

PANTIN See **PARIS**

89

PARAMÉ See **ST-MALO**

PARAY-LE-MONIAL
Saône-et-Loire

★★ **Trois Pigeons** 2 r d'Argaud
☎ 85810377
Mar-Dec
rm47(⇌🏠38) A29rm 🍴
Credit Cards ① ② ③

★★ **Vendages De Bourgogne** 🅻 5 r D-Papin ☎ 85811343
23 Mar-15 Feb Closed :Rest closed Sun pm & Mon lunch
rm14(⇌🏠13) 🍴 P30
Credit Cards ① ② ③

PARENTIS-EN-BORN
Landes

🛌★ **Larrieu** r de Stade ☎ 58784350 **P** Ren

PARIS
See plan pages 92–93
Population 9, 878, 500
Local Tourist Office
127 Avenue des Champs Élysées
☎ 47236172 (information only)
For information on making internal local calls, see page 23

'French cooking' is an international expression describing a style which is certainly an art. In Paris there are twenty districts, or arrondissements, each with a distinct character which is reflected in its restaurants. Most restaurants offer two types of meal – 'à la Carte' and 'le Menu'. The former gives an extensive choice and is more expensive, the latter offers a choice of several courses at a fixed price. The smartest and most expensive shops are in the Rue du Faubourg-St Honoré area, the more modest ones can be found in most districts of the city centre. The internationally renowned department stores 'Au Printemps' and 'Galeries Lafayette' are to be found in Boulevard Haussmann. The best way to see Paris is on a sightseeing tour booked through one of the many travel agents.

See also **AULNAY-SOUS-BOIS, BOBIGNY, BRETIGNY-SUR-ORGE, BUC, CHAMPS-SUR-MARNE, CHELLES, CONFLANS-STE-HONORINE, COURBEVOIE, ECOUEN, ÉPINAY-SUR-ORGE, ERMENONVILLE, ÉVRY, FONTENAY-SOUS-BOIS, GONESSE, LONGJUMEAU, MONTESSON, MONTMORENCY, MONTSOULT, NOISIEL, ORGEVAL, ORSAY, PALAISEAU, PLAISIR, PONTOISE, QUEUE-EN-BRIE(LA),**

France

RAMBOUILLET, ST-AUBIN, ST GERMAIN-EN-LAYE, SANNOIS, SEVRAN, SURESNES, SURVILLIERS-ST-WITZ, ULIS (LES), VERRIÈRES-LE-BUISSON, AND **VIRY-CHÂTILLON**

The distances shown after the locations following the 18th Arrondissement are measured from the Place de la Concorde.

1st Arrondissement
Opéra, Palais-Royal, Halles, Bourse

★★★★★ **Meurice** (Intercont) 228 r de Rivoli ☎ 42603860 tx 230673 PARIS plan **45**
⇌🏠187 P200 Lift 🎵
Credit Cards ① ② ③ ④ ⑤

★★★★★ **Ritz** 15 pl Vendôme ☎ 42603830 PARIS plan **54**
⇌🏠87 P18 Lift 🎵
Credit Cards ① ② ③ ④ ⑤

★★★★ **Lotti** 7 r de Castiglione ☎ 42603734 PARIS plan **40**
⇌🏠130 Lift
Credit Cards ① ② ③ ④ ⑤

★★★★ **Mayfair** 3 r R-de-l'Isle (n.rest) ☎ 426038141 tx 240037
⇌🏠53 Lift
Credit Cards ① ② ③ ⑤

★★★ **Cambon** 3 r Cambon (n.rest) ☎ 42603809 tx 240814 PARIS plan **16**
⇌🏠44 Lift 🎵
Credit Cards ① ② ③ ⑤

★★★ **Castille** 37 r Cambon ☎ 42615520 tx 213505 PARIS plan **18**
⇌🏠76 Lift 🎵
Credit Cards ① ② ③ ④ ⑤

★★★ **Duminy-Vendôme** 3 r Mont-Thabor (n.rest) ☎ 42603280. tx 213492 PARIS plan **21**
⇌🏠79 P Lift 🎵
Credit Cards ① ② ③ ④ ⑤

★★★ **Ladbroke France et Choiseul** 239 r St-Honoré, pl Vendôme ☎ 42615460 tx 680959 PARIS plan **69**
⇌🏠120 Lift 🎵
Credit Cards ① ② ③ ⑤

★★★ **Ladbroke Ste-Anne** 10 r Ste-Anne (n.rest) ☎ 2850544 tx 641025
⇌🏠86 Lift 🎵
Credit Cards ① ② ③ ⑤

★★★ **Louvre** pl A-Malraux ☎ 42615601 tx 220412 PARIS plan **41**
⇌🏠219 P Lift 🎵
Credit Cards ① ② ④ ⑤

★★★ **Montana-Tuileries** 12 r St – Roch ☎ 42603510 tx 214404 PARIS plan **47**
⇌🏠25 Lift 🎵
Credit Cards ① ② ③ ⑤

★★ **Family** 35 r Cambon (n.rest) ☎ 42615484 PARIS plan **24**
rm25(⇌🏠22) Lift 🎵

★★ **Timhotel Louvre** 4 r Croix des Petits Champs (n.rest) ☎ 42603486 tx 216405

⇌🏠56 Lift
Credit Cards ① ② ③ ④ ⑤

2nd Arrondissement
Opéra, Palais-Royal, Halles, Bourse

★★★★ **Westminster** 13 r de la Paix ☎ 42615746 tx 680035 PARIS plan **58**
Closed :Rest closed Sat, Sun & Aug
⇌🏠102 P8 Lift
Credit Cards ① ② ③ ⑤

★★★ **Horset Opéra d'Antin** 18 r d'Antin ☎ 47421301 tx 680564
rm60(⇌🏠57) Lift
Credit Cards ① ② ③ ⑤

★★ **France** 4 r du Caire (n.rest) ☎ 42333098 PARIS plan **27**
rm50(⇌🏠40) Lift 🎵

★★ **Timhotel Bourse** 3 r de la Banque (n.rest) ☎ 42615390 tx 214488
⇌🏠46 Lift
Credit Cards ① ② ③ ④ ⑤

5th Arrondissement
Quartier Latin, Luxembourg, Jardin-des-Plantes

★★ **Acacias Gobelins** 18 av des Gobelins (n.rest) ☎ 45358012 tx 206856 PARIS plan **97**
⇌🏠23 Lift
Credit Cards ① ② ③ ④ ⑤

★★ **Collège de France** 7 r Thénard ☎ 43267836 PARIS plan **76**
⇌🏠29 Lift
Credit Card ②

6th Arrondissement
Quartier Latin, Luxembourg, Jardin-des-Plantes

★★★★ **Lutetia Concorde** 45 bd Raspail (n.rest) ☎ 45443810 tx 270424 PARIS plan **42**
⇌🏠293 P1000 Lift 🎵
Credit Cards ① ② ③ ④ ⑤

★★★ **Aramis St Germain** (BW) 124 r de Rennes ☎ 45480375 tx 205098
⇌🏠42 P50 Lift 🎵
Credit Cards ① ② ③ ⑤

★★★ **Madison** 143 bd St-Germain (n.rest) ☎ 43297250 tx 201628 PARIS plan **43**
⇌🏠55 Lift 🎵
Credit Cards ① ②

★★★ **Senat** 22 r St-Sulpice (n.rest) ☎ 43254230 tx 206367 PARIS plan **59**
rm32(⇌🏠28) Lift 🎵
Credit Cards ① ② ③ ⑤

★★★ **Victoria Palace** 6 r Blaise-Desgoffe ☎ 45443816 tx 270557 PARIS plan **67**
⇌🏠110 🍴 P Lift 🎵
Credit Cards ① ② ③ ⑤

★★ **Angleterre** 44 r Jacob (n.rest) ☎ 42603472 PARIS plan **4**
⇌🏠29 Lift 🎵
Credit Cards ① ② ③ ⑤

7th Arrondissement
Faubourg-St-Germain, Invalides, École Militaire

★★★★ **Pont-Royal** (MAP/BW) 7 r Montalembert ☎ 45443827 tx 270113 PARIS plan **72**

France

Closed :Rest closed Sun
⇨🛏80 P450 Lift (
Credit Cards 1 2 3 5

★★★★ **Sofitel Bourbon** 32 r St-Dominique ☎ 45559180 tx 250019
⇨🛏112 P15 Lift (
Credit Cards 1 2 3 5

★★★ **Bourdonnais** 111-113 av Bourdonnais ☎ 47054542 tx 201416 PARIS plan **80**
Closed :Rest closed Sun
⇨🛏60 Lift (
Credit Cards 1 3 5

★★★ **Bourgogne & Montana** 3 r de Bourgogne ☎ 45512022 tx 270854 PARIS plan **12**
Closed :Rest closed Sat & Sun
⇨🛏35 Lift (
Credit Cards 1 2 3 5

★★★ **Cayré** 4 bd Raspail (n.rest)
☎ 45443888 tx 270577 PARIS plan **19**
⇨🛏130 Lift (
Credit Cards 1 2 3 4 5

★★ **Splendid** 29 av de Tourville
☎ 45592477 tx 201204 PARIS plan **62**
⇨🛏45 Lift

8th Arrondissement
Champs-Élysées, St-Lazare, Madeleine

★★★★★ **Bristol** (SRS) 112 fbg St-Honoré
☎ 42663145 tx 280361 PARIS plan **15**
⇨🛏188 P220 Lift (
Credit Cards 1 3 4 5

★★★★★ **George V** (Trusthouse Forte) 31 av George V ☎ 47235400 tx 650082 PARIS plan **30**
⇨🛏292 Lift (
Credit Cards 1 2 3 4 5

★★★★★ **Plaza-Athénée** (THF) 25 av Montaigne ☎ 47237833 tx 650092 PARIS plan **51**
⇨🛏218 Lift (
Credit Cards 1 2 3 4 5

★★★★★ **Prince de Galles** 33 av George V ☎ 47235511 tx 280627 PARIS plan **52**
⇨🛏171 Lift (
Credit Cards 1 2 3 4 5

★★★★★ **Royal Monceau** (CIGA) 35 av Hoche ☎ 45619800 tx 650361 PARIS plan **57**
⇨🛏220 Lift (⌕ 🖃
Credit Cards 1 2 3 4 5

★★★★ **Bedford** 17 r de l'Arcade
☎ 426622332 PARIS plan **10**
⇨🛏147 Lift (
Credit Cards 1 3

★★★★ **Castiglione** 40 r du fbg-St-Honoré
☎ 42650750 tx 240362 PARIS plan **17**
⇨🛏114 Lift
Credit Cards 1 2 3 5

★★★★ **Horset Astor** 11 r d'Astorg
☎ 42655656 tx 642737
⇨🛏128 Lift
Credit Cards 1 2 3 5

★★★★ **Horset Royal Malesherbes** 24 bd Malesherbes ☎ 42655330 tx 660190 PARIS plan **81**
⇨🛏102 Lift
Credit Cards 1 2 3 5

★★★★ **Lancaster** 7 r de Berri
☎ 43599043 tx 640991 PARIS plan **38**
⇨🛏66 P10 Lift (
Credit Cards 1 2 3 5

★★★★ **Pullman Windsor** 14 r Beaujon
☎ 45611532 tx 650902 PARIS plan **29**
Closed :Rest closed Sat & Sun
⇨🛏135 Lift (
Credit Cards 1 2 3 4 5

★★★★ **Trémoille** (THF) 14 r Trémoille
☎ 47233420 tx 640344 PARIS plan **64**
⇨🛏111 🕾 P Lift (
Credit Cards 1 2 3 4 5

★★★★ **Atala** 10 r Châteaubriand
☎ 45620162 tx 640576 PARIS plan **7**
Closed :Rest closed Sat & Sun
⇨🛏50 Lift
Credit Cards 1 2 3 5

★★★ **Élysées Marignan** (BW) 12 r de Mariganan ☎ 43595861 tx 6600018 PARIS plan **82**
⇨🛏72 Lift (
Credit Cards 1 2 3 4 5

★★★ **Élysées Ponthieu** 24 r de Ponthieu (n.rest) ☎ 42256870 tx 640053 PARIS plan **83**
⇨🛏62 Lift (
Credit Cards 1 2 3 4 5

★★★ **Royal** 33 av de Friedland (n.rest)
☎ 43590814 tx 280965 PARIS plan **56**
⇨🛏57 Lift
Credit Cards 1 2 3 4 5

★★ **Brescia** 16 r d'Edimbourg (n.rest)
☎ 45221431 tx 660714 PARIS plan **14**
⇨🛏38 Lift
Credit Cards 1 2 3 5

★★ **Élysée** 12 r Saussaies (n.rest)
☎ 42652925 tx 281665 PARIS plan **22**
⇨🛏32 Lift
Credit Cards 1 2 5

★★ **Europe** 15 r Constantinople (n.rest)
☎ 45228080 tx 280658 PARIS plan **23**
⇨🛏57 P Lift
Credit Cards 1 3

★★ **Ministère** 31 r de Surène (n.rest)
☎ 42662143 tx 375974 PARIS plan **46**
rm32(⇨🛏26) Lift (

★★ **Timotel** 13 r St-Lazare (n.rest)
☎ 142962828 tx 215350
rm91 Lift
Credit Cards 1 2 3 4 5

9th Arrondissement
Opéra, Gare du Nord, Gare de l'Est, Grands Boulevards

★★★★ **Ambassador Concorde** (GT) 16 bd Haussmann ☎ 42469263 tx 650912 PARIS plan **3**
⇨🛏300 Lift (

★★★★ **Grand** (Intercont) 2 r Scribe
☎ 42681213 tx 220875 PARIS plan **32**
⇨🛏515 Lift
Credit Cards 1 2 3 4 5

★★★ **Blanche Fontaine** 34 r Fontaine (n.rest) ☎ 45267232 tx 660311 PARIS plan **11**
⇨🛏49 🕾 P13 (
Credit Cards 2 3

★★★ **Caumartin** 27 r Caumartin
☎ 47429595 tx 680702 PARIS plan **84**
⇨🛏40 Lift (
Credit Cards 1 2 3 4 5

★★★ **Excelsior Opéra** 5 r la Fayette
(n.rest) ☎ 48749930 tx 283312
⇨🛏53 Lift
Credit Cards 1 2 3 5

★★★ **Franklin** (MAP/BW) 19 r Buffault
☎ 42802727 tx 640988 PARIS plan **28**
Closed :Rest closed Sat & Sun
⇨🛏64 Lift
Credit Cards 1 2 3 4 5

★★ **Havane** 44 r do Trévise (n rest)
☎ 47707912 tx 283462 PARIS plan **77**
⇨🛏53 Lift (
Credit Cards 1 3

★★★ **Hélios** 75 r de la Victoire (n.rest)
☎ 48742864 tx 283255 PARIS plan **33**
⇨🛏50 Lift (
Credit Cards 1 2 3 5

★★★ **Ladbroke Hamilton** 49 r Lafayette
☎ 2850544 tx 641025
⇨🛏93 Lift (
Credit Cards 1 2 3 5

★★ **Campaville** B1 bd de Clichy (n.rest)
☎ 48740112 tx 643572
⇨🛏78 Lift

★★ **Hotel Campaville** 11 bis r P-Sémard (n.rest) ☎ 48782894 tx 643861 PARIS plan **94**
⇨🛏47 Lift

★★ **Lorette** 36 r Notre-Dame de Lorette (n.rest) ☎ 42851881 tx 283877 PARIS plan **78**
⇨🛏83 P10
Credit Cards 1 2 3 5

★★ **Palmon** 30 r Maubeuge (n.rest)
☎ 42850761 tx 641498 PARIS plan **71**
⇨🛏38 🕾 Lift
Credit Cards 1 2 3 5

★ **Laffon** 25 r Buffault (n.rest) ☎ 48784991 PARIS plan **37**
25 Aug-25 Jul
rm45 Lift (
Credit Cards 1 3

10th Arrondissement
Opéra, Gare du Nord, Gare de l'Est, Grands Boulevards

★★★ **Horset Pavillon** 38 r de l'Echiquier
☎ 42461307 tx 641905 PARIS plan **89**
⇨🛏91 Lift
Credit Cards 1 2 3 5

★★★ **Terminus Nord** 12 bd Denain (n.rest)
☎ 42802000 tx 660615F PARIS plan **63**
⇨🛏220 Lift
Credit Cards 1 2 3 5

★★ **Altona** 166 r du fbg Poissonière
(n.rest) ☎ 48786824 tx 281436 PARIS plan **2**
rm55(⇨🛏50) Lift

★★ **Campaville** 26 r de l'Aqueduc (n.rest)
☎ 42392626 tx 216200 PARIS plan **95**
⇨🛏78 Lift →

91

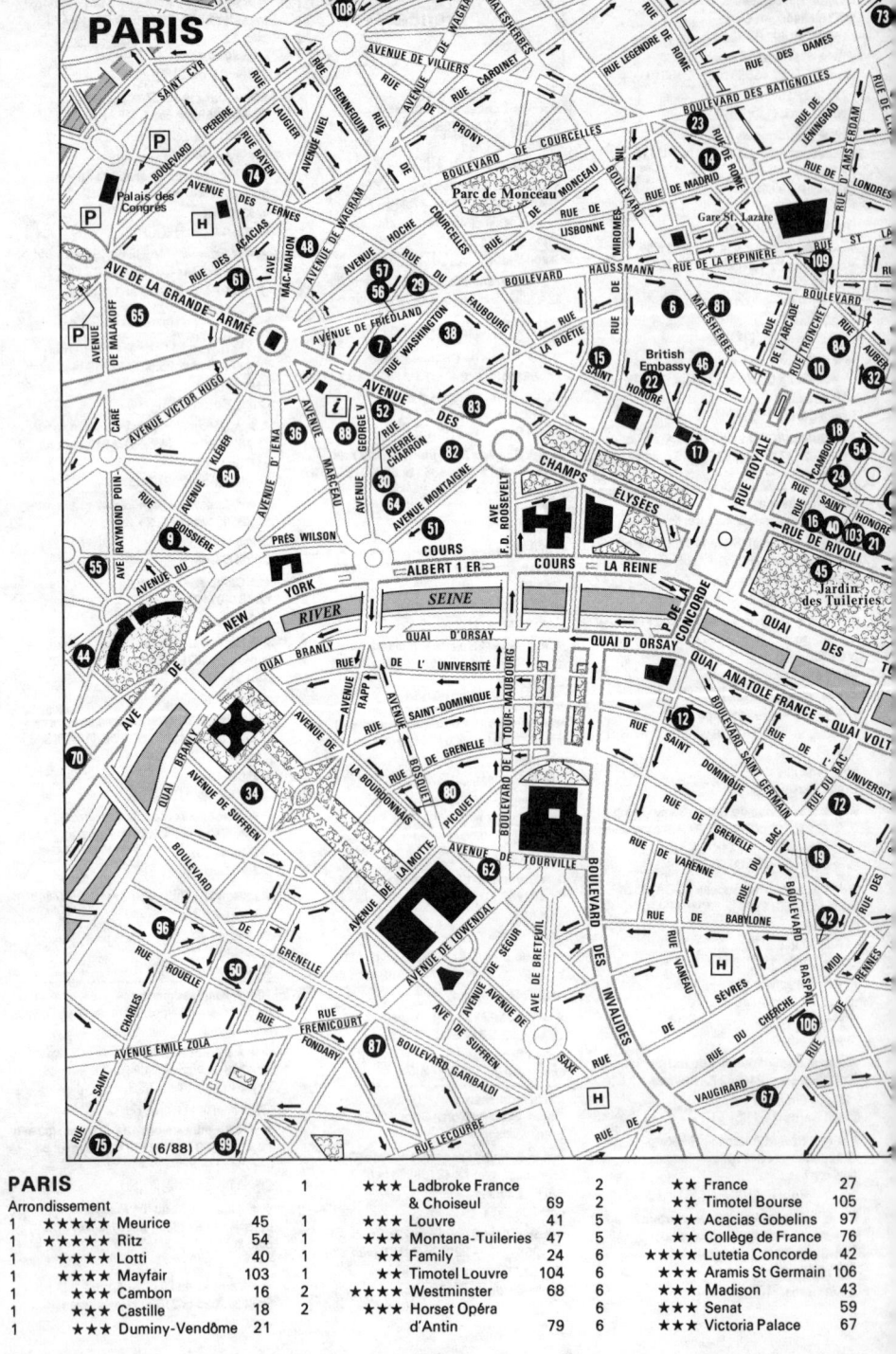

PARIS

Arrondissement

1	★★★★★ Meurice	45	1	★★★ Ladbroke France & Choiseul	69	2	★★ France	27
1	★★★★★ Ritz	54	1	★★★ Louvre	41	2	★★ Timotel Bourse	105
1	★★★★ Lotti	40	1	★★★ Montana-Tuileries	47	5	★★ Acacias Gobelins	97
1	★★★★ Mayfair	103	1	★★ Family	24	5	★★ Collège de France	76
1	★★★ Cambon	16	1	★★ Timotel Louvre	104	6	★★★★ Lutetia Concorde	42
1	★★★ Castille	18	2	★★★★ Westminster	68	6	★★★ Aramis St Germain	106
1	★★★ Duminy-Vendôme	21	2	★★★ Horset Opéra d'Antin	79	6	★★★ Madison	43
						6	★★★ Senat	59
						6	★★★ Victoria Palace	67

92

6	★★	Angleterre	4	8	★★★★★ Plaza-Athénée	51	8	★★★★ Pullman Windsor	29
7	★★★★	Pont Royal	72	8	★★★★★ Prince de Galles	52	8	★★★★ Trémoille	64
7	★★★	Bourdonnais	80	8	★★★★★ Royal Monceau	57	8	★★★ Atala	7
7	★★★	Bourgogne & Montana	12	8	★★★★ Bedford	10	8	★★★ Élysées Marignan	82
7	★★★	Cayré	19	8	★★★★ Castiglione	17	8	★★★ Élysées Ponthieu	83
7	★★★	Splendid	62	8	★★★★ Horset Astor	6	8	★★★ Royal	56
8	★★★★★	Bristol	15	8	★★★★ Horset Royal Malesherbes	81	8	★★ Brescia	14
8	★★★★★	George-V	30	8	★★★★ Lancaster	38	8	★★ Élysée	22
							8	★★ Europe	23

8	★★	Ministère	46
8	★★	Timotel Saint-Lazare	109
9	★★★★	Ambassador-Concorde	3
9	★★★★	Grand	32
9	★★★	Blanche Fontaine	11
9	★★★	Caumartin	84
9	★★★	Franklin	28
9	★★★	Havane	77
9	★★★	Hélios	33
9	★★	Campaville	94
9	★★	Campaville	100
9	★★	Lorette	78
9	★★	Palmon	71
9	★	Laffon	37
10	★★★	Horset Pavillon	89
10	★★★	Terminus Nord	63
10	★★	Altona	2
10	★★	Campaville	95
10	★★	Modern, Est	86
11	★★★★	Holiday Inn	90
11	★★	Campaville	107
13	★	Arts	5
14	★★★	Pullman St-Jacques	98
15	★★★★	Hilton	34
15	★★★★	Holiday Inn	91
15	★★★★	Sofitel Paris	75
15	★★★	Mercure Paris-Port de Versailles	99
15	★★	Arcade	87
15	★★	Campaville	96
15	★★	Pacific	50
15	★★	Timhotel Montparnasse	92
16	★★★★	Baltimore	9
16	★★★	Élysées Bassano	88
16	★★★	Frémiet	70
16	★★★	Massenet	44
16	★★★	Sevigné	60
16	★★	Keppler	36
16	★★	Rond Point de Longchamp	55
16	★★	Vermont	65
17	★★★★	Regent's Garden	74
17	★★★★	Splendid Étoile	61
17	★★	Neuville	108
17	★★	Neva	48
17	★	Verniquet	66
18	★★★★	Terrass	73
18	★★★	Mercure Paris-Montmartre	101
18	★★	Ibis Paris-Montmartre	102
18	★★	Timhotel Montmartre	93
	★★★	Novotel Paris-Bagnolet (At Bagnolet)	49
	★★	Ibis (At Bagnolet)	35

★★ **Campaville-Porte de Clichy** 4 r Marcelin Berthelot (n.rest) ☎ 47375298 tx 616844
⇨♖55 Lift

★★ **Modern 'Est** 91 bd de Strasbourg (n.rest) ☎ 46072472 tx 375974 PARIS plan **86**
⇨♖30 Lift
Credit Card [2]

11th Arrondissement
Bastille, République, Hôtel-de-Ville

★★★★ *Holiday Inn* Pn 10 pl de la République ☎ 43554434 tx 210651 PARIS plan **90**

France

⇨♖333 Lift (
Credit Cards [1] [2] [3] [4] [5]

★★ **Camanville** 9 r du Chemin-Vert (n.rest) ☎ 43385808 tx 218019
⇨♖170 Lift
Credit Card [3]

12th Arrondissement
Gare de Lyon, Bois de Vincennes

★★ **Campaville-Nation** 54 r du Rendezvous (n.rest) ☎ 43430152 tx 215771
⇨♖32 Lift

🏨 **Poniatowski** 57 bd Pontiatowski ☎ 43443732 **P** Ren

13th Arrondissement
Bastille, Gare d'Austerlitz, Place d'Italie

★★★ *Mercure Hamac* 21 r de Tolbiac (n.rest) ☎ 45846161 tx 250822
⇨♖71 🍴 P16 Lift
Credit Cards [1] [2] [3] [5]

★★ **Timhotel Italie** 22 r Barrault (n.rest) ☎ 45806767 tx 205461
⇨♖73 Lift
Credit Cards [1] [2] [3] [4] [5]

★★ **Timhotel Tolbiac** 35 r de Tolbiac (n.rest) ☎ 45837494 tx 201309
⇨♖54 Lift
Credit Cards [1] [2] [3] [4] [5]

★ **Arts** 9 r Coypel (n.rest) ☎ 47077632 PARIS plan **5**
rm38(⇨♖29) Lift
Credit Cards [1] [3]

14th Arrondissement
Vaugirard, Gare Montparnasse, Grenelle, Denfert-Rochereau

★★★ *Pullman St-Jacques* 17 bd St-Jacques ☎ 45898980 tx 270740 PARIS plan **98**
⇨♖798 🍴 P70 Lift (
Credit Cards [1] [2] [3] [4] [5]

★★ **Timotel** 146 av du Maine (n.rest) ☎ 43355760 tx 205036
rm91 Lift
Credit Cards [1] [2] [3] [4] [5]

15th Arrondissement
Vaugirard, Gare Montparnasse, Grenelle, Denfert-Rochereau

★★★★ *Hilton* 18 av Suffren ☎ 42739200 tx 200955 PARIS plan **34**
⇨♖489 🍴 Lift (

★★★★ *Holiday Inn* 69 bd Victor ☎ 45337463 tx 260844 PARIS plan **91**
⇨♖90 🍴 P50 Lift
Credit Cards [1] [2] [3] [5]

★★★★ *Sofitel Paris* 8-12 r L-Armand ☎ 40603030 tx 201432 PARIS plan **75**
⇨♖635 🍴 P300 Lift (⌂
Credit Cards [1] [2] [3] [4] [5]

★★★ *Mercure Paris-Porte de Versailles* r du Moulin ☎ 46429322 tx 202195 PARIS plan **99**

⇨♖391 🍴 P470 Lift
Credit Cards [1] [2] [3] [5]

★★ **Arcade** 2 r Cambronne ☎ 45673520 tx 203842 PARIS plan **87**
rm530 P50 Lift
Credit Card [3]

★★ **Campaville** 30 r Saint Charles (n.rest) ☎ 45786133 tx 203086 PARIS plan **96**
⇨♖76 Lift

★★ **Pacific** (Inter) 11 r Fondary (n.rest) ☎ 45752049 tx 201346 PARIS plan **50**
rm66(⇨♖49) Lift
Credit Cards [1] [3]

★★ **Timhotel Montparnasse** 22 r de l'Arrivée (n.rest) ☎ 45489662 tx 270625 PARIS plan **92**
rm58
Credit Cards [1] [2] [3] [4] [5]

16th Arrondissement
Passy, Auteuil, Bois de Boulogne, Chaillot, Porte Maillot

★★★★ *Baltimore* 88 bis av Kléber ☎ 45538333 tx 611591 PARIS plan **9**
⇨♖119 Lift (
Credit Cards [1] [2] [3] [4] [5]

★★★ *Élysées Bassano* 24 r de Bassano ☎ 47204903 tx 611559 PARIS plan **88**
⇨♖40 Lift (
Credit Cards [1] [2] [3] [4] [5]

★★★ *Frémiet* (MAP) 6 av Frémiet (n.rest) ☎ 45245206 tx 630329 PARIS plan **70**
⇨♖36 P Lift (⌂ ⛱ ▶ Sea Lake
Credit Cards [1] [2] [3] [5]

★★★ *Horset St-Cloud* 21 r Gudin (n.rest) ☎ 46519922 tx 610929
⇨♖47 Lift
Credit Cards [1] [2] [3] [5]

★★★ *Massenet* (MAP/BW) 5 bis r Massenet (n.rest) ☎ 45244303 tx 620682 PARIS plan **44**
rm41(⇨♖37) Lift (
Credit Cards [1] [2] [3]

★★★ *Sevigné* 6 r de Belloy (n.rest) ☎ 47208890 tx 610219 PARIS plan **60**
⇨♖30 P5 Lift
Credit Cards [1] [2] [3] [5]

★★ **Keppler** (Inter) 12 r Keppler (n.rest) ☎ 47206505 tx 620440 PARIS plan **36**
⇨♖59 Lift
Credit Cards [1] [2] [3]

★★ **Murat** 119 bis bd Murat (n.rest) ☎ 46511232 tx 648963
⇨♖28
Credit Cards [2] [3] [5]

★★ **Rond Point de Longchamp** (Inter) 86 r de Longchamp ☎ 45051363 tx 620653 PARIS plan **55**
Closed :Rest closed Sat & Sun
⇨♖58 Lift
Credit Cards [1] [2] [3] [5]

★★ **Vermont** 11 bis r Bois-de-Boulogne (n.rest) ☎ 45800497 tx 612208 PARIS plan **65**
rm28(⇨♖26) Lift
Credit Cards [1] [2] [3] [5]

17th Arrondissement
Clichy, Ternes, Wagram

France

★★★★ **Regent's Garden** (MAP/BW) 6 r P-Demours ☎ 45740730 tx 640127 PARIS plan **74**
🍴📞40 P40 Lift (
Credit Cards [1][2][3][5]

★★★★ **Splendid Étoile** 1 bis av Carnot
☎ 43801456 tx 280773 PARIS plan **61**
Closed :Rest closed Sun & Sat
🍴📞57 Lift (
Credit Cards [1][3][5]

★★ **Neuvillе** 3 r Verniquet ☎ 43802690
tx 648822 Not on plan
🍴📞28 Lift (
Credit Cards [1][2][3][5]

★★ **Neva** 14 r Brey (n.rest) ☎ 43802826
tx 649041 PARIS plan **48**
🍴📞35 Lift
Credit Cards [1][2][3][5]

🛏 Sarca 53-55 av de St Ouen
☎ 42283070 AR

18th Arrondissement
Montmartre, La Villette, Belleville

★★★★ **Terrass** (MAP/BW) 12 r J-de-Maistre ☎ 46067285 tx 280830 PARIS plan **73**
🍴📞106 Lift (
Credit Cards [1][2][3][5]

★★★ **Mercure Paris-Montmartre** 1-3 r Coulain Court (n.rest) ☎ 42941717
tx 640605
🍴📞308 Lift
Credit Cards [1][2][3][5]

★★ **Ibis Paris-Montmartre** 3 r Caulaincourt
☎ 42941818 tx 640428
🍴📞326 🍽 P Lift
Credit Cards [1][3]

★★ **Pigalle Urbis Paris** 100 bd Rochechouart (n.rest) ☎ 46069917
tx 290416
🍴📞67 Lift
Credit Cards [1][3]

★★ **Timhotel Montmartre** 11 pl E-Goudeau (n.rest) ☎ 42557479 tx 650508
PARIS plan **93**

rm63 Lift
Credit Cards [1][2][3][4][5]

At **BAGNOLET**(7km E)

★★★ **Novotel Paris-Bagnolet** 1 av de la République ☎ 43600210 tx 670216 PARIS plan **49**
🍴📞611 🍽 P160 Lift ⇌ ▶
Credit Cards [1][2][3][5]

★★ **Ibis** r J-Jaurès ☎ 43600276 PARIS plan **35**
🍴📞414 🍽 P Lift
Credit Cards [1][3]

At **BOULOGNE-BILLANCOURT**(7km W)

★★ **Campaville** 5 r Carnot (n.rest)
☎ 48252251 tx 631863
🍴📞57 Lift

🛏 **Parc Auto** 6 r de le Ferme
☎ 46216602 P

At **CACHAN**(11km S)

★★ **Climat** 2 r Mirabeau ☎ 45471800
🍴📞46 P50 Lift
Credit Cards [1][3]

At **CHESNAY**(16km W)

★★ **Urbis Versailles Quest** av du Dutartre 16Km W (n.rest) ☎ 39633793 tx 689188
🍴📞72 Lift
Credit Cards [1][3]

At **CRÉTEIL**(12km SE)

★★★ **Novotel** rte de Choissy RN186
☎ 42079102 tx 670396
🍴📞110 P50 Lift ⇌ Lake
Credit Cards [1][2][3][5]

★★ **Climat** Quartier de la Brèche, r des Archives ☎ 48992323 tx 262190
🍴📞51 P30 Lift
Credit Cards [1][2][3]

At **GENTILLY**(6km S)

★★ **Ibis** 13 r du Val-de-Marne ☎ 46641925
tx 250733
🍴📞296 Lift
Credit Cards [1][3]

At **KREMLIN-BICÊTRE**(6km SE)

★★ **Campanile** bd du Gl-de-Gaulle
☎ 46701186 tx 205026
🍴📞155 🍽 P40

At **LIVRY-GARGAN**(17km NE)

★★ **Climat** 119 bd R-Schuman
☎ 43854141
🍴📞43 P70 Lift
Credit Cards [1][2][3]

At **MONTROUGE**(6km S)

★★★ **Mercure Porte d'Orléans** 13 r F-Ory
☎ 46571126 tx 202528
🍴📞192 🍽 P130 Lift
Credit Cards [1][2][3][5]

★★ **Ibis** 33 r Barbès ☎ 47469595
tx 202527
🍴📞402 Lift
Credit Cards [1][3]

At **NEUILLY-SUR-SEINE**(8km W)

★★ **Maillot** 46 r de Sablonville (n.rest)
☎ 46242345
rm35(🍴📞34) P6 Lift (

🛏 **Reymond** 18 bd Vital-Bouhot
☎ 47471919

At **PANTIN**(7km NE)

★★★ **Mercure-Paris** 25 r Scandicci
☎ 230742
Closed :Rest closed Sat & Sun Lunch
🍴📞138 🍽 Lift
Credit Cards [1][2][3][5]

★★ **Campanile** av J-Lolive, ZAC "Îlôt 51"
☎ 47571111 tx 610016
🍴📞126 P Lift
Credit Card [3]

FOR YOUR HOLIDAY or PROFESSIONAL STAY
Hotel Le Loiret ★★★ 5, RUE DES BONS ENFANTS – 75001 PARIS
31 rooms in the very heart of PARIS
Tube-stations: LOUVRE or PALAIS ROYAL   Tel. (331) 42.61.47.31   42.96.34.34
Parking LOUVRE DES ANTIQUAIRES   Telex: HLOIRET 214 047 F

HOTEL des SOURCES
(★★ Logis de France)
88540 BUSSANG
Tel: (33) 29615194
Brochure on request.

Situated in the Vosges, at the entrance of the Alsace. (Altitude 600-1200m.) Very quiet hotel (9 rooms) in green surroundings. Gourmet dishes. Welcoming atmosphere. Close to important connection Paris-Basle N66.

HOTEL TRILLO ★★ NN

Situated right in the centre of the Montmartre, near the tube stations Abbesses and Blanche. You will be delighted by the personal welcome, pastel shaded rooms and breakfast buffet.
7, rue Aristide-Bruant – 75018 PARIS Tel. (1) 42.58.13.44

France

At **VILLENEUVE-LA-GARENNE**(16km N)
★★ *Climat* bd C-de-Gaulle ☎ 7995600 tx 692844
⇨♠37

PARIS AIRPORTS

BOURGET AIRPORT, LE
★★★ *Novotel-Paris Le Bourget* r le Pont Yblon (RN2) ☎ 48674888 tx 230115
⇨♠143 ☎ P300 Lift ⇨
Credit Cards ①②③⑤
★★ *Balladins* 134-136 av de la division, Leclerc ☎ 05355575 tx 649394
rm38 P38
Credit Cards ①②③④⑤

CHARLES-DE-GAULLE AIRPORT
At **ROISSY-EN-FRANCE**(2km E)
★★★★ *Holiday Inn* 1 allée du Verger ☎ 39880022 tx 695143
⇨♠240 P140 Lift
Credit Cards ①②③④⑤
★★★★ *Sofitel* ☎ 48622323 tx 230166
⇨♠352 ☎ P Lift ℓ ℛ ⇨
Credit Cards ①②③⑤
★★ *Arcade* 10 r du Verseau ☎ 48624949 tx 212989
⇨♠356 P150 Lift
★ *Ibis* av de la Raperie ☎ 39880046 tx 699083
⇨♠200 ☎ P Lift
Credit Cards ①③

ORLY AIRPORT
★★★★ *Hilton International* 267 Orly Sud ☎ 46873388 tx 25061
⇨♠380 P350 Lift ℓ
Credit Cards ①②③④⑤
★★ *Arcade* espl Aérogare Sud ☎ 46873350 tx 203121
⇨♠203 P80 Lift
Credit Card ③

At **ATHIS-MONS**(2.5km SE)
✻ *Bidaud* 59 rte de Fontainebleau ☎ 69388181 M/C **P** Peu

At **MORANGIS**(2.5km SW)
★★ *Campanile* 34 av F-de-Lesseps ☎ 64486130 tx 600832
⇨♠50 P50
★★ *Climat* r Lavoisier, ZI des Sables ☎ 44483155 tx 603215
⇨♠38
Credit Cards ①③

PARTHENAY
Deux-Sèvres
★★ *Grand* 85 bd de la Meilleraie (n.rest) ☎ 49640016
rm26(⇨♠20) ☎ P15
Credit Cards ①②③④⑤

PASSENANS See **SELLIÈRES**

PAU
Pyrénées-Atlantiques
★★★ *Continental* (MAP/BW) 2 r Ml-Foch ☎ 59296931 tx 570906
⇨♠100 ☎ P35 Lift ℓ
Credit Cards ①②③④⑤
★★★ *Roncevaux* (FAH) 25 r L-Barthou (n.rest) ☎ 59270844 tx 570849

rm44 P15 Lift
Credit Cards ①②③④⑤
★★ *Bristol* (Inter) 3 r Gambetta (n.rest) ☎ 59277298 tx 570317
rm24(⇨♠22) P15 Lift ℓ
Credit Cards ①②③④⑤
★★ *Campanile* bd de l'Aviation ☎ 59803233 tx 540208
⇨♠43 P43
★★ *Ibis* 45 r F-Garcia-Lorca ☎ 59803233 tx 540208
⇨♠83 ☎ P20 Lift

At **LESCAR**(7.5km NW)
★★★ *Novotel* (RN117) ☎ 59321732 tx 570939
⇨♠61 P80 ⇨ Mountain
Credit Cards ①②③④⑤
✻ *Morin* ZAC. Monhauba ☎ 59811881 **P** AR

PAYRAC
Lot
★★ *Hostellerie de la Paix* 🆑 ☎ 65379515 tx 521291
18 Feb-2 Jan
⇨♠50 P50 ⇨ Mountain
Credit Cards ①②③

PENNE-ST-MENET, LA See **MARSEILLE**

PÉRIGUEUX
Dordogne
★★★ *Domino* (Inter) 21 pl Francheville ☎ 53082580 tx 570230
rm37(⇨♠31) P15 Lift ℓ
Credit Cards ①②③
★★ *Campanile* ZI Carrefour Boulazac ☎ 53090037 tx 572705
⇨♠42 P42
Credit Card ③
★★ *Climat* "Le Breuil", Trelissac ☎ 53043636 tx 541707
⇨♠50 ℛ
Credit Card ①
★★ *Ibis* 8 bd Saumande ☎ 53536458 tx 550159
⇨♠89 Lift
Credit Cards ①③
✻ *Laroumedie* 182 rte de Bordeaux ☎ 53080827 Vol Mazda

PÉRONNE
Somme
★★ *St-Claude* 🆑 42 pl L-Daudre ☎ 22844600 tx 145618
rm36(⇨♠22) ☎ P15
Credit Cards ①②③⑤
★ *Remparts* 🆑 Pn 21 r Beaubois ☎ 22843821
rm16(⇨♠13) ☎ P6
Credit Cards ①②③⑤

At **ASSEVILLERS**(adj to A1)
★★★ *Mercure* (A1), r Beaubois ☎ 22841276 tx 140943
⇨♠100 P200 Lift ⇨
Credit Cards ①②③⑤

PÉROUGES
Ain
★★ *Vieux Pérouges* pl du Tilleul ☎ 74610088 tx 306898
⇨♠29 ☎ P Mountain
Credit Cards ①③

PERPIGNAN
Pyrénées-Orientales
★★★ *Mondial* (MAP) 40 bd Clemenceau ☎ 68342345 tx 500920
⇨♠40 P6 Lift
Credit Cards ①②③⑤
★★★ *Windsor* (Inter) 8 bd Wilson ☎ 68511865 tx 500701
⇨♠57 P Lift ℓ
Credit Cards ①③
★★ *Campanile* r A Levernan, Lotissement Porte d'Espagne ☎ 68567575 tx 505046
⇨♠43 P43
★★ *Christina* 50 cours de Lassus (n.rest) ☎ 68352461
rm37(⇨♠32) ☎ P5 Lift
Credit Cards ①③
✻ *Casadessus* 4 bd St-Assiscle ☎ 68540396 AR LR

At **RIVESALTES**(5km NW by N9)
★★★ *Novotel* ☎ 68640222 tx 500851
⇨♠85 P83 ⇨ Mountain
Credit Cards ①②③⑤
✻ *Guillouf* Zone Artisanale, r de l'Alzin ☎ 68644097

PERRIGNY-LÈS-DIJON See **DIJON**

PERROS-GUIREC
Côtes-du-Nord
★★★ *Trestraou* Pn bd J-le-Bihan, Trestraou ☎ 96232405 tx 741261
rm68(⇨♠66) A2rm P Lift Sea
Credit Cards ①②③⑤
★★ *Morgane* Pn 46 av Casino, Plage de Trestraou ☎ 96232280
Mar-20 Oct
rm32(⇨♠30) A5rm P32 Lift ⇨ ▶ Beach Sea
Credit Cards ①②③⑤
✻ *Côte* 39 r du Ml-Joffre ☎ 96232207 **P** Peu Tal

At **PLOUMANACH**(6km NW)
★★★ *Rochers* (FAH) Port de Ploumanach ☎ 96232302
Etr-Sep
⇨♠15 Sea
Credit Card ③

PESMES
Haute-Saône
★★ *France* 🆑 ☎ 84312005
⇨♠10 P20 ℓ
Credit Cards ①②③

PETITE-PIERRE, LA
Bas-Rhin
★★ *Vosges* 🆑 Pn 30 r Principale ☎ 88704505

France

15 Dec-15 Nov Closed :Rest closed Tue evening & Wed
rm30(⇌16) 🕿 P25 Lift Mountain
Credit Cards [1] [3]

PETIT-QUEVILLY, LE See **ROUEN**

PEYREHORADE
Landes
★★ **Central** pl A-Briand ☎ 58730322
Closed Feb :Rest closed Mon
⇌🛏17 P Lift Mountain
Credit Cards [1] [2] [3] [5]

PIED-DU-SANCY See **MONT-DORE, LE**

PIERRE-BUFFIÈRE
Haute-Vienne
★ **Providence** 20 r Nationale ☎ 55006016
15 Mar-15 Nov
rm11(⇌🛏8) 🕿
Credit Card [2]
🍴 R Gauthier 17 av de Toulouse
☎ 55006024 M/C **P** Cit

PIERRELATTE
Drôme
★★ **Hostellerie Tom II** L⁴ 5 av Gl-de-Gaulle (N7) ☎ 75040035
Closed :Rest closed Mon
⇌🛏15 🕿
Credit Cards [2] [3]
🍴 Mistral ZI rte de St-Paul ☎ 75040158
All makes

PITHIVIERS
Loiret
★★ **Climat** av du 8 Mai ☎ 48657061
⇌🛏26 P30
Credit Cards [1] [3] [5]
★ **Relais de la Poste** 10 Mail Quest ☎ 38304030
10 Jan-20 Dec Closed :Rest closed Sun evening & Mon
⇌🛏20 🕿 P5
Credit Cards [1] [2] [3] [4] [5]

PLAISIR
Yvelines
★★ **Campanile** ZI des Gâtines ☎ 30558150 tx 697578
⇌🛏50 P50
★★ **Climat** Lieudit le Hameau de la Chaine ☎ 30557737
rm38 P70
Credit Card [3]

PLEHEDEL See **LANVOLLON**
PLÉRIN See **ST-BRIEUC**
PLESSIS-CHENET, LE See **CORBEIL-ESSONNES**

PLOEREN
Morbihan
★★ **Climat** ZI de Luscanen ☎ 97409191
⇌🛏43 🕿 P50 Lift
Credit Card [2]

PLOËRMEL
Morbihan
★★ **Le Cobh** 10 r des Forges ☎ 97740049
⇌🛏13 A19rm 🕿 P6
★ **Commerce-Reberminard** L⁴ 70 r de la Gare ☎ 97740049

rm35(⇌🛏15) A20rm 🕿 P8
Credit Cards [1] [3]

PLOMBIÈRES-LES-BAINS
Vosges
★ **Abbesses** 6 pl de l'Église ☎ 29660040
May-sep
rm44(⇌🛏20) Mountain

PLOUGASTEL-DAOULAS See **BREST**
PLOUMANACH See **PERROS-GUIREC**

POITIERS
Vienne
★★★ **France** (MAP) 28 r Carnot ☎ 49413201 tx 790526
rm86(⇌🛏76) 🕿 P30 Lift (
Credit Cards [1] [2] [3] [4] [5]
★★★ **Royal Poitou** rte de Paris (3km N on N10) ☎ 49017286
⇌🛏32 P (
Credit Cards [1] [2] [3] [5]
★★ **Balladins** r A-Haller, Lot de la République ☎ 49415500 tx 649394
⇌🛏28 🕿 P28
Credit Cards [1] [3] [5]
★★ **Climat** Quartier de Beaulieu, r des Frères-Lumière ☎ 49613875 tx 792022
⇌🛏70 P90
Credit Cards [1] [2] [3]
★★ **Europe** 39 r Carnot (n.rest) ☎ 49881200
rm50(⇌🛏41) 🕿 P35 (
Credit Cards [1] [3]
★★ **Ibis** ZAC de Beaulieu, 'Les Maches' ☎ 49611102 tx 790354
rm33
Credit Cards [1] [3]
★★ **Ibis-Poitiers Sud** av du 8 Mai 1945 ☎ 49531313 tx 791556
⇌🛏112 Lift
Credit Cards [1] [3]
★★ **Relais Du Stade** 84-86 r J-Coeur (n.rest) ☎ 49462512
rm25(⇌🛏22) A4rm 🕿 P50 Lift
Credit Cards [1] [3]

At **BIARD**(2km W)
🍴 Barrault ZI de Larnay ☎ 49583543 P Vol

At **CHASSENEUIL-DU-POITOU**(8km N by N10)
★★★ **Novotel-Poitiers Nord** N10 ☎ 49527878 tx 791944
⇌🛏89 P250 Lift ⌬ ⌕
Credit Cards [1] [2] [3] [5]
★★★ **Relais de Poitiers** (N10) ☎ 49529041 tx 790502
⇌🛏97 P400 Lift ⌬ ⌕
Credit Cards [1] [2] [3] [5]
★★ **Campanile** ZI de Chasseneuil-de-Poitou, Voie Ouest ☎ 49528540 tx 791534
⇌🛏42 P42

POIX-DE-PICARDIE
Somme

★★ **Cardinal** pl de la République ☎ 22900823 tx 145379
⇌🛏35 P100
Credit Cards [1] [2] [3] [5]
★ **Poste** L⁴ 13 pl de la République ☎ 22900033
rm18(⇌🛏15) P18
Credit Cards [1] [3]

POLIGNY
Jura
★★ **Hostellerie des Monts de Vaux** (Relais et Châteaux) **Pn** Monts de Vaux (4.5km SE) ☎ 84371250
Jan-Oct
⇌🛏10 🕿 P20 ⌬
Credit Cards [1] [2] [3] [5]
★★ **Paris** L⁴ 7 r Travot ☎ 84371387
Feb-4 Nov
⇌🛏25 🕿 P ⌕ Mountain
★★ **Vallée Heureuse** L⁴ rte de Genève ☎ 84371213
rm12(⇌🛏9) 🕿 P12 Mountain
Credit Cards [1] [2] [3] [5]
🍴 Poix 1 & 3 av W-Gagnew ☎ 84371609 **P** For Fia

POLISOT
Aube
★ **Seine** L⁴ **Pn**
rm20(⇌🛏9) 🕿 P10
Credit Cards [1] [3]

PONS
Charente-Maritime
★★ **Auberge Pontoise** r Gambetta ☎ 46940099
1 Feb-20 Dec Closed :Rest closed Sun dinner & Mon in low sea
⇌🛏22 🕿 P15
Credit Cards [1] [3] [4]

PONT-A-MOUSSON
Meurthe-et-Moselle
★ **Européen** 158 av Metz ☎ 838100757
Closed :Rest closed Sun
rm30(⇌🛏9) A6rm 🕿 P40
★ **Poste DPn** 42 bis r V-Hugo ☎ 83810116
Closed :Rest closed Sun
rm25(⇌🛏16) A8rm 🕿 P8
Credit Cards [1] [3]

PONTARLIER
Doubs
★★ **Poste** 55 r de la République ☎ 81391812
Closed Nov
rm21(⇌🛏14) 🕿 P20 Lift
Credit Cards [1] [3]
🍴 Beau Site 29 av de l'Armée de l'Est ☎ 81392395 **P** Peu Tal

PONTAUBAULT
Manche
★★★ **13 Assiettes** L⁴ (1km N on N175) ☎ 33581403 tx 772173
15 Mar-15 Nov
rm36(⇌🛏27) A24rm P50
Credit Cards [1] [3]

PONT-AUDEMER
Eure
★★★ **Vieux Puits Pn** 6 r Notre-Dame du Pré ☎ 32410148 →

20 Jan-27 Jun & 7 Jul-20 Dec Closed :Rest closed Mon evening & Tue
rm12(⇌↑11) P10
Credit Cards 1 3

At **CORNEVILLE-SUR-RISLE**(6km SE)
★★★ **Cloches de Corneville** rte de Rouen
☎ 32570104
Closed :Rest closed Wed
⇌↑12 P
Credit Cards 1 2 3 5

At **FOURMETOT**(6km NE)
🛏 **Bacheley** ☎ 32574069 P Ren

PONTCHARRA
Isère

★★ **Climat** Lieudit "Le Gabion" RN90
☎ 76719184 tx 305551
⇌↑24 P30 ℛ Mountain
Credit Cards 1 3

PONT-D'AIN
Ain

★★ **Alliés** ☎ 74390009
20 Jan-20 Dec Closed :Rest closed Thu
rm18(⇌↑14) 🍴 P12
Credit Cards 1 3

★★ **Paris-Nice** 2 r du 1er Septembre 1944 (n.rest) ☎ 74390380
Closed Nov & Tue
rm20(↑2) 🍴 P25

PONT-DE-CLAIX See **GRENOBLE**

PONT-DE-L'ISÈRE
Drôme

★ **Portes du Midi** RN 7 ☎ 75846026
Mar-Oct
rm18(↑11) P50 Mountain
Credit Cards 1 2 3 5

PONT-DE-RHODES See **FRAYSSINET**

PONT-DU-GARD
Gard

★★ **Vieux Moulin** ☎ 66371435
10 Mar-11 Nov
rm17(⇌↑15) P30 Beach
Credit Cards 1 2 3 5

At **REMOULINS**(4km E)
★★ **Moderne Pn** pl des Grands-Jours
☎ 66372013
21 Nov-20 Oct Closed :Rest closed Sat
rm23(⇌↑15) 🍴
Credit Cards 1 2 3 5

PONTHIERRY
Seine-et-Marne

🛏 **Tractaubat** 78 av de Fontainebleau
☎ 60657039 Ren
🛏 **Trois Sept** 62 av de Fontainebleau
☎ 60657052 P

At **PRINGY**(2km SE)
★★ **Ibis** 4 rte de Melun ☎ 60655928 tx 690723
⇌↑32 P

PONTIVY
Morbihan

★★ **Porhoët** (Inter) 41 r du Gl-de-Gaulle (n.rest) ☎ 97253448
⇌↑28 P Lift
Credit Cards 1 2

France

🛏 **Jouan** 25 et 29 r du Gl-Quiniv
☎ 97250265 For

PONT-L'ÉVÊQUE
Calvados

★★ **Lion D'Or** pl Calvaire ☎ 31650155
⇌↑25 🍴 P30 (
Credit Cards 1 2 3 4 5

PONTOISE
Val-d'Oise

★★ **Campanile** r P-de-Coubertin
☎ 30385544 tx 698515
⇌↑50 P50
Credit Card 3

At **CERGY**(4km SW)
★★★ **Novotel** av du Parc, Ville Nouvelle
☎ 30303947 tx 697264
⇌↑195 P200 Lift
Credit Cards 1 2 3 5

★★ **Arcade** près Préfecture ☎ 30309393 tx 605470
Closed :Rest closed Sat & Sun
rm140 Lift
Credit Card 1

★★ **Balladins** 17 chaussée J-César
☎ 30321111
⇌↑28 P30
Credit Cards 1 2 3

★★ **Climat** Zac d'Eragny, r des Pinsons
☎ 30378600 tx 696149
⇌↑50 P
Credit Card 4

At **ST-OUEN-L'AUMÔNE**(5km SE)
★★★ **Cerf Hotel** 59 r Gl-Leclerc
☎ 34640313
22-7 Aug
⇌↑10
Credit Cards 2 3

PONTORSON
Manche

★★ **Montgomery** (FAH) DPn 13 r Couesnon ☎ 33600009 tx 171332
Etr-Oct
⇌↑32 🍴 P80
Credit Cards 1 2 3 5

PONT-SARRAZIN See **GAP**

PONTS-DE-CÉ, LES
Maine-et-Loire

★★ **Campanile** chemin du Moulin-Marcille
☎ 41449244 tx 720959
⇌↑41 P47
Credit Card 3

PONT-SUR-YONNE
Yonne

★★ **Ecu** 3 r Carnot ☎ 86670100
3 Mar-15 Jan Closed :Rest closed Mon evening & Tue
rm8(⇌↑6) P5
Credit Cards 1 2 3 5

PORNICHET
Loire-Atlantique

★★★ **Sud-Bretagne** 42 bd de la République ☎ 40610268 tx 701960
15 Mar-15 Jan
⇌↑30 🍴 P30 Lift (ℛ 🏖 🏊
Credit Cards 1 2 3 5

PORT-BLANC
Côtes-du-Nord

★ **Grand** ☎ 96926652
⇌↑26 P10 ℛ Sea
Credit Cards 1 2 3 5

PORTEL, LE
Pas-de-Calais See also **BOULOGNE-SUR-MER**

★ **Beau Rivage Et Armada** pl Mons-Bourgain ☎ 21315982
rm10(⇌↑6) Sea
Credit Cards 1 2 3

PORT-GRIMAUD See **GRIMAUD**

PORTICCIO
Corse-du-Sud See **CORSE (CORSICA)**

PORT-LA-NOUVELLE
Aude

🛏 **Pertil** bd Vals Francis ☎ 684880064 P

PORT-LOUIS
Morbihan

★★ **Avel Vor** (FAH/Inter) DPn 25 r de Locmalo ☎ 97824759 tx 950826
⇌↑20 Lift Sea
Credit Cards 1 2 3 5

PORTO-VECCHIO
Corse-du-Sud See **CORSE (CORSICA)**

POUILLY-EN-AUXOIS
Côte-D'or

🛏 **Jean-Luc Omont** ☎ 80907321 P For
🛏 **J J Jeannin** pl des Allies ☎ 80908211 P VW Peu
🛏 **P Orset** ☎ 80908045 P Ren

At **CHÂTEAUNEUF**(10km SE D18)
★★ **Hostellerie du Château** Pn
☎ 80492200
Mar-12 Nov
⇌↑17 A6rm
Credit Cards 1 2 3

POUILLY-SUR-LOIRE
Nièvre

★★ **Bouteille d'Or** Pn 13 bis rte de Paris ☎ 86391384
15 Feb-10 Jan
rm23(⇌↑3) A8rm
Credit Card 3

★ **Relais Fleuri** (0.5km SE on N7)
☎ 86391299
15 Feb-15 Jan Closed :Rest closed Wed evening & Thu
⇌↑9 🍴 P
Credit Cards 1 3

POULDU, LE
Finistère

★★ **Armen Pn** ☎ 98399044
28 May-21 Sep
⇌↑38 🍴 P45 Lift
Credit Cards 1 2 3 5

★★ **Castel Treaz** ☎ 98399111
10 Jun-10 Sep
⇌↑25 P19 Lift Sea

98

France

POUZAUGES
Vendée
★★ **Auberge de la Bruyère** L (FAH) r Dr-Barbanneau ☎ 51919346 tx 701804
rm30(⇌🛏26) P90 Lift 🌊 Beach
Credit Cards 1 2 3 5

POUZIN, LE
Ardèche
🚗 **M Pheby** N 86 ☎ 75638016 **P** Cit

PRINGY See PONTHIERRY

PROVINS
Seine-et-Marne
★★ **Ibis** Lieu Dit 'Les Palis' ☎ 60676667 tx 691882
⇌🛏51 P
Credit Cards 1 3

PUILBOREAU See ROCHELLE, LA

PUY, LE
Haute-Loire
★★★ **Christel** 15 bd A-Clair ☎ 71022434
⇌🛏29 P20 Lift (
Credit Cards 1 2 3

PUY-L'ÉVÊQUE
Lot
At **MONTCABRIER**(7km NW)
★★★ **Relais de la Dolce Pn** rte de Villefranche du Périgord ☎ 65365342
15 Apr-15 Oct
⇌🛏12 P ⇌
Credit Cards 1 2 5

PYLA-SUR-MER
Gironde
★★★ **Guitoune Pn** 95 bd de l'Océan ☎ 56227010
⇌🛏21 P20 (Sea
Credit Cards 1 2 3 4 5
★★ **Beau Rivage** 10 bd de l'Océan ☎ 56540182
Apr-Sep
rm22(⇌🛏8) A4rm
Credit Cards 1 3

QUARRÉ-LES-TOMBES
Yonne
★ **Nord et Poste** L DPn pl de l'Église ☎ 86322455
rm35(⇌🛏10) A22rm P

QUÉTIGNY See DIJON

QUETTREVILLE-SUR-SIENNE
Manche
★★ **Château de la Tournée** ☎ 33476291
⇌🛏10 P10
Credit Cards 1 3

QUEUE-EN-BRIE, LA
Val-de-Marne
★★ **Climat** ☎ 45946161 tx 262209
⇌🛏55 P60
Credit Cards 1 3

QUIBERON
Morbihan
★★★ **Sofitel Thalassa** Pointe de Goulvars ☎ 97502000 tx 730712
⇌🛏113 P150 Lift (🌊 Sea
Credit Cards 1 2 3 5

★★ **Ibis** av des Marroniers, Pointe de Goulvars ☎ 97304772 tx 951935
Closed 3 Jan-29 Jan
⇌🛏96 P110 ⇌ ⇌
Credit Cards 1 3
★★ **Océan** 7 quai de l'Océan ☎ 97500758
Etr-15 Nov
rm38(⇌🛏26) P30 Lift Sea
At **ST-PIERRE-QUIBERON**(4.5km N)
★★ **Plage** L DPn ☎ 97309210
Etr-Oct
rm49(⇌🛏48) P26 Lift Sea
Credit Cards 1 2 3

QUILLAN
Aude
★★ **Chaumière** L (Inter) bd Ch-de-Gaulle ☎ 68201790
rm38(⇌🛏30) A21rm 🚗 P20 Mountain
Credit Cards 1 3
★★ **Cartier** L (FAH) 31 bd Ch-de-Gaulle ☎ 68200514
15 Mar-15 Dec
rm33(⇌🛏27) 🚗 Lift Mountain
Credit Cards 1 3

QUIMPER
Finistère
★★★ **Griffon** (Inter) 131 rte de Bénodet ☎ 989803333 tx 940063
⇌🛏50 P50 🌊
Credit Cards 1 2 3 5
★★ **Balladins** rte de Coray Commune, d'Ergue-Gaberic ☎ 98595500 tx 649394
⇌🛏38 P38
Credit Cards 1 2 3
★★ **Gradlion** L 30 r Brest (n.rest) ☎ 98950439
⇌🛏25
Credit Cards 1 2 3 4 5
★★ **Ibis** r Gustave Eifel, Quartier de l'Hippodrome, Secteur Ouest ☎ 98905350 tx 940007
⇌🛏72 P72
Credit Cards 1 3
★★ **Ibis-Quimper** r G-Eiffel, ZI de l'Hippodrôme Secteur Ouest ☎ 98905380 tx 940007
⇌🛏70 Lift
Credit Cards 1 3
★★ **Ibis-Quimper Nord** Le Gourvily, rte de Brest ☎ 98957764 tx 940749
⇌🛏36 P50 (
★★ **Tour d'Auvergne** L (FAH) 11-13 r des Réguaires ☎ 98950870 tx 941100
rm43 A2rm 🚗 P Lift (
Credit Cards 1 2 3
🚗 **Auto Secours** 28 av A-de-Bretagne ☎ 98902805
🚗 **Kemper Automobile** 13 av de la Libération ☎ 98901849 AR

QUIMPERLÉ
Finistère

🚗 **Goc Automobiles** rte de Pont Scorff ☎ 98960793 **P** For

QUINCY-VOISINS
Seine-et-Marne
★★ **Auberge Demi Lune** N36 ☎ 60041109
Closed .Rest closed Wed
rm5 P Lift
Credit Card 1

RABOT, LE
Loir-et-Cher
★★★ **Bruyères** (N20) ☎ 54880570
⇌🛏36 A12rm ⇌ ⇌
Credit Cards 1 5

RAMBOUILLET
Yvelines
★★ **Climat** Lieu dit La Louvière ☎ 34856262 tx 695645
⇌🛏44 ⇌
Credit Cards 1 3
★★ **Ibis** Le Bel Air, N10 ☎ 30417850 tx 698429
⇌🛏62 Lift ⇌
Credit Cards 1 3
★★ **St-Charles** 15 r de Groussay (n.rest) ☎ 34830634
rm14(⇌🛏12) A2rm 🚗 P20

RANCOURT
Somme
★★ **Prieuré** N17 ☎ 22850443
25 Jan-20 Dec Closed :Rest closed Sun evening & Mon
⇌🛏28 🚗 P
Credit Cards 1 2 3

RAPHÈLE-LES-ARLES See ARLES

RAYOL, LE
Var
★★★★ **Bailli De Suffren** ☎ 94056767 tx 420535
Mar-Dec
⇌🛏46 P30 Lift Beach Sea
Credit Cards 1 2 3 5

RÉ, ILE DE
Charente-Maritime

FLOTTE, LA
★★ **Richelieu** 44 av de la Plage ☎ 46096070 tx 791492
Closed Jan
rm30 P Sea

RECOLOGNE
Doubs
★ **Escale** L (n.rest) ☎ 581213
Closed 2-31 Oct
⇌🛏11
Credit Card 2
At **LAVERNAY**(3.5km S)
🚗 **Pelot** Lavernay ☎ 81581224 **P** Peu Tal

REIMS
Marne
★★★★ **Altea Champagne** 31 bd P-Doumer ☎ 26885354 tx 830629
⇌🛏125 Lift
Credit Cards 1 2 3 5

★★★ **Mercure-Reims Est** Zise Les Essillards, rte de Châlons ☎ 26050008 tx 8302782
⇌🛏98 P200 Lift 🖂
Credit Cards [1][2][3][4][5]

★★★ **Paix** (Inter) 9 r Buirette ☎ 26400408 tx 830914
⇌🛏105 🍴 Lift ⇌
Credit Cards [2][3][5]

★★ **Balladins** r M-Hollande (n.rest)
☎ 26827210 tx 649394
⇌🛏34 P25
Credit Cards [1][2][3]

★★ **Campanile** av G-Pompidou
☎ 26366694 tx 830262
⇌🛏41 P41
Credit Card [3]

★★ **Climat** (Inter) r B-Russel, ZAC de la Neuvilletts ☎ 26096273
⇌🛏40 P50
Credit Cards [1][3]

★★ **Continental** 93 pl Drouet-d'Erlon (n.rest) ☎ 26403935 tx 830585
⇌🛏60 P Lift
Credit Cards [1][2][3][4]

★★ **Dom Pérignon** 14 r des Capucins
☎ 26473364
⇌🛏10 P (

★★ **Europa** 8 bd Joffre (n.rest)
☎ 26403620 tx 840777
5 Jan-22 Dec
rm32(⇌🛏23) Lift
Credit Cards [1][2][3][4][5]

★★ **Grand du Nord** 75 pl Drouet-d'Erlon (n.rest) ☎ 26473903 tx 842157
4 Jan-23 Dec
⇌🛏50 Lift (
Credit Cards [1][2][3][4][5]

★★ **Touring** 17 ter bd Gl-Leclerc (n.rest)
☎ 26473815
⇌🛏14
Credit Cards [1][2][3]

★★ **Univers** (Inter) 41 bd Foch
☎ 26886808 tx 842120
rm41(⇌🛏36) Lift (
Credit Cards [1][2][3][5]

★★ **Welcome** 29 r Buirette (n.rest)
☎ 26473939 tx 842145
5 Jan-20 Dec
rm68(⇌🛏60) Lift
Credit Cards [1][2][3]

At **TINQUEUX**(4km W off N31)
★★★ **Novotel** rte de Soisson ☎ 26081161 tx 830234
⇌🛏127 P150 ⇌
Credit Cards [1][2][3][5]

★★ **Campanile** Zone de Camp Paveau, av S-Bernard ☎ 26040946 tx 842038
⇌🛏50 P50
Credit Card [3]

★★ **Ibis** (A4) ☎ 26046070 tx 847116
⇌🛏51 Lift
Credit Cards [1][3]

REMIGEASSE, LA See **OLÉRON, ILE D'**

REMIREMONT
Vosges

At **ST-NABORD**(5km N on N57)

France

★★★ **Montiroche** (N57) (n.rest)
☎ 293620659
Apr-Oct
rm14(⇌🛏13) P50 Mountain

REMOULINS See **PONT-DU-GARD**

RENAISON
Loire
★ *Jacques Coeur* LE rte Vichy ☎ 77642534
Mar-Jan
rm10(🛏6) P
Credit Cards [2][3][5]

RENNES
Ille-et-Vilaine
★★★ **Altea** pl du Colombier, r du Cpt-Maignan ☎ 99315454 tx 730905
⇌🛏140 P Lift
Credit Cards [1][2][3][5]

★★★ **Guesclin** 5 pl de la Gare (n.rest)
☎ 99314747 tx 740748
⇌🛏68 Lift
Credit Cards [1][2][3][5]

★★★ **Novotel-Rennes Alma** av du Canada
☎ 99506132 tx 740144
⇌🛏98 P ⇌
Credit Cards [1][2][3][5]

★★★ **Président** 27 av Janvier (n.rest)
☎ 99654222 tx 73004
⇌🛏34 🍴 Lift (
Credit Cards [1][2][3][5]

★★ **Campanile** 120 r Eugène Pottier, ZAC de Cleunay ☎ 99304545 tx 741154
⇌🛏45 P45
Credit Card [3]

★★ **Climat** ZAC de Beauregard Sud
☎ 99541203 tx 741544
⇌🛏42 P35
Credit Cards [1][2][3][4][5]

★★ **Urbis** 1/3 bd Solferino (n.rest)
☎ 99673112 tx 730625
⇌🛏60 Lift
Credit Cards [1][3]

🏨 **Europe** 73-75 av du Mail ☎ 99590152
For

🏨 **J Huchet** 316 rte de St-Malo
☎ 99591122 P AR BMW

At **CESSON-SÉVIGNÉ**(6km E)
★★ **Ibis-Rennes** Centre Hotelier, La Perrière ☎ 99839393 tx 740378
⇌🛏76 Lift
Credit Cards [1][3]

★★ **Ibis-Rennes Beaulieu** rte de Paris
☎ 99833172 tx 740321
⇌🛏35
Credit Cards [1][3]

RESSONS-SUR-MATZ
Oise

At **CUVILLY**(3km NW on N17)
🏨 *Brecqueviller* r Planché (N 17)
☎ 44850016 P

RETHEL
Ardennes

★★ *Moderne* LE pl de la Gare ☎ 24384454
⇌🛏25 🍴 P8 (
Credit Cards [1][2][3][4][5]

REZÉ-DE-NANTES
Loire-Atlantique
★★ **Fimotel** Impasse Ordronneau
☎ 40042030 tx 700429
⇌🛏42 P60
Credit Cards [1][2][3][5]

RIGNAC See **GRAMAT**

RIVE-DE-GIER
Loire
★★ **Hostellerie de la Renaissance** 41 r Marrel ☎ 77750431
⇌🛏8 P25
Credit Cards [1][2][3][5]

RIVESALTES See **PERPIGNAN**
RIXHEIM See **MULHOUSE**

ROANNE
Loire
★★ **France** 19 r A-Roche ☎ 77712117
rm46(⇌🛏18) 🍴
Credit Cards [1][2]

★★ **Ibis** ZI du Côteau ☎ 77683622
tx 300610
⇌🛏51 Lift
Credit Cards [1][3]

★★ *Troisgros* 22 cours de la République
☎ 77716697 tx 307507
Feb-4 Aug & 20 Aug-Dec Closed :Rest closed Tue & Wed lunchtime
⇌🛏24 🍴 P20 Lift (
Credit Cards [1][2][3][5]

At **ST-GERMAIN-L'ESPINASSE**(10km NW on N7)
★★★ *Relais de Roanne* (FAH/Inter)
☎ 77719735 tx 307554
⇌🛏30 🍴 P50 Mountain
Credit Cards [1][2][3][5]

ROCAMADOUR
Lot
★★★ **Beau Site & Notre Dame** (MAP/BW) r R-le-Preux ☎ 65336308 tx 520421
rm55(⇌🛏51) A5rm 🍴 P15 Lift Mountain
Credit Cards [1][2][3][5]

★★★ *Château* LE (FAH) rte de Château
☎ 65336222 tx 521871
25 Mar-12 Nov
⇌🛏58 A24rm P100 ℘

★★ **Ste-Marie** r Grand Escalier, , pl des Sehnal ☎ 65336307
Etr-10 Oct
⇌🛏22 A5rm 🍴 P Mountain

★ **Lion d'Or** LE Porte Figuier ☎ 65336204
Etr-1 Nov
rm32(⇌🛏28) A6rm P10 Lift Mountain
Credit Cards [1][3][4]

ROCHEFORT
Charente-Maritime
★★★ **Remparts Fimotel** 43 r C-Pelletan
☎ 46871244 tx 290258
⇌🛏73 P80 Lift
Credit Cards [1][2][3][5]

🏨 *Central* 31 Av la Fayette ☎ 46990065
AR

🏨 *Zanker* 76 r Gambetta ☎ 46870755 For

ROCHELLE, LA
Charente-Maritime
★★★ ***Brises*** chemin Digue Richelieu
(n.rest) ☏ 46438937 tx 790754
15 Jan- 15 Dec
⇨🛏46 🍴 P Lift Sea
Credit Cards [1] [3]

★★★ ***France et d'Angleterre*** (MAP/BW)
22 r Gargoulleau ☏ 46413466 tx 790717
rm76(⇨🛏67) P35 Lift (
Credit Cards [1] [2] [3] [5]

★★★ ***Yachtman*** 23 quai Valin
☏ 46412068 tx 790762
⇨🛏40 P10 Lift ⇌
Credit Cards [1] [3] [5]

★★ ***Campanile*** rte de Paris, Fief des
Ardennes Ouest ☏ 46340729 tx 791286
⇨🛏32 P32

★★ ***Ibis*** pl du Cdt-de-la-Motte-Rouge
☏ 46416022 tx 791431
⇨🛏76 Lift
Credit Cards [1] [3]

★★ ***St-Nicolas*** (Inter) 13 r Sardinerie
(n.rest) ☏ 46417155 tx 793075
⇨🛏76 🍴 P45 Lift
Credit Cards [1] [2] [3] [5]

★★ ***Urbis*** r Vieljeux et Chef de Ville (n.rest)
☏ 46506868 tx 791726
rm77(⇨🛏67) Lift
Credit Cards [1] [3]

★ ***Trianon et Plage*** (FAH) 6 r de la Monnaie
☏ 46412135

France

Feb-23 Dec
⇨🛏25 P20 (
Credit Cards [1] [2] [3] [5]

At **PUILBOREAU**(4km NE)

★★ ***Climat*** Zone Commerciale de
Beaulieu, RN11 ☏ 46673737
⇨🛏48 P50
Credit Cards [1] [3]

🍴 **Depan Auto** Zone Commerciale de
Beaulieu ☏ 46671616 M/C **P**

ROCHE-POSAY, LA
Vienne
★ ***Parc*** av Fontaines ☏ 49862002
May- Sep
rm80(⇨🛏58) 🍴 P50 Lift ♪

ROCHES-DE-CONDRIEU, LES
Isère
★★ ***Bellevue*** Pn 1 quai du Rhône (n.rest)
☏ 74564142
Closed Mon & Sun pm
rm18(⇨🛏14) A3rm 🍴 P15 Lake
Credit Cards [1] [2] [3] [4] [5]

ROCHE-SUR-YON, LA
Vendée
★★ ***Campanile*** Les Bazinières, rte de
Nantes ☏ 51372786 tx 701766

⇨🛏42 P42
Credit Card [3]

★★ ***Ibis*** bd Arago ☏ 51362600 tx 700601
⇨🛏63 Lift
Credit Cards [1] [3]

🍴 **Baudry** bd Lavoisier ☏ 51362235 For

ROCROI
Ardennes
★★ ***Commerce*** pl A-Briand (n.rest)
☏ 24541115
10 Feb -5 Jan
⇨🛏12 🍴

RODEZ
Aveyron
★★★ ***Broussy*** (MAP/BW) 1 av V- Hugo
☏ 6568187 tx 520198
⇨🛏46 🍴 P10 Lift
Credit Cards [1] [2] [3] [5]

★★★ ***Tour Maje*** (Inter) bd Gally
☏ 65683468
rm48(⇨🛏45) P Lift (
Credit Cards [1] [2] [3] [5]

ROISSY-EN-FRANCE
See **PARIS AIRPORTS** under **CHARLES-DE-GAULLE AIRPORT**

ROMANS-SUR-ISÈRE
Drôme
★★ ***Terminus*** (Inter) 48 av P-Sémard
(n.rest) ☏ 75024688
5 Jan-22 Feb
rm32(⇨🛏18) Lift
Credit Card [1]

TERMINUS HOTEL ★★

Place de la Carretta
46500 ROCAMADOUR
Tél.: 65.33.62.14
65.33.65.00 (off season)

In the heart of the town, in a rustic setting, the Hotel Terminus reserves a family welcome for you.

We will introduce you to gastronomic cuisine based on local produce in the purest Quercy tradition.

From our terrace we offer you a wonderful view overlooking the valley. Facilities for seminars and business functions.

TERMINUS HOTEL ★★
Restaurant

France

ROMILLY-SUR-SEINE
Aube

★★ *Climat* av Diderot (N19) ☎ 25249240 tx 692844
⇨♠35 P

ROMORANTIN-LANTHENAY
Loir-et-Cher

★★ **Colombier** 🆕 18 pl Vieux Marché
☎ 54761276
15 Feb-15 Sep & 22 Sep-15 Jan
⇨♠10 🍴 P10
Credit Cards ①②③④⑤

★★ **Lion D'Or** (Relais et Châteaux) 69 r G-Clemenceau ☎ 54760028 tx 750990
Closed Jan-mid Feb
⇨♠16 🍴 P16 Lift
Credit Cards ①②③⑤

ROQUEBRUNE-CAP-MARTIN
Alpes-Maritimes

★★★ **Victoria & Plage** 7 prom du Cap
☎ 93356590
19 Feb-4 Nov
rm30(⇨♠8) 🍴 P7 (Sea
Credit Cards ①②③④⑤

★★ **Westminster** 14 av L-Laurens, quartier Bon-Voyage ☎ 93350068
10 Feb & 20 Oct
⇨♠31 A4rm P8 Sea
Credit Cards ①③

ROQUE-GAGEAC, LA
Dordogne

★ **Belle Étoile** 🆕 ☎ 53295144
Etr-15 Oct
rm17(⇨♠16) 🍴 Lake
Credit Card ③

ROQUES-SUR-GARONNE See **TOULOUSE**

ROSCOFF
Finistère

★★★ **Gulf Stream** r Marquise-de-Kergariou ☎ 98697319
13 Apr-Nov
⇨♠32 P50 Lift ♪ Sea
Credit Cards ①③

★★ **Talabardon** pl Église ☎ 98612495 tx 940711
15 Mar-15 Nov Closed :Rest closed Sun evening
⇨♠38 🍴 P Lift Beach Sea
Credit Cards ①③

★ **Bains** pl Église ☎ 98612065
May-Oct
rm30(⇨♠8) 🍴 Lift Sea
Credit Cards ①③

ROSIERS, LES
Maine-et-Loire

★★ **Jeanne de Laval** (N152) ☎ 41518017
15 Feb-8 Dec
rm12(♠1) A7rm 🍴 P20
Credit Cards ①②③④⑤

ROSPORDEN
Finistère

★★★ **Bourhis** 🆕 (FAH) pl Gare
☎ 98592389 tx 914808
Apr-15 Nov & Dec-9 Mar Closed :Rest closed Mon & Sun evening
⇨♠27 P20 Lift
Credit Cards ①②③⑤

ROUBAIX
Nord

★★★ **Grand Altea** 22 av J-Lebas
☎ 20734000 tx 132301
⇨♠92 Lift
Credit Cards ①②③⑤

At **VILLENEUVE-D'ASCQ**(6km S)

★★ **Balladins** Quartier de l'Hôtel-de-Ville, angle bd de Valmy/r Entre Deux, Villes
☎ 20670720
⇨♠38 P25
Credit Cards ①②

★★ **Campanile** La Cousinerie, av de Canteleu ☎ 20918310 tx 133335
⇨♠50 P50
Credit Cards ①③

★★ *Climat* Quartier de Triolo, r Trudaine
☎ 20050403 tx 692844
⇨♠37
Credit Cards ①③

★★ **Ibis-Lille** Quartier de l'Hôtel-de-Ville, , Rocade Est ☎ 20918150 tx 160626
⇨♠80 P100 Lift
Credit Cards ①③

ROUEN
Seine-Maritime

★★★★ **Pullman Albane** r Croix-de-Fer
☎ 35980698 tx 180949
⇨♠125 P80 Lift (
Credit Cards ①②③⑤

★★★ **Dieppe** (MAP/BW) pl B-Tissot
☎ 35719600 tx 180413
⇨♠42 Lift (
Credit Cards ①②③④

★★ **Arcade** 20 pl de l'Église St-Sever
☎ 35628182 tx 7706725
⇨♠144 P200 Lift
Credit Cards ①③

★★ **Cardinal** 1 pl de la Cathédrale (n.rest)
☎ 35702442
4 Jan -18 Dec
⇨♠22 Lift
Credit Cards ①③

★★ **Cathédrale** 12 r St-Romaine (n.rest)
☎ 35715795
⇨♠24 Lift
Credit Cards ①③

★★ **Europe** 87 r aux Ours (n.rest)
☎ 35708330 tx 172172
rm27(⇨♠17) P27 Lift (
Credit Cards ①②③

★★ **Ibis Rouen Centre** 56 quai Gaston Boulet ☎ 35704818 tx 771393
⇨♠88 P30 Lift
Credit Cards ①③

★★ *Nord* (Inter) 91 r Gros-Horloge (n.rest)
☎ 35704141 tx 771938
⇨♠62 P100 Lift

★★ **Normandie** (Inter) 19 & 21 r du Bec
☎ 35715577 tx 771350
⇨♠23 Lift
Credit Cards ①②③⑤

★★ **Paris** (Inter) 12-14 r de la Champmeslé (off quai de la Bourse) (n.rest) ☎ 35700926 tx 771979
rm24(⇨♠23) 🍴 P10 Lift
Credit Cards ①②③⑤

★★ *Québec* 18-24 r Québec (off r de la République) (n.rest) ☎ 35700938
5 Jan -20 Dec
rm38(⇨♠34) P4 Lift
Credit Cards ①②③

★★ **Viking** (Inter) 21 quai du Havre (n.rest)
☎ 35703495 tx 180503
⇨♠37 🍴 P Lift Sea
Credit Cards ①②③

★ *Arcades* 52 r des Carmes (n.rest)
☎ 35701030
rm16(♠5)
Credit Card ②

★ **Vieille Tour** 42 pl Haute Vieille Tour (n.rest) ☎ 35700327
rm23(⇨♠14) P23 Lift (
Credit Cards ②③

🍴 *Guez* 135 Rue Lafayette ☎ 35727684
For

At **BARENTIN**(17km NW)

★★ **Campanile** Lotissement de la Carbonnière ☎ 35926404 tx 741680
⇨♠49 P (

★★ **Ibis** Rte Nationale 15 ☎ 35910123 tx 180810
⇨♠40 P
Credit Cards ①③

At **BOIS-GUILLAUME**(5Km NE)

★★ *Climat* av de l'Europe ☎ 35616110 tx 172902
⇨♠42 P42
Credit Cards ①③④

At **MONT-ST-AIGNAN**(2km N)

★★ **Campanile** ZAC de la Vatine, rte d'Hauppeville ☎ 35597500
⇨♠41 P

At **PETIT-QUEVILLY, LE**

★★ **Fimotel** 112 av Jean-Jaurès
☎ 35623850 tx 770132
⇨♠42 P12 Lift
Credit Cards ①②③⑤

At **ST-ÉTIENNE-DU-ROUVRAY**(2km S)

★★★ **Novotel-Rouen Sud** Le Madrillet
☎ 35665850 tx 180215
⇨♠135 P180 Lift ♪ ⇨
Credit Cards ①②③⑤

★★ **Campanile** r de la Mare aux Sangsues
☎ 35640416 tx 172145
⇨♠49 P49
Credit Card ③

★★ **Ibis-Rouen Sud** av Maryse-Bastie
☎ 35660363 tx 771014
⇨♠108 Lift
Credit Cards ①③

At **TOURVILLE-LA-RIVIÈRE**(10km SE)

★★ *Climat* Le Clos aux Antes ☎ 35784948 tx 771189
⇨♠35
Credit Card ①

ROUFFACH
Haut-Rhin

France

At **BOLLENBERG**(6km SW)
★★ **Bollenberg** ☎ 89496247 tx 880896
⇌ 🛏 50 P50 ♨ Mountain
Credit Cards ① ② ③ ⑤

ROUFFILLAC See **ST-JULIEN-DE-LAMPON**

ROUSSILLON
Isère
★ **Garrigon** rte St-Saturnin d'Apt
☎ 90056322
⇌ 🛏 8 P20 ⇌ ♨ Mountain
Credit Cards ① ② ③ ⑤
✉ **Guillon** 133 rte de la Chapelle
☎ 74862436 **P** Ope

At **CHANAS**(6km S on N7)
✉ **Modern** N7 ☎ 74842191 **P** Sko

ROYAN
Charente-Maritime
★★ **Grand De Pontaillac** 195 av de Pontaillac (n.rest) ☎ 46390044
Etr-Sep
rm55(⇌🛏 50) A10rm 🍴 P4 Lift (Sea
Credit Cards ① ③
✉ **Richard** rte de Saintes ZC, 38 r Lavoister ☎ 46050355 Peu Tal

At **CONCHE-DE-NAUZAN**(2.5km NW)
★★★ **Résidence De Rohan** Parc des Fées (n.rest) ☎ 46390075
Etr-15 Nov
⇌ 🛏 41 A19rm P20 (℘ Sea
Credit Cards ② ③

ROYAT
Puy-de-Dôme
★★★ **Métropole** 4 bd Vaquez
☎ 73358018
May-Sep
Lift (Mountain
Credit Card ①

ROYE
Somme
✉ **Dallet** 5 pl de la République
☎ 22871089 **P** For

RUFFEC
Charente
★ **Toque Blanche** 16 r du Gl-Leclerc
☎ 45310016
⇌ 🛏 20 P25 (
Credit Cards ① ③

RUNGIS
Val-de-Marne See also **ORLY AIRPORT** under **PARIS AIRPORTS**
★★★★ **Holiday Inn** 4 av C-Lindbergh
☎ 46872666 tx 204679
⇌ 🛏 168 P200 Lift ℘ ⇌
Credit Cards ① ② ③ ④ ⑤
★★★★ **Pullman Paris Orly** 20 av C-Lindbergh ☎ 46873636 tx 260738
⇌ 🛏 206 🍴 P130 Lift ⇌
Credit Cards ① ② ③ ⑤
★★ **Campanile** angle r du Pont-des-Halles, r du Mondetours ☎ 46873529 tx 261163
⇌ 🛏 49 P49
Credit Card ③
★★ **Ibis** r Baltard bis Zone-de-Delta
☎ 46872245 tx 261173

⇌ 🛏 119 ⌐ Lift
Credit Cards ① ③

SABLES-D'OLONNE, LES
Vendée
★★ **Residence** 36 prom Clemenceau (n.rest) ☎ 51320666
Mar-3 Nov
rm35(⇌🛏 30) 🍴 Sea
Credit Cards ① ② ③ ⑤

At **CHÂTEAU-D'OLONNE**(4km E on D36)
✉ **Tixier** La Mouzinère ☎ 51324104 VW Aud

SABLES-D'OR-LES-PINS
Côtes-du-Nord
★★★ **Bon Accueil** allée des Acacias
☎ 96414219
Etr-Sep
rm39(⇌🛏 25) P12 Lift
Credit Cards ① ③
★★ **Ajoncs d'Or** allée des Acacias
☎ 96414212
15 May-Sep
rm75(⇌🛏 44) A40rm P20 Sea
Credit Card ③
★★ **Diane** av Brouard ☎ 96414207
12 Apr-Sep
rm45(⇌🛏 40) A10rm P60 Sea Lake
★★ **Dunes d'Armor et Mouettes** (n.rest)
☎ 96414206
May-Oct
⇌ 🛏 54 P30 Sea
★★ **Voile d'Or** r des Acacias ☎ 96414249
15 Mar-15 Nov
rm18(⇌🛏 16) A4rm P20 Sea
Credit Cards ① ③

SABLÉ-SUR-SARTHE
Sarthe
★★ **Campanile** 9 av Ch-de-Gaulle
☎ 43953053
⇌ 🛏 31 P31
Credit Card ③
★ **St-Martin** 3 r Haute St-Martin
☎ 43950003
Apr-Mar Closed :Rest closed Fri evening
rm10(⇌🛏 5) P8

At **SOLESMES**(3km NE on D22)
★★★ **Grand** (FAH) ☎ 43954510 tx 722903
Closed Feb
⇌ 🛏 34 A2rm Lift
Credit Cards ① ② ③ ⑤

SACLAY See **ORSAY**

ST-AFFRIQUE
Aveyron
★★ **Moderne** 43 av A-Pezet ☎ 65492044
15 Jan-15 Dec
rm39(⇌🛏 33) A11rm 🍴 P15 Mountain
Credit Cards ① ③

ST-AIGNAN
Loir-et-Cher
★★ **St-Aignan** ☎ 7-9 quai J-J-Delorme
☎ 54751804

Feb-Dec Closed :Rest closed Tue midday & Sun pm(winter)
rm23(⇌🛏 17) 🍴 P18
Credit Cards ① ③

ST-ALBAIN See **MÂCON**

ST-AMOUR
Jura
★★ **Alliance** ☎ rte Ste-Marie ☎ 84487494
Feb-Nov Closed :Rest closed Mon & Sun evening
rm16(⇌🛏 8) P7
Credit Cards ① ③ ⑤
★ **Commerce** ☎ pl Chevalerie ☎ 84487305
rm15(⇌🛏 7) 🍴 P5 ℘ ⇌ Mountain
Credit Card ③

ST-ANDRÉ-LES-ALPES
Alpes-de-Haute-Provence
✉ **Chabot** rte de Nice ☎ 92890001 **P**
✉ **J Rouvier** 202 rte Nationale
☎ 92890302 **P** Peu

ST-ANDRÉ-LES-VERGERS See **TROYES**

ST-APOLLINAIRE See **DIJON**

ST-AUBIN
Essonne
★★ **Climat-Paris Sud** pl de la Mairie
☎ 69412055
⇌ 🛏 29
Credit Cards ① ③

ST-AUBIN-SUR-MER
Calvados
★★ **St-Aubin** ☎ r de Verdun ☎ 31973039
Feb-Nov Closed :Rest closed Sun evening & Mon (winter)
rm26(⇌🛏 20) Sea
Credit Cards ② ③

ST-AVOLD
Moselle
★★★ **Novotel** RN33 ☎ 87922593
⇌ 🛏 61 P ⇌
Credit Cards ① ② ③ ⑤

ST-BRIEUC
Côtes-du-Nord
★★★ **Alexandre l'er** 19 pl du Guesclin
☎ 96337945
⇌ 🛏 43 P Lift
Credit Cards ① ② ③ ⑤
★★★ **Griffon** (Inter) r de Guernsey
☎ 96945762 tx 950701
⇌ 🛏 48 🍴 P50 Lift ℘
Credit Cards ① ② ③ ⑤

At **PLÉRIN**(2km N via N12)
★★ **Chêne Vert** ☎ (FAH/Inter) r de St Laurent ☎ 96746320 tx 741323
Closed :Rest closed Sun
⇌ 🛏 50 🍴 ℘
Credit Cards ① ② ③ ⑤

At **YFFINIAC**(5km W)
★ **Fimotel de la Baie** Aire de Repos (N12)
☎ 96726410
Closed :Rest closed Mon & Sat midday
⇌ 🛏 42 P Lift
Credit Cards ① ② ⑤

ST-CAST-LE-GUILDO
Côtes-du-Nord →

103

★ *Angleterre et Panorama* r Fosserole (n.rest) ☎ 96419144
Jul-7 Sep
rm40 🍽 P45 ♟ Sea

At **GARDE-ST-CAST, LA**(2 km SE)
★★★ *Ar Vro* 10 bd de la Plage (n.rest) ☎ 96418501
5 Jun-6 Sep
rm47(⇌🛏42) 🍽 P40 Lift Sea
Credit Cards ①②③⑤

ST-CÉRÉ
Lot

★★ *Coq Arlequin* Pn 1 bd du Dr-Roux ☎ 65380213
Mar-Dec
⇌🛏32 🍽 P10 ♟ ⇌ Beach
Credit Cards ①③

ST-CHAMANT
Corrèze

★ *Roche de Vic* les quatre rtes d'Albussac ☎ 55281587
Mar-Dec
⇌🛏14 🍽 P20
Credit Cards ①③

ST-CHÉLY-D'APCHER
Lozère

★ *Lion d'Or* 132 r T-Roussel ☎ 66310014
Closed 1-20 Jan
rm30(⇌🛏5) 🍽

ST-CYPRIEN
Pyrénées-Orientales

★★ *Ibis* Bassin Nord du Port ☎ 68213030 tx 500459
⇌🛏34 P
Credit Cards ①③

ST-DENIS
Seine-St-Denis

★★ *Climat* 212 av du Prés-Wilson ☎ 48099685 tx 230737
⇌🛏57 P Lift
Credit Cards ①③

★★ *Fimotel* 20 r J-Saulnier ☎ 48094810 tx 230046
⇌🛏60 P60 Lift 〔
Credit Cards ①②③

ST-DENIS-SUR-SARTHON
Orne

★★ *Faïencerie* rte Paris-Brest ☎ 33273016
Etr-Oct
⇌🛏18 P Mountain
Credit Card ③

ST-DIZIER
Haute-Marne

★★★ *Gambetta* (Inter) 62 r Gambetta ☎ 25565210 tx 842365
⇌🛏63 🍽 P40 Lift 〔
Credit Cards ①②③⑤

★★★ *Soleil d'Or* (MAP) 64 r Gambetta ☎ 25056822 tx 840946
⇌🛏60 P Lift ⇌

★★ *Champagne* 19 r P-Timbaud ☎ 25056754
Closed :Rest closed Sun
⇌🛏28 P25
Credit Card ③

France

★ *Auberge la Bobotte* rte Nationale 4 (3km W on N4) ☎ 25562003
Etr-Dec
⇌🛏10 🍽 P6 〔

🚗 **Dynamic-Motors** rte de Bar-Le-Duc ☎ 25560398 For

ST-DOULCHARD See **BOURGES**

STE-ADRESSE See **HAVRE, LE**

STE-ANNE-LA-PALUD
Finistère

★★★ *Plage* (Relais et Châteaux) La Plage ☎ 98925012 tx 941377
Apr-Oct 12
⇌🛏30 A6rm P50 Lift ♟ ⇌ Sea
Credit Cards ①②③

STE-CATHÉRINE See **BRIANÇON**

STE-FOY-LES-LYONS See **LYON**

ST-ÉGRÈVE See **GRENOBLE**

ST-ÉLOY-LES-MINES
Puy-de-Dôme

★★ *Ibis* r J-Jaurès ☎ 73852150 tx 392009
Closed :Rest closed wknds in winter
⇌🛏29 P40
Credit Cards ①③

STE-MAXIME
Var **See also BEAUVALLON**

★★★ *Beau Site* 6 bd des Cistes ☎ 94961963 tx 970080
11 Apr-Sep
⇌🛏36 Lift ♟ ⇌ Sea
Credit Cards ①②③⑤

ST-ÉMILION
Gironde

★★★ *Hostellerie de la Plaisance* pl Clocher ☎ 57247232
⇌🛏12
Credit Cards ①②③⑤

STE-ENIMIE
Lozère

★★ *Commerce* (FAH) RN586 ☎ 66485001
Apr-Sep
⇌🛏20 A10rm 🍽 P 〔
Credit Cards ①②③

SAINTES
Charente-Maritime

★★★ *Commerce Mancini* r des Messageries ☎ 46930561 tx 791012
rm39(⇌🛏32) P18 〔
Credit Cards ①②③⑤

★★★ *Relais du Bois St-Georges* rte de Royan ☎ 46935099 tx 790488
⇌🛏31 🍽 P80 〔 ♟ ⇌ Lake
Credit Cards ①③

★★ *Ibis* rte de Royan ☎ 46743634 tx 791394
⇌🛏71 P90
Credit Cards ①②③

★★ *Messageries* (Inter) r des Messageries (n.rest) ☎ 46936499 tx 793132

rm36(⇌🛏33) 🍽 P19 〔
Credit Cards ①②③⑤

★★ *Terminus* espl de la Gare (n.rest) ☎ 46743503
10 Jan-15 Dec
⇌🛏28 🍽 〔
Credit Cards ①②③⑤

SAINTES-MARIES-DE-LA-MER, LES
Bouches-du-Rhône

★★ *Mirage* 14 r C-Pelletan (n.rest) ☎ 90978043
20 Mar-15 Oct
⇌🛏27

ST-ÉTIENNE
Loire

★★★★ *Altea Parc de l'Europe* Rond Point de l'Europe, r de Wuppertal ☎ 77252275 tx 300050
⇌🛏120 P15 Lift
Credit Cards ①②③⑤

★★★ *Grand* 10 av Libération ☎ 77329977 tx 300811
⇌🛏66

★★★ *Terminus du Forez* (FAH) 31 av Denfert-Rochereau ☎ 77324847 tx 307191
rm66(⇌🛏62) 🍽 P36 Lift 〔
Credit Cards ①②③④⑤

★★ *Ibis* 35 pl Massenet ☎ 77933187 tx 307340
⇌🛏57 🍽 P80 Lift
Credit Cards ①②③⑤

ST-ÉTIENNE AIRPORT
Loire

At **ANDRÉZIEUX-BOUTHÉON**(2km W of N82)

★★★ *Novotel* Centre De Ville (N82) ☎ 77365563 tx 900722
⇌🛏98 P150 Lift ⇌
Credit Cards ①②③⑤

ST-ÉTIENNE-DE-BAIGORRY
Pyrénées-Atlantiques

★★ *Arcé* ☎ 59374014
15 Mar-11 Nov
⇌🛏27 A5rm 🍽 P40 ♟ ⇌ Mountain Lake
Credit Cards ①②③

ST-ÉTIENNE-DU-ROUVRAY See **ROUEN**

ST-FLORENTIN
Yonne

★ *Est* 7 r fbg St-Martin (n.rest) ☎ 86351035
⇌🛏18 A7rm 🍽 P15
Credit Cards ①②③⑤

At **VENIZY**(5.5km N)

★★ *Moulin des Pommerats* ☎ 86350804
⇌🛏20 A18rm P25 ♟
Credit Cards ①③⑤

ST-FLOUR
Cantal

★★★ *Étape* 18 av de la République ☎ 71601303
⇌🛏34 A11rm 🍽 Lift Mountain
Credit Cards ①②③④⑤

★★★ *Europe* DPn 12-13 Cours Spy-des-Ternes ☎ 71600364
13 Mar-Nov
rm45(⇌🛏41) 🍽 P100 Lift Sea Mountain
Credit Card ①

France

★★ **Nouvel Bonne Table** (MAP) 16 av de la République ☎ 71600586 tx 393160
Apr-Oct
rm48(⇌↑47) 🕿 P60 Lift ♪ Mountain
Credit Cards 1 2 3 4 5

★★ **St-Jacques** (FAH) 8 pl Liberté ☎ 71600920
15 Jan-11 Nov
⇌↑28 🕿 P10 Lift ⇌ Mountain
Credit Cards 1 3 4

★★ **Voyageurs** 25 r Collège ☎ 71603444
Etr-Nov
rm35(⇌↑25) 🕿 P Lift Mountain
Credit Cards 1 2 3 5

ST-GAUDENS
Haute-Garonne

★★ **Ferrière & France** 1 r Gl-Leclerc (n.rest) ☎ 61891457
rm15(⇌↑12) 🕿 P8
Credit Cards 1 2 3 5

At **VILLENEUVE-DE-RIVIÈRE**(6km W on D117)
★★ **Cèdres** ☎ 61893600
⇌↑20 P30 ♪ Mountain
Credit Cards 1 3

ST-GENIS-LAVAL See LYON

ST-GENIS-POUILLY
Ain

★★ **Climat** Lieudit le Marais ☎ 50420520
⇌↑42 P50 Mountain
Credit Cards 1 3

ST-GERMAIN-DE-JOUX
Ain

★ **Reygrobellet** ☎ 50598113
⇌↑10 🕿 Mountain
Credit Cards 3 5

ST-GERMAIN-EN-LAYE
Yvelines

★★★ **Ermitage des Loges** (MAP) 11 av des Loges ☎ 34518886 tx 697112
Closed : Rest closed Sun evening
⇌↑34 P Lift
Credit Cards 1 2 3 5

★★ **Campanile** rte de Mantes, Maison Forestière ☎ 34515959 tx 697547
⇌↑54 P54
Credit Card 3

At **CHAMBOURCY**(4km NW)
★★ **Climat** r du Mur du Parc ☎ 30744261
⇌↑46 P100 ⇌
Credit Cards 1 3

ST-GERMAIN-L'ESPINASSE
See **ROANNE**

ST-GERVAIS-EN-VALLIÈRE
Saône-et-Loire

★★ **Moulin d'Hauterive** ☎ 85915556 tx 801391
Feb-15 Dec Closed :Rest closed Mon & Sun evening
⇌↑22 A2rm P ♪ ⇌ U
Credit Cards 1 2 3 5

ST-GERVAIS-LA-FORÊT See BLOIS

ST-GERVAIS-LES-BAINS
Haute-Savoie

★★★ ***Splendid*** (n.rest) ☎ 50782133
⇌↑20 Lift Mountain

ST-GILLES
Gard

At **SALIERS**(4Km E on N572)
★★★ ***Cabanettes en Camargue*** (MAP) ☎ 66873153 tx 480451
Closed 15 Jan-20 Feb
⇌↑29 🕿 P50 ⇌
Credit Cards 1 2 3 5

ST-GILLES-CROIX-DE-VIE
Vendée

★★ ***Embruns*** 16 bd be la Mer (n.rest) ☎ 51551140
Closed :Rest closed Sat
⇌↑17 🕿 Sea
Credit Cards 1 3

ST-GIRONS
Ariège

★★★ ***Eychenne*** (MAP/BW) 8 av P-Laffont ☎ 61662055 tx 521273
Feb-22 Dec
rm48(⇌↑43) 🕿 P30 (Mountain
Credit Cards 1 2 3 5

★★★ **Hostellerie la Truite Dorée** L 28 av de la Résistance ☎ 61661689
Mar-Oct
⇌↑15 🕿 P30 (🖾 Mountain Lake
Credit Cards 2 3 5

ST-HERBLAIN See NANTES

ST-HILAIRE-DU-HARCOUËT
Manche

★★ **Cygne** L 67 r Waldeck-Rousseau ☎ 33491184 tx 171455
10 Jan-15 Dec
A25rm 🕿 P7 Lift
Credit Cards 1 2 3 5

★ **Lion d'Or** L 120 r Avranches ☎ 33491082
rm20(⇌↑16) 🕿 P25
Credit Cards 1 3

★ ***Relais de la Poste*** 11 r de Mortain ☎ 33491031
Closed :Rest closed Mon
rm12(⇌↑8)
Credit Card 1

ST-JEAN-CAP-FERRAT
Alpes-Maritimes

★★★★ **Grand Cap Ferrat** bd Gl-de-Gaulle ☎ 93760021 tx 470184
3 May-19 Oct
⇌↑65 🕿 P60 Lift (♪ ⇌ Sea Mountain
Credit Cards 1 2 3 5

ST-JEAN-DE-LUZ
Pyrénées-Atlantiques

★★★★ **Chantaco** rte d'Ascain ☎ 59261476 tx 540016
Apr-Oct
⇌↑24 P50 (♪ ♭ Mountain Lake
Credit Cards 1 2 5

★★★ **Poste** 83 r Gambetta (n.rest) ☎ 59260453 tx 540140
rm34(⇌↑21) (
Credit Cards 1 2 3 5

★★ **Paris** 1 bd Passicot (n.rest) ☎ 59260062
Feb-Dec
rm29(⇌↑14) Lift Mountain
Credit Cards 1 3

★ **Continental** 15 av Verdun ☎ 59260123
⇌↑21 Lift Mountain
Credit Cards 1 2 3 5

At **CIBOURE**(1km SW)
★ ***Hostellerie de Ciboure*** 10 av J-Jaurès ☎ 59470057
rm22(⇌↑16) P ⇌

ST-JEAN-DE-MAURIENNE
Savoie

★★ **St-Georges** 334 r République (n.rest) ☎ 79640106
rm22(⇌↑20) P10 Mountain
Credit Cards 1 2

ST-JEAN-DE-MONTS
Vendée

★★ **Plage** espl de la Mer ☎ 51580035
Mar-Sep
rm50(⇌↑48) P15 Lift Sea
Credit Cards 1 2 3

🐚 **G Vrignaud** rte de Challens ☎ 51582674 **P** Ren

ST-JEAN-LE-THOMAS
Manche

★★ **Bains** Face Post ☎ 33488420 tx 170380
15 Mar-10 Oct
rm31(⇌↑24) A8rm P50 ⇌
Credit Cards 1 2 3 5

ST-JEAN-PIED-DE-PORT
Pyrénées-Atlantiques

★★★ **Continental** 3 av Rénaud (n.rest) ☎ 59370025
Etr-15 Nov
⇌↑22 P20 Lift Mountain
Credit Cards 1 2 3

★★ **Central** (FAH) 1 pl Ch-de-Gaulle ☎ 59370022
5 Feb-23 Dec
rm14(⇌↑7) Mountain
Credit Cards 1 2 3 5

★★ **Pyrénées** pl Marché ☎ 59370101
22 Dec-3 Jan & 20 Jan-20 Nov
⇌↑27 P5 Lift Mountain
Credit Cards 1 2 3

ST-JULIEN-DE-LAMPON
Dordogne

At **ROUFFILLAC**(N of river)
★★ ***Cayre*** DPn (n.rest) ☎ 53297024
Closed Oct
⇌↑20 A12rm 🕿 P50 ♪ ⇌ Mountain

ST-JULIEN-EN-BEAUCHÊNE
Hautes-Alpes

★★ **Bermond-Gauthier** rte Nationale 75 ☎ 92580352
Feb-20 Dec
rm20(⇌↑10) 🕿 P10 ⇌ Mountain
Credit Cards 1 3 5

France

ST-JULIEN-EN-GENEVOIS
Haute-Savoie

★ *Savoyarde* DPn 15 rte de Lyon
☎ 50492579
rm10(⇌1) P

ST-JUNIEN
Haute-Vienne

★★ *Concorde* L 49 av H-Barbusse
(n.rest) ☎ 55021708
15 Jan-15 Dec
⇌26 P20
Credit Cards 1 2 3

★★ *Relais de Comodoliac* (FAH) 22 av S-Carnot ☎ 55022726 tx 590336
⇌28 P40
Credit Cards 1 2 3 5

ST-LARY-SOULAN
Hautes-Pyrénées

★★ *Terasse Fleurie* ☎ 62395148
tx 520360
15 Dec- 15 Apr & 15 Jun-15 Sep
rm28(⇌19) P20 Mountain
Credit Card 2

ST-LAURENT-DE-COGNAC See **COGNAC**

ST-LAURENT-DU-VAR See **NICE**

ST-LAURENT-SUR-SÈVRE
Vendée

At **TRIQUE, LA**(1km N)

★★★ *Baumotel et la Chaumière*
☎ 51678081 tx 701758
⇌20 A3rm P40
Credit Cards 1 2 3 5

ST-LÉONARD-DES-BOIS
Sarthe

★★★ *Touring* (MAP) ☎ 43972803
tx 722006
15 Feb-15 Nov
⇌33 P Lift Mountain
Credit Cards 1 2 3 5

ST-LIEUX-LES-LAVAUR See **LAVAUR**

ST-LÔ
Manche

★★ *Marignan* pl Gare (n.rest) ☎ 33051515
Closed Feb
rm18(⇌12) P
Credit Cards 1 2 3 5

★★ *Terminus* 3 av Briovère ☎ 33050860
15 Jan -15 Dec
rm15(⇌12) P
Credit Cards 1 3

★★ *Univers* 1 av Briovère ☎ 33051084
rm24(⇌21) P20
Credit Cards 1 2 3 5

★ *Armoric* 15 r de la Marne (n.rest)
☎ 335717447
20 Feb-26 Dec
rm21(⇌7) P Lift

★ *Cremaillère* DPn 27 r du Belle, pl de la Préfecture ☎ 33571468
⇌12 P15
Credit Cards 1 2 3

ST-LOUIS
Haut-Rhin

At **HUNINGUE**(2km E D469)

★★ *Climat* 4 av de Bâle ☎ 89698610
⇌43
Credit Cards 1 3

ST-MALO
Ille-et-Vilaine

★★★ *Central* (MAP/BW) 6 Grande r
☎ 98408770 tx 740802
⇌46 Lift (
Credit Cards 1 2 3 5

★★★ *Duguesclin* 8 pl Duguesclin (n.rest)
☎ 99560130 tx 740802
⇌22 P30 Lift Sea
Credit Cards 1 2 3

★★★ *Mercure* chaussée du Sillon (n.rest)
☎ 99568484 tx 740583
⇌70 P27 Lift Sea
Credit Cards 1 2 3 5

★★ *Ibis* L r Gl-de-Gaulle, qtr de la Madeleine ☎ 99821010 tx 730626
⇌73 Lift
Credit Cards 1 3

★★ *Louvre* 2-4 r de Marins (n.rest)
☎ 99408662 tx 740802
15 Feb-25 Nov
rm45(⇌40) Lift
Credit Cards 1 3 4

★ *Noguette* 9 r de la Fosse ☎ 99408357
rm12(6) P
Credit Cards 1 3

At **GOUESNIÈRE, LA**(12km SE onD4)

★★ *Gare* ☎ 99891046 tx 740896
18 Jan- 18 Dec
⇌50 A24rm P50
Credit Cards 2 3 5

At **PARAMÉ**(1km E)

★★ *Rochebonne* 15 bd Châteaubriand
☎ 99560172 tx 740802
15 Feb- 15 Jan Closed :Rest closed Mon
⇌38 Lift
Credit Cards 1 3

ST-MARTIN-DE-BELLEVILLE
Savoie

★★★ *Novotel* Val Thorens ☎ 79000404
tx 980230
Dec-Apr & Jul-Aug
⇌104 Lift Mountain
Credit Cards 1 2 3 5

ST-MARTIN-EN-BRESSE
Saône-et-Loire

★★ *Au Puits Enchante* ☎ 85477196
Mar-Dec Closed :Rest closed Sun evening & Tue
⇌15 P15
Credit Card 1

ST-MAURICE-SUR-MOSELLE
Vosges

★★ *Relais des Ballons* L rte Benelux-Bâle (N66) ☎ 29251109

⇌17 P20 Mountain
Credit Cards 1 2 3 5

★ *Bonséjour* L ☎ 29251233
rm15(⇌2) P

ST-MAXIMIN-LA-STE-BAUME
Var

Auto Real Mont Fleury ☎ 94780358 P Fia

ST-MICHEL-DE-MAURIENNE
Savoie

★★ *Savoy* L 25 r Gl-Ferrié ☎ 79565512
rm22(⇌20) P6 Mountain
Credit Cards 1 2 3

ST-MICHEL-SUR-ORGE
Essonne

★★★ *Delfis-Bois-des-Roches* 17 r Berlioz
☎ 60154640 tx 692032
⇌80 Lift
Credit Cards 1 2 3 5

ST-NABORD See **REMIREMONT**

ST-NAZAIRE
Loire-Atlantique

★★ *Dauphin* 33 r J-Jaurès (n.rest)
☎ 40665961
rm20(⇌16) (
Credit Cards 1 3

Hougard 30 r J-B-Marcet ☎ 40901008 AR

ST-NICHOLAS See **ARRAS**

ST-OMER
Pas-de-Calais

★★ *Bretagne* (FAH) 2 pl Vainquai
☎ 21382578 tx 133290
rm43 A3rm P25
Credit Cards 1 2 3 5

★★ *Ibis* r H-Dupuis ☎ 21931111 tx 135206
⇌45 Lift
Credit Cards 1 3

★★ *St-Louis* 25 r d'Arras ☎ 21383521
Closed :Rest closed Sun
⇌30 P17
Credit Cards 1 3

At **TILQUES**(4km NW of N43)

★★ *Vert Mesnil* (FAH) (1.5km E of N43)
☎ 21932899 tx 133360
10 Jan- 18 Dec
rm70 A37rm P300 Lake
Credit Cards 1 2 3 4 5

ST-OUEN-L'AUMÔNE See **PONTOISE**

ST-PALAIS-SUR-MER
Charente-Maritime

★★★ *Courdouan* av Pontaillac
☎ 46231033
Apr-15 Oct
rm30 A7rm P6 Sea
Credit Cards 1 3

ST-PARDOUX-L'ORTIGLER
See **DONZENAC**

ST-PAUL
Alpes-Maritimes

★★★★ *Mas d'Artigny* (Relais et Châteaux) rte de la Colle ☎ 93328454
tx 470601

⇨♠83🅿 P120 Lift (♪ 🖼 ⇌ Sea
Mountain
Credit Cards ① ③
★★ *Climat* rte de la Colle ☎ 93329424
rm19 P190 ⇌ Sea

ST-PAUL-DE-LOUBRESSAC
Lot
★ *Relais de la Madeleine* Ⓛ 65219808
10 Jan-Nov
rm16(⇨♠8) P ♪
Credit Card ③

ST-PÉE-SUR-NIVELLE
Pyrénées-Atlantiques
★★ *Pyrénées Atlantiques* (N618)
☎ 59540222
rm33(⇨♠32) P30 Mountain
Credit Card ②

ST-PIERRE-DE-CHARTREUSE
Isère
★★ *Beau Site* Ⓛ ☎ 76886134
⇨♠33 ⇌ Mountain
Credit Cards ① ③ ⑤

ST-PIERRE-DU-VAUVRAY See **LOUVIERS**

ST-PIERRE-QUIBERON See **QUIBERON**

ST-POL-DE-LÉON
Finistère
🐟 *E Charetteur* pl du Creisker
☎ 98690208 Ren

ST-POL-SUR-TERNOISE
Pas-de-Calais
★ *Lion d'Or* 68 r Hesdin ☎ 21031293
rm35(⇨♠25) 🍴
Credit Cards ① ② ③ ⑤

ST-PONS
Hérault
★★ *Château de Ponderach* rte de
Narbonne ☎ 67970257
Apr-Oct
rm11(⇨9) 🍴 P40 Mountain
Credit Cards ① ② ③ ⑤
★ *Pastre* av Gare ☎ 67970054
Feb – Dec Closed : Rest closed Sat durning
Jan
rm20(⇨♠8) Mountain
Credit Card ①

ST-POURÇAIN-SUR-SIOULE
Allier
★ *Chêne Vert* (FAH) 35 bd Ledru-Rollin
☎ 70454065
rm30(⇨♠25) A15rm 🍴 P12
Credit Cards ① ② ③ ⑤
★ *Deux Ponts* Ⓛ (FAH) Ilot de Tivoli
☎ 70454114
15 Dec – 15 Nov
rm27(⇨♠14) Sea
Credit Cards ① ② ③ ⑤

ST-QUAY-PORTRIEUX
Côtes-du-Nord
★★ *Gerbot d'Avoine* 2 bd Littoral
☎ 96704009 tx 950702
rm26(⇨♠17) P25
Credit Cards ① ③
★ *Bretagne DPn* 36 quai de la République
(n.rest) ☎ 96704091
rm16(♠6) Sea

France

ST-QUENTIN
Aisne
★★★ *Grand* 6 r Dachery ☎ 23626977
tx 140225
⇨♠24 P12 Lift (
Credit Cards ③ ⑤
★★ *Campanile* ZAC de la Vallée, r C-
Naudin ☎ 23092122 tx 150596
⇨♠40 P40
Credit Card ③
★★ *France et Angleterre* 28 r E-Zola
(n.rest) ☎ 23621310 tx 140986
rm28(⇨♠20) 🍴 P17
Credit Cards ① ② ③
★★ *Paix & Albert Ier* 3 pl de Huit Octobre
☎ 23627762 tx 140225
rm82(⇨♠64) P12 Lift
Credit Cards ① ② ③ ⑤
🐟 *Auto* 418 rte de Paris ☎ 23623423 P
Peu Tal
🐟 *Moderne* r du Cdt-Raynal ☎ 23671490
For

ST-QUENTIN-EN-YVELINES
Yvelines
★★ *Fimotel* ☎ 34605024 tx 699235
⇨♠81 P60 Lift
Credit Cards ① ② ③ ⑤

ST-RAMBERT-D'ABLON
Drôme
★★ *Ibis* 'La Champagnère', RN7
☎ 75030400 tx 345958
⇨♠46 Lift
Credit Cards ① ③

ST-RAPHAËL
Var
★★★ *Continental* prom du Prés-Coty
(n.rest) ☎ 94950014 tx 970809
⇨♠49 P Lift Sea
★★ *Beau-Séjour* prom du Prés-Coty
☎ 94950375
⇨♠40 Lift Sea
Credit Cards ① ③ ⑤
★★ *Provençal* 197 r de la Garonne (n.rest)
☎ 94950152
⇨♠28 (Mountain
Credit Cards ① ③
🐟 *Agay* av Gratadis ☎ 94820616 AR
🐟 *R Bacchi* 658 av de Verdun
☎ 94959851 Cit

ST-RÉMY-DE-PROVENCE
Bouches-du-Rhône
★★★ *Antiques* 15 av Pasteur (n.rest)
☎ 90920302
Apr – Oct
⇨♠27 A10rm P50 ⇌
Credit Cards ① ② ③ ⑤
★★ *Castelet des Alpilles* pl Mireille
☎ 90920721
20 Mar – 10 Nov
rm19(⇨♠17) P30 ♪ ⇌ ▶ ∪ Beach
Mountain

Credit Cards ① ② ③ ⑤

ST-SATUR
Cher
★★ *Laurier* Ⓛ r du Commerce
☎ 48541720
Dec-Jan & Mar- 15 Nov
rm9(⇨♠6) P4
Credit Cards ① ③

ST-SERNIN-SUR-RANCE
Aveyron
★★ *Carayon* Ⓛ (Inter) pl du Fort
☎ 65996026
⇨♠37 🍴 P12 Lift Mountain
Credit Cards ① ② ③ ⑤

ST-TROJAN-LES-BAINS See **OLÉRON,
ILE D'**

ST-TROPEZ
Var
★★★★ *Byblos* av P-Signac ☎ 94970004
tx 470235
4 Mar-Oct
⇨♠107 🍴 P30 Lift (⇌ Sea
Credit Cards ② ③ ⑤
★★★ *Coste* (Inter) Port du Pilon (n.rest)
☎ 94970064
15 Mar-3 Nov
⇨♠30 P Sea
Credit Cards ① ② ③ ④ ⑤
★★★ *Ermitage* av P-Signac (n.rest)
☎ 94975233
rm30(⇨♠7) P16 (Sea Mountain
Credit Cards ② ⑤
🐟 *Fabbri* 6 r J-Mermoz ☎ 94970510 AR

ST-VAAST-LA-HOUGUE
Manche
★★ *France et des Fuschias* Ⓛ DPn 18 r
Ml-Foch ☎ 33544226
Mar-3 Jan Closed : Rest closed Mon
rm33(⇨♠29) A12rm
Credit Cards ① ② ③ ⑤

ST-VALERY-EN-CAUX
Seine-Maritime
★★★ *Altea St-Valery* av Clemenceau
☎ 35973548 tx 172308
⇨♠157 P20 Lift Sea
Credit Cards ① ② ③ ⑤

SALBRIS
Loire-et-Cher
★★★ *Mapotel Du Parc* Ⓛ (MAP) 10 av
d'Orléans ☎ 54971853 tx 751164
⇨♠27 🍴 P50 (
Credit Cards ① ② ③ ⑤
★ *Dauphin* Ⓛ 57 bd de la République
☎ 54970483
Feb-Dec Closed : Rest closed Sun evening
& Mon
rm10(⇨♠5) P18
Credit Cards ① ③

SALERS
Cantal
★ *Beffroi* r du Beffroi ☎ 71407011
Apr-Oct
⇨♠10 P15 Mountain

SALIERS See **ST-GILLES**

SALLANCHES
Haute-Savoie →

France

★★ **Ibis** av de Genève ☎ 50581442 tx 385754
Closed :Rest closed Sun evening
⇨♪56 Lift
Credit Cards 1 3

SALON-DE-PROVENCE
Bouches-du-Rhône

★★ **Ibis** rte d'Aix-Pelissanne, RN 572
☎ 90422357 tx 441591
⇨♪48 P35 ⌒
Credit Cards 2 3

◐◑ **Bagnis** 144 allée de Craponne
☎ 90534397 **P** Col

◐◑ **Beaulieu Autos** bd du Roy René
☎ 90533537 M/C **P AR**

At **BARBEN, LA**(8km SE)

★ **Touloubre** ☎ 90551685
15 Jan-15 Nov
⇨♪16 P100
Credit Cards 2 3

At **LANÇON-PROVENCE**(9km SE on A7)

★★★ **Mercure** ☎ 90539070
Closed :Rest closed Nov-Feb
⇨♪100 P20 Lift ⌒ Mountain
Credit Cards 1 2 3 5

SALSES
Pyrénées-Orientales

★★★ **Relais Roussillon** ☎ 68386067
⇨♪56 P ⌒ Mountain

SANARY-SUR-MER
Var

★★ **Tour** 24 quai de Gaulle ☎ 94741010
⇨♪28 P4 Sea
Credit Cards 1 3 5

SANCÉ-LES-MÂCON See MÂCON

SANCERRE
Cher

★★ **Rempart** Ŀ Rempart des Dames
☎ 48541018 tx 783541
⇨♪13 ☎ P50
Credit Cards 1 2 3 5

SANNOIS
Val-d'Oise

★★ **Campanile** ZUP d'Ermont Sannois, av de la Sadernaude ☎ 34137957 tx 697841
⇨♪49 P49
Credit Card 3

SARAN See ORLÉANS

SARLAT-LA-CANÉDA
Dordogne

★★★ **Hostellerie de Meysset** r des Éyzies ☎ 53590829
26 Apr-4 Oct
⇨♪26 P30
Credit Cards 1 2 3 5

★★★ **Madeleine Pn** 1 pl de la Petite-Rigaudie ☎ 53591041
15 Mar-Dec
⇨♪22 Lift
Credit Cards 1 3

★★★ **Salamandre** r Abbé Surguier (n.rest)
☎ 53593598 tx 550059
⇨♪40 ☎ P30 ⌒ Beach
Credit Cards 1 2 3 5

★ **Lion d'Or** 48 av Gambetta ☎ 53593598
rm26(⇨♪20) A4rm

◐◑ **St-Michel** rte de Brive ☎ 53310888 **P AR** Vol

◐◑ **Scarlet Auto** rte de Vitrac ☎ 53591064 Cit

SARREBOURG
Moselle

◐◑ **Deux Sarre** pl de la Gare ☎ 87033260 For

SARREGUEMINES
Moselle

◐◑ **Schwindt** 62 rte de Nancy
☎ 87982677 **P** Ren

SATOLAS AIRPORT See LYON

SAULCE-SUR-RHÔNE
Drôme

★★ **Ibis-Montélimar Nord** quartier Fraysse (n.rest) ☎ 75630960 tx 345960
⇨♪29
Credit Cards 1 3

◐◑ **J P Frey** RN 7 ☎ 75630038 **P** Cit

SAULIEU
Côte-D'or

★★★ **Poste** Ŀ (Inter) 2 r Grillot
☎ 80640567 tx 350540
⇨♪48 P35 Lift (
Credit Cards 1 2 3 4 5

SAULX-LES-CHARTREUX See LONGJUMEAU

SAUMUR
Maine-et-Loire

★★ **Londres** 48 r Orléans (n.rest)
☎ 41512398
rm28(⇨♪27) P15
Credit Cards 1 2 3 5

★ **Croix-Verte** 49 r de Rouen ☎ 41673931
2 Feb-20 Dec Closed :Rest closed Sun & Mon evening
rm18(⇨♪5) P12
Credit Cards 1 3 5

At **BAGNEUX**(1.5km SW)

★★ **Campanile** Côte de Bournan
☎ 41501440 tx 722709
⇨♪43 P43
Credit Card 3

At **CHÊNEHUTTE-LES-TUFFEAUX**(8km NW)

★★★ **Prieuré** (Relais et Châteaux)
☎ 41679016 tx 720379
⇨♪35 A16rm P50 (♪ ⌒
Credit Cards 1 3

SAUSHEIM See MULHOUSE

SAUT-DES-CUVES See GÉRARDMER

SAUZET See MONTÉLIMAR

SAVERNE
Bas-Rhin

★★ **Geiswiller** 17 r Côte ☎ 88911851
⇨♪38 ☎ P15 Lift
Credit Cards 1 2 3 5

★ **Boeuf Noir** 22 Grand' r ☎ 88911053 tx 890098
Closed :Rest closed Tue
rm20(⇨♪5) ☎ P10 Mountain
Credit Cards 1 3

★ **Chez Jean DPn** 3 r de la Gare ☎ 88911019
10 Jan-22 Dec
rm27(⇨♪24) P25 Lift Mountain
Credit Cards 1 2 3 5

SAVIGNAC-LES-ÉGLISES
Dordogne

HOTEL RESTAURANT **LES ARDILLIERES** ★★★
Route de Lacanau (D6), 33160 BORDEAUX SALAUNES
Tel. (56) 58.58.08-58.54.54 Télex: ITAG 540 495 (D 89)

A 6ha park in midst of the Gironde region. All rooms equipped with bath, toilet, telephone and television. We recommend our hotel for all your receptions, conferences, business meals, business meetings and exhibitions. Swimming pool in midst of wood, private tennis court in park. Table tennis – pétanque – horse-riding club 2 km.
Member of HOTEL DE VIGNOBLE CHAIN

HOTEL CHATEAU DE SAULON DE LA RUE HOTEL – RESTAURANT
Route de la Seurre – 21910 SAULON LA CHAPELLE. Tel.: 80.36.61.70 – Telex: Château 350 571 F
33 quiet rooms with bath, wc, tel. and tv. Restaurant with shady terrace. Large car park. 27 ha. forest.
Water plans. Tennis. At 10 minutes for Dijon.

France

★★ **Parc** ☎ 53050811 tx 570335
May-Oct
rm14(⇨♠12) P15 🅿 🛆
Credit Cards ①②③④⑤

SAVONNIÈRES See **TOURS**

SÉES
Orne

★ **Cheval Blanc** Ⓛ **DPn** 1 pl St-Pierre
☎ 33278048
rm9(♠2)
Credit Cards ①③

★ **Dauphin** Ⓛ **Pn** 31 pl Halls ☎ 33278007
rm9
Credit Cards ①②③⑤

SELLIÈRES
Jura See also **POLIGNY**

At **PASSENANS**(6km SE)
★★ **Domaine Touristique du Revermont** Ⓛ
Passenans ☎ 844446102
Mar-Dec
⇨♠28 🅿 P50 Lift 🅿 🛆
Credit Cards ①③

SEMUR-EN-AUXOIS
Côte-d'Or

★★ **Lac** (3km S on D1036 at Lac-de-Pont)
☎ 80971111
Feb-15 Dec Closed :Rest closed Sun evening & Mon
rm23(⇨♠20) 🅿 P30 Lake
Credit Cards ①③⑤

★ **Côte d'Or** Ⓛ **DPn** 3 pl G-Gaveau
☎ 80970313
18 Mar-10 Jan Closed :Rest closed Wed
rm14(⇨♠13) 🅿 P3
Credit Cards ①②③④

★ *Gourmets* Ⓛ 4 r Varenne ☎ 80970313
15 Mar -15 Nov Closed Rest closed Wednesday
⇨♠15 🅿 P8
Credit Cards ①②③

SÉNAS
Bouches-du-Rhône

★ **Luberon DPn** 17 av A-Aune ☎ 90572010
15 Dec-15 Oct Closed :Rest closed Tue
rm7(⇨♠4) P5
Credit Cards ①③

🏁 **Testud** 31 av A-Aune ☎ 90590449 P

SENLIS
Oise

★★ **Campanile** r E-Gazeau ☎ 44600507
tx 155028
⇨♠49 P49
Credit Card ③

★★ **Ibis** RN324 ☎ 44537050 tx 140101
⇨♠50 Lift
Credit Cards ①③

🏁 **Delacharlery** 3-5 av Foch ☎ 44530818 Ren

SENNECEY-LE-DIJON See **DIJON**

SENNECY-LE-GRAND
Saône-et-Loire

★ **Lion d'Or Pn** r de la Gare ☎ 85448375
Dec-Oct
rm10(♠8) P
Credit Cards ①②

SENONCHES
Eure-et-Loir

★ **Forêt** Ⓛ pl Champ de Foire ☎ 37377850
rm12(⇨♠9) P

SENS
Yonne

★★★ **Paris et Poste** (MAP/BW) 97 r de la République ☎ 86651743 tx 801831
⇨♠30 🅿 Ⓒ
Credit Cards ①②③⑤

SEPT-SAULX
Marne

★★ **Cheval Blanc DPn** r du Moulin
☎ 26039027 tx 830885
15 Feb-15 Jan
⇨♠22 P20 🅿
Credit Cards ①②③⑤

SERRES
Hautes-Alpes

★ **Alpes DPn** av Grenoble ☎ 92670018
Apr-Nov
rm20(⇨♠9) P12 Mountain
Credit Cards ①②

🏁 **Gonsolin** 8 av M-Meyers ☎ 92670360
M/C **P** Peu Tal

SÈTE
Hérault

★★★ **Grand** 17 quai Ml-Lattre-de-Tassigny ☎ 67747177 tx 480225
⇨♠51 🅿 Lift ⚓ Sea
Credit Cards ①②③⑤

★★★ **Imperial** (MAP/BW) pl E-Herriot (n.rest) ☎ 67532832 tx 480046
⇨♠44 🅿 Lift
Credit Cards ①②③⑤

🏁 **Port** 36 quai de Bosc ☎ 67744894 P For

SEVRAN
Seine-Maritime

★★ **Campanile** 5 r A-Léonour ☎ 43846777
tx 233030
⇨♠58 P58
Credit Card ③

★★ **Climat** av R-Dautry, ZAC de Sevran
☎ 43834560 tx 692844
⇨♠43 P50
Credit Cards ①③

SEVRIER
Haute-Savoie

★ **Robinson** ☎ 50525411
Apr-Oct
rm12(⇨4) 🅿 P20 🅿 🛆 Mountain Lake
Credit Cards ①②⑤

SEYSSEL
Ain

★★ **Rhône** Ⓛ ☎ 50532030
15 Feb-15 Nov Closed :Rest May-Sept
rm11(⇨♠10) A5rm 🅿 Mountain
Credit Cards ②③④⑤

SÉZANNE
Marne

★★ **Croix d'Or** Ⓛ 53 r Notre-Dame
☎ 26806110
Closed 31 Dec-15 Jan :Rest closed Mon
⇨♠13 🅿 P13
Credit Cards ①②③④⑤

SIGEAN
Aude

★ **Ste-Anne** Ⓛ ☎ 68482438
rm12(♠3) P28

SIORAC-EN-PÉRIGORD
Dordogne

★ *Scholly* Ⓛ r de la Poste ☎ 53316002
tx 550787
⇨♠33 P40
Credit Cards ①②③④⑤

SISTERON
Alpes-de-Haute-Provence

★★★ **Grand du Cours** av de la Liberation, pl de l'Église (n.rest) ☎ 92610451
tx 405923
10 Mar-10 Nov
⇨♠50 🅿 P30 Lift Mountain Lake
Credit Cards ①②③⑤

SOCHAUX
Doubs

★★ **Campanile** r de Pontarlier
☎ 81952323 tx 361036
⇨♠42 P42
Credit Card ③

SOISSONS
Aisne

★★ **Lions** rte de Reims ☎ 23732983
⇨♠28 P35
Credit Cards ①②③⑤

★★ **Picardie** 6 r Neuve St-Martin
☎ 23532193
⇨♠33 P40 Lift
Credit Cards ①②③⑤

★★ **Rallye** 10 bd de Strasbourg (n.rest)
☎ 23530047
rm12(⇨♠6) 🅿 P
Credit Cards ①③

SOLESMES See **SABLÉ-SUR-SARTHE**

SOSPEL
Alpes-Maritimes

★★ *Étrangers* Ⓛ 7 bd Verdun
☎ 93040009
⇨♠35 A5rm P Lift 🅿 🛆 Mountain
Credit Cards ①③

SOUILLAC
Lot

★★ **Ambassadeurs** Ⓛ 7-12 av Gl-de-Gaulle ☎ 65327836
Nov-Sep Closed :Rest closed Fri eve Sat ex Jul-Sep, hol
⇨♠28 A10rm 🅿 P20 Mountain
Credit Cards ①③

★★ **Auberge du Puits** Ⓛ ☎ 65378032
Closed Nov-Dec :Rest closed Sun evening & Mon
rm16(⇨♠9) P
Credit Cards ①③

★★ **Périgord** Ⓛ (FAH) 31 av Gl-de-Gaulle
☎ 65327828
1st May – 30 Sep
rm38(⇨♠35) A7rm 🅿 P30 🛆
Credit Cards ①③

109

France

★★ **Renaissance** (FAH) 2 av J-Jaurès
☎ 65327804
Apr-2 Nov
⇨♠30 🍴 P20 Lift ⇨
Credit Cards [1][3]

★★ **Roseraie** L 42 av de Toulouse
☎ 65378269
15 Apr-15 Oct
⇨♠16 🍴 P10 Lift
Credit Card [3]

★ **Nouvel** 21 av Gl-de-Gaulle (n.rest)
☎ 65378272
Apr-Oct
rm28(⇨♠21) P40
Credit Cards [3][5]

SOUPPES-SUR-LOING
Seine-et-Marne

🍴 **Cornut Osmin** 115 av Ml-Leclerc
☎ 64297032 P Ren

SOURCE, LA See **ORLÉANS**

SOUSCEYRAC
Lot

★ **Déjeuner de Sousceyrac** ☎ 65330056
Mar-15Jan Closed :Rest closed Mon in high season
rm10(⇨♠9)
Credit Cards [1][3]

SOUSTONS
Landes

★★ **Bergerie** av du Lac ☎ 58411341
Apr-15 Nov
⇨♠30 A17rm P40
Credit Cards [1][2]

STAINVILLE
Meuse

★★★ **Grange** L ☎ 29786015
15 Feb-15 Dec
⇨♠10 🍴 P6
Credit Cards [1][2][3][4][5]

STRASBOURG
Bas-Rhin

★★★★ **Grand** 12 pl de la Gare (n.rest)
☎ 88324690 tx 870011
rm90(⇨♠87) Lift (
Credit Cards [1][2][3][4][5]

★★★★ **Hilton International** av Herrenschmidt ☎ 88371010 tx 890363
⇨♠246 P100 Lift
Credit Cards [1][2][3][4][5]

★★★★ **Holiday Inn** 20 pl de Bordeaux
☎ 88357000 tx 890515
⇨♠170 P200 Lift ℘ 🞴
Credit Cards [1][2][3][4][5]

★★★★ **Sofitel** pl St-Pierre-le-Jeune
☎ 88329930 tx 870894
Closed :Rest closed Sun
⇨♠182 🍴 P70 Lift 🞴
Credit Cards [1][2][3][5]

★★★ **Altea de l'Europe** Parc du Rhin
☎ 88610323 tx 870833
⇨♠93 P 🞴 ⇨
Credit Cards [1][2][3][5]

★★★ **France** 20 r du Jeu des Enfants (n.rest) ☎ 88323712 tx 890084
⇨♠70 🍴 Lift
Credit Cards [1][2][3][5]

★★★ **Hannong** (FAH) 15 r du 22 Novembre ☎ 88321622 tx 890551
Closed 23-30Dec:Rest closed Sat midday & Sun
⇨♠70 P16 Lift (
Credit Cards [1][2][5]

★★★ **Monopole-Métropole** L 16 r Kuhn (n.rest) ☎ 88321194 tx 890366
Closed 25Dec-1Jan
⇨♠94 🍴 P18 Lift
Credit Cards [1][2][3][4][5]

★★★ **Novotel-Centre Halles** quai Kléber ☎ 88221099 tx 880700
⇨♠97 🍴 P Lift
Credit Cards [1][2][3][5]

★★★ **Terminus-Gruber** (MAP/BW) 10 pl de la Gare ☎ 88328700 tx 870998
rm78(⇨♠70) P20 Lift (
Credit Cards [1][2][3][4][5]

★★ **Arcade** 7 r de Molsheim ☎ 88223000 tx 880147
rm244 P30 Lift
Credit Cards [1][3][4]

★★ **Climat** pl A-Maurois, Maille Irène, ZUP Hautepierre ☎ 88263923
⇨♠38 P50
Credit Card [3]

★★ **Ibis** 1 r Sebastopol, quai Kléber
☎ 88221499 tx 880399
⇨♠97 🍴 P Lift
Credit Cards [1][3]

★★ **Vendôme** (Inter) 9 pl de la Gare
☎ 88324523 tx 890850
⇨♠48 Lift
Credit Cards [1][2][3][5]

At **GEISPOLSHEIM**(12km SE N83)

★★ **Campanile** 20 r de l'Ill ☎ 88667477 tx 890797
⇨♠50 P50
Credit Card [3]

At **ILLKIRCH-GRAFFENSTADEN**(7km S)

★★★ **Mercure-Strasbourg Sud** r du 23 Novembre, Ostwald ☎ 88662156 tx 890142
⇨♠76 P100 🞴
Credit Cards [1][2][3][5]

★★★ **Novotel-Strasbourg Sud** rte de Colmar (N83) ☎ 88662156 tx 890142
⇨♠76 P 🞴
Credit Cards [1][2][3][5]

SULLY-SUR-LOIRE
Loiret

★★ **Grand Sully** L 10 bd Champ-de-Foire
☎ 38362756
15 Jan-15 Dec
rm11(⇨9) 🍴 P11
Credit Cards [1][2][3][5]

★★ **Poste** (Inter) 11 r fbg St-Germain
☎ 38362622
Mar-25 Jan
rm27(⇨♠26) A10rm P25
Credit Cards [1][2][3]

SURESNES
Hauts-de-Seine

★★ **Ibis** 6 r de Bourets ☎ 45064488 tx 614484
⇨♠62 Lift
Credit Cards [1][3]

SURVILLIERS-ST-WITZ
Val-d'Oise

★★★ **Mercure-Paris-St-Witz** r J-Noulin
☎ 34682828 tx 695017
⇨♠115 🍴 P150 Lift ℘ 🞴
Credit Cards [1][2][3][4][5]

★★★ **Novotel-Paris Survilliers** Autoroute A1/D16 ☎ 34686980 tx 695910
rm79 P 🞴

TAIN-L'HERMITAGE
Drôme

★★★ **Commerce** 69 av J-Jaurès
☎ 75086500 tx 345573
⇨♠50 🍴 P40 Lift (🞴 Mountain
Credit Cards [1][2][3][4][5]

🍴 **Billon** 30 av de Prés-Roosevelt
☎ 75082810 P Peu Tal

🍴 **45e Parallele** Pont de l'Isère
☎ 75846004 M/C P Ope

TALANGÉ See **METZ**

TALLOIRES
Haute-Savoie

★★★ **Cottage Pn** rte G-Bise ☎ 50607110 tx 309454
Mar & Apr-Oct
rm36(⇨♠32) A14rm P20 Lift Lake
Credit Cards [2][5]

★★ **Beau Site** ☎ 50607110 tx 309454
23 May-5 Oct
⇨♠38 A28rm 🍴 P40 ℘ Mountain Lake
Credit Cards [1][2][3][5]

★★ **Vivier** ☎ 50607054
Apr-Oct
⇨♠30 🍴 P

TAMARISSIÈRE, LA See **AGDE**

TAMNIÈS
Dordogne

★★ **Laborderie** L ☎ 53296859
15 Mar-15 Nov
⇨♠30 A15rm P50 🞴
Credit Cards [1][3]

TARARE
Rhône

★ **Mère Paul** ☎ 74631457
:Rest closed 6 Sep
rm10(⇨♠9) P10
Credit Cards [1][3]

TARASCON-SUR-ARIÈGE
Ariège

★★ **Poste** L DPn 16 av V-Pilhès
☎ 61056041
rm30(⇨20) Mountain
Credit Cards [1][2][3][5]

TARASCON-SUR-RHÔNE
Bouches-du-Rhône

★★ **Terminus** pl du Colonel-Berrurier
☎ 90911895
Closed 15 Jan-15 Feb
rm23(⇨♠14)
Credit Cards [1][3]

★ *Provençal* 12 cours A-Briand (n.rest)
☎ 90911141
Mar-Oct
⇨♃22 ☎ P10 ⟨
Credit Cards ①②③④⑤

TARBES
Hautes-Pyrénées
★★★ *Président* (MAP/BW) 1 r G-Faure
☎ 62939840 tx 530522
⇨♃57 ☎ Lift ⇨ Mountain
Credit Cards ①②③④⑤
★★ *Campanile* Lotissement Longchamp,
rte de Lourdes (4 km SW on N21)
☎ 62938320 tx 530571
⇨♃42 P42
Credit Card ③
★★ *Croix Blanche* pl Verdun (n.rest)
☎ 62321313
rm32(⇨♃12)
Credit Card ①
★ *Henri-IV* (Inter) 7 bd B-Barère (n.rest)
☎ 62340168
⇨♃24 ☎ P15 Lift ⟨
Credit Cards ①②③④⑤
☙ *Auto Selection* 2 bd du Juin
☎ 62936930 P Toy

THÉOULE-SUR-MER
Alpes-Maritimes
★★ *Guerguy La Galère* La Galère
☎ 93754454
Feb-Nov Closed :Rest closed Wed
⇨♃14 P30 Sea
★ *Hermitage Jules César* 1 av C-Dahon
☎ 93499612
15Mar-15Oct
rm18(⇨♃16) Sea Mountain

THIERS
Puy-de-Dôme
★★ *Fimotel* rte de Clermont-Ferrand
☎ 73806440 tx 392000
⇨♃40 P40 Lift
Credit Cards ①②③④⑤

THIONVILLE
Moselle
★★ *Balladins* Forum 3000 Zone du Val
Marie, Face Zone Industrielle et
Commerciale du Linkling ☎ 82530416
tx 649394
⇨♃38 P38
Credit Cards ①②③
☙ *R Dillman* 18 rte de Garche
☎ 82532925 P Cit
☙ *Fort* r des Artisans ☎ 82561174 AR
Lan

THOISSEY
Ain
★★★ *Chapon Fin* (Relais et Châteaux) r
du Champ de Foire ☎ 74040474 tx 305728
beg Feb – beg Jan Closed :Rest closed
Tues
rm25(⇨♃18) ☎ P100 Lift
Credit Cards ①③⑤
★ *Beau-Rivage Pn* av Port ☎ 74040166
15 Mar-15 Oct Closed :Rest closed Mon
⇨♃10 Mountain
Credit Cards ①③

France

THONON-LES-BAINS
Haute-Savoie
★★ *Ibis* av d'Evian ☎ 50712424 tx 309934
rm67 Lift Mountain Lake
Credit Cards ①③

THOUARS
Deux-Sèvres
★★ *Climat* les Moulins à Vent ☎ 49681321
⇨♃24 P20
Credit Cards ①③

THURY-HARCOURT
Calvados
★ *Relais de la Poste* rte Caen ☎ 31797212
Feb-20 Nov
⇨♃11 ☎ P
Credit Cards ①②③④⑤

TILQUES See **ST-OMER**

TINQUEUX See **REIMS**

TONNERRE
Yonne
★★★ *Abbaye St-Michel* (Relais et
Châteaux) Montée St-Michel ☎ 86550599
tx 801356
Feb-20 Dec
⇨♃11 P30
Credit Cards ②③⑤

TORCY See **CREUSOT, LE**

TOUL
Meurthe-et-Moselle
☙ *Dalier Fils* rte de Pont-a-Mousson
☎ 83430613 For

TOULON
Var
★★★★ *Altea Tour Blanche* bd Aml-Vence
☎ 94244157 tx 400347
⇨♃92 P50 Lift ♪ Sea
Credit Cards ①②③⑤
★★ *América* 51 r J-Jaurès (n.rest)
☎ 94923219 tx 400479
⇨♃30 Lift
Credit Cards ①②③⑤
☙ *Azur* av de l'Université ☎ 94210400
For
☙ *Soleil* 42 r A-Chenier Prolongée
☎ 94204090 P

At **CAMP-ST-LAURENT**(7.5km W)
★★★ *Novotel Toulon* B52-Sortie Ollioules
☎ 94630950
⇨♃86 P90 Lift ⇨
Credit Cards ①②③⑤
★★ *Ibis* Autoroute (B52) ☎ 94632121
tx 400759
⇨♃60 Lift
Credit Cards ①③

At **FARLÈDE, LA**(8.5km NE)
★★ *Climat* quartier de L'Auberte
☎ 94487421
⇨♃39 P40
Credit Cards ①③

At **GARDE, LA**(3Km W)
★★ *Fimotel* (N98) ☎ 94632121 tx 400759
⇨♃86 P90 Lift ⇨
Credit Cards ①②③⑤

At **VALETTE-DU-VAR, LA**(7km NE)
★★ *Balladins* Zona d'Activité des
Espaluns ☎ 05355575 tx 649394
rm38 P38
Credit Cards ①②③④⑤
★★ *Campanile* ZA des Espaluns
☎ 94211301 tx 430978
⇨♃50 P50
Credit Card ③

TOULOUSE
Haute-Garonne
★★★ *Caravelle* (MAP/Best Western) 62 r
Raymond-IV (n.rest) ☎ 61627065
tx 530438
⇨♃30 ☎ P10 Lift ⟨
Credit Cards ①②③⑤
★★★ *Compagnie du Midi* Gare Matabiau
☎ 61628493 tx 530171
⇨♃65 Lift
Credit Cards ②③
★★★ *Concorde* 16 bd Bonrepos (n.rest)
☎ 61624860 tx 531686
⇨♃97 P Lift ⟨
★★★ *Diane* 3 rte de St-Simon
☎ 61075952 tx 530518
⇨♃35 P35 ♪ ⇨
Credit Cards ①②③⑤
★★★ *Mercure* r St-Jérome ☎ 61231177
tx 520760
⇨♃170 Lift
Credit Cards ①②③⑤
★★ *Ibis* r J Babinet ☎ 61408686 tx 520805
⇨♃89 P80 Lift
Credit Cards ①③
★★ *Ibis Toulouse* 27 bd des Minimes
☎ 61226060 tx 530437
⇨♃130 Lift
Credit Cards ①③
★★ *Voyageurs* (Inter) 11 bd Bonrepos
(n.rest) ☎ 61628979 tx 532305
⇨♃34 ☎ Lift
Credit Cards ①②③④⑤
☙ *Lormand* 306 rte de Revel
☎ 61200916 P Peu Tal
☙ *Vie* 57-59 allée C-de-Fitte ☎ 61429911
Peu Tal

At **LABÈGE**(11km SE)
★★ *Campanile* Face carrefour
☎ 61340189 tx 532007
⇨♃49 P
Credit Card ③

At **MIRAIL, LE**
★★ *Climat* av du Mirail, 2 r A-Coutét
☎ 61448644 tx 521980
⇨♃43 P50
Credit Cards ①③
★★ *Ibis* r J-Babinet ☎ 61408686
tx 520805
⇨♃89 Lift
Credit Cards ①③

At **ROQUES-SUR-GARONNE**(6km SW)
★★ *Campanile* Le Chemin des Moines →

France

☏ 61725151 tx 521426
⇨♫50 P50
Credit Card ③

TOULOUSE AIRPORT
★★★★ **Altea** 7 r de Labéda (n.rest)
☏ 61212175 tx 530550
⇨♫95 🍴 Lift
Credit Cards ①②③④⑤

★★★ **Novotel-Toulouse Purpan** 23 r de Maubec ☏ 61493410 tx 520640
⇨♫123 P Lift ♀ ⇋
Credit Cards ①②③⑤

At **BLAGNAC**(7km NE)
★★ **Balladins** ZAC du Grand Noble, Carrefour Didier Dauret ☏ 05355575 tx 649394
rm38 P38
Credit Cards ①②③④⑤

★★ **Campanile** 3 av D-Daurat ☏ 61300340 tx 530915
⇨♫42 P42
Credit Card ③

TOUQUES See DEAUVILLE

TOUQUET-PARIS-PLAGE, LE
Pas-de-Calais
★★★ **Côte d'Opale** 99 bd Dr J-Pouget, bd de la Mer ☏ 21050811
beg Mar-Dec
rm28(⇨♫20) (Sea
Credit Cards ①②③⑤

★★★ **Novotel-Thalamer** La Plage
☏ 21098500 tx 160480
rm104 P Lift ♀ ⇋ Sea
Credit Cards ①②③④⑤

★★★ **Westminster** (Inter) av Verger
☏ 21054848 tx 160439
1 Mar-18 Nov
⇨♫115 🍴 Lift (⇋
Credit Cards ①②③⑤

★★ **Forêt** 73 r de Moscou (n.rest)
☏ 21050988
⇨♫10
Credit Card ②

★★ **Ibis** Front de Mer ☏ 21098700 tx 134273
⇨♫90 Lift Sea
Credit Cards ①③

★★ **Plage** 13 bd de la Mer (n.rest)
☏ 21050322
15 Mar-15 Nov
rm29(⇨♫24) (Sea
Credit Cards ①③⑤

★★ **Windsor-Artois** 7 r St-Georges (off r de la Paix) ☏ 21050544
Apr-Sep
⇨♫25 Lift

★ **Chalet** 15 r de la Paix ☏ 21845555
1 Feb-15 Nov

rm18(⇨♫11) Sea
Credit Cards ①③

★ **Robert's** 66 r de Londres ☏ 21051198
Apr-Sep
rm14(⇨♫3)

★ **Touquet** 17 r de Paris (n.rest)
☏ 21052254
rm16(⇨♫10)

At **GOLF LINKS**(3km S)
★★★ **Manoir** av du Golf Links
☏ 21052022 tx 135565
4 Mar-Jan
⇨♫42 P ♀ ⇋
Credit Cards ①②③

TOURCOING
Nord
★★★ **Novotel Neuville** Autoroute Lille-Grand ☏ 20940770 tx 131656
⇨♫118 P Lift ⇋

★★ **Fimotel** 320 bd Gambetta ☏ 20703800 tx 131234
⇨♫40 🍴 P30 Lift
Credit Cards ①③

★★ **Ibis** centre Gl-de-Gaulle, r Carnot
☏ 20248458 tx 132695
⇨♫102 Lift
Credit Cards ①③

TOUR-DU-PIN, LA
Isère
At **FAVERGES-DE-LA-TOUR**(10km NE)
★★★★ **Château de Faverges**
☏ 74374252 tx 300372
May-Oct Closed :Rest closed Mon
⇨♫46 A26rm P Lift ♀ ⇋ ⊩ Mountain
Credit Cards ①②③⑤

TOURNUS
Saône-et-Loire
★★★ **Rempart** 2 & 4 av Gambetta
☏ 855811056 tx 351019
⇨♫30 A8rm 🍴 P16 Lift
Credit Cards ①②③⑤

★★★ **Sauvage** (MAP/Best Western) pl du Champ de Mars ☏ 85511445 tx 800726
Jan-14 Nov & 16-31 Dec
⇨♫30 🍴 Lift (
Credit Cards ①②③⑤

★ **Terrasses** L 18 av du 23-Janvier
☏ 85510174
Closed :Rest closed Sun & Mon
⇨♫12 🍴 P
Credit Cards ①③

♫ **Pageaud** 3 rte de Paris ☏ 85510705 P Ren

TOURRETTES See **FAYENCE**

TOURS
Indre-et-Loire See also **JOUÉ-LÈS-TOURS**
★★★ **Bordeaux** L 3 pl du Ml-Leclerc
☏ 47054032 tx 750414
⇨♫50 Lift ♀ ⇋
Credit Cards ①②③⑤

★★★ **Central** 21 r Berthelot (n.rest)
☏ 47054644 tx 751172
rm42(⇨♫32) 🍴 P42 Lift
Credit Cards ①②③⑤

★★★ **Châteaux de Loire** 12 r Gambetta (n.rest) ☏ 47051005
23 Jan-17 Dec
⇨♫32 🍴 Lift (
Credit Cards ①②③⑤

★★★ **Meridien** 292 av de Grammont
☏ 47280080 tx 750922
⇨♫125 P150 Lift ♀ ⇋
Credit Cards ①②③④⑤

★★★ **Royal** 65 av de Grammont (n.rest)
☏ 47647178 tx 752006
⇨♫35 🍴 Lift
Credit Cards ①②③⑤

★★★ **Univers** 5 bd Heurteloup
☏ 47053712 tx 751460
Closed :Rest closed Sat
⇨♫89 🍴 Lift (
Credit Cards ①②③⑤

★★ **Arcade** 1 r G-Claude ☏ 47614444 tx 751201
⇨♫139 P28 Lift

★★ **Armor** L 26 bis bd Heurteloup
☏ 47052437 tx 752020
rm48(⇨♫27) 🍴 P9 Lift
Credit Cards ①②③⑤

★★ **Balladins** La Petite Arche, av Maginot
☏ 5355575 tx 649394
rm38 P38
Credit Cards ①②③④⑤

★★ **Climat** Zl les Granges Galand (N76), St-Avertin ☏ 47277117 tx 37170
⇨♫38 P35
Credit Cards ①③

★★ **Cygne** 6 r du Cygne (n.rest)
☏ 47666641
rm19(⇨♫11) 🍴 P6
Credit Cards ①③⑤

★★ **Ibis** la Petite Arche, av A-Maginot
☏ 47543220 tx 751592
⇨♫60 Lift
Credit Cards ①③

★★ **Mondial** L 3 pl de la Résistance (n.rest) ☏ 47056268
rm18(⇨♫7)
Credit Cards ①③⑤

★ **Balzac** 47 r de la Scellerie ☏ 47054087
rm20(⇨♫13) A8rm
Credit Cards ①③

Hôtel Le Bristol ★★ NN

Ascot bar. **17, Grande Rue – 62520 Le Touquet. Tel.: 21.05.49.95**

48 rooms with direct dial telephone, TV, and bathroom. Garden. Elevator. Totally renovated. 100 m. from the beach. Open the whole year. Big style "Britanny".

★ *Choiseul* 12 r de la Rôtisserie (n.rest)
☎ 47208576
⇨♪16
Credit Cards ①③

★ *Colbert* 78 r Colbert (n.rest) ☎ 4766156
rm18(⇨♪15)
Credit Cards ①②③⑤

★ *Foch* 20 r MI-Foch (n.rest) ☎ 47057059
rm15(⇨♪12) A2rm
Credit Cards ①②③

🛏 *Depannage-Auto-Touraine* 151 av A-Maginot ☎ 47411515 **P**

🛏 *Pont* ZAC La Vrillonnerie ☎ 47392533
For

At **CHAMBRAY-LES-TOURS**(6km S)
★★★ *Novotel Tours Sud* ZAC de la Vrillonerie ☎ 47274138 tx 751206
⇨♪125 Lift ⇨

★★ *Ibis* La Vrillonnerie, N10 ☎ 47282528
tx 751297
⇨♪80 Lift
Credit Cards ①③

At **SAVONNIÈRES**(10km W D7)
★ *Faisan Pn* ☎ 47500017
Mar-1Nov
rm13(⇨♪10) P60 ♪
Credit Cards ①②③④⑤

TOURVILLE-LA-RIVIÈRE See **ROUEN**

TRANS-EN-PROVENCE
Var

★★ *Climat* quartier de Cognet
☎ 94708211
⇨♪34 P50
Credit Card ①

TRÉBEURDEN
Côtes-du-Nord

★★★ *Manoir de Lan Kerellec* (Relais et Châteaux) **Pn** allée de Lan Kerellec
☎ 96235009 tx 741172
15 Mar-15 Nov Closed :Rest closed Mon lunch
⇨♪12 P20 ♪ Sea
Credit Cards ①②③⑤

★★ *Family* L⁺ 85 r des Plages
☎ 96235031
Closed :Rest closed Oct-Mar
rm25(⇨♪19) 🍴 P15 Sea
Credit Cards ①②③

★★ *Ker an Nod* L⁺ r Pors-Termen
☎ 96235021
Etr-1 Nov
rm21(⇨♪14) Sea
Credit Cards ①③

TRÉGASTEL-PLAGE
Côtes-du-Nord

★★★ *Belle Vue* L⁺ (FAH) **Pn** 20 r des Calculots ☎ 96238818

France

Ctr 26 Sep
rm33(⇨♪31) P35 Sea
Credit Cards ①③

★★ *Beau Séjour* L⁺ (Inter) **Pn** ☎ 96238802
10 Mar-10 Oct
rm18(⇨♪14) P15 Sea
Credit Cards ①②③⑤

★★ *Mer et Plage* ☎ 96238803
May-Sep
rm40(⇨♪24) P12 Sea
Credit Cards ①③

TRÉGUIER
Côtes-du-Nord

★★ *Kastell Dinec'h* L⁺ (FAH) rte de Lannion ☎ 96924939
15 Mar-Dec
⇨♪15 P20 ⇨
Credit Cards ①③

TRÉPORT, LE
Seine-Maritime

★ *Rex* 50 quai Francois-1er ☎ 35862655
rm17(⇨♪14) P Mountain

TRÉVOL
Allier

★★ *Relais d'Avrilly* L⁺
☎ (03460)70426141 tx 392999
⇨♪42 P100 Lift ⇨
Credit Cards ①③

TRIGNAC
Loire-Atlantique

★★ *Campanile* ZAC de la Fontaine au Brun ☎ 40904444 tx 701243
⇨♪48 P48
Credit Card ③

★★ *Ibis* 5 r de la Fontaine au Brun ☎ 40903939 tx 701231
⇨♪45 Lift
Credit Cards ①③

TRIMOUILLE, LA
Vienne

★ *Hostellerie de la Paix* r de la Liberté
☎ 49916050 tx 791316
rm12(⇨♪7)
Credit Cards ①②③⑤

TRINITÉ-SUR-MER, LA
Morbihan

★★ *Rouzic* L⁺ 17 cours de Quais
☎ 97557206
15 Dec-15 Nov
⇨♪32 Lift Sea
Credit Cards ①②③⑤

TRIQUE, LA See **ST-LAURENT-SUR-SÈVRE**

TROIS-ÉPIS, LES
Haut-Rhin

★★★★ *Grand* (MAP/BW) ☎ 89498065
tx 880229
⇨♪50 P50 Lift 《 ⇨ Mountain
Credit Cards ①②③⑤

TRONCHET, LE
Ille-et-Vilaine

★★ *Hostellerie l'Abbatiale* ☎ 99589321
tx 740802
15 Feb-Dec
⇨♪72 P ♪ ⇨ Lake

TROUVILLE-SUR-MER
Calvados

★★★ *Flaubert* r G-Flaubert (n.rest)
☎ 31883923
Mar-15 Nov
rm33(⇨♪26) Lift 《
Credit Cards ①②③⑤

★★ *Reynita* 29 r Carnot ☎ 31881513
Closed Jan
rm26(⇨♪21) 🍴 《
Credit Cards ①②③⑤

TROYES
Aube

★★★ *Grand* (Inter) 4 av MI-Joffre
☎ 25799090 tx 840582
⇨♪95 P Lift
Credit Cards ①②③⑤

★★ *Fimotel* bd G-Pompidou ☎ 42615014
tx 215269
⇨♪42 P Lift
Credit Cards ①②③⑤

★★ *Paris* (Inter) 54 r R-Salengro (n.rest)
☎ 25731170
rm27(⇨♪20) 🍴 P9
Credit Cards ①③⑤

🛏 *Ets Belin* (25) 2 Mail des Charmilles
☎ 25805419 **P** LR

At **BUCHÈRES**(6km SW)
★★ *Campanile* Le Haut de Caurgerennes, (RN71) ☎ 25496767 tx 840840
⇨♪42 P42
Credit Card ③

At **ST-ANDRÉ-LES-VERGERS**
🛏 *Juszak* 37 rte d'Auxerre
☎ 25824655 **P** AR

TROYES AIRPORT
At **BARBEREY**(6km NW on N19)
★★★ *Novotel-Troyes Aéroport* RN19
☎ 25745995 tx 8407259
⇨♪84 P120 ⇨
Credit Cards ①②③④⑤

TULLE
Corrèze →

Hôtel de la Scellerie

In the heart of Tours, a traditional hotel with welcoming atmosphere.
22, rue de la Scellerie – 37000 TOURS

Tel.: (47) 05.38.84   Telex 750 008 La Scellerie

France

★★★ **Limouzi** 19 quai République
☏ 55264200
Closed 1-7 Jan :Rest closed Sun dinner
⇌♪50 ☎ Lift
Credit Cards ① ② ③ ④ ⑤

🛏 **Ets Carles** rte de Brive ☏ 55200805 **P**
For

ULIS, LES
Essonne

★★ **Campanile** ZA de Courtaboeuf
☏ 69286060 tx 603094
⇌♪50 P50
Credit Card ③

★★ **Climat** av des Andes ☏ 64460506
⇌♪42

URY See FONTAINEBLEAU

UZERCHE
Corrèze

★★ **Ambroise** av de Paris ☏ 55731008
tx 590845
Dec-Oct Closed :Rest closed Sat & Sun (ex.
Jul & Aug)
⇌♪20 ☎ P20
Credit Cards ① ② ③

★★ **Teyssier** r Pont-Turgot ☏ 55731345
Mar-10 Jan Closed :Rest closed Wed
rm17(⇌♪10) ☎ P25
Credit Cards ① ③

🛏 **Renault** rte de Limoges ☏ 55731333 **P**
Ren

UZÈS
Gard

★ **Provençale** 3 r Grande Bourgade
☏ 66221106
⇌♪10 Lift

VAISON-LA-ROMAINE
Vaucluse

★★ **Beffroi** r de l'Evêche ☏ 90360471
tx 306142
15 Mar-15 Nov & 15 Dec-5 Jan Closed
:Rest closed Mon & Tue lunchtime
rm22(⇌♪18) A10rm P11 Mountain
Credit Cards ① ② ③ ⑤

VAÏSSAC
Tarn-et-Garonne

★ **Terrassier** ☏ 63309460
rm12(♪4) ⛱

VAL-ANDRÉ, LE
Côtes-du-Nord

★ **Bains** 7 pl Gl-de-Gaulle ☏ 96722011
20 May-20 Sep
rm26 P7 Sea

VALBONNE
Alpes-Maritimes

★★★ **Novotel Sophia Antipolis**
☏ 93333800 tx 970914
⇌♪97 P Lift ♌ ⛰ Mountain

★★ **Ibis Sophia Antipolis** r Albert-Caquot
☏ 93653060 tx 461263
⇌♪99 Lift
Credit Cards ① ③

VALDAHON
Doubs

★★ **Relais de Franche Comté** Ŀ (Inter)
☏ 81562318

15 Jan-20 Dec
⇌♪20 ☎ P100
Credit Cards ① ② ③ ⑤

VAL-DE-REUIL See LOUVIERS

VAL D'ISÈRE
Savoie

★★★★ **Sofitel** ☏ 79060830 tx 980558
Dec-5 May & Jul-25 Aug
⇌♪53 ☎ P Lift ⛱ ⛰ Mountain
Credit Cards ① ② ③ ⑤

★★★ **Aiglon DPn** ☏ 79060405
1 Dec-1 May
⇌♪21 Mountain
Credit Cards ① ② ③ ⑤

★★ **Savoie** ☏ 79060530
rm36(⇌♪34) Lift Mountain

★ **Vieux Village** Ŀ ☏ 79060379 tx 980077
Dec-5 May
⇌♪24 P10 Mountain
Credit Cards ① ③

VALENÇAY
Indre

★★★ **Espagne** (Relais et Châteaux) 8 r du
Château ☏ 5400002 tx 751675
Mar-Dec
⇌♪18 P18 ⛱ ♌ ⛱
Credit Cards ① ② ③

★ **Lion d'Or** pl Marché ☏ 54000087
rm15(⇌♪8) ☎ P14
Credit Cards ① ② ③ ⑤

VALENCE
Drôme

★★★ **Novotel Valence Sud** 217 av de
Provence (N7) ☏ 75422015 tx 345823
⇌♪107 P150 Lift ♌ ⛱
Credit Cards ① ② ③ ④ ⑤

★★ **Campanile** r du Dr-Abel ☏ 75569280
tx 346304
⇌♪42 P42
Credit Card ③

★★ **Ibis** 355 av de Provence ☏ 75444254
tx 345384
⇌♪86 Lift
Credit Cards ① ③

★★ **Park** (Inter) 22 r J-Bouin (n.rest)
☏ 75433706
⇌♪21 ☎
Credit Cards ① ② ③ ⑤

★★ **Pic** (Relais et Châteaux) 285 av V-Hugo ☏ 75441532
Closed Aug & Feb school hols
⇌♪4 ☎
Credit Cards ① ② ③ ⑤

🛏 **Anayan** 170 r du Chateauvert
☏ 75441685 **P** Cit

🛏 **Bastien** 38-40 r Gustave Eiffel
☏ 75434268 **P** Peu Tal

🛏 **Brun Valence** 73-79 av de Verdun
☏ 75556060 Ope

🛏 **Costechareyre** 31 av des Aureates
☏ 75440109 **P** All makes

🛏 **J Jaurès** 410 av de Chabeuil
☏ 75421266 **P** Audi VW

🛏 **Minodier** rte de Benuvallon ZI
☏ 75443124 **P** Cit

🛏 **Molière** 164 av V-Hugo ☏ 75441137 **P**
Por Col

🛏 **Vinson et Verde** 35 r de la Cartoucherie
☏ 75430192 **P** Peu Tal

At **BOURG-LÈS-VALENCE**(1km N)

★★ **Climat** rte de Chateauneuf-sur-Isère
☏ 75427746 tx 692844
⇌♪42 P

★★ **Le Soleil D'or** Montée du Long RN7
☏ 75560229 tx 346710
⇌♪37 P40 Mountain
Credit Cards ① ③

★★ **Seyvet** Ŀ (Inter) 24 av M-Urtin
☏ 75432651 tx 346338
rm32 A3rm ☎ P40 Lift ⛱ Mountain
Credit Cards ① ② ③ ⑤

VALENCE-D'AGEN
Tarn-et-Garonne

★★ **Tout-Va-Bien** 35-39 r de la République
☏ 63395483
Feb-Dec Closed :Rest closed Mon
rm22(⇌♪21)
Credit Cards ① ③

VALENCE-SUR-BAÏSE
Gers

★★ **Ferme du Flaran** ☏ 61285822
Feb-Dec Closed :Rest closed Mon
⇌♪15 P30 Beach
Credit Cards ① ② ③

VALENCIENNES
Nord

★★★ **Grand** (MAP/Best Western) 8 pl de
la Gare ☏ 27463201 tx 110701
⇌♪96 Lift ⛱
Credit Cards ① ② ③ ⑤

★★★ **Novotel Valenciennes-Ouest DPn**
Autoroute Paris-Bruxelles, N2 (n.rest)
☏ 27442080 tx 120970
⇌♪76 ⛱
Credit Cards ① ② ③ ④ ⑤

★★ **Campanile** Valenciennes Aérodrome
☏ 27440123 tx 810288
⇌♪42 P42
Credit Card ③

★★ **Ibis** A2, Sortie Valenciennes Ouest
(n.rest) ☏ 27445566 tx 160737
⇌♪65 Lift
Credit Cards ① ③

VALETTE-DU-VAR, LA See TOULON

VALLOIRE
Savoie

★★ **Grand de Valloire et Galibier**
☏ 79590095 tx 980553
15 Jun-15 Sep & 18 Dec-15 Apr
⇌♪43 P40 Lift Mountain
Credit Cards ② ④

VALOGNES
Manche

★★ **Louvre** 28 r Réligieuses ☏ 33400007
4 Jan-Nov Closed :Rest closed Sat
rm20(⇌♪9) ☎ P20

114

VALS-LES-BAINS
Ardèche

★★★ **Vivarais** (MAP/BW) 5 r C-Expilly
☎ 75946585 tx 345866
Closed :Rest closed 1 Feb-6 Mar
⇌♠40 P60 Lift (ℒ ⇌ Beach Mountain
Credit Cards [1][2][3][4][5]

★★ **Europe** 🄻 (FAH) 86 r J-Jaurès
☎ 75374394 tx 346256
10 Apr-10 Oct
rm33(⇌♠29) Lift
Credit Cards [1][2][3][5]

VAL-SUZON
Côte-d'Or

★★★ **Val-Suzon** ☎ 80356215
Feb-Dec Closed Rest clo Wed Thus Lunchtime HS
⇌♠7 A10rm P30
Credit Cards [1][3]

VANDOEUVRE-LES-NANCY See NANCY

VANNES
Morbihan

★★★ **Marebaudière Pn** 4 r A-Briand
☎ 97473429 tx 951975
6 Jan-18 Dec Closed :Rest closed Etr
⇌♠41 P60
Credit Cards [1][2][3][5]

★★ **Aquarium** Le Parc du Golfe
☎ 97404452 tx 850926
Closed :Rest closed Sun evening
⇌♠48 ☎ P50 Lift Sea
Credit Cards [1][2][3][5]

★★ **Ibis Vannes** r E-Jourdan, ZI de Ménimur Est ☎ 97636111 tx 950521
⇌♠59 Lift
Credit Cards [1][3]

★★ **Image Ste-Anne** (FAH) 8 pl de la Libération ☎ 97632736 tx 950352
rm32(⇌♠28) P10
Credit Cards [1][3]

★ **Marée Bleue Pn** 8 pl Bir-Hakeim
☎ 97472429 tx 951975
6 Jan-18 Dec Closed :Rest closed Etr
rm16(♠8) P60
Credit Cards [1][2][3][5]

🍽 **Autorep** 41 r du Vincin ☎ 97631035 **P** For

🍽 **Poulichet** 126 bd de la Paix
☎ 97540325 Alf Fia Toy

VARCES
Isère

★★ **Escale** (Relais et Châteaux) pl de la République (n.rest) ☎ 76728019
Closed Jan
⇌♠11 P10 ℒ Mountain
Credit Cards [1][2]

VARENGEVILLE-SUR-MER
Seine-Maritime

★★ **Terrasse** 🄻 **DPn** ☎ 35851254
15 Mar-15 Oct
⇌♠28 ℒ Sea
Credit Cards [1][3]

VARENNES-VAUZELLES See NEVERS

VARETZ See BRIVE-LA-GAILLARDE

VAULX-EN-VELIN
Rhône

France

★★ **Fimotel** 9 r N-Carmellino ☎ 78807226 tx 305964
⇌♠42 P20 Lift
Credit Cards [1][2][3][5]

VAUVENARGUES
Bouches-du-Rhône

★ **Moulin de Provence Pn** ☎ 42660222 tx 410777
5 Mar-Oct Closed :Rest closed Mon
rm12(⇌♠9) P20 Mountain
Credit Cards [1][3]

VENCE
Alpes-Maritimes

★★★★ **Domaine St-Martin** (Relais et Châteaux) rte de Coursegoules
☎ 93580202 tx 470282
mid Mar-mid Nov
⇌♠25 ☎ ℒ ⇌ Sea
Credit Cards [1][2][3][5]

★★ **Diana** av Poilus (n.rest) ☎ 93582856
⇌♠25 ☎ Lift (Mountain
Credit Cards [1][2][3][5]

🍽 **Simondi** 39 av Foch ☎ 93580121 **P** Peu Tal Mer

VENDIN-LE-VIEL See LENS

VENDÔME
Loir-et-Cher

★★ **Vendôme** 15 fbg Chartrain
☎ 54770288 tx 750383
5 Jan-19 Dec
⇌♠35 ☎ Lift
Credit Cards [1][3]

VENIZY See ST-FLORENTIN

VERDUN
Meuse

🍽 **M Rochette** r V-Schleiter
☎ 29865049 **P** For

At **CHATTANCOURT**(14km NW D38)

🍽 **M Riboizi** ☎ 29843286 M/C **P** Ren

VERETZ
Indre-et-Loire

★ **St-Honoré** 🄻 ☎ 47503006
Closed Jan. :Rest closed Sun evening
rm9(⇌♠6)
Credit Cards [1][2][3][5]

VERNET-LES-BAINS
Pyrénées-Orientales

★★ **Angleterre DPn** 9 av de Burnay
☎ 68055058
2 May-26 Oct
rm20(⇌♠11) Mountain
Credit Cards [1][3]

VERNEUIL-SUR-AVRE
Eure

★★★ **Clos** (Relais et Châteaux) 98 r Ferte Vidame ☎ 32322181 tx 172725
Feb-Nov
⇌♠11 A3rm P40
Credit Cards [1][2][3][5]

★★ **Saumon** 🄻 (FAH) 89 pl de la Madeleine ☎ 32320236 tx 172770
5 Jan-22 Dec
rm28(⇌♠24) A18rm
Credit Cards [1][3]

🍽 **Martin** ☎ 32321327 **P** Peu Tal

VERRIÈRES-LE-BUISSON
Essonne

★★ **Climat** ZAC des Prés Houts, av G-Pompidou ☎ 69307070
⇌♠38 P
Credit Cards [1][3]

VERSAILLES
Yvelines

★★★ **Trianon Palace** 1 bd de la Reine
☎ 39503412 tx 698863
⇌♠120 P200 Lift (ℒ ⇌
Credit Cards [1][2][3][4][5]

★★ **Cheval Rouge Pn** 18 r A-Chenier
☎ 39500303
10 Jan-20 Dec
rm40(⇌♠22) P22

★★ **Clagny** 6 Impasse Clagny (n.rest)
☎ 39501809
rm21(⇌♠18) (

★★ **St-Louis** 28 r St-Louis (n.rest)
☎ 39502355
⇌♠27 Lift
Credit Cards [1][3]

VERT-ST-DENIS See MELUN

VERVINS
Aisne

★★★ **Tour du Roy** 45 r Gl-Leclerc
☎ 23980011 tx 155445
15 Feb-15 Jan
⇌♠13 P20 ℒ
Credit Cards [1][2][3][4][5]

★ **Cheval Noir** 33 r de la Liberté
☎ 23980415
Closed 25 Dec & 1 Jan
rm18(⇌♠12) ☎ P6
Credit Cards [1][2][3]

VESOUL
Haute-Saône

★★ **Nord** r Aigle Noir 7 ☎ 84750256
rm33(⇌♠30) Lift (U Beach Sea Mountain Lake
Credit Cards [1][2][3][5]

★★ **Relais N19** (Inter) rte de Paris
☎ 84764242
12 Jan-22 Dec
⇌♠22 ☎ P40
Credit Cards [1][2][3][5]

🍽 **Franche Comte** ZI Quest
☎ 84762366 **P** AR

🍽 **Vesoul** av Pasteur, Echanoz la Meline
☎ 84752801 **P** Dat

VEURDRE, LE
Allier

★★ **Pont Neuf** 🄻 (FAH) **Pn** rte de Lurcy-Levis ☎ 70664012 tx 392978
Closed School holidays & Rest Sun dinner
⇌♠25 A10rm ☎ P35 ⇌
Credit Cards [1][2][3][5]

VEYRIER-DU-LAC
Haute-Savoie →

115

France

★ **Auberge du Colvert** ☎ 50601023
Apr-15 Nov
⇌♪10 P20 Mountain Lake
Credit Cards [1] [3]

VEYS, LES See **CARENTAN**

VICHY
Allier

★★★ **Pavillon Sévigné** (BW) 10 pl Sévigné
☎ 70321622
Apr-Oct
⇌♪37 P10 Lift (
Credit Cards [1] [2] [5]

🍴 **Imperial** 59 av Thermale
☎ 70986771 P For

At **BELLERIVE-SUR-ALLIER** (2Km SW)

★★ **Campanile** av de Vichy ☎ 70593223
tx 392985
⇌♪49 P49
Credit Card [3]

🍴 **Vasseur** 93 av de Vichy ☎ 70320367
Peu

VIC-SUR-CÉRE
Cantal

★★ **Beauséjour** L av du Parc
☎ 71475027
15 May – 1 Oct Closed Rest clo 1 Oct – 15 May
rm75(⇌♪65) A18rm P60 Lift Mountain
Credit Cards [1] [3]

At **COL-DE-CUREBOURSE** (6km SE on D54)

★ **Relais des Morezes** L Col-de-Curebourse ☎ 21475171
15 Jan – 15 Oct Closed Rest clo 15 Jan – 15 Jan
rm30(⇌27) A4rm P30 Mountain
Credit Card [1]

VIENNE
Isère

★ **Nord** (Inter) 11 pl Miremont ☎ 74857711
⇌♪43 ⬤ P22 Lift (
Credit Cards [1] [2] [3] [5]

🍴 **Societe du Central** 76 av du Gl-Leclerc
☎ 74531344 For

At **CHONAS-L'AMBALLAN** (9km S on N7)

★★ **Relais 500 de Vienne** ☎ 74580144
tx 380343
⇌♪44 ⬤ P100 ⬚
Credit Cards [1] [2] [3] [5]

VILLARS
Loire

★★ **Campanile** r de l'Antisaneet
☎ 77935248 tx 307101
⇌♪42 P42
Credit Card [3]

VILLEDIEU-LES-POÊLES
Manche

★★ **St-Pierre et St-Michel** L DPn 12 pl de la République ☎ 33610011
Closed :Rest closed Fri
rm23(⇌♪16) ⬤ P8
Credit Cards [1] [3]

VILLEFRANCHE-DU-PÉRIGORD
Dordogne

★★ **Bruyères** L ☎ 53299797
⇌♪10 A4rm
Credit Cards [1] [2] [3]

VILLEFRANCHE-SUR-MER
Alpes-Maritimes

★★★ **Provençal** 4 av Ml-Joffre
☎ 93017142 tx 970433
Closed :Rest closed 1 Nov-20 Dec
rm45(⇌♪43) Lift (Sea
Credit Cards [1] [2] [3] [4] [5]

★★★ **Welcome** (MAP/BW) 1 quai Courbet
☎ 93767693 tx 470281
15 Dec-15 Nov
rm32(⇌28) ⬤ Lift Sea
Credit Cards [1] [2] [3] [5]

★★ **Coq-Hardi** L 8 bd de la Corne d'Or
☎ 93017106
15 Dec-Oct
⇌♪20 ⬤ P15 ⬚ Sea

VILLEFRANCHE-SUR-SAÔNE
Rhône

★★★ **Plaisance** (FAH) 96 av de la Libération (n.rest) ☎ 74653352 tx 375746
2 Jan-24 Dec
⇌♪68 A6rm ⬤ P20
Credit Cards [1] [2] [3] [5]

★★ **Campanile** 210 r Georges-Mangin, La Ferme de Poulet ☎ 74680758 tx 310208
⇌♪43 P43
Credit Card [3]

★★ **Climat** rte de Riotter le Péage
☎ 74629955 tx 300712
⇌♪43 P50
Credit Cards [1] [2] [3]

★★ **Ecu de France** 35 r d'Anse
☎ 74683448
⇌♪26 ⬤ P
Credit Cards [1] [2] [3] [5]

★ **Ibis** Le Péage-Commune de Limas
☎ 74682273 tx 370777
⇌♪113 Lift
Credit Cards [1] [3]

🍴 **Europe** r Ampère ☎ 74655059 Aud / VW

VILLEFRANQUE See **BAYONNE**

VILLENEUVE-D'ASCQ See **ROUBAIX**

VILLENEUVE-DE-MARSAN
Landes

★ **Europe** L 1 pl Foirai ☎ 58452008
⇌♪15 (⬚
Credit Cards [1] [2] [3] [5]

VILLENEUVE-DE-RIVIÈRE See **ST-GAUDENS**

VILLENEUVE-LA-GARENNE See **PARIS**

VILLENEUVE-LÈS-AVIGNON
Gard

★★★ **Magnaneraie** 37 r Camp-de-Bataille ☎ 90251111 tx 432640
rm25(⇌20) (♫ ⬚
Credit Cards [1] [2] [3] [5]

★★★ **Prieuré** 7 pl Chapître ☎ 90251820 tx 431042
15 Mar-15 Nov
⇌♪36 P60 Lift (♫ ⬚
Credit Cards [1] [2] [3] [5]

VILLENEUVE-LOUBET-PLAGE See **CAGNES-SUR-MER**

VILLENEUVE-SUR-LOT
Lot-et-Garonne

★★★ **Parc** (MAP/BW) 13 bd de la Marine ☎ 53700168 tx 550379
⇌♪42 ⬤ P50 Lift (
Credit Cards [1] [2] [3] [5]

★★ **Prune d'Or** pl de la Gare ☎ 5390050
rm17(⇌♪11) ⬤ P20

VILLENEUVE-SUR-YONNE
Yonne

★ **Dauphin** 14 r Carnot ☎ 86871855
Closed 1 Jan & 25 Dec
⇌♪11 ⬤ P10

VILLERS-LES-POTS See **AUXONNE**

VILLERS-COTTERÊTS
Aisne

★★ **Ibis** rte de Vivières ☎ 23962680
tx 145363
⇌♪62 Lift
Credit Cards [1] [3]

VILLERS-SEMEUSE See **CHARLEVILLE-MÉZIÈRES**

VILLERS-SUR-MER
Calvados

★★★ **Bonne Auberge** Pn 1 r du Ml-Leclerc
☎ 31870464
Mar-Jan
rm14(⇌♪11) A3rm Sea
Credit Cards [1] [3]

🍴 **Meridien** 13 r de Gl-Leclerc
☎ 31870213 Peu Tal

VINAY See **ÉPERNAY**

Hôtel ★★★ *Saint Estève*

Rue E. Duhamel – **06230** Villefranche-sur-mer Tel. 93 01 72 59
With its ideal situation close to the very lively harbour, it is an ideal stopover between NICE (4km) and MONACO (12 km). 17 rooms with bath or shower, toilet, radio, direct dial phone, TV-room. Lock-up garage in basement.

VINEUIL See **BLOIS**

VIRE
Calvados
★★ **Cheval Blanc** L (FAH) 2 pl du 6 Juin 1944 ☎ 31680021 tx 170428
Closed 21 Dec-19 Jan
rm22(⇨12)
Credit Cards [1] [2] [3] [5]

VIRONVAY See LOUVIERS

VIRY-CHÂTILLON
Essonne
★★ **Climat** r Octave-Longuet ☎ 69442121 tx 603478
⇨♠38 Lake
Credit Cards [1] [2] [3]

VITRAC
Dordogne
★ **Plaisance** L Au Port (N703) ☎ 53283304
1 Feb-20 Nov Closed :Rest closed Fri
⇨♠38 A8rm P15 ♀
Credit Cards [1] [2]

VITRÉ
Ille-et-Vilaine
★ **Chêne Vert DPn** 2 pl du Gl-de-Gaulle ☎ 99750058
Jan-22 Sep & 22 Oct-Dec Closed :Rest closed Sat
rm22(⇨♠8) ☎

VITROLLES See **MARSEILLE AIRPORT**

VITRY-LE-FRANÇOIS
Marne
★ **Bon Séjour** 4 fbg L-Bourgeois ☎ 26740235
Feb-Dec Closed :Rest closed Sat
rm20(⇨♠12) ☎ P16
Credit Cards [1] [3]

France

★ **Cloche** 34 r A-Briand ☎ 26740384
rm24(⇨19) ☎ P20
Credit Cards [1] [2] [3] [5]

★ **Nancy** 22 Grand' r de Vaux ☎ 26740937
rm15(⇨♠7) ☎
Credit Cards [1] [2] [3]

VIZILLE
Isère
★ **Parc** 25 av A-Briand ☎ 76680301
rm24(⇨♠16) P4 Mountain
Credit Cards [2] [3]

VOGELGRUN See **NEUF-BRISACH**

VOREPPE See **GRENOBLE**

VOUVRAY
Indre-et-Loire
★ **Grand Vatel** L av Brûle ☎ 47527032
Closed 15 Dec-15 Mar :Rest closed Mon
⇨♠7 P10
Credit Cards [2] [3]

WALHEIM See **ALTKIRCH**

WAST, LE
Pas-de-Calais
★★ **Château de Tourelles** ☎ 21333478
Closed :Rest closed Mon Lunchtime
⇨♠16 A6rm P25
Credit Cards [1] [2] [3] [5]

WIMEREUX
Pas-de-Calais
★★ **Atlantic** Digue de Mer ☎ 21324101
Apr-1 Oct
rm11(⇨10) ☎ P35 Lift Sea
Credit Cards [1] [3] [5]

★★ **Paul et Virginie** 19 r Gl-de-Gaulle ☎ 21324212
20 Jan-15 Dec
rm18(⇨♠16)
Credit Cards [1] [3]
★ **Centre** 78 r Carnot ☎ 21324108
20 Jan-20 Dec Closed :Rest closed Mon
rm25(⇨♠18) ☎

WITTENHEIM See **MULHOUSE**

WOIPPY See **METZ**

YENNE
Savoie
★ **Logis Savoyard** pl C-Dullin ☎ 79367038
Closed :Rest closed Fri
rm9 A4rm P4

YFFINIAC See **ST-BRIEUC**

MONACO

MONTE CARLO
★★★★★ **Paris** pl du Casino ☎ 93508080 tx 469925
⇨♠300 P Lift ☐ ♦ Sea
★★★★ **Hermitage** sq Beaumarchais ☎ 93506731 tx 479432
⇨♠260 P50 Lift (☐ Sea
Credit Cards [1] [2] [3] [4] [5]
★★★ **Alexandra** 35 bd Princesse Charlotte (n.rest) ☎ (93)506313 tx 489286
⇨♠55 Lift
Credit Cards [1] [2] [3] [5]
🚗 **British Motors** 15 bd Princesse Charlotte ☎ 93256484 RR Ast DJ AR

At MONTE-CARLO BEACH
★★★★ **Beach** 22 av Princesse Grace ☎ 93309880 tx 479617
⇨♠320 ☎ P120 Lift (☐ Beach Sea Mountain
Credit Cards [1] [2] [3] [5]

SYMBOLS and ABBREVIATIONS

ENGLISH

★★★	Hotel classification
O	Hotel likely to be open during the currency of this annual guide
⇌	Private baths
♉	Private showers
P	Parking for cars
🚗	Garage and/or lock-up
♩	Night porter
⚲	Tennis court(s) (private)
▶	Golf (private)
U	Riding stables (private)
▭	Indoor swimming pool
⌒	Outdoor swimming pool
🐞	Breakdown service
☏	Telephone number
DPn	Demi-pension
Pn	Full pension
(n.rest)	Hotel does not have its own restaurant
tx	Telex
rm	Number of bedrooms (including annexe)
A	Annexe, followed by number of rooms
Ŀ	Logis de France
M/c	Motorcycle repairs undertaken
Beach	Hotel has private beach
Sea/Mountain/Lake	Rooms overlook sea, mountain(s) or a lake
→	Entry continued overleaf
Plan	Number gives location of hotel on town plan
Credit cards	(see page 30)

For a more detailed explanation refer to 'About the Gazetteer' pages 29–33

FRANÇAIS

★★★	Classement des hôtels
O	Hôtels qui doivent ouvrir prochainement
⇌	Salles de bain privées
♉	Douches privées
P	Parking pour voitures
🚗	Garage et/ou garage avec serrure
♩	Portier de nuit
⚲	Court(s) de tennis (privé)(s)
▶	Golf (privé)
U	Equitation (privée)
▭	Piscine couverte
⌒	Piscine en plein air
🐞	Service dépannage
☏	Numéro de téléphone
DPn	Demi-pension
Pn	Pension complète
(n.rest)	Hôtel sans restaurant
tx	Télex
rm	Nombre de chambres (annexes comprises)
A	Annexe suivie par nombre de chambres
Ŀ	Logis de France
M/c	Réparations de cyclomoteurs possibles
Beach	Hôtel a une plage privée
Sea/Mountain/Lake	Chambres avec vue sur la mer, les montagnes ou un lac
→	Suite au verso
Plan	Chiffre indique l'emplacement de l'hôtel sur le plan de la ville
Cartes de crédit	(voir page 30)

Pour plus amples informations veuillez vous référer à 'About the Gazetteer' voir pages 29–33

DEUTSCH

★★★	Hotelklassitizierung
O	Hotel wird während der Laufzeit dieses Führers eröffnet
⇌	Privatbad
♉	Privatdusche
P	Parken
🚗	Garage bzw verschliessbare Parkeinheit
♩	Nachtportier
⚲	Tennisplatz (Privat)
▶	Golfplatz (Privat)
U	Reitgelegenheiten (Privat)
▭	Hallenbad
⌒	Freibad
🐞	Pannendienst
☏	Telefonnummer
DPn	Demipension
Pn	Vollpension
(n.rest)	Hotel ohne eigenes Restaurant
tx	Telex
rm	Zimmeranzahl (einschliesslich Nebengebaude)
A	Nebengebaude und danach Zimmeranzahl
Ŀ	Logis de France
M/c	Motorradreparaturen
Beach	Hotel hat Privatstrand
Sea/Mountain/Lake	Zimmer mit einem Blick auf das Meer, die Gebirge oder einen See
→	Fortsetzung siehe umseitig
Plan	Nummer gibt den Standort des Hotels auf dem Stadtplan
Kreditkarten	(siehe Seite 30)

Für weitere Angaben beziehen Sie sich auf 'About the Gazetteer' siehe Seiten 29–33

ITALIANO

★★★	Classificazione alberghi
O	Alberghi che saranno aperti durante il periodo di validita della guida
⇌	Bagni privati
♉	Docce private
P	Parcheggio macchine
🚗	Garage e/o box
♩	Portiere notturno
⚲	Campi da tennis (privati)
▶	Golf (privato)
U	Scuola d'equitazione (privata)
▭	Piscina coperta
⌒	Piscina all'aperto
🐞	Servizio assistenza stradale
☏	Numero telefonico
DPn	Mezza pensione
Pn	Pensione completa
(n.rest)	Albergo senza ristorante
tx	Telex
rm	Numero di camere (compresa la dependance)
A	Dependence, seguita dal numero di camere
Ŀ	Logis de France
M/c	Si riparano motociclette
Beach	L'albergo è provvisto di spiaggia privata
Sea/Mountain/Lake	Le camere guardano sul mare/i mont/il lago
→	La lista delle voci continua a tergo
Plan	Il numero indica la posizione dell'albergo sulla cartina della città
Carte di credito	(vedere pagine 30)

Per una splegazione plé dettagliata, consultare la sezione 'About the Gazetteer' vedere pags 29–33

SYMBOLS *and* ABBREVIATIONS

ESPAÑOL

★★★	Clasificación de hoteles	(n.rest)	El hotel no tiene restaurante
O	Hoteles a ser inaugurados durante la vigencia de estaguia	tx	Telex
		rm	Número de habitaciones (incluso el edificio anexo)
⇋	Baños en cada habitación	A	Edificio anexo, seguido por el número de habitaciones
♠	Duchas en cada habitación		
P	Aparcamiento para automóviles	L	Logis de France
🚗	Garaje y/o garaje individual con cerradura	M/c	Se reparan motocicletas
		Beach	El hotel tiene playa privada
D	Conserje nocturno	Sea/Moun-tain/Lake	Las habitaciones tienen vista al mar/a las montañas/al lago
♀	Pistas de tenis (privadas)		
▶	Golf (privado)	→	La lista de simbolos continúa a la vuelta
U	Escuela hipica (privada)	Plan	El número indica la posición del hotel en el plano de la ciudad
▣	Piscina cubierta		
≈	Piscina al aire libre	Tarjetas de crédito	(véase página 30)
🛎	Servicio de asistencia avenas		
☎	Número de teléfono		
DPn	Media pensión		
Pn	Pensión completa		

Para una explicación más detallada, consúltese la sección 'About the Gazetteer' (véase el indice de materias) véase paginas 29–33

Opening doors to the World of books

BOOK TOKEN

Book Tokens

Book Tokens can be bought and exchanged at most bookshops

ACCOMMODATION REPORT

To: The Automobile Association,
Hotel and Information Services,
Fanum House, Basingstoke,
Hants RG21 2EA.

Town, hotel

Your star rating Location Date of stay

Food Room(s)

Service Sanitary arrangements Value for money

General remarks

Town, hotel

Your star rating Location Date of stay

Food Room(s)

Service Sanitary arrangements Value for money

General remarks

Town, hotel

Your star rating Location Date of stay

Food Room(s)

Service Sanitary arrangements Value for money

General remarks

Name (block letters)

Address (block letters)

Membership no. (if any) (For office use only) Acknowledged Recorded

CUT ALONG DOTTED RULE

ACCOMMODATION REPORT

To: The Automobile Association,
Hotel and Information Services,
Fanum House, Basingstoke,
Hants RG21 2EA.

Town, hotel

Your star rating Location Date of stay

Food Room(s)

Service Sanitary arrangements Value for money

General remarks

Town, hotel

Your star rating Location Date of stay

Food Room(s)

Service Sanitary arrangements Value for money

General remarks

Town, hotel

Your star rating Location Date of stay

Food Room(s)

Service Sanitary arrangements Value for money

General remarks

Name (block letters)

Address (block letters)

Membership no. (if any) (For office use only)
 Acknowledged Recorded

CUT ALONG DOTTED RULE

ACCOMMODATION REPORT

To: The Automobile Association,
Hotel and Information Services,
Fanum House, Basingstoke,
Hants RG21 2EA.

CUT ALONG DOTTED RULE

Town, hotel

Your star rating — Location — Date of stay

Food — Room(s)

Service — Sanitary arrangements — Value for money

General remarks

Town, hotel

Your star rating — Location — Date of stay

Food — Room(s)

Service — Sanitary arrangements — Value for money

General remarks

Town, hotel

Your star rating — Location — Date of stay

Food — Room(s)

Service — Sanitary arrangements — Value for money

General remarks

Name (block letters)

Address (block letters)

Membership no. (if any) — (For office use only) Acknowledged — Recorded

ACCOMMODATION REPORT

To: The Automobile Association,
Hotel and Information Services,
Fanum House, Basingstoke,
Hants RG21 2EA.

CUT ALONG DOTTED RULE

Town, hotel

Your star rating   Location   Date of stay

Food   Room(s)

Service   Sanitary arrangements   Value for money

General remarks

Town, hotel

Your star rating   Location   Date of stay

Food   Room(s)

Service   Sanitary arrangements   Value for money

General remarks

Town, hotel

Your star rating   Location   Date of stay

Food   Room(s)

Service   Sanitary arrangements   Value for money

General remarks

Name (block letters)

Address (block letters)

Membership no. (if any)   (For office use only) Acknowledged   Recorded

ACCOMMODATION REPORT

To: The Automobile Association,
Hotel and Information Services,
Fanum House, Basingstoke,
Hants RG21 2EA.

CUT ALONG DOTTED RULE

Town, hotel

Your star rating Location Date of stay

Food Room(s)

Service Sanitary arrangements Value for money

General remarks

Town, hotel

Your star rating Location Date of stay

Food Room(s)

Service Sanitary arrangements Value for money

General remarks

Town, hotel

Your star rating Location Date of stay

Food Room(s)

Service Sanitary arrangements Value for money

General remarks

Name (block letters)

Address (block letters)

Membership no. (if any) (For office use only) Acknowledged Recorded